The Spirit of the Game

The Spirit of the Game

American Christianity and Big-Time Sports

PAUL EMORY PUTZ

OXFORD
UNIVERSITY PRESS

OXFORD
UNIVERSITY PRESS

Oxford University Press is a department of the University of Oxford.
It furthers the University's objective of excellence in research, scholarship,
and education by publishing worldwide. Oxford is a registered trademark of
Oxford University Press in the United Kingdom and in certain other countries.

Published in the United States of America by Oxford University Press
198 Madison Avenue, New York, NY 10016, United States of America.

© Oxford University Press 2024

CIP data is on file at the Library of Congress

ISBN 9780190091064

DOI: 10.1093/9780190091095.001.0001

Printed by Marquis Book Printing, Canada

For Bethany, Leighton, Lynndon, and Louison

Contents

Acknowledgments

This book exists because so many people have poured some part of their lives into making it possible.

From kindergarten through twelfth grade, I had teachers in McCook, Nebraska, who invested in me. Linda Crandall, my high school journalism teacher, deserves special mention. She helped me believe that kids from small-town Nebraska could write words that truly mattered in the world. My high school basketball coach, Joel Hueser, inspired me to begin thinking about the connections between sports and the Christian life. And two classmates, Jordan Bass and Willie Williams, became lifelong friends as we developed a love for sports that continues to this day.

Omaha, Nebraska, was a special place, too. At Grace University I played basketball for Thad Mott, and in the classroom I learned from outstanding professors like Michelle Lundgren, Susan Alford, Jon Hood, Joy Schulz, Mark Linder, Joe Harder, and James Eckman. I began my educational career as a social studies teacher at Millard North High School—I have so many fond memories of my time there. In my master's program at Nebraska-Omaha, professors like Maria Arbeláez, Michael Tate, Moshe Gershovich, Mark Scherer, and John Grigg helped me move from teaching and learning *about* history to considering the possibility that I could actually *do* history myself.

I could not have picked a better place to learn how to be a historian than Baylor. In my Ph.D. program I took classes with brilliant professors like Barry Hankins, Tommy Kidd, Andrea Turpin, Beth Allison Barr, George Gawrych, Michael Parrish, Joe Stubenrauch, Philip Jenkins, and David Bebbington. My dissertation committee was an American religious history dream team: Barry, Tommy, Andrea, and Elesha Coffman, and, outside Baylor, Darren Dochuk. The generosity was remarkable. I could always count on Barry to quickly read drafts of my work, send meaningful feedback, and offer guidance and support. My regular lunches with Tommy shaped how I thought about the craft of history in important ways. And I will always be thankful for Beth's leadership of the history program. When I came to her after my fourth year, academic job offer in hand, to let her know that I needed to turn down the position, Beth supported my decision because she supported me as a person. This book would not exist without the fifth year of funding that Beth made possible.

My grad student colleagues also made Baylor an excellent place to learn: Nick Pruitt, Tim Grundmeier, Adina Kelley, Taylor Sims, Brendan Payne, Paul

Gutacker, Elise Leal Henreckson, Ryan Butler, Alyssa Craven, Liz Marvel, Matt Millsap, Lynneth Miller Renberg, Skylar Ray, Benjamin Leavitt, David Roach, Joel Iliff, and Sam Kelley. I am proud to be part of a learning community with them.

The institutional support of Baylor made this book possible as well. The indispensable Baylor library staff fulfilled countless interlibrary loan requests. The Guittard Fellows program provided funding for my first year of doctoral work. And Baylor's Graduate School offered travel support during my dissertation research.

Several fellowship programs provided additional research funding. The University of Chicago's Robert L. Platzman Memorial Fellowship, the Presbyterian Historical Society's Research Fellowship, and the Billy Graham Center's Evangelism Research Grant allowed me to travel to the respective libraries of those institutions for archival materials that shaped the heart of this book. The librarians and archivists at several other libraries, including the Library of Congress, Archives of the Episcopal Church, and Michigan State University Archives & Historical Collections, also provided help and support. And staff members at the national headquarters of the Fellowship of Christian Athletes and Athletes in Action graciously allowed me to browse through published material kept on site.

In the initial stages of this project I thought I might pursue an oral history route. While I decided to focus on published sources and archival material, interviews and conversations with Gary Demarest, Gary Warner, Donn Moomaw, Ken Schmitz, Cindy Smith, Randy St. Clair, Geoff Stoner, Janice Stoner, Bill Glass, and several others provided background and context that informed my research in helpful ways.

I had the good fortune to start doctoral work in 2013, in the heyday of the Religion in American History blogging community built by Paul Harvey and friends. Paul championed young scholars like me; my writing at the blog in turn connected me with a broad network of historians, both online and in the conference circuit, who shaped my approach to American religious history. It has been incredible to be part of an intellectual community with brilliant and kind scholars and thinkers (some can play basketball, too—Christopher Jones and Benjamin Park among them).

Several scholars have provided meaningful words of affirmation at various points in the process, including Seth Dowland, Annie Blazer, Randall Balmer, Jeff Scholes, Aaron Griffith, and Jemar Tisby. My dissertation committee offered important suggestions that helped me transform the dissertation into a book—and Barry Hankins stayed with me through it all, reading every version of the manuscript. Jesse Curtis, Art Remillard, Nick Pruitt, Tommy Kidd, and Hunter Hampton have provided helpful feedback on portions of the book manuscript, and a conversation with Leah Payne reframed my understanding of the uniqueness of sports as a cultural space. I also owe a special thanks to Heath Carter. Not only did he come up with the title for the book, but also his constant encouragement, friendship, and exhortation to "go big" helped me expand the scope of the project.

My editor, Theo Calderara, has believed in this book from the beginning and shaped it in key ways. I am grateful for his patience and support and for the work of the Oxford University Press team. The two reviewers assigned by Theo made this book better in every way. They were models for constructive criticism, examples of the collaborative labor that makes academic history special. After the review process was over, Matt Sutton informed me that he was one of the reviewers. To know that a historian of Matt's caliber read my work and offered incisive feedback was a major boost of confidence. Thanks also to Tucker Adkins, a fellow historian, for his work creating the index to this book.

My scholarly home was in American religious history, but I wanted this to be a sports history book, too. Reading from a distance, I found historians Randy Roberts, Johnny Smith, and Amy Bass to be models for how I wanted to write about sports. I am also grateful for Benjamin Rader, who read an early draft of my manuscript. In the online space, the Sport in American History blog, founded by Andrew McGregor, welcomed me as part of their community, while Derrick White and Louis Moore have been a consistent source of inspiration for publicly engaged scholarship. I am also thankful for Chad Carlson, who has become a friend and collaborator.

It was while working at Messiah University in 2018–2019 that I signed the book contract. Although my time there was short, it was significant. My students asked great questions, John Fea offered invaluable advice and guidance, and Todd Allen became a good friend. Just up the road, at Bucknell and Saint Francis, Art Remillard and Brantley Gasaway allowed me to share some of my ideas with their students and colleagues.

This book was completed after I returned to Baylor in 2019 to work with the Faith & Sports Institute (FSI) at Truett Seminary. I am grateful for my Truett colleagues and especially for Todd Still's leadership and support. FSI staff and students, past and present, have also been an important part of my life. John and Cindy White deserve special thanks for their vision to start FSI and for bringing me to the team. And my students, too, continually impress and inspire me with their insights and desire to learn—a special shout-out to Brian, Bre, Adam, Zakk, Ashlee, Tyler, and Drew.

Baylor is a hub for thoughtful conversations on history, culture, faith, sports, and the life of the mind. Conversations with my former history professors (now colleagues) as well as Baylor people like Ron Johnson, Bob Elder, Julie deGraffenried, Shawn Varghese, David Nanninga, Elijah Jeong, Jonathan Tran,

Sean Strehlow, Bob Elder, Andy Meyer, Perry Glanzer, John Maurer, Holly McKenzie, Sophia Young-Malcolm, Marcus Sedberry, Kevin Goll, George Schroeder, Dustin Benac, Jon Sisk, Rusty Freeman, Juliana Smith, Jason Carter, Ben Simpson, Isaac Lee, Elizabeth Bounds, Abby Lee, Matt Kim, Daniel Hill, and Malcolm Foley have helped me expand my imagination and consider new ideas. In Malcolm's case, it has also allowed me to share in the joys and struggles of the book-writing process. Erik Ellefsen has been a constant source of encouragement and inspiration, too, along with Bill Sterrett, Jon Eckert, and the rest of the Baylor Center for School Leadership team.

Outside of Baylor, Gene Habecker, John Vaughn, Eddie Waxer, Valerie Gin, Roger Lipe, Andy Parker, and several others have provided wisdom and support over the past few years. So have the many people I have connected with (online and off) who share a passion for the intersection of sports and religion—I wish I had space to list all of you here.

Throughout my life, my church homes have helped me stay rooted as a follower of Jesus. It began with Cornerstone Fellowship in McCook, pastored by my dad, and continued with Coram Deo in Omaha and now Mosaic Church in Waco. I know that my particular tradition within Christianity, evangelical Protestantism, is one small strand of the global church. But it is the tradition that has formed me. I continue to seek to live into what is best about it while also naming and giving account for its—and my—failures.

My faith has also been shaped by some of the organizations that I write about in this book, particularly the Fellowship of Christian Athletes (FCA). My high school basketball coach, Joel Hueser, introduced me to the FCA, and both Coach Hueser and the FCA have played a positive role in my development as a person. I continue to have friendships with sports ministry staff members, some of whom have been my students. At the same time, I also have friendships and work with those who have had negative experiences and concerns with evangelical sports ministry organizations. Their insights have enriched my thinking and perspective.

Ultimately, although my interpretations are undoubtedly shaped in some ways by my personal experiences, I have tried in this book to carry out what John Fea calls the "the task of the historian": "to pursue the truth, wherever it may lead" by turning to primary sources and seeking, as best I can, to "reconstruct the past in all its complexity and fullness."[1] I hope the story that readers encounter in the following pages does justice to the broader cultural and social contexts that have shaped the contours of Christian engagement with sports in the modern United States—and also to the multiplicity of meanings that individual people have found from within.

Finally, and most importantly, this book would not be possible without the love and support of my family.

My parents, Rob and Cherri, have always cheered me on, no matter what, and instilled in me a love of reading and learning. My siblings—Sara, Joel, Hannah, Leah, and Ben, and their significant others, Nathaniel, Chris, and Sam—are the best brothers and sisters a person could ask for. My in-laws—Clark and Dawna, and also Seth, Sandy, Bryson, Hope, Kendra, and Willie— have fully welcomed me into the Bates family and provided encouragement along the way. My grandparents, aunts, uncles, and cousins have been a constant source of encouragement, too. Susan, Todd, and Kevin in particular have shared with me the joys and miseries of rooting for the Cornhuskers. Emory and Lucille Putz and Arnott and LaVonne Buxton have passed on, but their love continues to shape who I am.

And then there are the people who have been with me every single day through the highs and lows of the writing process. Most important is Bethany. We are just two pastor's kids from McCook, Nebraska, doing our best to figure things out along the way. Seventeen years after we first fell in love, it feels like our love grows deeper by the year. This book is not possible without her love and support across three states over the course of ten years while raising three beautiful children together: Leighton, Lynndon, and Louison. I am so proud of them and the gifts they bring to the world.

For those named and the many more who are unnamed, I hope this book honors in some small way the incredible support you have given me. Its shortcomings are mine. Whatever is good and true in the pages that follow belongs to you.

Introduction

Two National Religions

> Beyond the winning and the goal,
> Beyond the glory and the fame,
> He feels the flame within his soul,
> Born of the spirit of the game
> —Grantland Rice, "The Great Competitor"*

Famed sportswriter Grantland Rice penned the verses above for a 1925 article in *Collier's* magazine. Entitled "There's No Such Thing as Quit," the article was an ode to the "competitive spirit" that supposedly undergirded the success of Babe Ruth, Ty Cobb, Jack Dempsey, and other sports celebrities of the 1920s. The poem summed up the message that Rice's article sought to convey: There was something noble and spiritual about competitive athletics, and the ingredients that went into success in sports—discipline, determination, concentration— were also the ingredients needed for success in the modern world.

As a work of sports boosterism, Rice's poem was hardly unique. Sportswriters produced countless pieces like this. What *was* significant was that these sentiments reflected—and helped drive—the explosion of organized athletics in the United States. During the 1920s, sports were transformed from an accepted part of society to a commercial spectacle on an unprecedented scale. Attendance at college football games jumped 119 percent, to over ten million by 1930; in Major League Baseball, annual attendance surged past nine million, a new record; in boxing, the first million-dollar fights took place. Meanwhile, newspapers dramatically expanded their sports coverage, and general interest magazines, newsreels, radio, and advertising agencies made athletes into national celebrities. This surge of interest led some observers to dub the 1920s the "golden age" of sports; it caused others to wonder whether America's love of sports had gone too far.[1]

Despite this, scholars who have written about the intersection of sports and Christianity in American history rarely focus sustained attention on the 1920s. Instead, most of their focus has been on an earlier development, known as "muscular Christianity." In its American form, muscular Christianity sought

The Spirit of the Game. Paul Emory Putz, Oxford University Press. © Oxford University Press 2024.
DOI: 10.1093/9780190091095.003.0001

to counter the supposed feminization of the Protestant church by presenting a more masculine image—one fit for the "strenuous" age of American expansion. Linking religion with masculinity, racial hierarchy, and national progress, white Protestant leaders called for vigorous, courageous action to solve the nation's problems and maintain white male authority. Black Protestants, meanwhile, developed their own version of muscular Christianity, which emphasized racial equality and challenged white supremacy.[2]

Athletics became an important part of the movement, helping attract men to church and mold them into the rugged Christian leaders that the times demanded. It was in part through the muscular Christian movement that Protestants overcame their suspicion of games and recreation and came to embrace such organized sports as football, baseball, and the newly invented basketball as wholesome—and holy—endeavors.[3]

According to the typical historical narrative, muscular Christianity began to fade after World War I, just when America's sports obsession was ramping up, reappearing periodically when a new Christian athlete or coach received widespread publicity.[4] In *The Spirit of the Game*, however, I argue that muscular Christianity did not disappear. Instead, the 1920s are critical for understanding how American Protestants both carried forward and reshaped muscular Christian approaches to sports. It was during this decade that Protestants were forced to confront a crucial reality: They would not be able to shape sports in their own image, as the earlier generation of muscular Christians had hoped to do. If they wanted to maintain a place within the commercialized world of big-time sports while also upholding the moral value of athletics—the "spirit of the game"—they would need to accommodate and adapt.

This book details how a group of Protestant men (and women, after the 1970s) accomplished this task and built a lasting movement. In the midst of the cultural changes of the 1920s, they transformed muscular Christianity, reframing commercialized sports as a form of middlebrow culture through which they could promote a vision for American society rooted in "traditional" nineteenth-century values like self-discipline, industriousness, and personal faith while also incorporating supposedly "modern" twentieth-century values of consumerism, cooperation, and pluralism.[5]

After forging and maintaining links between Protestant religion and big-time sports in the 1920s, they began to organize after World War II, launching new institutions that brought structure and meaning to the diffuse community of Christian athletes. By the 1970s this growing movement had enmeshed itself within the sports industry, forming an evangelical sports subculture dubbed "Sportianity" by *Sports Illustrated*'s legendary Frank Deford. This subculture— what I call the "Christian athlete movement"—continues to shape the meanings that many Christians ascribe to sports today.[6]

What This Book Does

The relationship between American Protestantism and big-time sports is the primary focus of this book.[7] I hope that by unpacking this story, I can contribute to several conversations.

First, while sports historians have documented and analyzed the cultures, organizational infrastructures, and social influence of modern American sports, they have mostly neglected the role of Protestant Christianity in the story.[8] *The Spirit of the Game* aims to fill this gap, showing how Christian coaches, athletes, and ministry leaders, working over the span of the twentieth century, developed their own networks and organizations within American sports—particularly at the highest levels of the nation's "big three" team sports of football, baseball, and basketball. The organizational infrastructure of the Christian athlete movement—comprised of groups like the Fellowship of Christian Athletes, Athletes in Action, Pro Athletes Outreach, and Baseball Chapel—shaped the development of American sporting institutions and ideologies while also advancing particular ways of making meaning through athletics.[9]

I also hope to show how sports can help us see the transformation of American Protestantism over the course of the twentieth century, as the balance of power shifted from the ecumenical/mainline establishment that held sway until the 1960s to the evangelicalism that has claimed to represent the mainstream since.[10] Sometimes this story is told as if there were two mutually exclusive Protestant tracks: the liberal "mainline" or the conservative "evangelicalism."[11] I emphasize instead that the boundaries between "mainline" and "evangelical" Protestants could be messy, particularly when we look at a grassroots cultural setting like sports.[12]

By emphasizing these messy boundaries, I offer a different narrative than the typical story told about the rise of the Christian athlete movement. Scholars who write about the movement's history usually trace its roots through Billy Graham and post–World War II neoevangelicalism.[13] But I show how mainline Protestants were central to the story. From the 1920s through the 1950s, they were the primary drivers of Protestant engagement with big-time sports, providing the foundation on which the Christian athlete movement would be built.

To be sure, the mainliners I analyze were not the intellectuals and social reformers commonly associated with the mainline; rather, these were the people in the pews and the popularizers who sought to reach them. I call this nebulous group "middlebrow Protestants" to distinguish them as a subset within mainline Protestantism and to signal what they held in common: a cultural sensibility in which Northern and Midwestern white Protestants saw themselves as the respectable center of American society, seeking to uphold "traditional" values in a modern consumer culture while embracing a practical faith that offered guidance for everyday living.

With little interest in academic theology, what made them middlebrow was in part precisely that they did not emphasize deep commitments to particular points of doctrine. They were, instead, committed to an optimistic, big-tent Protestantism, one large enough and vital enough for the American nation it supposedly represented—yet still centered on white, middle-class men. This religious sensibility, historian Matthew Hedstrom has shown, is best described as "middlebrow."[14]

After the 1960s, the center of gravity for sports-friendly Protestantism shifted from its mainline roots to the Sunbelt, where Southern white Protestantism and neoevangelicalism converged, with a small cadre of Black Christian leaders included as well. Yet, the imprint and involvement of middlebrow mainline Protestantism remained, helping to influence evangelical sports ministries—and thus evangelicalism as a whole.[15]

By including a range of voices throughout my narrative—liberals and conservatives, white Southerners and African Americans, fundamentalists and mainliners—I point to the diverse strands and contested nature of American Protestant identity. Even after the Christian athlete movement embraced evangelicalism in the 1970s, contradictions and conflicts remained, with ongoing debates over "God's way" of doing sports. At the same time, the story of the Christian athlete movement is one of convergence. By tracing how some mainline Protestants came to identify and affiliate with evangelicalism through their involvement in sports, I highlight the cultural sensibilities that could bind different Protestant groups together despite theological differences.[16]

Importantly, those sensibilities had a gendered component, shaped by a desire to foster certain ideas about Protestant masculinity. Historian Kristin Kobes Du Mez's *Jesus and John Wayne* has brought attention to a militant strand of masculinity that gained traction among white evangelicals in the twentieth century. While this was present in some sections of the Christian athlete movement, it was often tempered by a desire to cultivate well-rounded men who possessed tenderness and empathy as well as strength. Men were encouraged to be responsible husbands and fathers, though rarely in ways that challenged male-centered gender norms, and always with the assumption that heterosexuality was the only option available to Christian men.[17]

The focus on men in this book is not to suggest that women were absent from sports. Throughout the twentieth century Christian women sought out opportunities to compete. Yet, leagues for women were local or regional in orientation, with no big-time sports infrastructure commensurate with the high-level collegiate and professional leagues for men. Not until the 1970s, after the passage of Title IX, would this situation begin to change. Accordingly, women feature most prominently in the chapter covering the years after Title IX.[18]

Finally, precisely because my book is about sports and religion, it is also about American pluralism and the public spaces we share together. Protestantism and sports have each been identified as the United States' informal "national religion." Yet, while some historians of American identity and nationalism have included sports in their analyses, and some have included religion, only recently have they begun to bring the two together.[19] In *The Spirit of the Game*, I highlight the fault lines within the Christian athlete movement over American identity and belonging. I focus special attention on racial differences, showing how sports provided a cultural space in which Christian athletes and coaches both challenged and supported the colorblind racial ideology that increasingly held sway in American society after the 1960s.[20] At the same time, I show how the leaders of the movement to connect Protestantism and sports saw their efforts as an attempt to keep the United States aligned with their vision for society, one in which "ordinary" men like themselves were entrusted with the care and guidance of the American project.

In one sense, it is remarkable how much the Christian athlete movement achieved. A strong case can be made that there is no public workplace or industry in American culture today with a greater concentration of organized and committed Christians than big-time sports. While many sectors of American public life, including education and entertainment, have tended to move in a more secular direction, in sports the opposite is true. Compared with one hundred years ago, there are far more athletes and coaches today willing to publicly champion Christianity as a formative influence in their lives.

In another sense, however, the success of the Christian athlete movement remains tenuous. Unlike other forms of evangelical popular culture—such as music, books, and movies—evangelicals cannot simply create their own big-time sports leagues. The pluralistic nature of the sports industry means that evangelicals have to participate within an organizational infrastructure whose boundaries and priorities they do not dictate. Accommodation is required, and accommodation is sometimes anathema to the increasingly zero-sum culture war approach that has shaped the public face of evangelicalism since the 1980s.

This need to fit within a pluralistic space means that the Christian athlete movement is marked by both power (the ability to define and set the terms for what it means to be a Christian in sports) and precarity (access to big-time sports that is never secure). It is a central paradox that looms over the past, present, and future of the movement.

* * *

When I first began this project in 2014, I was inspired in part by a desire to know my own story. I grew up in Nebraska, in a community strongly shaped by the Fellowship of Christian Athletes (FCA). One of the most important people in my life was my high school basketball coach, who was also the FCA advisor in our school. As I became a historian, I thought that studying the FCA and other sports ministries could provide a unique lens through which to view transformations in American Protestantism and American culture over the course of the twentieth century. But I also wanted to study the creation of Christian networks in American sports because I wanted to explore the origins and development of the ideas I had been taught about what it means to be a Christian athlete.

My research for this book has only confirmed my sense that sports matter in ways that resonate beyond the field of play—that we should take sports seriously as a site of intellectual inquiry and moral formation. Sports are not simply an escape from "real" life but instead are always both a reflection of the culture in which they exist and a force shaping and transforming that very culture. Through sports, Americans (including me) have learned what they should value, what type of person they should become, and what type of world they should help to build.

In telling the story of the Christian athlete movement, I have tried to recognize the significance of the mundane and the ordinary, with faith often providing practical guidance for everyday living. But I have also attempted to situate those personal meanings within a broader cultural and political context. Upholding the moral value of big-time sports—defending the "spirit of the game"—may have meant different things to different people, but it was rarely a politically or culturally neutral act. It was almost always entwined with visions for an American society in which Protestant coaches, athletes, and sports ministers saw themselves as men in the arena, carefully and cautiously guiding the United States into the future while preserving the so-called traditional values of their imagined Protestant past.

The rise of big-time sports once seemed to threaten Christianity, creating a rival for the time and attention of Americans. By carving out a home within this world, the leaders of the Christian athlete movement turned that threat into a vehicle for maintaining their influence in a secularizing American society. This book explains how it happened—and, in the process, what sports can tell us about transformations in American Protestantism over the last 100 years.

1

The Terrific Urge to Win

In 1928, sportswriter John R. Tunis was fed up with the American sports scene. Unwilling to let the sports craze that had swept the nation go unchallenged, Tunis published *$port$: Heroics and Hysterics*, a scathing indictment of the American system of organized athletics. Blasting the "myth" that sports instilled positive moral values, Tunis railed against the commercialization of athletic competition, the deification of star athletes, and the way that sports in the 1920s had been turned "into a kind of national religion."[1]

Tunis was not the first—and would certainly not be the last—to describe sports as a religion. Nor was he the first critic to take aim at American sports culture. But his description of sports as the "national religion" marked a sharp contrast with America's other unofficial national religion: mainline Protestantism. Internally fractured by the fundamentalist/modernist debates and openly scorned by intellectuals, precocious college students, and fast-living celebrities, by the late 1920s Protestantism's hold on American life seemed to be in decline.[2] All the while, the spectacle of sport grew in public acclaim and attention. In 1929, Congregationalist minister Charles Sheldon contrasted the devotion of sports fans with that of church members. "I couldn't help wondering," Sheldon wrote after witnessing a sold-out college basketball game on a stormy winter night, "how many church members would be in the fifty different churches at a prayer meeting on a night like that, and paying a dollar apiece for the privilege of going."[3]

It is in part because of reactions like this that some scholars have viewed the 1920s as a time of Protestant "disengagement" from sports.[4] Yet, suspicion of big-time sports is only part of the story. Where some Protestants saw commercialized athletics as a rival for authority, others saw sports as an opportunity, a means of maintaining the influence of Protestant values and institutions in American life. These "middlebrow" Protestants were part of the mainline—the predominantly white, predominantly Northern denominations and networks that viewed themselves as the nation's primary guardians of morality. Typically, mainline Protestants are associated with intellectualism, social activism, and bureaucracy.[5] But middlebrow Protestants were different. They were laypeople and popular ministers, representatives (or so they thought) of the "man in the street." Embracing the business-friendly culture of the 1920s, they sought to find a place

The Spirit of the Game. Paul Emory Putz, Oxford University Press. © Oxford University Press 2024.
DOI: 10.1093/9780190091095.003.0002

for the older moral values of nineteenth-century Protestantism in a new age of mass consumption. And sports were a key part of their strategy.

No two men stand out more as emblems of middlebrow Protestant engagement with sports in the 1920s than football coach Amos Alonzo Stagg and baseball executive Branch Rickey. They made their living within and contributed to the expansion of the two most popular team sports of the decade, college football and professional baseball. At the same time, both men used their increased national fame to defend white Protestant values and practices, providing evidence that one could be both a committed Christian and a successful leader in big-time sports. In the face of a postwar consumer society that seemed to challenge traditional Protestant morality, Stagg and Rickey offered reassurance to anxious white Protestants that their values still had a place within American culture.

As an organized network, the Christian athlete movement was not launched until the 1950s. Yet, the cultural and religious sensibilities and ideas that led to its formation were forged in the 1920s by men like Stagg and Rickey. The accommodationist strategies they and other middlebrow Protestants developed to maintain their faith and promote moral values within commercialized athletics were critical to the development of long-lasting patterns of Protestant engagement with big-time sports.

Amos Alonzo Stagg and "Classic" Muscular Christianity

Decades before Protestants grappled with the ethics of living faithfully in the "golden age" of sports, muscular Christianity taught them to embrace athletic competition. Amos Alonzo Stagg was not only formed by this movement; he was practically its embodiment. Stagg was from the Northeast, born in New Jersey in 1864. An avid reader of *Tom Brown's Schooldays*, the mid-nineteenth-century English novel that popularized the links between schoolboy sports and moral formation, Stagg attended the elite private schools of Phillips Exeter Academy (1883–1884) and Yale University (1884–1889), where he starred on the baseball diamond and football field. Along with Harvard and Princeton, Yale pioneered the development of organized intercollegiate athletics in the late nineteenth century, with athletes from the "Big Three" often serving as emblems of the well-rounded muscular Christian man fit for national leadership.[6]

Stagg also participated in YMCA work, joining the organization while at Yale. In contrast to Protestant ministers who viewed sports as a worldly activity full of vice and sin, key YMCA leaders embraced the idea that physical recreation (including competitive sports) was every bit as important as spiritual and intellectual growth in developing well-rounded Christian men. "It is by means of the physical that men are brought under the influence of the spiritual," wrote Luther

Gulick, superintendent of physical education for the International YMCA Training School, in 1889. "[A]nd it is the spiritual that teaches men that their bodies are sacred to noble ends, and that the gymnasium is one of the means to the accomplishment of those ends." In 1891 Gulick's student, James Naismith, put those ideas into practice when he created basketball as a game designed to form Christian character.[7]

The rise of modernist theology, which tended to break down divisions between "sacred" and "secular" spheres of life by stressing God's presence in human society, influenced the YMCA's shift toward character building through sports. If God, through the efforts of Christian men and women, was present and at work within secular areas of life, then athletic endeavor itself could be a Christian activity and not merely a way to attract people to the "real" Christian message of personal conversion.[8]

Racial paternalism (the "white man's burden") and American imperialism also shaped the emerging muscular Christian ideology. Only if "young men became Christians and aggressive ones," Stagg suggested in an 1888 talk for the YMCA, could America's "heritage of freedom handed down to the present generation" be preserved from threats posed by immigrants and foreign ideologies.[9]

The YMCA's national infrastructure helped to spread the sports-friendly tenets of muscular Christianity from their home in the urban Northeast.[10] Stagg was a case in point. In 1890, he enrolled in the YMCA's International Training School in Springfield, Massachusetts (now Springfield College), where he studied under Luther Gulick alongside James Naismith and also served as an instructor and coach. Two years later, he moved to the Midwest, taking a position as football coach and director of the Department of Physical Culture and Athletics at the newly created University of Chicago. Stagg did not think that he was turning away from a life of Christian service in his new role. Football *was* his ministry. As he explained in his 1927 autobiography, he believed he "could influence others to Christian ideals more effectively on the field than in the pulpit."[11]

With a fierce competitiveness, attention to detail, and spartan discipline—once asked by a national magazine to share his favorite meal, he responded with "crackers and milk"—Stagg became a central figure in both the growth of college football and the development of the coaching profession.[12]

As Stagg built a football powerhouse at the University of Chicago in the early twentieth century, evidence of Protestants' growing affinity for athletics abounded. They created Sunday School Athletic Leagues, built gyms at churches and YMCA buildings, and invited star athletes like pitcher Christy Mathewson to speak about faith. A wide range of Protestants—including revivalist and former big-league outfielder Billy Sunday and leading liberal theologian Shailer Mathews—extolled the joys and virtues of baseball. Church-affiliated colleges participated in intercollegiate athletics, and Ivy League schools continued to support the muscular Christian tradition.[13] While ongoing debates remained, by World War I the question of *whether* Christians could or should participate in sports had been settled. Now, it was mostly a question of *how*.

YMCA leader Richard Henry Edwards accurately diagnosed this situation in 1915. "The meaning of loyalty and basic morality enters the very fiber of American youth through well conducted athletics," he declared in *Christianity and Amusements*, adding that "their moral and mental values are now recognized." Yet, Edwards was worried about "certain tendencies" in sports. Among those problems: the "spirit of commercialism," an overemphasis on winning, and the tendency toward violence and animosity among players. Edwards urged his readers to apply the principles of Jesus to athletic participation in order to preserve its moral value.[14]

The trends Edwards identified at the outbreak of World War I only grew afterward, as the popularity of commercialized sports surged. For the militaristic, sports offered a way to train future soldiers; for the pacifists, a safer channel for the competitive instincts of men; for spectators, a consumerist escape from the demands of modern life and the recent horrors of war. Fans increasingly flocked to professional baseball, college football, and boxing, while daily newspapers, general interest magazines, newsreels, and radio (a new technology) dramatically expanded their sports coverage.[15]

Like commercialized sports more broadly, Stagg saw his star rise after the war. He developed a national reputation as a defender of the value of athletics and, more importantly, built teams that won games.[16] From 1921 until 1924 his Chicago Maroons compiled a 22-4-4 record, winning two Big Ten championships.[17] This run brought Stagg's name into the pantheon of 1920s sports heroes. He did not quite have the star power of athletes like Babe Ruth, Jack Dempsey, and Red Grange, but among coaches only Notre Dame's Knute Rockne had greater renown.[18] Sports fans across the nation knew Stagg's name—and there were far more sports fans than ever before.

Stagg's intimate involvement with the commercialized and nationalized spectacle of big-time sports is what made him different in the 1920s from the muscular Christian leaders of the pre–World War I years. Muscular Christians in the Progressive Era lauded sports for two main reasons: they hoped it would attract young men and boys to Protestant churches, and they believed it developed well-rounded Christian character in the boys who participated. However, this Christian formation could only happen if young people participated as amateurs with pure, idealistic motivations. Playing sports in order to make money or win acclaim corrupted the idealism that made sports an engine of positive moral formation. The class-based assumptions behind the amateur ideal went unstated—those who did not need to earn money for themselves or their family had a much easier time participating in athletics organized around the amateur ideal.[19]

The excessive commercialization of sports in the 1920s led some muscular Christians to consider the concerns Richard Henry Edwards had identified in 1915 and question the landscape of big-time college athletics. Correspondence in 1921 between Stagg and A. J. "Dad" Elliott, a YMCA leader in Chicago, helps to illustrate this. A YMCA-trained muscular Christian and a former college football star, Elliott believed that athletics could be put to Christian use. But he felt compelled to bring troubling details about college football to Stagg's attention. The sport, he claimed, was now "built up on the fundamental premise first, of winning games—to win honestly if you can, but if you can't win honestly, win." This obsession with winning led to direct payments to standout football players and a lowering of academic standards to keep football players enrolled. It was "very difficult to grow Christian character in the kind of soil that our present athletic situation is responsible for," Elliott wrote, and he asked to meet with Stagg about the problem.[20]

Stagg undoubtedly agreed with Elliott's desire to uphold the principle of amateur sport. Yet, the "fundamental premise" that Elliott identified as the problem— the emphasis on winning—was not as much of a concern for Stagg. "The British play a game for the game's sake; [Americans] play to win," Stagg explained in his 1927 autobiography.[21]

To be sure, Stagg believed that football players must be able to accept a loss with dignity, and that they must not cheat to win. Stagg also believed coaches should not be hired or fired because of their win–loss records, and he complained about alumni who took a win-at-all-costs attitude.[22] But Stagg helped to create the incessant demand for winning in the first place, and he remained convinced that the intense will to win was an essential trait in male leaders that needed to be cultivated through athletic competition. An exchange recorded in a 1931 interview emphasizes this point. "This terrific urge to win," the author asked, "you don't agree with some of the reformers who say it's low and unworthy?" Stagg responded indignantly, "Low and unworthy! Low and unworthy, to want to win? Golly, man, isn't that what life's all about?"[23]

Stagg's obsession with the "will to win" went hand in hand with his staunch support for amateur athletics. He continued to believe that if players received financial compensation, the character-building value of the game would be destroyed. Only if players participated with idealistic motivations—love of their alma mater and duty to their teammates—could football's man-making potential stay intact.

Yet, Stagg also aided and abetted the commercialization of college football that expanded to dramatic new heights in the 1920s. It was Stagg, after all, who broke Big Ten conference regulations by taking his Chicago Maroons east to play Princeton in an intersectional game in 1921, intensifying the surge of interest in such matchups.[24] It was Stagg, too, who serialized his autobiography in one of the nation's most popular magazines, the *Saturday Evening Post*, in 1926, pioneering a trend followed by other football coaches. For each of the eight articles, Stagg received $1,000 (adjusted for inflation, equal to about $15,000 today).[25] Thus, Stagg contributed to what scholar Michal Oriard calls "the contradiction at the heart of big-time college football . . . college football players were student amateurs, despite their participation in a multimillion-dollar business."[26]

This ambivalent stance ultimately served Stagg well. On the one hand, his defense of the amateur ideal and his support for measures to curb the recruitment of players made him stand out as a throwback to an earlier, purer age compared with other major coaches in the 1920s.[27] On the other hand, his continued participation in and defense of big-time football distinguished him from reform-minded critics who sought to greatly diminish football's cultural power.

As the sports boom of the 1920s enhanced Stagg's fame, his close identification with the muscular Christian movement received new life, in part because he stood as a contrast with Protestant leaders concerned about the influence of sports. "Where is this going to stop?" one Protestant minister worried in 1930. "Is sport going to displace religion?"[28] Fears of slowing church growth were coupled with the fear that America no longer valued the "old-time" individualistic virtues of the Victorian era that many Protestants held dear—traits such as self-reliance, perseverance, and self-control.[29]

For his part, Stagg often blasted the "exaltation of luxury and pleasure seeking" in America's postwar consumer society.[30] Yet, rather than viewing sports as a problem, he thought it was the solution, the means of instilling in American youth the increasingly discarded old virtues. "Instead of going to church to learn how to live, the youngsters nowadays go anywhere they want to," Stagg said in 1931. "Thank God, they like to go to football games!" In Stagg's view, young Americans were learning "temperance, self-control, fair play, sportsmanship, courage, and the Golden Rule from athletes and athletic directors and coaches."[31]

Although Stagg believed sports could promote religious values outside the structure of the church, he remained closely linked with mainline Protestant symbols and institutions.[32] A Presbyterian while at Yale, at Chicago he followed his wife, Stella, into a Northern Baptist church and then switched to the Methodists when he moved to California in 1933. If his denomination shifted over the years, his theology leaned toward modernism. While at Chicago, Stagg faithfully attended Hyde Park Baptist Church, pastored from 1910 until 1928 by Charles W. Gilkey, a champion of liberal Protestantism and a close associate of leading modernist pastor Harry Emerson Fosdick. When Stagg moved to California, he joined the local Methodist church in part because the Baptist pastor in town was, in Stagg's words, "strongly fundamentalist."[33]

Despite his modernist disposition, Stagg won support from Protestants of competing theological opinions. Sensational ecclesiastical battles may have cast the 1920s as a time of polarizing debate, but many Northern white Protestants continued to share the same set of cultural and moral values and practices.[34] No cultural issue loomed larger or united Protestants more than Prohibition. It was, as Sydney Ahlstrom put it, "*the* great Protestant crusade of the twentieth century."[35] Stagg jumped into the fray, joining organizations that sought to mobilize support for the enforcement of Prohibition and testifying before Congress on its behalf in 1926 and 1930.[36] Both times, letters of support from Protestants flooded Stagg's mailbox. "Even though your ministry has not been in the pulpit, your life has been one long Christian ministry," one man wrote, "and of late, you have been doing some fine, effective talking in the Prohibition crisis."[37]

Stagg also frequently encouraged young people to personally abstain from alcohol and smoking. He framed the issue as a matter of achieving peak physical health and developing Christian character; he did not focus on drinking and smoking as sins, as some conservative Protestants did. Nevertheless, Stagg's promotion of clean living through athletics—and his criticism of gambling and swearing—resonated with a broad Protestant moral consensus.[38]

Practices of Protestant piety, especially prayer, also served as a way for Stagg to publicly demonstrate his faith.[39] Of course, Protestants did not have a monopoly on prayer. For Catholics, Notre Dame's blend of gridiron success and publicized piety served as a powerful source of identity in the 1920s.[40] For Protestants, Centre College of Danville, Kentucky, dubbed the "Praying Colonels," served as a prototype for the "praying football team" genre, earning widespread publicity in 1920 thanks to their pregame ritual.[41] In 1924 Army's star center Eddie Garbisch became the new poster boy for gridiron piety. Inspired by Harry Emerson Fosdick's *The Meaning of Prayer*, Garbisch gathered his teammates before games, asking God "to permit us to go into action with a clean heart, acquit ourselves like men, and maintain a Christian sportsmanlike attitude."[42] In 1927 Stagg himself got into the action, as reports told of Stagg kneeling before a pregame talk in order to ask God "that I might be able to speak the words I ought to have said, and for the fortitude to bear the result."[43]

For many Protestants, publicized prayers of football players and coaches served as proof that men could be religious and masculine at the same time. In this way, the anxieties over masculinity that defined muscular Christianity in the Progressive Era continued in the 1920s. An Indiana newspaper editor, for example, pointed to stories of praying football players as a "blow" to the idea that public prayer was "a sign of weakness and womanishness."[44] But to a greater degree than in the Progressive Era, the stories of praying athletes in the 1920s also served as evidence that religion still mattered in American society. Articles published in the YMCA's national periodical, *Association Men*, highlighted this theme. In 1925, after recounting examples of praying athletes, sportswriter Robert Kelley exclaimed, "What an answer this thing has been to those who have been feeling that religion and prayer are dying out of the country!"[45]

Stagg's public support for Prohibition, prayer, and other widely shared Protestant moral standards made him a respected figure in Protestant circles. A 1931 assessment in the liberal *Christian Century* lauded Stagg as a man who "glorified everything that was clean, wholesome, and character-building in sports."[46] Meanwhile, an editorial in the conservative *Presbyterian* singled out Stagg as a man of "sterling Christian character."[47]

While Stagg rarely spoke of a need for conversion in the 1920s, emphasizing instead that Christian character could be cultivated and nurtured over time, he championed causes that Protestants understood as symbols of sincere religious conviction. In this, Stagg was not alone. College football players like Eddie Garbisch and coaches such as Fielding Yost and Glenn Thistlethwaite also attended Protestant churches and spoke in support of Protestant causes. But no coach reached the same level of national fame as Stagg. With professional football a regional affair at the time, Stagg emerged as the most important and visible symbol of the links between Protestantism and big-time football in the interwar years. As for the other team sport that reigned in the 1920s—Major League Baseball—it, too, had its Protestant champion.[48]

Branch Rickey and Midwestern Muscular Christianity

If Stagg exemplified the elite Northeastern origins of American muscular Christianity, Branch Rickey symbolized its westward diffusion and democratization. Born and raised in small-town Ohio, Rickey starred in baseball and football at Ohio Wesleyan in the early 1900s. While Ivy League muscular Christians placed great emphasis on maintaining amateur purity—Stagg famously refused to sign a lucrative professional baseball contract—Rickey played semiprofessional baseball while in college, followed by three years in Major League Baseball (1905–1907). He went on to coach college football and baseball before settling into a role as manager of baseball's St. Louis Browns in 1913.[49]

Although Rickey was well known in the baseball world before World War I, the 1920s sports boom propelled Rickey to a national stage. Rickey worked as manager and general manager of the St. Louis Cardinals from 1919 until 1925, and then exclusively as general manager of the team until 1942. On Rickey's watch the Cardinals reversed three decades of futility; from 1926 until 1934 they won five National League pennants and two World Series crowns. That success, combined with Rickey's pioneering role in developing new scouting and player development tactics, earned him widespread fame.

Through it all, Rickey maintained his religious commitments. A lifelong Methodist, Rickey taught a Sunday school class at Grace Methodist Church in St. Louis, served as vice president of the Methodist Brotherhood Commission in the 1920s and 1930s, and spoke often at Methodist men's clubs.[50] Other mainline Protestant groups capitalized on Rickey's fame, including the Federal Council of Churches and the Interdenominational Men's Congress.[51] At the same time, thanks to his friendship with Ohio Wesleyan classmate Homer Rodeheaver (Billy Sunday's musical director), Rickey spoke at the Winona Lake summer meetings frequented by fundamentalists and introduced Billy Sunday when the revivalist came to St. Louis in 1928.[52] Like Stagg, Rickey exemplified the continued similarities that united Northern white Protestants of competing theological persuasions in the 1920s.

Despite the obvious similarities, there were key differences between Rickey and Stagg. Perhaps of first importance were the divergent sports contexts. While Stagg worked within college athletics, Rickey operated in professional baseball, dealing with men who, for the most part, had already been "made." The amateur idealism that Stagg and others placed at the heart of the college football enterprise had little sway in the blatantly and openly commercialized world of professional baseball.

To be sure, Rickey attempted to bring idealism into Major League Baseball. In St. Louis he helped to organize a club for young Cardinals fans dubbed the "Knothole Gang." By giving free tickets to boys and encouraging them to watch and play the sport, Rickey hoped to "cultivate in the minds of American youth clean sportsmanship" through baseball.[53] But character formation was not viewed as an intrinsic part of professional baseball, as it was with college football.[54] At best the sport could inspire young boys to follow their heroes and participate in athletics; at worst, it could corrupt them with the gambling, drinking, and swearing commonly associated with professional athletes. While most college football coaches at least paid lip service to the importance of traditional moral values, in professional baseball Rickey stood out as "a trifle too good, too religious, too strict, too Puritanical."[55]

Rickey also faced the problem of Sunday. In the nineteenth century strict Sabbath observance—or the Puritan Sabbath—had been, in historian George Marsden's words, the "distinctive symbol of evangelical civilization in the English-speaking world."[56] In the 1920s it remained a major issue of concern for Protestants and a symbol of sincere Protestant faith. In 1920, for example, the General Assembly of the Presbyterian Church in the United States of America passed a resolution declaring that the Assembly "emphatically disapproves all secular uses of the Sabbath Day, including games and sports . . . and the Sunday game propaganda of powerful baseball leagues."[57] Despite the passage of resolutions and the preaching of sermons against Sabbath desecration, the 1920s witnessed the widespread disintegration of "blue laws" that restricted Sunday activities. Put simply, Americans' desire for leisure and recreation on Sunday proved stronger than the pronouncements of Protestant ministers.[58]

Some church leaders responded by doubling down and attempting to re-establish strict community-wide Sabbath laws. Others accepted cultural defeat and focused on privatizing Sabbath observance, making it a mark of one's personal Christian commitment. Still others sought a middle ground, seeking to narrow the target of prohibited activities on Sundays, banning only "commercialized" leisure activities. In New York City, Episcopalian Bishop William T. Manning caused a stir in December 1925 when he encouraged participation in "wholesome" sport on Sundays. His remarks received criticism across the country from strict Sabbath observers. Yet, Manning refused to sanction professional baseball on Sunday. He believed that a money-making spectacle attracting thousands of paying spectators would not only violate the sacred spirit of the day but also disturb the Sabbath rest of residents who did not attend the game.[59]

Because college football games took place on Saturday, Stagg rarely faced the question of involvement in Sunday sports. Not so with Rickey. If he participated in Sunday games, many Protestants would question his religious sincerity. If he did not, it would be difficult for him to have a place in professional baseball. Because of this dilemma, by the 1920s sabbatarian professional baseball players had become a rarity. "Only two or three such birds still remain among us," a St. Louis sportswriter remarked in 1919.[60]

Rickey was one of these "birds." He stayed away from the ballpark on Sundays during his time as manager of the St. Louis Cardinals (1919–1925), forcing the team to utilize a Sunday manager. When the Cardinals removed Rickey from his managerial duties after the 1925 season (keeping him as general manager), Rickey continued to avoid Sunday games.[61] With sabbatarian professional baseball players an endangered species, Rickey's position on Sunday sports took on great symbolic importance for Protestants. In *Middletown*, Robert and Helen Lynd's sociological study of Muncie, Indiana, in the early 1920s, the authors reported that when Rickey came to speak at a Ministerial Association event, the promotional materials made sure to note that "Mr. Rickey never plays on Sunday."[62]

Protestant resistance to commercialized Sunday baseball remained strong until the 1930s, placing Rickey in a unique position. His success in the country's most popular professional sport brought him national recognition and fame, while his Sabbath convictions strengthened his Protestant credentials beyond those of most other Christian baseball players and managers. Like Stagg, Rickey's ability to balance the demands of the two worlds—to combine leadership in the operations of a big-time, commercialized sport with the public promotion of his

Protestant faith—made him stand out compared with other baseball-friendly muscular Christians. Billy Sunday merely drew upon his nineteenth-century past as a baseball player in order to win souls to Christ; Branch Rickey was a sports industry insider. And while there were other Protestant baseball insiders—men like manager Bill McKechnie and pitcher Vic Keen—they lacked Rickey's national prominence.

Along with the professional sports context in which he operated, Rickey also differed from Stagg in his theological priorities. By the 1920s Stagg's practical modernist theology led him to view the Christian life primarily as a process of character formation. By cultivating traits like self-mastery, industriousness, and piety, Stagg believed, Christians could become productive, respectable, and successful citizens. The Bible verse Stagg identified as his favorite captured this idea: "Whatsoever thy hand findeth to do, do it with thy might" (Eccles. 9:10). After encountering that verse as a young man, Stagg put it into practice in "my studies and in my play and whatever work I had to do."[63]

Rickey shared Stagg's emphasis on character development, and he promoted similar nineteenth-century values. Yet, while Stagg rarely mentioned Jesus, Rickey viewed him as the centerpiece of his faith and the exemplar of the ideals Rickey sought to emulate. "Perhaps Jesus is a dormant, subjective ideal to many people," Rickey wrote in an article for the *Christian Advocate* in 1931, "but He is a living, objective fact to those who try Him out . . . He is also a dynamic principle that seeks laboratory demonstration."[64] In an interview the same year, Rickey declared that Jesus "means everything." "I want to live the ideals of Christ every day, in business and on the athletic field," he said.[65]

Rickey's adulation of Jesus was common among a new generation of muscular Christians in the early twentieth century. Biographies that sought to emphasize Jesus's humanity proliferated, from Harry Emerson Fosdick's *The Manhood of the Master* (1913) to Bruce Barton's *The Man Nobody Knows* (1925).[66] Rickey was shaped by this literature; in 1915, for example, he drew on Fosdick's book in a YMCA talk about Jesus.[67]

His favorite book in the genre was Giovanni Papini's *Life of Christ*. Translated from Italian and published in English in 1923, it was a bestselling book in the United States for the next few years.[68] Papini's rejection of "dogmatic proofs and learned discussions" when it came to Jesus resonated with Rickey. Papini wanted to "make Christ more living . . . to make us feel Him as actually and eternally present in our lives."[69] That was Rickey's focus as well. While he maintained core evangelical convictions regarding the deity of Christ, he rarely framed his religious appeals as a matter of salvation from sin; rather, he sought a vibrant practical faith. By encountering the awe-inspiring Jesus and putting his ideals into practice, Rickey believed, people would develop "empirical knowledge" of religion's usefulness upon which their faith could stand.[70]

This understanding of Jesus as a dynamic and inspirational personality fit in with a broader cultural trend in the early twentieth century, often described as a shift from a "culture of character" that prized the nineteenth-century values of self-discipline and self-denial to a "culture of personality" that focused more on self-fulfillment and therapeutic growth.[71] The contrast between Stagg and Rickey is emblematic of this shift. The elder Stagg spoke often of developing Christian character but rarely spoke of Jesus as a dynamic personality. At the same time, it is important to note the continued emphasis on character for "culture of personality" types like Rickey. In Jesus, they saw a personality who could inspire others to embrace the old virtues associated with nineteenth-century Protestantism.[72]

Middlebrow Engagement with Sports

Through their religious activities in the 1920s, Stagg and Rickey made it clear that the spectacle of big-time sports could promote Protestant institutions and cultural values. Some Protestant leaders, however, were not convinced. They expressed concern over the very cultural trend that brought Stagg and Rickey to fame: the commercialized, mass-marketed sports scene.

The debate was not confined to Protestant circles. Scholars have shown that the 1920s witnessed a reversal in the attitudes of leading intellectuals and reformers who had embraced sports in the Progressive Era. Many turned against the excesses of commercialized athletics in the 1920s, criticizing America's obsession with sports in general and the crass commercialism and violence of football in particular.[73]

The journal for liberal Protestant intellectuals, the *Christian Century*, brought these concerns into the religious sphere. In 1926, an editorial admonished Stagg (without naming him) for taking football too seriously and thus contributing to America's overemphasis on athletics. The following year the same magazine took aim at Stagg's claim that sports cultivated moral values. "[L]ife is not essentially a game," it declared. "Qualities learned in one field cannot be carried over into another without loss in the transition."[74] Three years later, after the publication of the Carnegie Report—which documented widespread hypocrisy in big-time football, including blatant player recruitment and low academic standards—the *Christian Century* blasted college football's "dishonest professionalism."[75]

Conservative Protestants who shared the *Christian Century*'s intellectual orientation also took issue with athletic excess. As early as 1925, editorials in *The Presbyterian*, a theologically conservative journal, urged readers not to magnify sports "over the acquisition of valuable knowledge and skill."[76] By 1931 the concern expressed in *The Presbyterian* had escalated. "Until we can reduce the sport idea, we will be in moral peril," editor W. Courtland Robinson warned, concluding in another editorial that "athletics have been too thoroughly organized, professionalized, and commercialized to do much good, and may do much harm."[77]

There were differences between the concerns of conservative and liberal Protestants. The latter were far more likely to critique sports for its capitulation to the competitive logic of capitalism, while the former were more likely to lament sports' tendency to detract from church attendance and Sunday worship. Yet, both camps spoke of sports' excesses with a scholarly disposition and a concern that America's obsession with athletics was either an empty and materialistic distraction or an activity that could form destructive habits and values. They found it difficult to see how the winning-obsessed, mass spectacle of sports could form the type of thoughtful, virtuous men they believed the country needed.

For Protestants like Stagg and Rickey who were involved in big-time sports, such criticism was difficult to accept. To do so would undermine the very foundations on which their careers and livelihoods stood. Instead, they defended the potential moral usefulness of commercialized athletics, working to reconcile the older notions of the character-building value of sports with the mass consumerism enveloping their athletic institutions. In short, they claimed a "middlebrow" cultural space, standing in between the supposedly unthinking "lowbrows," who looked at sports as an escapist diversion, and the "highbrows" with their detached intellectualism, looking down their noses at the hypocrisies of big-time sports.[78]

This middlebrow space, historian Joan Shelley Rubin has argued, emerged in the 1920s with the aim of embracing elements of modern consumer society while preserving the values associated with the genteel tradition of the nineteenth century—notions of moderation, self-control, self-sacrifice, and inward virtue.[79] While the broader middlebrow movement often had an implicit Protestant identity, there was also a more distinctly Protestant subset that scholars Erin Smith and Matthew Hedstrom have described as a "religious middlebrow" culture. According to Hedstrom, religious middlebrow leaders used the tools of a mass consumer society to "promote a tolerant, practical, and modern spirituality" while also looking nostalgically to the Protestant-dominated small-town life of the past.[80] Smith, meanwhile, emphasizes the ways that middlebrow Protestants promoted a practical individualism, presenting religion as a means of finding "guidance for everyday life."[81]

While the nebulous middlebrow movement was not confined to men, it did have a particular emphasis on masculinity.[82] One could find it articulated in interdenominational religious periodicals like the *Christian Herald* or the YMCA's *Association Men,* as well as in general interest magazines like *Collier's* and *American Magazine.* It was also present in the businessmen's service clubs—Rotary, Kiwanis, and Lions—that expanded throughout the 1920s.[83] And one could find it in bestselling books like Bruce Barton's *The Man Nobody Knows* (1925). Eschewing theological specifics and doctrinal debates, Barton's popular book focused on how religion could be useful in one's everyday life. He depicted an up-to-date, broad-minded, masculine Jesus—comfortable with sports and business—while also seeking to give readers a sense that faith still had meaning in the modern world, and that the old virtues like self-sacrifice still mattered.[84]

Barton's book, like middlebrow Protestants more broadly, advocated for a popularized modernism—a practical, nondogmatic faith. Hedstrom effectively summarized its components: "optimism regarding human nature, emphasis on moral education and ethics, and an overarching faith in human progress."[85] However, it was a cultural sensibility more than a coherent theology, one that could be embraced by everyone from modernist minister Harry Emerson Fosdick on the left to Daniel Poling, pastor and editor of the *Christian Herald*, on the right.[86]

Standing in contrast to the chastened postwar realism and suspicion of capitalism articulated by mainline Protestant intellectuals, middlebrow Protestants preferred to focus on the individual and to accentuate the positive. A 1929 poem by syndicated newspaper columnist Edgar Guest, a middlebrow favorite, aptly summed up this sensibility. In the poem, titled "Wreckers," a man considers the ease with which a crew of men can destroy a structure compared with the time it takes to build it. In that contrast, Guest and his readers saw a metaphor to explain their own social position and responsibility as guardians of the American project. They sought to be a "builder" who was "patiently doing the best I can" rather than a "wrecker" focused on "the labor of tearing down."[87]

To critics, of course, middlebrow Protestants were hardly enlightened leaders; rather, they were conformity-minded boosters, uncritically embracing a materialistic culture while seeking to impose their outdated views on others. The popularity of Sinclair Lewis's trio of satirical novels aimed at middlebrow culture—*Main Street* (1920), *Babbitt* (1922), and *Elmer Gantry* (1927)—shows that this assessment resonated with many Americans.[88]

Critics like Lewis hit the mark with some of their claims, but they also trafficked in hyperbole, glossing over the ways middlebrow Protestants sought to advance more inclusive understandings of faith and nation. Unlike the dogmatism of fundamentalists, the strict segregation of conservative white Southerners, or the extreme nativism of the Ku Klux Klan, middlebrow Protestants often projected an ecumenical image of broadmindedness, including support for the emerging trifaith "goodwill" movement that sought to encourage cooperation among Jewish, Catholic, and Protestant communities.[89]

Even so, despite pronouncements of inclusion, the middlebrow rhetoric of pluralism remained tethered to white Protestant authority. Stagg, for example, may not have advocated for segregation, but he maintained a belief in a racial hierarchy. While a few Black athletes competed for his track and field teams at Chicago, a Black player never made the football roster. In 1926 Stagg explained why. In response to a letter from a Black sportswriter, he claimed that Black men were "less likely to be as good in that sport [football], where fearlessness, aggressiveness, and dogged determination play a large part in the selection of positions."[90]

Stagg's views were not shared by all middlebrow Protestants, but they were firmly in the mainstream. And even for those who might have embraced the idea of racial equality, challenging racist structures in church and sports was a bridge too far. Branch Rickey would famously go on to help upend racial segregation in Major League Baseball. But in the 1920s and 1930s, he took no direct actions to end the practice. To do so would subvert the middlebrow sensibility, in which the structures of American society and culture were considered sound. Rather than the disruption that might come from serious reconstruction and reform, middle-brow Protestants preferred building on the foundations already in place.[91]

This sensibility shaped how middlebrow Protestants connected their faith to sports. With their desire to affirm individualism, they sought, first, to reach as many individuals as possible. Congregationalist minister S. Parkes Cadman, chair of the Religious Book Club's (RBC's) editorial board—a key middlebrow organization—explained in 1927 that the RBC's target audience was "the man in the street, who often seems concerned only with the stock market and the World Series" but who "is really immensely interested in religion."[92] Methodist minister William Stidger—friends with Branch Rickey, for whom he had played college football—similarly emphasized reaching a mass audience in a 1929 article on preaching. "There ought never to be a football season go by that the preaching of the minister of God is not touched every Sabbath with figures from the high-school and college football field," he instructed. "Why? Because so many thousands of young boys and girls and men and women are watching football and are fascinated with it."[93]

Having reached "the man in the street," the next step was to instill Protestant values. This was a key distinguishing feature of the middlebrow sensibility: the idea that commercialized consumer culture continued to possess pedagogical spiritual value, with the potential to teach life lessons and cultivate moral virtue.

One organization carrying out this work was the Sportsmanship Brotherhood. Founded in 1923 (Stagg later became a member), the group sought to promote the "spirit of sportsmanship," which "is in essence the Golden Rule." As historian Barbara Keys writes, the Brotherhood "saw sportsmanship as a manifestation of Christian brotherly love."[94] With an expansive agenda, the Brotherhood aimed to help young athletes "obtain in sport . . . something spiritual that will draw them closer to each other in a sense of brotherhood making for greater justice and well being." In order to accomplish this, members distributed literature, established local clubs, and collaborated with existing sports agencies.[95] They also defended the value of sports. A 1928 editorial for *Sportsmanship*, the group's official magazine, addressed arguments about the "over-emphasis of sport" by claiming that the sports boom was a "blessing in disguise." The more that people watched sports, the argument went, the more they would learn from the examples of sportsmanship that permeated athletic competition.[96]

The national magazine for the YMCA, *Association Men*, provides another example of middlebrow support for sports. By the 1920s the YMCA no longer occupied a place at the forefront of elite athletic competition, focusing more on health and recreation for the general population. In its main magazine, however, star athletes and coaches were identified with the moral values that supposedly led to business success.[97] Franklin G. Smith, a Cleveland-based manufacturer, explained in 1926 that college football "is replete with acts of sportsmanship" and that such players will "be successful in business largely because of this quality."[98] Similarly, a 1927 *Association Men* article titled "Are Athletes Good Business Risks?" answered in the affirmative, quoting former Michigan track star Floyd Rowe to explain that sports "teach sportsmanship, teamwork, co-ordination" and "those are about all the essentials a young man needs to succeed in life."[99]

Sports-friendly middlebrow Protestantism also found expression in magazines that lacked official religious affiliations, including *American Magazine*. A general interest monthly periodical that topped two million subscribers in the late 1920s, *American Magazine*'s basic message was described by frequent contributor Bruce Barton this way: "Life is a game; and success consists in making the most of what you have, without complaint or whimpering; with modesty when the luck comes your way and no alibis when the cards run bad."[100] This ideology of "true success" sought to root success not in the material signs of achievement (money, fame, possessions) but, rather, in the cultivation of character. Yet, *American Magazine* inevitably turned to people with material achievements— including coaches and athletes—to proclaim its message and to link commercialized sports with moral values.[101]

In *American Magazine* and other middlebrow Protestant publications, the main focus was on the way Christian formation could occur *through* sports. Sometimes, however, there was also an emphasis on the practical usefulness of religion *within* sports. Glenn Clark, a professor of creative writing and a track and field coach at Macalester College in Minnesota, offered an especially developed example of this.

Clark came to national attention in 1924 when *Atlantic Monthly* published his essay on prayer, "The Soul's Sincere Desire," which provided the basis for a bestselling book with the same title the following year.[102] Influenced by a range of sources, including Christian mysticism, liberal Protestantism, and New

Thought, Clark promised to help readers tap into the infinite power of God through the practice of prayer.[103] His advice intentionally mirrored regimens of physical exercise. "Prayer should be for the spirit exactly what calisthenics should be for the body," Clark explained, "something to keep one in tune, fit, vital, efficient and constantly ready for the next problem of life."[104]

This blending of athletics and prayer went beyond simply applying sports discipline to one's spiritual life. Clark also suggested that following his prayer methods would provide tangible results on the playing field. The key, Clark said, was to pray for a "Condition of Consciousness"—for a spirit of love and joy to pervade one's inner being. If a coach or athlete prayed in this way, without an inner desire for victory, then love and joy would release divine power, allowing the athlete to perform their best.[105]

In *Power of the Spirit on the Athletic Field* (1929), Clark expanded on this idea, suggesting that athletes should structure their prayer life around major athletic events so that they would build up the "condition of consciousness" necessary to become "in tune with God" by the time of the event. Drawing on popularized concepts from the emerging field of psychology, Clark also suggested that anxiety, guilt, and jealousy could hinder an athlete's performance. Athletes needed to throw away such "useless ballast" and "tune in" to love, joy, and peace in order to reach peak performance. As proof, Clark claimed that the University of Minnesota achieved an upset victory over Red Grange's University of Illinois in 1924 because the Minnesota players met before the game, cleared the air of jealousies that had been causing discord, and prayed together.[106]

Clark's interest in applying religion to the on-field performance of Christian athletes fit in with the middlebrow Protestant aim of making religion useful and practical to people's everyday lives. In a 1931 letter to his son Paul, Amos Alonzo Stagg expressed a similar idea. Written in response to Paul's apparently disappointing tennis performance, Stagg urged his son to work on his spiritual preparation. A spiritually prepared athlete, Stagg claimed, would be able to focus, maintain intensity, and cultivate the "will to win" that would enable success. Stagg even gave an example from his own college baseball career in the 1880s. "I stimulated my 'will to win' during the progress of the game by frequently praying 'Help me to do my best,'" he said. Spiritual preparation, Stagg told Paul, was the final piece needed to "win your conference matches."[107]

* * *

Stagg's letter to his son—with its reference to Stagg's time at Yale—suggests continuity between the muscular Christianity that formed Stagg in the 1880s and the middlebrow uses of sport that developed in the 1920s. Yet, there were key differences. In 1887, when he spoke to reporters about praying on the baseball field, Stagg described it as a matter of Christian duty: "Even if we were defeated, I knew that we were doing our best, our Father's duty."[108] In 1931, Stagg emphasized prayer as a spiritual technique, a means of cultivating a psychological edge for competitive success.

This shift closely tracked with the growth and development of big-time sports, a culture in which winning was currency. Still, Stagg's emphasis on the "will to win" was not simply about sports; it spoke to the qualities that were formed in the people who competed. In an era when both conservative and liberal Protestants worried that big-time sports were undermining Americans' commitment to Protestant values and authority, middlebrow Protestants like Stagg took another path. For them, commercialized sports still offered a way to cultivate character and promote Protestant ideas and institutions.

It was this accommodation with American cultural trends, this willingness to abide tension and contradiction in the name of influence, that allowed middlebrow Protestants to maintain a space within big-time sports in the 1920s. Authors like Bruce Barton and Glenn Clark, magazines like *Association Men* and *American Magazine*, and prominent sports leaders like Amos Alonzo Stagg and Branch Rickey did not entirely ignore the ethical concerns that swirled around sports. But they championed the good in athletic competition, focusing on the ways sports could be made useful for white Protestant purposes in American culture.

This approach provided a foundation on which Protestant leaders would build as they worked to institutionalize their faith within sports after World War II. But mainline Protestants were not the only game in town. Outside the establishment, on the margins of national cultural power and influence, there were other Protestant communities engaging with athletics in the 1920s. While these Protestants did not have a place of prominence within big-time sports—at least not yet—they developed their own patterns of athletic engagement that would prove influential in the years to come.

2

Unless the Playing Interferes
with the Praying

Nearly seven thousand people packed into Atlanta's civic auditorium on November 21, 1927, to witness the funeral service for Tiger Flowers, a Black middleweight boxer. Just one year earlier, Flowers had defeated Harry Greb to win the world middleweight championship; now, five days after a botched medical operation, Flowers was dead. Despite the heavy hand of Jim Crow, the passing of the former champion resonated beyond Atlanta's Black population: an estimated seven hundred white residents attended the funeral, including prominent Atlanta sportswriter Morgan Blake, who delivered a eulogy. Blake lauded Flowers as a model Christian, declaring him a clean fighter who was a credit not only to his race, but to the city of Atlanta and the state of Georgia.[1]

The interracial audience and the white praise for Flowers did not challenge the power of white supremacy in the Jim Crow South. As a member of what was then the Colored Methodist Episcopal Church (now the Christian Methodist Episcopal Church, or CME Church) and nicknamed the "Georgia deacon," Flowers had a reputation for piety that softened the aggression typically associated with boxers. It was precisely because Flowers seemed safe that white Atlanta residents felt compelled to pay their respects. But while Blake's presence at Flowers's funeral did not pose a threat to segregation, it did highlight the potential of sports and religion to provide a sense of shared identity across the color line.

The prominence of the two men also highlighted Protestant engagement with sports in the 1920s that extended beyond the Northern-based mainline. The religious groups connected to Blake and Flowers—fundamentalists, white Southern Protestants, and Black Protestants—stood outside the national Protestant establishment to varying degrees and for a variety of reasons, ranging from racism, to region, to theology. Yet, despite their outsider status, they established important patterns of involvement with sports that both overlapped with and diverged from the middlebrow approach.

Understanding the ideologies and emphases that these "outsider" groups developed in the 1920s and 1930s provides a fuller sense of the multiple ways Protestants engaged with the golden age of sports—and also the directions that

The Spirit of the Game. Paul Emory Putz, Oxford University Press. © Oxford University Press 2024.
DOI: 10.1093/9780190091095.003.0003

the Christian athlete movement, launched after World War II, would eventually take.

Moral Purity and Missionary Idealism

After World War I, as Americans' obsession with athletics reached unprecedented heights, a group of white Protestants who thought of themselves as defenders of "old-time" religion rallied under the banner of fundamentalism. While fundamentalists had no cohesive organizational structure, central to the movement was a network of ministers and religious entrepreneurs who advocated a brand of premillennialism labeled "dispensationalism"—the belief that God had divided history into ages, or dispensations, and that Jesus's Second Coming to earth would initiate the final dispensation (the millennium). The task for Christians was to watch, work, and wait in a sinful world, searching the biblical prophecies for signs that Jesus's return was imminent. Unlike middlebrow Protestants, who held to an optimistic view of human progress and American culture, premillennialists usually viewed the world around them with suspicion and nurtured a more aggressive emphasis on evangelism. While not all fundamentalists were dispensational premillennialists, the doctrine was especially important to the movement.[2]

Meanwhile, at the level of spiritual devotion, Keswick spirituality often held sway. Also called the "Higher Christian Life" or "Victorious Christian Life," Keswick theology divided Christians into "carnal" and "spiritual" categories. The former were nominal believers who might attend church but who had not fully surrendered their lives to Christ; the latter were those who were consecrated, or fully committed, to the Christian life. This commitment was experienced through continual postconversion encounters with the Holy Spirit and expressed by prioritizing the spiritual over the worldly—by consistently and earnestly practicing spiritual disciplines like prayer and Bible study, carefully following the behavioral standards of nineteenth-century evangelical Protestantism, and serving Christ through evangelism.[3]

Dispensational premillennialism and Keswick spirituality were central to the fundamentalist community, but it was the battle against modernist theology in Northern denominations and modernist tendencies in public life (particularly the teaching of evolution) that defined the public face of the movement in the 1920s. Believing that modernism stripped away the transcendent claims of Christianity, fundamentalists championed the defense of what they saw as traditional Christian doctrines, including the inerrancy of Scripture, the historical truth of its claims about Jesus's miracles, and the exclusive path to salvation offered by Jesus's death and resurrection.[4] In this conflict fundamentalists allied with those uninterested in or opposed to dispensational premillennialism, including "antimodernist evangelicals" like William Jennings Bryan and "churchly conservatives" like J. Gresham Machen.[5] Through the mid-1920s this broad fundamentalist coalition waged a fierce battle for control of the Northern Baptist and Presbyterian denominations and campaigned against teaching evolution in public schools.[6]

By the second half of the decade, fundamentalists had been defeated in their efforts to purge their denominations of modernists, and in the aftermath of the Scopes trial (1925) they were increasingly consigned to the margins of cultural legitimacy.[7] But while fundamentalists may have withdrawn from aggressive efforts to control their denominations, they did not retreat from public life. As a mostly white movement, they sat atop the racial hierarchy that plagued American society; meanwhile, their premillennial theology drove them to remain engaged in American culture and politics, following Jesus's command to "occupy until I come."[8] Throughout the 1930s, fundamentalists expanded their network of Bible institutes, summer Bible conferences, radio programs, publishing ventures, foreign mission societies, and businessmen's clubs.[9] Still, fundamentalists self-consciously positioned themselves on the peripheries of mainstream American life. "To be a fundamentalist in the 1930s," historian Joel Carpenter writes, "was to bear the social and psychic burden of an outsider."[10]

That outsider status extended to the world of big-time sports. There were at least two factors at play. First, fundamentalists maintained a zealous emphasis on evangelism that other Northern white Protestants lacked. Fundamentalists believed that a true Christian needed to have a supernatural salvation experience. And to be saved, one needed to hear the message of salvation preached. Fundamentalists prized athletes-turned-evangelists more than they prized athletes or coaches who made sports their profession.

Billy Sunday, a pro baseball outfielder who retired in 1891 to become a full-time minister, exemplified this fundamentalist priority.[11] Two runners who competed in the 1924 Olympics—the American Ray Buker and the Scottish Eric Liddell—became heroes, too, when they followed their Olympic success by dedicating their lives to missionary service. (Although Liddell was not himself a fundamentalist, his refusal to compete on Sunday during the Olympics resonated with the movement).[12] William Borden, a former college athlete at Yale who died on the mission field in 1913, earned acclaim as well. In *Borden of Yale '09: The Life That Counts* (1926), Borden is depicted as an all-around man who surrenders to Christ and leaves behind his comfortable life for overseas evangelism.[13] The "missionary idealism" expressed in *Borden of Yale* pervaded fundamentalist culture.[14] Most fundamentalists had no problem with young men playing sports, but they reserved their greatest praise for those who made full-time Christian service their life's work.

Along with a missionary zeal that prized "spiritual" vocations (missionary service) over "secular" ones (working within sports), fundamentalists' desire to avoid worldliness also limited their ability to engage with big-time sports. Fundamentalists believed they were "in the world, but not of it," with a greater emphasis on the latter than their fellow Protestants. To guard against worldliness, fundamentalists held themselves to strict standards of behavior: dancing, swearing, smoking, drinking, playing cards, and breaking the Sabbath were all regarded as sins. While other Protestants might have frowned on those activities, they tended to be less militant or to frame their behavioral standards as matters of character development rather than adherence to a biblical command.[15]

The Sabbath issue alone meant that even if fundamentalists could get over the drinking, swearing, and gambling associated with professional sports, they could not participate in Major League Baseball (MLB). Writing for *Moody Monthly* in 1921, one minister made it plain there was no room for compromise: "[E]very baseball player and every baseball 'fan'. . . who on the Sabbath day lures the people from worship is doing what he can to undermine the religious foundations of national life."[16] In 1929 the *Alliance Weekly*—the periodical of the Christian and Missionary Alliance, a fundamentalist missionary network that later became an evangelical denomination—explained that participation in Sunday sports indicated "that we are either 'dead in trespasses and sins' or sadly backslidden and desperately in need of revival."[17] While mainline Protestants began dropping strict Sabbath observance by the 1930s, in fundamentalist circles maintaining the sanctity of Sunday remained a major area of concern into the 1960s.

Yet even if the fundamentalist desire to prioritize evangelism and avoid association with sinful practices limited their participation in big-time sports, they continued to view amateur sports as a wholesome use of time and a way to develop strong Christian men.[18] In 1922 a reader asked *Moody Monthly* if it was appropriate for Christian ministers to organize a church-based baseball league. "Does not the Christian life call for an entire separation from the world?," the reader inquired. The *Moody Monthly* editor responded that although churches should prioritize preaching over recreation programs, "it is proper for clergymen to mingle with their men and boys in their sports" because "it forms an excellent 'point of contact.'"[19]

Even fiery opponents of sports spectacles made sure to clarify that they approved of wholesome athletics. Fundamentalist minister John Roach Straton's criticism of the 1921 prizefight between Jack Dempsey and Georges Carpentier is often cited as an example of fundamentalists' antipathy to popular culture.[20] Yet in the same sermon in which he blasted the fight as a sign of moral degeneracy and a "relapse into paganism," he took time to reassure his audience that he appreciated "real sport." People, he said, need "relaxation and recreation and play," and "there is a place for all of these things in any right scheme of human life."[21]

The close connections between competitive athletics and masculinity provided another reason for fundamentalists to stay engaged in sports: it allowed them to project an image of assertive Christian manhood. This strategy had considerable appeal in the interwar years, as fundamentalist leaders sought to portray themselves as "vigorous and energetic" men who defended traditional gender roles against the proliferation of flappers and other cultural symbols of the new independent woman.[22] Billy Sunday once again was the most famous representative of this style. Although his playing days were long over by the 1920s, throughout the decade Sunday continued to enhance his appeal by drawing on his sports career.[23] "Fightin'" Bob Shuler, John R. Rice, J. Frank Norris, and numerous other fundamentalist leaders expressed an affinity for sports as well.[24] Even the more relaxed Charles Fuller, radio host of *The Old Fashioned Revival Hour*, had captained the football team at Pomona College, a fact that a sympathetic fundamentalist biographer made sure to highlight in 1940.[25]

While an athletic past could help fundamentalist ministers project a masculine image, it could also provide them with metaphors to promote their spiritual message. Paul Rader, a former boxer and college football coach who pastored Moody Memorial Church from 1915 until 1921 and served as president of the Christian and Missionary Alliance from 1919 until 1924, was especially adept at this.[26] In 1920 Rader drew on his knowledge of football and boxing to show readers that faith "is an offensive, an active element in the Christian life." Referring to his days as a college coach, Rader described to his readers how he had improved his team by teaching his players to adopt an attacking, aggressive style of defense. Then he turned to a more controversial example: heavyweight champion Jack Dempsey. Rader found in Dempsey's boxing style a lesson for Christians in their spiritual lives. "Instead of being on the defensive and receiving a blow, [Dempsey] gives a blow to defend himself with," Rader noted. "This is what we have in Scripture in a remarkable way." Christians, Rader declared, should realize they "are never on the defensive in God's word."[27]

Rader's discussion of boxing and football reveals an intimate familiarity with those sports that not all fundamentalists shared. But his use of sports to highlight spiritual lessons was common. After all, the Apostle Paul had used athletic metaphors about "running the race" to illustrate his vision for the Christian life. And for those attuned to the "victorious Christian life" themes of Keswick spirituality, athletic metaphors had special resonance. Thus, a 1920 *Alliance Weekly* article compared "full consecration and sanctification" to a star athlete receiving his second wind in the heat of competition.[28]

At the same time, fundamentalist support for sports had its limits. Rader, who had no problem encouraging Christians to pattern their spiritual lives after Jack

Dempsey, made it clear that athletics should be subordinate to "the only task of the Christian"—winning souls to Christ.[29] The basic fundamentalist position on sports was summed up by John C. Page in a 1922 *Moody Monthly* article: "We believe that Christians should play as well as pray, unless the playing interferes with the praying."[30]

Throughout the interwar years fundamentalists did not always agree on where to draw the line between playing and praying. At Wheaton College, after initial resistance to football, leaders in the 1920s embraced the sport as a way of developing Christian manhood. Yet Bob Jones College went the other way, electing to drop football in the 1930s because of its connection with rowdiness, gambling, drinking, and other vices.[31] Despite these variations, fundamentalists generally sought to encourage wholesome athletic participation while working to keep it secondary to the higher priorities of evangelism, spiritual discipline, and adherence to nineteenth-century evangelical Protestant behavioral standards. They may not have fully engaged in big-time sports, a culture dominated by men who violated most of the standard markers of fundamentalist morality. But, in their own way, they upheld the value of athletic competition.

Regional Insiders

While fundamentalists harbored a sense of estrangement from the Northern Protestant establishment, in the South a different Protestant establishment wielded power, even as it stood outside the center of national life. Led by the Southern Baptist Convention (SBC; which claimed 2.7 million members in the 1930s), the Methodist Episcopal Church, South (just over 2 million members), and the Presbyterian Church of the United States (500,000 members), established white Southern denominations mostly avoided the bitter theological controversies that divided Northern Protestants, preaching an evangelical gospel of "uplift and respectability" while upholding the segregated status quo.[32] Although they maintained a sense of Southern distinctiveness, in the early twentieth century many middle- and upper-class white Southern Protestants also sought to move closer to the mainstream of American life.

One sign of the South's growing involvement in national culture came via athletics. Although the South did not have a MLB team (the closest teams were in Washington and St. Louis), it did have high-level minor league baseball, with the Southern Association and Texas League cultivating regional pride and developing Southern talent destined for the big leagues. Southerners like Ty Cobb had already made their mark in the majors before 1920; by the end of the 1920s, more than one-third of the players on MLB rosters hailed from the South.[33] The

Sabbath convictions of Southern Protestant clergy meant that full-fledged support for professional baseball was limited. Yet some Southern players publicized their religious convictions at a local and regional level, including St. Louis Cardinals star Pepper Martin and Boston Braves pitcher Bob Smith, both of whom were Southern Baptists.[34]

Baseball was no match for the enthusiasm with which white Southern Protestants embraced college football in the interwar years. Protestant clergy in the region had vigorously opposed the sport in the late nineteenth century, in part because of its close connections with elite Northern institutions. Although they could not keep the game from spreading throughout the South, these religious leaders succeeded in banning football at denominational colleges like Wake Forest (Baptist), Furman (Baptist), and Trinity (Methodist, now known as Duke). By 1920, however, many of the bans had been reversed and the Protestant-led opposition to the sport weakened dramatically. Football became a "focal point for denominational pride, boosterism, and a bit of harmless hedonism" for most white Southern evangelicals.[35]

An early indication of the South's entrance into the world of big-time football came from the "Praying Colonels" of Centre College, a small Presbyterian school in Danville, Kentucky. In 1917 Centre College graduate Robert L. Myers took over as athletic director, with the goal of bringing athletic glory to his alma mater. Myers had previously coached an undefeated high school football team in Fort Worth, Texas, and he convinced five of those players, including star Bo McMillin, to bring their talents to Danville. Myers also recruited Charley Moran, a Kentucky-born athletic journeyman with experience as a player, coach, and referee, to take over coaching duties for the team in 1917.[36]

With an experienced coach and a soon-to-be superstar in McMillin, the 1917 .season marked the beginning of Centre College's rise to prominence. National attention came two years later, in 1919, when Centre College upset West Virginia. The win immediately captured the interest of the national sports press because West Virginia had beaten traditional football power Princeton the previous week. Curious editors dispatched reporters to Kentucky to inquire about the upstart team. There, they discovered Centre College's pregame ritual of prayer, a practice that the local Kentucky press had been aware of since it began in 1917.[37] After *Association Men*, the YMCA's national publication, published a March 1920 article on the "Praying Kentuckians," the mythology of the Praying Colonels was firmly in place.[38]

The 1920 and 1921 seasons took the Praying Colonels legend to new heights. At the time, the elite "Big Three" of Harvard, Yale, and Princeton commanded the greatest prestige in the sport.[39] When Harvard, at the suggestion of a Boston sports editor, added Centre College to its schedule, the Praying Colonels earned a shot at national glory.[40] They put up a respectable showing in a loss to Harvard in 1920 and then returned the following year to shock the college football world with a 6-0 victory. According to historian Michael Oriard, Centre's win over Harvard "was the decisive event in launching the age of intersectionalism," with games featuring schools from different regions attracting substantial attention. Although Centre began to drop off the football map after the 1924 season, throughout the 1920s Southern schools like Georgia, Georgia Tech, and Alabama carried the regional banner.[41]

Centre College caught the attention of the Northern sports press not just because of its underdog status, but also because of the growing popularity of the Lost Cause myth. This reinterpretation of the Civil War downplayed the horrors of slavery, framing the Confederacy as a noble effort and Reconstruction as a disaster because it placed Black and white people as social equals. While Lost Cause mythology was first propagated by white Southerners in the late nineteenth century, it was widely embraced by white people across the nation in the early twentieth century, diffused through popular media like the 1915 blockbuster film *The Birth of a Nation*.[42]

In the hands of sportswriters, college football offered a cultural narrative that could be shaped to fit the contours of the Lost Cause. Themes highlighting Centre College's Southern identity and alluding to the Civil War proliferated (even though Kentucky had been a divided border state). As this narrative developed in the sports press, Centre's pregame prayers became a way of highlighting the team's reliance on the supposedly simple and sincere values of the romanticized Old South.[43]

One novel echoed these themes as well. In *First Down, Kentucky!* (1921), Yale graduate Ralph D. Paine wrote a fictionalized account of the Praying Colonels that closely followed real life events. His book culminated with a 1920 game against Harvard, a "bold raid" that stirred "the spirit of Dixie-Land."[44] Throughout the book Paine used the team's pregame prayers to signify the nostalgia for simpler times that pervaded much of the Old South mythology. While the "shrewd practical No'therners" associated with Harvard had "the efficiency of a large business corporation" and viewed prayer as "sentimental drivel," at Centre College, football "had been largely builded [sic] upon sentiment."[45] Although Centre College lost its matchup against Harvard in *First Down, Kentucky!*, Paine depicted the loss in Lost Cause hues, with defeat bringing honor to Centre College and the South.

Other denominational schools in the South attempted to follow Centre College's model. Centenary College, a Methodist school in Shreveport, Louisiana, went directly to the source by hiring Bo McMillin as its head coach in 1922, paying him $2,000 more than the school president.[46] "Universities which had not heard of Centenary twelve months ago, have begged in vain for a place on [our football] schedule," the school's leadership gloated, while the student body penned a new song culminating in the lines "Great 'Bo' is coming here / Glory, Glory, Hallelujah! / Great 'Bo' is coming here!"[47]

Henry T. Carley, editor of the Methodist church's *New Orleans Christian Advocate*, also caught the spirit of excitement. After McMillin announced his plans to take the helm of Centenary football, Carley introduced him to Louisiana by lauding McMillin's character. "Bo's philosophy of life may be summed up in these words," Carley concluded, "hard work, brotherly love, team-spirit, fair play, prayer—and that's a pretty good philosophy."[48]

Centenary did not quite replicate Centre College's success, but the team did win ninety percent of its games during McMillin's three seasons as coach.[49] However, for Centenary as for Centre, the resources required to pursue football glory proved too great a burden. The loose academic standards under McMillin threatened Centenary's accreditation, and they let him go after three years. Centre considered hiring its former star player, but, like Centenary, it ultimately decided that McMillin's costly salary and penchant for lowering a school's academic reputation were not worth the potential football success. By the late 1920s both Centenary and Centre had faded from football relevance, although they continued to field teams.[50]

Other denominational schools in the South had lasting success with football. Duke University, with Methodist affiliations, snatched Alabama coach Wallace Wade in 1930, leading to a football renaissance for a school that had banned the sport from 1895 until 1920. Southern Methodist University, which opened its doors in 1915, became a football power in the 1930s, battling the Disciples of Christ–affiliated Texas Christian University and the Baptist-affiliated Baylor University in the Southwest Conference. The example of Centre College was not forgotten by its successors. In 1930 Baylor's student newspaper, the *Daily Lariat*, praised the Praying Colonel teams of the early 1920s for successfully advertising Centre College. The editorial encouraged Baylor to follow the same path.[51]

Not all white Protestant leaders went along with the growing football craze. Methodist Bishop Warren Candler, long a fierce opponent of football, continued his opposition in the 1920s. He blasted schools that used sports as advertisements, warning that football was "defiling and defeating" higher education.[52] Candler's screeds did not sway many, but he managed to control his own kingdom: as president of Emory University, he made sure the school did not build a football program.

The Baptist-affiliated Mercer University successfully stiff-armed football as well. Spright Dowell, a devoted Baptist and president of Auburn University from 1920 until 1927, was forced out of Auburn due in part to his de-emphasis of football. At his new post as president of Mercer, Dowell kept the football program under control, shutting it down entirely during World War II and electing not to bring it back after the war.[53]

Other Baptist leaders were also ambivalent. After the Carnegie Report was published in 1929, detailing the excessive commercialization of college football, the *Baptist Standard* published several articles urging Southern Baptists to take note and "seek a sane solution" to "this very grave problem."[54] Opposition to big-time football persisted among rural evangelicals and members of radical holiness and Pentecostal churches, too—which distinguished themselves from other evangelicals with their belief that the active and supernatural power of the Holy Spirit could be experienced in a personal way, expressed through spiritual gifts like speaking in tongues and divine healing.[55]

Yet, most middle-class white Protestants in cities and college towns across the region embraced the sport.[56] F. M. McConnell, editor of the *Baptist Standard*, recognized this fact. In 1931 when a reader suggested that Baptists should abolish football on their campuses, McConnell rejected the proposal as too extreme. "[T]he vast majority of the people of the United States are in favor of athletics," McConnell noted. Instead of ending football, McConnell urged readers to "make athletics healthful and as safe as possible"—to control athletics instead of allowing athletics to control Baptist institutions.[57]

Exhortations to control college football's excesses offered one path for Southern clergy. But as the sport became a regional obsession and moved into the national spotlight, white Southern Protestants also sought to capitalize on the sport's popularity. The SBC proved especially adept at this. Flush with money from a fundraising campaign launched after World War I, the SBC hired Frank Leavell in 1922 to launch a college ministry aimed at enlisting "the thousands of Baptist college and university students" in the South toward "a distinctive denominational student movement."[58] Taking the name Baptist Student Union (BSU), Leavell spent the next two decades forging the BSU into a vibrant organization that reached nearly every college and university in the South.

Leavell was not a former football player himself—baseball was his sport of choice—but he recognized the importance of the game to college life. In the pages of the *Baptist Student*, the monthly periodical of the BSU, cover images in the fall months frequently depicted a heroic young football star while articles like "Football and Religion" and "Success Essentials on the Gridiron" featured Southern football coaches promoting the religious values of the game, not unlike the middlebrow uses of sports for mainline Protestants. Star athletes involved with the BSU were promoted as well. Joe Hall of Florida, J. C. "Abe" Barnett of Baylor, and Casey Cason of Oklahoma all received praise for their athletic prowess and their involvement in Baptist life, as did numerous athletes from smaller colleges.[59]

A similar brand of sports boosterism, Southern identity, and Christian faith came from the typewriter of Morgan Blake, sports editor of the *Atlanta Journal* throughout the 1920s. After a conversion experience in 1922, Blake joined the

Baptist Tabernacle in Atlanta and soon after began teaching a popular men's Bible class, broadcast over the radio from 1928 until World War II.[60] He frequently combined his connections in sports to his passion for evangelism. In 1923, for example, Blake joined with Georgia Tech's star running back "Red" Barron to lead revival services at a Baptist church in Atlanta. In 1929, during a trip to Nashville to cover Georgia Tech's football game against Vanderbilt, Blake stayed for an extra day to speak with a local Bible class. He secured Vanderbilt football coach Dan McGugin to introduce him before launching into one of his standard evangelistic talks: "Football and Life."[61]

Like the *Atlanta Journal*, which claimed that it "Covers Dixie like the Dew," Blake's Southern identity was never far from view.[62] When speaking in 1929 at a meeting of the National Federation of Men's Bible Classes, Blake took aim at an unnamed writer (likely H. L. Mencken) who "had referred to the South as a vast, ignorant section, where the people still believed in a personal God." Blake accepted the charge as true, declaring that "another war between the States would be brought about if an attempt were made to introduce another God than a personal God across the Mason and Dixon line."[63] In his autobiography, when Blake discussed his vision of the ideal athletic man, his list included typical national heroes like Jack Dempsey, Knute Rockne, and Teddy Roosevelt—but it also featured Nathan Bedford Forrest, a Confederate general who had helped create the Ku Klux Klan.[64]

Blake's Southern identity did not preclude him from drawing on Northern theological influences. As a member of Baptist Tabernacle Church in Atlanta, which had connections to the fundamentalist movement, Blake established a relationship with Billy Sunday and counted Donald Barnhouse, a Philadelphia-based fundamentalist Presbyterian minister, as a good friend and spiritual mentor.[65] Yet Blake did not fully fit the fundamentalist mold. He generally focused on a positive articulation of the gospel message rather than militant opposition to modernist trends, and he participated in sports activities that fundamentalists (and many Southern Baptists) saw as sinful: attending baseball games on Sundays, watching prizefights, and defending Christians who did the same.[66] He also argued that Christians should support the "social gospel," by which he meant uplift programs and charities for the betterment of humanity.[67] In this way, Blake combined the optimistic view of culture advanced by middle-brow Protestants with the fundamentalist message of sin and salvation, all while linking it with a strong sense of regional identity.

Importantly, this regional identity was tethered to white supremacy. White denominational colleges, like all schools in the South, remained strictly divided along the color line. In intersectional games, too, white Southern colleges asked integrated Northern teams to bench their Black football players—a request that Northern schools in the 1920s usually obliged.[68] Throughout the 1920s, neither

Blake nor other Southern white Protestants in sports sought to change this. While the *Baptist Student*—relatively moderate in its racial views compared with other white Southern publications—agreed that African Americans sometimes faced unfair prejudice, writers for the periodical defended segregation, claiming that "[n]o two races have ever lived together and each continue to prosper" and "[n]either the Negro nor the white man is pleading for 'social equality.'"[69]

Respectability and Race Advancement

Whatever differences existed between the various white Protestant groups in the 1920s, they all shared the insider status afforded by their racial identity. Few of their leaders saw opposition to segregation as a moral priority. This was true even for white Protestants in the North, who chose to follow the so-called gentleman's agreement rather than challenge segregation. In MLB this meant accepting the unwritten rule that barred Back players from the league; in college football this meant benching Black players when playing against a white Southern team. Other religious groups may have felt marginalized. For Black Protestants, their marginalization was imposed on them and by design.

Still, racism and segregation did not eliminate Black agency, with Black churches in particular becoming a space for support and solidarity. In the early twentieth century, Methodist and Baptist denominations formed the heart of the Black Protestant landscape, with African Methodist Episcopal (AME), African Methodist Episcopal Zion (AME Zion), CME, National Baptist Convention, USA, and National Baptist Convention of America churches providing support and meaning for Black communities. Black congregations associated with pre-dominantly white Presbyterian, Episcopalian, and Methodist denominations—functioning like a denomination within a denomination—served Black neighborhoods as well. And newer holiness and Pentecostal denominations also emerged, none more important than the Church of God in Christ (COGIC).[70]

In sports, too, Black leaders, educators, and entrepreneurs built their own spaces to encourage and promote athletic competition within their communities. While the lack of economic resources made professional leagues difficult to sustain, by the 1920s the establishment of Negro League baseball, traveling basketball teams, college conferences, rivalry football games, and expanded sports sections in Black newspapers converged to form what historian Derrick White describes as a "sporting congregation": an informal community of Black players, coaches, fans, and sportswriters who articulated meaning and significance through their shared sports experiences.[71]

This "sporting congregation" was not defined by religion, but it made room for a Black version of muscular Christianity. Black muscular Christians shared several tenets with their white counterparts: the focus on male leadership, the middle-class emphasis on self-discipline and gentlemanly refinement, and even the sense that the destiny of the United States rested, at least in part, on their shoulders. But Black muscular Christians reframed the movement to fit their reality as people living in a society shaped by white supremacy. By cultivating Black pride and working toward racial integration—what scholar Patrick Miller calls "muscular assimilation"—they saw sports as a way to challenge racist assumptions and gain a seat at tables of power in American society.[72]

The YMCA, though it remained segregated until 1946, served as an important incubator for Black muscular Christianity. With sports as a key part of their strategy, Black YMCA leaders built their own wing within the organization, advocating for the moral and physical benefits of athletic participation.[73] Some eventually moved on to wider fields of service. Edwin Henderson, a lifelong Baptist and one of the most important Black athletic leaders of the early twentieth century, worked with the YMCA to organize basketball teams in Washington, DC. Henderson also directed and facilitated high school and college leagues while simultaneously writing and raising awareness about Black sports. Through it all, he encouraged Christian support for athletics. "The health and morals of our race may be improved through athletic recreation," he wrote in 1912, urging Black "churchmen" to "exert an influence actively and intelligently for athletics and healthy recreation."[74]

Joining with the efforts of the YMCA, historically Black colleges and universities (HBCUs) also built sporting institutions and cultivated muscular Christian ideas. College football was especially important in this effort. As Derrick White explains, the sport helped to nurture "a version of Black manhood that tied student-athletes to the ideology of racial uplift and, eventually, to the mantle of racial leadership."[75] Because many HBCUs had church roots and affiliations, their football programs were often linked with the broader religious aims of their institutions. Samuel H. Archer, a professor and football coach at Atlanta Baptist College (later renamed Morehouse College), articulated the basic muscular Christian ethos in 1906 when he linked the growth of football on HBCU campuses with the development of well-rounded moral leaders for the Black community, men with "courage and gentleness, daring and sympathy, strenuous endeavor and just consideration."[76]

By the 1920s, muscular Christianity had infused the institutions and organizations of the Black "sporting congregation" for several decades. Its influence continued in the golden age of sports, as did the religious identification of key Black sports leaders. Jake Gaither is one example. The son of a Methodist minister, Gaither enrolled at Knoxville College, a Presbyterian-affiliated HBCU in Tennessee. As a student, Gaither played on the football team and became an advocate for the sport, writing articles for the student newspaper on the moral value of the game. By the time he graduated in 1927, Gaither had decided to make football his life's work and his mission field. As he later told an interviewer, he believed one of football's key purposes was to provide athletes with "a belief in prayer, a faith in God."[77] Although widespread acclaim did not arrive until Gaither was coaching at Florida A&M in the 1940s, he developed his Christian coaching style and ideology through his involvement in Black sporting spaces in the 1920s.

Success in integrated competition—muscular assimilation—was also important to the sporting congregation. Writing about the "colored college athlete" in *The Crisis* in 1911, Edwin Henderson laid out the logic and challenge. Black athletes who excelled at predominantly white colleges, he said, could win "the respect and admiration of thousands" and thus shape "the minds of thousands of Americans." Yet, success in white spaces came with a cost: "He [the Black athlete] must fight the prejudiced attacks of Negro haters" while also going above and beyond in both athletic ability and strength of character. "Nearly every Negro athlete of prominence in college has been a gentleman, has worn his honors with modesty," Henderson wrote, "and has gained respect by playing the game and ignoring the taunts of prejudiced opponents."[78]

In the 1920s, as in the decades before, several Black athletes followed the path laid out by Henderson, excelling at predominantly white Northern schools. For some of these athletes, Christian faith was a central part of their identity. John Howard Johnson, the son of Harlem-based Episcopalian priest John Wesley Johnson, learned basketball through his father's church, St. Cyprian. With a gym and a sponsored team (the "Speed Boys"), St. Cyprian was one of several Black churches that played a key role in the emergence of Harlem's Black basketball community in the 1910s, helping to infuse "a religious ethos of ultimate worth and community uplift into the game."[79]

The younger Johnson took the game he learned at his father's church and earned a starring role on the Columbia University basketball teams of the early 1920s. A *Chicago Defender* article in 1921 described him as the team's leading scorer and "one of the brainiest players in the game."[80] Following his time at Columbia, Johnson became an Episcopal minister himself, leading St. Martin's parish. There, he remained involved in the sports world. He counted Effa and Abe Manley, owners of a National Negro League franchise, as friends. Bob Douglas, founder of the famed New York Renaissance professional basketball team—the best Black basketball team of the time—was also a friend and a member of St. Martin's.[81] For Johnson, whether as an athlete or a minister, sports and faith were complementary. "Both demand cleanliness in personal life," he explained to a reporter in 1928. "The fight in an athletic contest is analogous to the fight in life."[82]

While Johnson was well known in New York, greater national fame came to William DeHart Hubbard, track star for Michigan. Born and raised in

Cincinnati, Hubbard developed his athletic abilities through the YMCA and his public high school before enrolling at Michigan. An exceptional all-around athlete, he could have contributed in basketball or football if not for unwritten bans on Black involvement in those sports at Michigan—bans supported by football coach and athletic director Fielding Yost.[83]

In the individual sport of track and field, however, white Northern schools demonstrated greater flexibility with regard to the color line. Hubbard quickly asserted himself after arriving in Ann Arbor, winning conference titles as a sprinter and setting records in the long jump. In 1924, his ability in the latter event earned him a trip to the 1924 Olympics, where he brought home a gold medal—the first for an African American in an individual event.[84]

The Black sporting congregation celebrated Hubbard's feat. "Americans may want to deny him," Roscoe Simmons wrote in the *Chicago Defender*, "but they CAN'T deny that American flag he wore."[85] The *Afro-American*, based in Baltimore, reported on a welcome party featuring hundreds of young people that greeted Hubbard upon his return. To his impressionable audience, Hubbard revealed the secrets to his success: hard work and clean living, which included avoiding tobacco and alcohol.[86] Hubbard continued to preach his muscular Christian message in the years to come. "Competition on a high plane develops healthy minds and bodies," he explained in 1925. "It develops fair play that should be inborn in the youth of our race."[87] And Hubbard did his part to promote this type of competition: he worked with the YMCA, wrote sports columns, organized basketball and baseball leagues, and developed youth recreation programs.[88]

While Hubbard and Johnson nurtured an all-American image associated with respectability and racial uplift, they did not remain quiet when it came to racism. In one of his first games at Columbia, Johnson traded punches with an opposing player, a white Southerner who apparently was frustrated with Johnson's defensive intensity. An article recounting the incident a few years later compared Johnson's actions to "Jesus when he drove the money lenders out of the Temple" and gloated that Johnson's fists "did much to calm that Dixie rashness."[89]

Hubbard, meanwhile, used his sports column to call out racial inequalities. He criticized white heavyweight champion Jack Dempsey for refusing to face Black challengers, and when Northwestern football coach Glenn Thistlethwaite—a Methodist coach at a Methodist school—asked a Black player on his team to sit in the stands for a game against the Southern school Tulane, Hubbard called out the "deplorable" incident.[90] By bringing attention to racial injustices, Black muscular Christians differentiated themselves from their fellow Protestants across the color line.

Despite the ongoing links between faith and sports represented by Hubbard, Johnson, and Gaither, there was also tension and debate among Black Protestants over the role of sports. Like white Protestant congregations, Black churches included a range of theological and cultural perspectives. For the highly educated Black Protestant elite, sports could be considered a diversion from more important educational priorities needed to "advance the race." Accordingly, some church leaders followed the path of Black intellectuals associated with the Harlem Renaissance, criticizing or distancing themselves from an excessive focus on sports. Others worried about professionalization and the decline of the amateur ideal—like their white counterparts, they believed amateurism unlocked the character-building potential of sports.[91] Those associated with conservative revivalist traditions, meanwhile, often warned against the "worldly" sins and vices associated with sports, ranging from gambling, to drinking, to breaking the Sabbath.[92]

For Black Protestants in the sporting congregation, however, the rising popularity of sports in the 1920s provided an opportunity to link Christian faith with racial uplift and muscular assimilation. Writing in 1928, Edwin Henderson admitted that some unhealthy tendencies had developed among Black sports fans, including an obsession with winning. But he believed that sports were "almost as essential as religion for the masses" and he praised coaches for upholding the moral values and citizen-making ideals of athletic competition. Like white middlebrow Protestants, Henderson believed that even in the midst of commercialization, sports could "become a great molder of ideals and attitudes to prepare the boy for the real struggles of life."[93]

In general, prominent Black Protestant support for sports in the 1920s came from men like Henderson and churches that reflected his sensibility: educated, middle-class, with a theology that emphasized respectability and the cultivation of Christian character. Writing in the *Southern Workman* in 1926, Charles H. Williams credited "progressive" Black ministers who possessed a "social vision" for the growth in church support for sports and recreation.[94] Yet this trend crossed theological boundaries. Williams also revealed in his article that a survey of eighty Black Protestant ministers, representing a range of theological perspectives, showed widespread support for youth sports: eighty-one percent of the ministers approved of football, ninety-one percent approved of basketball and baseball, and seventy-six percent approved of boxing.[95]

The Reverend James M. Gates, a Baptist minister from rural Georgia, highlights the ways that conservative Black Protestants could find meaning in sports. Gates moved to Atlanta in the 1910s and in the 1920s became a breakout star for his sermons recorded on phonograph and distributed in Black communities across the country. Historian Lerone Martin points out that Gates's sermons reflected "rural and southern forms of black expression" that offered a traditional gospel message. But his old-time message came packaged in the context of urban life in the Jazz Age, with frequent references to popular cultural trends, including sports.[96] In a 1928 sermon titled "The Ball Game of Life," Gates offered a traditionalist spin on a common metaphor. In Gates's vivid imagery, the Devil stood on the mound seeking to "strike out" Christians who let their guard down. The four bases, meanwhile, represented the path to salvation: listeners were told that to reach first base they needed to repent; for second base, believe; third base was be baptized; and home plate was making it to eternal glory.[97]

Gates's sermon may have drawn on the popularity of sports, but it was not necessarily an endorsement of sports as it existed in the 1920s. On the other side of the record, however, Gates included another sports-related sermon: a tribute to the recently deceased middleweight boxer Tiger Flowers, whom we met at the beginning of this chapter. Gates eulogized Flowers as a "clean sport" and "title holder" who was a "gentleman and a citizen" as well as "a man that held up for his race."[98]

That Flowers could be recognized as a "title holder" was remarkable. At the heavyweight division in boxing, segregation reigned through the 1920s. White Americans, haunted by the specter of the confident and boastful former heavyweight champion Jack Johnson, made sure that between 1915 and 1935 no African Americans had a shot at the title.[99] As white boxers Jack Dempsey and Gene Tunney attracted hundreds of thousands of fans to their bouts and became national celebrities, Black heavyweight fighters remained on the margins. Flowers faced similar barriers at the middleweight division, but he managed to earn a shot at the title, defeating champion Harry Greb in 1926. Flowers lost the title later that year in a controversial decision and then died in 1927 before he had another chance to regain it.

Despite his short run among the boxing elite, Flowers earned the admiration and respect of Black supporters and at least some white fans. Central to his widespread appeal was his religious identity. With roots among the lower classes, Flowers—like Gates—publicly embraced more traditional forms of piety common in the rural South. He spoke often about his devotional life and his adherence to traditional markers of evangelical morality. "I make it a practice to read three verses of the New Testament each morning and afternoon of my life, never train for a contest on the Sabbath, and happen to be a steward of the Methodist church in my home town," he wrote in a 1925 article for the *Chicago Defender*. Numerous articles in both the Black and white press emphasized these practices, describing Flowers as a Bible reader and a church member committed to his faith.[100]

But while Flowers's appeal cut across racial divides, there were differences in the meanings assigned to him. A 1926 profile of Flowers published in the *Indianapolis Recorder*, an African American weekly, noted that Flowers eschewed "wine, women, and song," and that he was "an exceptional clean liver, a religious man, deacon in his church, and owner of much real estate."[101] Here, the key focus was on Flowers as a strong and independent Black man, one who achieved success while maintaining traditional moral values.[102]

For white audiences, Flowers's independence and even his Blackness were downplayed. Instead, white journalists often used a description first coined by Flowers's white promoter: "the whitest black man in the game." They emphasized his subservience—Flowers, according to one white Southern sportswriter, "learned to obey the every wish of his manager and to take orders without a word of comment."[103] Morgan Blake drew on these ideas, too, when he eulogized Flowers. The middleweight champion, Blake declared, was "as gentle as a woman" with "the faith of a little child."[104]

These descriptions of Flowers as the anti–Jack Johnson created space for some white support. Yet, while white Protestants from all backgrounds might find something to affirm in Flowers—for fundamentalists his Bible reading; for middlebrow mainliners his clean living; for white Southerners his roots in Atlanta—they generally stopped short of assigning moral value to his success against white opponents. To use sports to challenge racism—to cross the color line—was moral ground on which Black Protestants stood mostly alone among American Christians during the golden age of sports.

* * *

As white Southern Protestants, fundamentalists, and Black Protestants navigated popular trends in American culture in the 1920s, they developed distinct patterns of engagement with sports. Fundamentalists enjoyed and enthusiastically participated in athletics, but they prioritized evangelism, piety, and separation from the world to such an extent that success in sports at an elite level was difficult to achieve. White Southern Protestants comfortably blended the evangelistic emphasis of fundamentalists with the character-building and establishment sensibility of middlebrow Protestants, all the while connecting sports success with Southern identity. Black Protestants shared with white Protestants the emphasis on using athletics to build character and promote traditional behavioral expectations. Yet, they added to this a focus on cultivating Black pride and working for muscular assimilation.

Despite these differences, into the 1930s all three groups remained on the peripheries of big-time sports in varying ways. No major professional sports teams existed in the South, and fundamentalists continued to abstain from professional sports on Sundays. Black Protestants, meanwhile, faced segregation and racism that limited their access to predominantly white spaces. As a result, middlebrow Protestants remained best positioned for influence within big-time sports.

That position would prove essential for the developments to come. As a series of global crises began to envelop American life in the 1930s, leading to World War

II and the dawn of the Cold War, a new movement emerged to mobilize Christian athletes for the protection of the "American way." Middlebrow Protestants, as sports industry insiders, led the charge—but they were not alone. The new Christian athlete movement would also be shaped by religious communities that had been on the margins of 1920s sports culture: fundamentalists, Black Protestants, and white Southern Protestants.

3

Christian Democracy Is Being
Tackled for a Loss

On a summer night in 1956, at a camp center in the mountains near Estes Park, Colorado, Branch Rickey took the podium. His task: to deliver an address to the 250 young men gathered for the inaugural Fellowship of Christian Athletes (FCA) summer conference.

Earlier that evening a ceremony honoring Amos Alonzo Stagg for his "Christian ministry in the world of sport" had set the stage for Rickey. Well into his seventies, the aging baseball executive felt himself swept up in the moment. "I don't think I've ever been faced with a situation that seemed to me to be so pregnant with the immediate possibilities of a great crowd of young men coming to feel the presence of God and the duty of service to the King of Kings," he announced. Rickey's excitement stemmed from his hopes for the future—a future in which the American nation would be preserved and upheld by people of faith. "There is an honor in this government, and we have got to keep it," he told the crowd of young athletes. "If this group here tonight were to find themselves dedicated to a common cause," he claimed, they could transform the United States "before the next generation is over."[1]

Rickey's speaking role on the first night of the conference reflected his importance to the fledging FCA, a relationship that began in August 1954 when an unheralded twenty-nine-year-old college basketball coach named Don McClanen met with the baseball executive, sharing his vision for an organization of athletes mobilized to instill Christian values in America's youth. "If athletes can endorse shaving cream, razor blades, and cigarettes," McClanen reasoned, "surely they can endorse the Lord." When Rickey responded enthusiastically to the idea, McClanen had the final piece needed to launch his movement. The organization that became the Fellowship of Christian Athletes was born.[2]

The significance of Rickey's support for the FCA can hardly be exaggerated. Dating back to the 1920s, Rickey was the most prominent symbol of Christian faith in America's most popular team sport. His involvement with the FCA provided legitimacy and respectability that the organization desperately needed. At the same time, the FCA provided something Rickey keenly desired: hope for a

The Spirit of the Game. Paul Emory Putz, Oxford University Press. © Oxford University Press 2024.
DOI: 10.1093/9780190091095.003.0004

future in which Americans embraced the blend of moral and religious values that Rickey saw as essential to the nation's success.

How was a little-known junior college basketball coach able to create an organization full of celebrity athletes and coaches who advertised their faith as they operated within the world of big-time sports? The shared sense that they were fighting for the soul of America was a crucial factor. By gathering Christian athletes under one banner, the founding of the FCA marked the beginning of a new era and the launch of a movement—the rise of a religious sports subculture that would come to define and shape what it meant to be a "Christian athlete" in the decades to come.

Before Branch Rickey's speech announced the beginning of a new movement, however, historical and cultural forces helped to pave the way, heightening the significance of religion and sports to American identity. For fundamentalists and mainliners, white Southerners and Black Protestants, the existential challenges of the 1930s and 1940s made it clear that sports had an important role to play in shaping the American present and future. The question was which visions of America and of Christianity would prevail.

While the movement that the FCA launched would eventually become identified with evangelicalism, this was not the case in the beginning. It was, instead, driven primarily by the same forces that shaped the religious sensibility of Branch Rickey: middlebrow culture and mainline Protestant institutions.

Defining the "American Way" with Sports

Born in New Jersey in 1925, Don McClanen came of age as American leaders were grappling with a worldwide economic crisis and the rise of totalitarian governments across the globe. The imminent sense of change stirred fierce debates about American identity. For some white Americans, the 1930s brought about a reactionary turn, with racist and nativist notions of America as a white Protestant (or white Christian) nation growing in popularity.[3] Softer versions of white Protestant identity rooted in a nostalgia for small-town life also flourished. In 1936, Bob Feller, a seventeen-year-old pitcher from tiny Van Meter, Iowa, became a national sensation when he debuted for the Cleveland Indians. *Time* featured the young ballplayer on its cover, deeming him the "schoolboy wonder," and newspapers followed his every move. Feller's allure derived from his farm boy image, his rootedness in the "real" America of small towns and country villages—an image of which Protestantism was an integral part.[4]

Yet if the 1930s brought a yearning for a return to an imagined white Protestant past, there was also considerable support for more inclusive understandings of an American way that defined itself against the totalitarian governments of

Germany and the Soviet Union. As Wendy Wall has shown, there were competing visions for how and in what way greater diversity should be pursued. One version of the American way came from those friendly to Franklin Roosevelt's New Deal program. This group pushed for a more equal distribution of power, viewing pluralism as a way to unite Americans behind social, political, and economic reform. Another version came from those more suspicious of the New Deal who used symbols of pluralism to promote civility and teamwork while maintaining the economic status quo—or reversing New Deal trends.[5] The latter group turned to voluntary interfaith "goodwill" endeavors like the National Conference on Christians and Jews (NCCJ) to encourage social harmony within the existing structures of America's capitalist system.[6]

Debates over the American way extended into sports. The two leading magazines for high school and college coaches in the 1930s—*Athletic Journal* and *Scholastic Coach*—illustrate the divide. *Athletic Journal*, edited by Big Ten commissioner John Griffith, represented a continuation of the business-friendly middlebrow Protestantism of the 1920s. Griffith used the pages of his journal to express suspicion of the encroaching welfare state and to emphasize the importance of high-stakes, money-making college sports for the development of future business and professional leaders.[7]

Scholastic Coach, on the other hand, edited by sportswriter and basketball official Jack Lippert, urged coaches and athletic directors to "control the game" and to keep it "free of the kind of training that was once regarded as most suitable for young Americans who would become successful in business."[8] While Lippert did not seek to eliminate competition, he spoke out against its excesses in a way that Griffith and the *Athletic Journal* did not, using *Scholastic Coach* to encourage readers to modify amateur athletics in order to fit in with the New Deal order. "As in government," one *Scholastic Coach* contributor wrote regarding sports, "we are trying to conserve the good of the old and to combine it with the valuable of new experiments."[9]

Most of the prominent white Protestants within athletics, including Amos Alonzo Stagg and Branch Rickey, came down on the *Athletic Journal's* side.[10] Speaking at a major Methodist conference in Chicago in 1938, Rickey made this perspective plain. Tasked with providing a layman's view of the church, Rickey highlighted the swirling global uncertainty, with "the ideals of democracy questioned." He then turned to his sports experience to offer a solution: "When teams are demoralized on a field of competition, they are ready to accept quick, though voluntary leadership." The emphasis on *voluntary* mirrored anti–New Deal messaging and was a clear signal to listeners that Rickey did not fully support Franklin Roosevelt's program. So was his explanation of what this voluntary leadership needed to provide: "something constructive and yet intensely personal."[11]

The individualistic pragmatism offered by Rickey was countered by others who focused more on social conditions and structures. Liberal Protestant intellectuals and student activists, building on the highbrow critiques of sports from the 1920s, generally followed *Scholastic Coach* in connecting New Deal reform to athletics.[12] Social concerns shaped the perspective of some Black Protestant leaders, too, particularly when it came to racism and segregation.

Participating on the same panel as Rickey in Chicago, a young African American minister named Karl Downs spoke on "What Youth Expects from the Church." Like Rickey, he framed his thoughts in relation to global events. Fascism and communism, he argued, challenged Christianity by seeking the complete loyalty of their adherents. The answer to this, for Downs, came not just in a personal faith, but also in an all-encompassing vision of a Christian social order—a "Christ-set world." With this goal in mind, Downs urged the church to speak with conviction about ethical issues including war, poverty, and racism. "Racial prejudice is a problem that is very close to some of us," he declared. "We must constantly speak out against it . . . as fearlessly as Christ would have spoken upon this evil."[13]

In the years to come, Downs and Rickey would join forces to help dismantle the color line in Major League Baseball—Downs by mentoring a college student named Jackie Robinson through his Pasadena church, and Rickey by signing Robinson to a contract in 1945. But in 1938, as he sat next to Downs on the Methodist panel in Chicago, Rickey remained silent on the problem of racial segregation. Continuing with the booster/builder approach preferred by middlebrow Protestants, he shied away from disrupting the status quo. It was instead Black leaders like Downs and a small but growing number of sympathetic white people—including liberal and left-wing mainline Protestants—who pushed the issue. And a key part of their strategy was the use of sports to project an image of a pluralistic and inclusive American way that contrasted with Nazi Germany's doctrine of racial purity.

An early sign of this strategy came in 1934 when Michigan and Georgia Tech prepared to meet for a football game. One of Michigan's star players, Willis Ward, was a Black man. But Georgia Tech, like most white Southern teams, refused to play against Black players. For most of the 1920s, as part of the "gentleman's agreement," white Northern teams usually benched their Black players in situations like this.[14] The two men who scheduled the game, Michigan athletic director Fielding Yost and Georgia Tech coach William Alexander, expected that this pattern would continue.

In the weeks leading up to the game, however, Black sportswriters and NAACP leaders drew attention to the game and urged Michigan not to bow to Jim Crow. On campus, a group of Michigan students demanded that Ward be allowed to play or the game be canceled; a petition they circulated received over one thousand signatures. The agitation only strengthened Yost's resolve. He hired private detectives to dig up information and disrupt any potential protests, and when the game kicked off on October 20, 1934, Ward was out of uniform and outside the stadium, not even allowed to stand with his team on the sidelines.[15]

Crucially, the debates that swirled around the Tech game involved not just notions of American identity, but also different conceptions of Christianity. Yost and Alexander were respectable Protestants with reputations as clean-living Christian men. Yost in particular frequently publicized his faith. A devoted Methodist with Southern roots, he participated in local church events, wrote articles for Protestant magazines, and spoke up for Protestant causes like Prohibition.[16] Through it all, Yost believed Black players lacked the leadership qualities needed for football. Like his Big Ten counterpart, Amos Alonzo Stagg, when Yost was a coach he never recruited a Black football player; Ward was only allowed to join the Michigan team in the 1930s because head coach Harry Kipke maneuvered behind the scenes to work around Yost's objections.[17]

For Yost and Alexander, racial segregation was entirely compatible with firm Christian convictions. In their view, benching Ward was the appropriate Christian response, since it would protect him from potential injury and demonstrate Christian hospitality to the segregationist traditions of the South.[18] Yost also criticized the ideological commitments of Ward's supporters. "The agitation was developed by a committee of five Jewish sophomore students, four of them from New York City and vicinity," Yost wrote to Alexander after the game. "They did it in the name of 'The United Front Committee on Ward.'" By painting the movement to play Ward as a plot by Jewish "outsiders," Yost implied that direct challenges to the gentleman's agreement were outside the bounds of acceptable Protestant behavior.[19]

Yet, the other side claimed Christian support, too. The Ann Arbor Ministerial Association, made up primarily of Protestant ministers, issued a statement urging Michigan to let Ward play, claiming that benching him would be "contrary to the finer principles of religion and democracy."[20] Ward himself was a member of a Baptist church in Detroit, and many of the Black leaders defending him had Christian commitments. An editorial in the *Chicago Defender* took Yost's dismissive claim that only "radicals" wanted Ward to play and flipped it around by linking radicalism with the Christian faith. "To be a radical is to say that there is something in the Golden Rule, in the Christian religion, in the law of universal brotherhood," it argued. "To be a radical is to stand firm for the principles of justice and of humanity."[21]

Such rhetoric did not win the day for Ward, but it did point to growing divides over American identity and the place of sports and Christianity in expressing ideas about national belonging. On the one hand, Ward's humiliating experience highlighted the continuation of the segregated status quo.[22] This social order was supported by many rank-and-file white Protestants, including Yost and Alexander. On the other hand, the substantial support Ward received revealed cracks in the foundation of white solidarity. These cracks emerged in large part out of a desire to differentiate the democratic American way from the authoritarian regimes gaining strength abroad. "In our own Land of the Free," Jack Lippert wrote in *Scholastic Coach* when commenting on Ward's plight, "we are far from innocent of the prejudice and discrimination of which Germany stands accused."[23]

New opportunities to assert an inclusive national identity through sports developed in the coming years. In 1936, Black track star Jesse Owens dominated the Olympic games in Germany; two years later Black heavyweight boxer Joe Louis defeated German Max Schmeling to defend his heavyweight title. For some Black Protestants, these athletic achievements carried religious significance. "God was with Joe Louis," a Black minister wrote to the *Chicago Defender* in 1938. "Schmeling represents Nazi Germany. Germany represents prejudice, hatred, race animosity, anti-democracy, anti-Christianity."[24]

Writing in his groundbreaking 1939 book, *The Negro in Sports*, Edwin Henderson made a similar point. He argued that one of the great benefits of sports was the potential to "develop a real Christian brotherhood among men of the minority and majority groups in our cosmopolitan American life." As evidence, he pointed to the achievements of Owens and Louis, particularly their victories over Germany.[25]

To be sure, the vast majority of white Southerners continued to uphold the color line, and few white Americans in any region advocated for substantial racial reform. Even so, a growing number of white Americans were willing to cheer on the success of a Black athlete and to claim that success on behalf of the nation.[26] A white reader from Kansas exemplified this trend in a letter to the *Emporia Gazette* after Louis's victory in 1938. "Can you imagine a negro being given an opportunity in Germany?" he asked. "Hardly: The United States is where such a thing could happen."[27]

White support was often predicated on images of respectability and exemplary moral conduct. "[Louis] is a clean, wholesome boy with no bad habits," white Atlanta sportswriter Morgan Blake wrote in 1937. "As long as he keeps that attitude he will find that the white people will respect him."[28] With these expectations in mind, Joe Louis's promoters took the Tiger Flowers route, carefully curating his image with publicized visits to churches and widely distributed photographs of Louis reading a Bible. The publicity helped to establish Louis as an inspirational hero to Black youth and a safe Black man to white audiences.[29] That reputation was only strengthened when the United States entered World War II and Louis became a spokesman for the war effort, encouraging Americans to see the conflict as a sacred struggle between good and evil, with the United States standing "on God's side."[30]

Religion, however, was not simply a public prop or a marketing tool. Black Christians in sports drew on their faith for personal sustenance and meaning, while also finding in it the imperative to challenge segregation. At HBCUs, coaches like Jake Gaither continued to infuse their athletic programs with Black muscular Christian ideas as they developed future "race leaders."[31] In Black churches, some ministers drew on the experience and rhetoric of sports to campaign against racism. John Howard Johnson, the Episcopal priest who had starred on the basketball court for Columbia in the 1920s, helped Negro League baseball owner Effa Manley organize and lead a campaign in 1934 aimed at getting white-owned businesses in Harlem to hire more Black employees. Linking their advocacy with sports imagery—they took the name "Citizen's League for Fair Play"—Johnson formally launched the campaign with a sermon entitled "Don't Buy Where You Can't Work."[32]

Some Black churches also used sports to reach young people and encourage community development. Soon after Karl Downs spoke at the Methodist conference in 1938, he returned to his church in Pasadena and launched a sports and recreation program that caught the attention and involvement of Jackie Robinson, then a college athlete. "Those of us who had been indifferent church members began to feel an excitement in belonging," Robinson later wrote.[33] Downs's support for sports extended into the broader Black community of Pasadena. In 1940, he helped form the Pasadena Athletic Club, with Robinson installed as its first president. The goals for the club included promoting "unity among the Negro youth of our community" as well as "cultural and athletic development" and "love for the Christian ideals of our American democracy."[34]

For Downs, the coming of World War II provided new ways to put those Christian ideals into practice. His 1943 book, *Meet the Negro*, echoed the rhetoric of the Double V campaign, focusing on victory over fascism abroad and over racism at home. The book was organized around biographical vignettes, with profiles devoted to several athletes, including Joe Louis, Henry Armstrong, Jesse Owens, and Satchel Paige. While acknowledging the persistence of racism—he noted that Black Americans had experienced fascism, harassment, and lynching "before ever Hitler was born"—Downs emphasized the inherent dignity of Black people. "True democracy, potent Christianity and genuine brotherhood lie enshrouded within the bloom of the 'Negro Possibility,'" he declared.[35]

Published with a white Methodist press, Downs's book added fuel to the growing support for desegregation in sports among Protestant intellectuals and liberal ministers. In 1942 when the Pittsburgh Pirates announced plans to offer four African American players a tryout, the *Christian Century* commented with excitement, arguing that integration in baseball would "make the ordinary

American more conscious that a new day in race relations is at hand than any hundred resolutions on racial good will adopted by church assemblies."[36] The problem was that intellectuals associated with the *Christian Century* had little influence in sports. Middlebrow Protestant coaches, athletic directors, and executives, on the other hand, had the power and access needed to bring change—they simply lacked the will.

The basketball program at the University of Kansas faced this reality. The program traced its origins back to the father of basketball, James Naismith. A Presbyterian minister and leading muscular Christian, Naismith had invented the game at a YMCA college in 1891. Seven years later he arrived at Kansas and coached the first basketball teams at the school. But Naismith cared little about winning or the high-stakes competition of big-time sports; when he stepped down from coaching in 1907 he had a losing record, the only men's basketball coach in Kansas's history with that distinction. One of his players, Forrest "Phog" Allen, took a different approach. After taking over as coach of Kansas in 1919 (his second stint at the school), the churchgoing Methodist built Kansas into a regional power and advocated for greater organization and publicity for the college game. Meanwhile, Naismith remained at Kansas, teaching in the physical education department.[37]

The differences between the two men were expressed in their relationship with John McLendon, a Black student who enrolled at the school in the 1930s. McLendon wanted to coach basketball, but Allen rejected his attempts to get involved with the team, adhering instead to the gentlemen's agreement that barred Black players from competing at Kansas. Naismith, however, took McLendon under his wing, mentoring the aspiring coach and helping him navigate the everyday experiences of racism at the school. After graduating from Kansas, McLendon launched a Hall of Fame coaching career while advocating for racial integration in college basketball. "Dr. Naismith said I owed it to myself, to my profession and to those I was coaching to be the best example of Jesus Christ and his teaching that I could be," McLendon would later explain. "I've tried to do so."[38]

Both Naismith and Allen were mainline Protestants and part of the muscular Christian tradition, but only the one whose career was centered in the classroom rather than the bright lights of the basketball court supported an aspiring Black coach. For Allen and other white Protestants within big-time sports in the 1930s, the desire to operate within their given structures—even if those structures were segregated—usually overruled any moral concerns they felt about racial exclusion.

That pattern began to change during and after World War II, as several middlebrow Protestants used their influence within sports to support desegregation. Most famously, in 1945 Branch Rickey signed Jackie Robinson to a contract.

Robinson's Christian faith and moral convictions, cultivated under the mentorship of Karl Downs, appealed to Rickey. During the first meeting between the two men, Rickey turned to his favorite biography of Jesus, Giovanni Papini's *Life of Christ*, reading from its passages about "turning the other cheek" as an exhortation for Robinson. When the news of Robinson's signing was finally made public, Rickey's fellow mainline Protestants applauded. "[D]on't forget that it was Branch Rickey, the much-derided churchman, who took the first, decisive step," the *Christian Century* crowed.[39]

Of course, a variety of motivations undergirded Rickey's move, including racial paternalism, financial incentives, and an interest in taking advantage of a supposedly untapped source of talent.[40] At the same time, a desire to work toward gradual racial equality, rooted in Rickey's Christian commitments, influenced his decision. So did his long-standing opposition to communism. Throughout the 1930s and into the 1940s, communists in the United States had vigorously supported desegregation in baseball. For segregationists, this made anyone who advocated for racial integration guilty of communism by association. Rickey seemed to follow this line for a time, but eventually he reversed course; he saw communist support for desegregation not as a reason to avoid racial integration, but instead as a reason for capitalism's supporters to act first. By working through voluntary means within the existing structure of sports, Rickey sought to claim the moral high ground for American free enterprise.[41]

Black Christian leaders like Edwin Henderson, John Howard Johnson, and Karl Downs had advocated for desegregation in sports long before Rickey. In Jackie Robinson, they saw signs of hope that their understanding of true Christianity—one that advocated for racial equality—was advancing in American society. Yet Robinson's success in the big leagues also revealed the costs of racial integration, with Black athletes finding themselves within a white-centered narrative and organizational structure that could use the very success of Black athletes to downplay the need for broader social change—or to pit Black people against each other.

Robinson experienced this most acutely in 1949 when Black actor and singer Paul Robeson, a former All-American football player, reportedly claimed that the Soviet Union had done more than the United States for the cause of Black freedom. Coming during the heat of the early Cold War, Robeson's words ignited a firestorm and set off hearings by the House Un-American Activities Committee (HUAC) aimed at discrediting Robeson. Asked to testify, Robinson reluctantly agreed, recognizing that he was being cast as the "good" Black American in contrast to the "dangerous" Robeson.[42]

One year earlier, Robinson's pastor and mentor, Karl Downs, had died at age thirty-five following a botched medical procedure—just weeks after setting in motion events that would lead to the publication of one of the classic texts inspiring the civil rights movement, Howard Thurman's *Jesus and the Disinherited* (1949).[43] Unable to lean on the support and guidance of Downs, Robinson weighed his remarks to Congress carefully and attempted to thread the needle between two points. First, he noted that he and most other Black Americans did not support communism; second, he pointed out that those who opposed racial discrimination were not communist sympathizers, as some white segregationists claimed.

"The fact that it is a Communist who denounces injustice in the courts, police brutality, and lynching when it happens doesn't change the truth of those charges," he told the committee. "I am a religious man. Therefore I cherish America where I am free to worship as I please, a privilege which some countries do not give," Robinson concluded. "But that doesn't mean that we're going to stop fighting race discrimination in this country until we've got it licked."[44]

It is unclear whether Don McClanen read the newspaper reports about Robinson's testimony or cheered on Robinson's exploits on the baseball field. What *is* clear is that as McClanen came of age and began to develop the ideas that would lead to the FCA, the meaning of sports in the United States had been transformed to reflect debates about national identity and belonging. Sports stars took on greater significance as symbols of what it meant to be an American; these symbols, always contested, were often infused with religious meaning, particularly as the Cold War took shape and the threat of nuclear war hovered over American life.

Mobilizing Religion

With racial diversity a cause of division among American Protestants, another piece of the emerging American way ideology provided more common ground: the anticommunist religious nationalism that sprouted in the 1930s and fully bloomed in the early Cold War years. Jackie Robinson hinted at it in his testimony for HUAC when he identified himself as "a religious man" who was thankful for the freedom to worship. Told that communism was at heart an atheistic and godless ideology, many Americans came to see faith in God as a central aspect of their national identity. To protect Americans from the appeal of communism, they believed, personal belief in God was key—and the world of sports offered an important way to spread the message.[45]

The 1938 Methodist conference in Chicago attended by Branch Rickey and Karl Downs offered an early example of the ways that sports could be mobilized for religious nationalism. Near the beginning of the conference, baseball phenom Bob Feller joined his hometown pastor Charlie Fix at a session for Methodist youth, encouraging the awestruck audience to remain faithful in their church attendance.[46] Branch Rickey's involvement at the conference was notable, too. As we have seen, Rickey used his session to encourage a voluntary and constructive approach to solving problems. But he also emphasized the need for personal religious belief. The church, Rickey said, needed to help people see Jesus as a "live, dynamic force, willing to be put to the practical field test." Only by developing a "personal working faith" could Americans withstand the tumult of the age.[47]

Rickey's ideas found organized expression seven years later with *Guideposts* magazine, a project he helped to launch. The magazine's founding editor, Norman Vincent Peale, was a well-known opponent of the New Deal whose religious ideology combined elements from 1920s-style middlebrow Protestants Bruce Barton and Glenn Clark. Like the latter, he emphasized the need for self-surrender as a way to tap into spiritual power and meet psychological needs. Like the former, he preached a practical, business-friendly message, embracing modernist theology while seeking to preserve nineteenth-century Protestant values.[48] Peale claimed that he founded *Guideposts* to restore a sense of American identity derived from three sources: the Bible, McGuffey's Readers, and Horatio Alger stories. It was also, as he explained in a letter to Branch Rickey, intended to "preserve freedom by undergirding American life with religion" and by opposing "collectivist doctrines . . . that have been undermining our country."[49]

Similar in many ways to the success-oriented themes of *American Magazine* in the 1920s, *Guideposts* featured testimonials from famous men and women highlighting the importance of religion to their personal lives. As the *Guideposts* masthead explained, it was "an inspirational monthly magazine for all faiths" where "men and women from every walk of life tell how they overcame obstacles, rose above failures, met sorrow, learned to conquer themselves, and became more effective people through direct application of the religious principles by which they live."[50] The middlebrow Protestant emphasis on the practical and the positive reigned supreme.

The magazine's ecumenical approach to religion aligned with mainline Protestant priorities, but *Guideposts* did not cater to the sophisticated intellectuals who read the *Christian Century*.[51] Consider, for example, the contrasting responses to the college sports scandals of 1951. In the wake of revelations of widespread point fixing in college basketball and a cheating scheme among Army football players, the *Christian Century* responded with editorials on "the sickness in intercollegiate athletics" that suggested a "year's moratorium on all college athletics might be a good way to begin" to deal with the issues.[52] *Guideposts*, on the other hand, presented a positive counterimage for sports. "It just seems to me that because of all the scandals that have been brought to light recently in the sports field," a *Guideposts* editor wrote to Branch Rickey in 1951, "a wonderful article could be written on the fact that baseball has proved itself to be a clean sport, entitled to the respect and enthusiasm which it has generated in the American people." The editor noted that they had published a story by football star Doak Walker in a previous issue to provide a public relations boost for football.[53]

Dozens of sports figures joined Rickey and Walker on the pages of *Guideposts*. In 1954, when *Guideposts* published an anthology titled *Faith Made Them Champions*, more than twenty sports celebrities were featured. The testimonials reflected an ecumenical sensibility, featuring Catholics, Mormons, and Protestants, and included African American athletes Dan Towler and Jackie Robinson. Although Robinson's article (first published in 1948) addressed racism, it did so in typical *Guideposts* fashion, presenting the United States as, at its core, a land of racial harmony and opportunity. "As Mr. Rickey says," Robinson concluded in his article, "a champion is a champion in America, black or white."[54]

By 1952 *Guideposts* had a subscriber base of two hundred thousand, with a healthy portion of the subscriptions coming from business leaders who bought in bulk for their employees. After the 1952 release of Peale's bestselling *The Power of Positive Thinking*, the subscriber base picked up dramatically, reaching one million people by 1961.[55] And *Guideposts* was not alone. Although it was the most popular source of stories about religious athletes in the 1940s and 1950s, it was one part of a much larger cultural ecosystem that historian Jonathan Herzog has described as a "spiritual-industrial complex." Seeking to "inoculate" Americans against atheistic communism, an array of cultural products including movies, books, billboards, magazines, radio and television programs, dollar bills, and the Pledge of Allegiance all proclaimed religion's importance to American identity.[56]

Christian communities outside of the mainline Protestant camp also engaged in these efforts, with the sense of impending global catastrophe opening up space for more traditional forms of revivalism to gain traction. Sports stars like Gil Dodds helped to lead the charge. A runner and a minister-in-training, Dodds emphasized evangelism, premillennialism, and fundamentalist piety. He came to fame in 1943 when he broke American records in the mile and won the James E. Sullivan Award as the nation's outstanding amateur athlete.[57]

Dodds represented a shift in the fundamentalist landscape. By the 1940s, a neoevangelical wing of the movement had emerged, seeking to temper the reactionary and separatist edges of fundamentalism in order to claim a greater place of respectability in American life. Shedding the "fundamentalist" label and embracing "evangelical" instead, the movement was represented by the National Association of Evangelicals (NAE), a new organization that positioned itself as an alternative to the mainline's Federal Council of Churches (FCC). But it was truly driven on the ground level by parachurch organizations like Youth for Christ (YFC). Blending modern communication and marketing strategies with an old-time emphasis on soul winning, YFC became a national phenomenon at the end of World War II, preaching to youth rallies that attracted thousands. Attuned to the popular appeal of celebrities, YFC recruited athletes to its cause, including Dodds, who began to preach under the YFC banner in 1944.[58]

Other neoevangelical organizations expanded on YFC's affinity for sports. Campus Crusade for Christ, founded in 1951 by Bill Bright, strategically targeted college athletes at the University of California, Los Angeles (UCLA), in its early years. After All-American football player Donn Moomaw had a born-again experience, Bright immediately put his star recruit to use, sending him out to promote Campus Crusade in speaking engagements and television interviews.[59]

Similarly, in 1952 a team of athlete-evangelists made up primarily of basketball players from Taylor University, an evangelical college, traveled to Taiwan for a series of games, with evangelistic messages delivered at halftime. Sponsored by missionary Dick Hillis under the auspices of his new Formosa Crusades organization (later named "Orient Crusades" and eventually "One Challenge"), the basketball missionaries were led by Taylor coach Don Odle and included Wheaton College star Bud Schaeffer. The 1952 campaign became an annual event, leading to the creation of Venture for Victory (later named Sports Ambassadors) as the sports wing of Hillis's missionary organization.[60]

The original "Crusade" names of both Bright's and Hillis's organizations reflected the undertones of the Cold War era, with neoevangelicals linking their evangelistic efforts with the holy war between communism and capitalism. By winning souls to Christ, neoevangelicals claimed, they were supporting the American side in the global battle for influence and power. "Christ or Communism—which shall it be?" Bright asked in an early statement of purpose for his new organization.[61] Don Odle, too, believed basketball was "secondary to bringing the message of Christ to Far Eastern neighbors as an answer to Communism."[62] Although Campus Crusade did not focus exclusively on sports and Venture for Victory/Sports Ambassadors was primarily connected to small Christian colleges, the two organizations provided important precedents for subsequent sports evangelism efforts.

Another YFC product, Billy Graham, also earned a sports-friendly reputation. He had been a serviceable high school baseball player, leading YFC promotional materials to describe him as a former star athlete. In 1947, after Graham set off on his own as an evangelist, he leaned into his sports affinities, recruiting Gil Dodds to boost one of his rallies with a running exhibition and testimony. During Graham's 1949 crusade in Los Angeles—the revival that put him on the national map—former U.S. Olympic runner Louis Zamperini accepted Christ and the following evening was brought on stage to share his story.[63]

Graham's use of sports stars tapped into neoevangelical trends, but it also resonated with the white Southern Protestant culture in which the North Carolina–born Graham had been raised.[64] These dual identities were on display in 1950 when Graham led a revival in Atlanta. During one of the revival nights, Morgan Blake, the former sports editor of the *Atlanta Journal*, teamed up with Graham, delivering a dramatic recitation of the famed poem "Casey at the Bat," followed by Graham preaching a sermon based on the poem. "Every man, woman, boy, and girl here tonight is at the bat," Graham declared. "[S]omeday the Umpire of the Ages is going to let the ball go by you for the last time and He is going to call you 'Out.'" For the Atlanta residents in attendance, Graham's blending of sports and faith echoed familiar refrains they had heard from Blake for the past three decades.[65]

They had also seen it from Southern Baptist college students. Near the end of World War II, the Baptist Student Union launched a youth-led revival movement that quickly spread throughout the South.[66] It featured a prominent athlete-evangelist in Jack Robinson, a basketball All-American who enrolled at Baylor in 1945. Robinson spent the winter months leading the school to basketball prominence and the summers leading revival tours across the South. In 1948 Robinson's star rose when he earned a place on the U.S. Olympic basketball team. Dispatches from London in the *Baptist Student* gloried in the basketball-playing minister's success and connected it with American responsibility amid global turmoil. "In the face of what people around the world are up against," Robinson told editor Frank Leavell, "I found my Christ adequate again."[67]

Few Southern Baptist athletes earned the national acclaim afforded Robinson, but year after year the *Baptist Student* featured stories of star athletes who led revivals, worked with the Baptist Student Union, or were otherwise clean-living, churchgoing young men.[68] While this continued a long-standing tradition, the ease with which white Southern Protestants blended evangelism and sports in the 1940s also connected with national trends: by encouraging Southerners to return to God, young Baptist athletes could protect the American way of life.

The FCA Idea

As Jack Robinson was receiving acclaim for his play on the 1948 Olympic basketball team, Don McClanen was in Stillwater, Oklahoma, attending Oklahoma A&M (now Oklahoma State). McClanen enrolled at the school in 1946 after serving in the Navy. With an eye toward coaching, he majored in physical education and took a position as manager for the basketball team. Led by legendary coach Henry Iba, Oklahoma A&M had one of the nation's best basketball programs in the 1940s—in fact, two of Jack Robinson's Olympic teammates were Oklahoma A&M graduates. Few schools were better positioned to equip McClanen for a career in coaching.[69]

Yet, for McClanen, coaching needed to be tethered to a higher purpose. He was haunted by the existential questions that loomed over American society, and he and his wife, Gloria, turned to religion for answers. They attended a Presbyterian (Presbyterian Church USA [PCUSA]) church in Stillwater, participating in its campus ministry. There, in 1947, McClanen was confronted with a question that captured his imagination and changed his life: What would it look like to make his vocation Christian?

From that moment, he began to develop an idea. If young people were so influenced by sports, McClanen reasoned, why not organize Christian athletes and coaches to project a Christian image to admiring fans? The idea grew into a hobby. As he advanced through his program at Oklahoma A&M (he graduated in 1950) and began his own coaching career at Eastern Oklahoma State, McClanen scoured newspapers and magazines for stories about Christians in sports, clipping any articles that he could find and stashing them in a dresser drawer. Given the surging interest in religion throughout American culture, McClanen had plenty of material to find. And no publication provided more clippings than *Guideposts*, from which McClanen derived most of his material.[70]

While the diffuse cultural reach of middlebrow Protestantism provided one important source for McClanen's FCA idea, the institutional structures and programs of mainline Protestantism—particularly those within the Presbyterian Church USA and the National Council of Churches (NCC)—served as another. Like fundamentalists and Southern Baptists, who ramped up their outreach efforts in the 1930s and 1940s, mainline Protestants also advocated for an enhanced focus on evangelism. Writing for the *Christian Century* in 1939, Methodist missionary E. Stanley Jones explained the need. "This generation of youth is living on leftovers from a previous generation and most of it is thin, precarious and inadequate," he argued. "They need God for themselves to give basis for personal living, for social change, for morality, and for a meaning to their universe."[71]

Mainline Protestant leaders had a different vision for evangelism than the revivalist style preferred by fundamentalists, Southern Baptists, and evangelical Black Protestants. The death of Billy Sunday in 1935 illustrated these differences. An editorial in the *Christian Century* described the famed baseball revivalist as "the last of his line" and the "final expression" of revivalism—the last gasp of "the desperate and hopeless condition of the evangelical type of piety."[72] While this assessment proved to be naive, it did reveal mainline Protestant sensibilities. Instead of Sunday's masculine showmanship and aggressive altar calls, many mainline leaders preferred an evangelistic style that Richard Pierard describes as "evangelical and ecumenical": shorn of emotionalism, tied to both denominational and interdenominational Protestant church structures, and linked with social concern.[73]

In the years immediately after Sunday's death, mainline leaders sought to expand this approach with initiatives like the University Christian Mission (UCM).

Launched in 1937 under the auspices of the Federal Council of Churches, UCM attempted to reach college students at state-supported colleges and universities. The goal was simple: "win students to an active Christian life and service in the Church" with speakers who presented "the personal and the social gospel in a living blend."[74] To do this, UCM expanded on the existing tradition of holding Religious Emphasis Weeks. Working with college administrators, UCM leaders came to selected campuses and planned an entire week of meetings, seminars, lectures, and worship services led by a team of nationally known Protestant leaders. In order to steer clear of accusations of Protestant bigotry or preferential treatment, UCM presented itself as the Protestant wing of a trifaith Religious Emphasis Week. Jews and Catholics were encouraged to select and schedule their own speakers if they so desired.[75]

From its first mission in 1938 until its dissolution in 1961, UCM concerned itself primarily with developing and enhancing Religious Emphasis Weeks (or similarly named programs like "Religion in Life Weeks"). In 1949, while McClanen was a junior, its influence reached Oklahoma A&M. That year, UCM director James Stoner, later a prominent leader in the FCA, arrived on campus to expand the annual event at the school. This proved consequential five years later when famed pastor Louis H. Evans Sr. received an invitation to speak at the school's enhanced Religious Emphasis Week.[76]

As the PCUSA minister-at-large, Evans stood at the vanguard of mainline Protestant public witness. His national reputation emerged during his time at Hollywood Presbyterian Church, which Evans led from 1941 until 1953.[77] Evans's ministry hewed toward the conservative side of the middlebrow Protestant approach. Although he preached the necessity of individual conversion to Christ, he rejected premillennialism, connected religion with business success, denounced bigotry and racial intolerance, and encouraged work toward achieving the "fatherhood of God and the brotherhood of man."[78] He was a former college athlete, too, often sprinkling sports metaphors and themes into his sermons.[79] In a typical example, Evans began his 1952 book, *The Kingdom Is Yours*, with these lines: "In football a man may fumble a ball, even be tackled for a loss, but there is no excuse for a man's not knowing where the goal is or knowing what it is to score."[80]

Believing that Evans's charisma, speaking ability, and leadership skills made him an ideal face for the denomination, PCUSA leaders created the new position of national minister-at-large specifically for him. Evans served in that role from 1953 until 1962, taking on preaching and teaching engagements across the country, launching a television program, and writing a number of books.[81] For Presbyterian leaders, Evans's "voice and vision" served "not only the Presbyterian Church but the whole Protestant Church"—by which they meant mainline Protestants in sympathy with the National Council of Churches (an expanded version of the FCC formed in 1950).[82] This required Evans to distance himself from fundamentalist and neoevangelical challengers. Writing privately in 1953, Evans informed a colleague that "I have refused to have anything to do officially with the National Association of Evangelicals."[83]

Yet, even if Evans had sterling credentials as a Presbyterian churchman and even if he avoided official association with the neoevangelicals of the NAE, he had fundamentalist connections and influences. His father, William Evans, taught at Moody Bible Institute for several decades while earning a reputation as a popular Bible teacher in fundamentalist circles.[84] And at Hollywood Presbyterian, Evans benefited from the remarkable work of Henrietta Mears, the church's director of Christian education. Beginning in 1928, thirteen years before Evans's arrival, Mears revitalized the church's Sunday school and college ministry with an approach that stressed soul winning, Keswick spirituality, and Bible reading, while also demonstrating an openness to popular culture. Mears's leadership and influence resonated far beyond the church, reaching most of the youth-oriented fundamentalist organizations that emerged in the 1930s and 1940s, including YFC and Campus Crusade for Christ.[85]

While Evans's ministry illustrated the potential overlap between "mainline" and "fundamentalist" Protestants, the emerging neoevangelical movement had little influence on Don McClanen at the time. The basketball coach read about Evans and his love of sports in a 1953 article in *Life*; mainline Protestant networks and institutions did the rest. As part of Oklahoma A&M's UCM-enhanced Religious Emphasis Week, Evans came to visit McClanen's alma mater in 1954. While there, Evans had dinner with Presbyterian campus minister Bob Geller, who had been McClanen's college pastor. As it happened, Geller had invited McClanen over for dinner that night as well. Sitting across the table from one of the men featured in his dresser drawer, McClanen shared his dream: a national organization of Christian athletes and coaches that would publicize their faith. Evans enthusiastically endorsed the plan.[86]

With one of America's most respected and famous ministers offering his support, McClanen had the prestige and name recognition he needed to get his endeavor off the ground. As for Evans, in one of his first speaking engagements after his meeting with McClanen, he dusted off one of his standby talks, "The Game of Life," urging his young listeners to look to God as their coach and to think of their Christian mission in life as a march down the football field.[87]

Gathering the Christian Athletes

A month after his visit with Evans, McClanen sent out a letter of inquiry to twenty athletes and coaches.[88] In just over two pages of text (along with four additional pages of enclosures), McClanen presented his vision for an organization of Christian athletes. He made sure to reference Louis Evans early in the letter, and he summarized his basic idea this way:

> Some type of an organization which would provide an opportunity for those of us (athletes and coaches) who are so inclined to speak and witness for Christ and the wholesome principles of good character and clean living to the youth of our nation.

The need for such an organization, he claimed, existed because "too many of our youth are not being reached and influenced in the proper way." Since youth "are hero worshippers," McClanen believed they would listen to famous athletes and coaches.[89]

McClanen's letter did not offer a concrete plan, but it did reveal a number of key assumptions. First, McClanen viewed the organization as a distinctly American and masculine project. Like other programs in the early Cold War era, McClanen wanted to save the country by instilling religious values in the nation's young men. Second, McClanen's goals of witnessing for Christ and promoting good character and clean living erected a broad tent into which Protestants from a variety of backgrounds could fit. The language reflected typical middlebrow Protestant talking points. While it did not exclude soul-winning fundamentalists, it did not privilege their priorities. Third and finally, McClanen envisioned his organization as a publicity machine, dispensing written and spoken testimonials by well-known athletes on the importance of faith. His original vision viewed famous athletes not as a constituency to be served, but as a force to be mobilized.

Within weeks of sending his letter McClanen had heard back from fourteen of the recipients. Most expressed support for the idea, but because McClanen did not have a clear vision for his next step, there were no binding commitments. So McClanen got to work. During the summer of 1954 McClanen and his family (wife Gloria and two children, Michael and Judy) traveled across the Midwest and Northeast in hopes of getting face-to-face visits with as many potential supporters as possible. He met in person with Cleveland Browns quarterback Otto Graham, stopping in at the insurance agency that employed the All-Pro in the off-season. In Philadelphia, he tracked down Brooklyn Dodgers pitcher Carl Erskine in a hotel lobby. Both star athletes were struck with McClanen's sincerity and passion and agreed to participate.

Meanwhile, McClanen continued to discuss his plans with Louis Evans, and he also made contact with James Stoner, director of the University Christian Mission, and Len LeSourd, managing editor for *Guideposts*.[90] Stoner had been an athlete in college, and he offered his support. Because of his work for the NCC, Stoner's association added another level of Protestant prestige and respectability, allowing McClanen to move in mainline Protestant circles that might have otherwise been suspicious of an upstart parachurch organization. *Guideposts*, meanwhile, had been one of the main sources of inspiration for McClanen's project in the first place. LeSourd recognized the similarities between McClanen's mission and that of *Guideposts*, providing McClanen with contact information for additional athletes who had published their stories in his magazine. That list allowed McClanen to send out more invitations.[91]

McClanen's summer trip enabled him to establish a core group of supporters and hone the organization's identity and mission. By July he had tentatively named his movement the "Fellowship of Christian Athletes" and outlined an organizational framework. He envisioned three basic components: an Advisory Board made up of ministers who were former athletes; a Program Board composed of a core group of Christian athletes and coaches; and Associated Workers, a group of volunteers who worked to carry out FCA activities on local and regional levels. McClanen scheduled meetings of the Advisory and Program Boards for late September in Oklahoma City and December 31 (the day before the Rose Bowl) in Pasadena, California. He also drummed up financial support from a few Oklahoma businessmen. By mid-August, as McClanen prepared to travel back to Oklahoma for the start of the school year, his fledgling organization had made substantial progress.[92] But there was one essential piece still missing: the support of Branch Rickey.

Recent events in Rickey's life had primed him for exactly the sort of organization McClanen was putting together. Like many business-friendly middlebrow Protestants, Rickey had long opposed communism and socialism. In the spring of 1953, however, as Senator Joseph McCarthy's anticommunist hearings dominated newspaper headlines, Rickey was exposed to a more militant anticommunist campaign led by Verne Kaub of the American Council of Christian Laymen and Carl McIntire, the fundamentalist editor of the *Christian Beacon*. Kaub and McIntire took special aim at mainline Protestant leaders, including Methodist bishop G. Bromley Oxnam. Rickey apparently read some of the attacks on Oxnam and grew concerned.[93] In June 1953, he fired off a letter to a Methodist official, asking about "the apparent socialistic tendencies" of some Methodist ministers and "the obvious identification of some of our theological professors with Socialism."[94]

Throughout 1953 Rickey's concerns about communist sympathizers within Methodism festered. Then in November Rickey's faith received another shock during a meeting with his pastor (Robert Howe) and Methodist bishop Lloyd Wicke. Over lunch the bishop discussed the incompatibility of the four New Testament gospel accounts and nonchalantly noted that no one really believed that Jesus was born of a virgin. When Rickey returned home he reflected on Wicke's comments, growing more and more disturbed. He finally decided to lay out his frustration in a letter to Howe.

How could Bishop Wicke, Rickey wondered, lead his congregation in reciting the Apostles' Creed? How could he shepherd a Christian denomination when he did not believe basic Christian doctrines the laity took for granted? Rickey thought of his mother and father. "Neither of them would have been able to understand Bishop Wicke," Rickey wrote, "but they always felt, I am sure, that they understood what Jesus said and by practicing what he preached they continuously increased their happiness and their belief in Jesus as the Christ." Rickey contrasted the bishop's view of Jesus as a "social prophet" with his own view of a Jesus who "ministered to individuals, and right now." The Sermon on the Mount, Rickey explained "really makes me wish to be a good man—a better man. All of Matthew makes me believe that He is interested in me personally." Having vented his frustrations, Rickey ended his letter by resigning from First Methodist Church.[95]

Despite Rickey's frustration, he stopped short of placing the letter in the mail. Rickey's Methodist commitments were too strong, and the letter remained filed away with the rest of his papers.[96] But even if Rickey's letter did not reach its intended audience, it is a significant document for understanding Rickey's motivations. First, it reflected Rickey's continued reliance on a middlebrow Protestant ethos that measured religion based on its practical usefulness in an individual's life. Rickey contrasted the bishop's view of Jesus as a "social prophet" with his own individualistic conception of religion, highlighting throughout the letter what he called the "empirical knowledge" that grounded his and his parents' belief in Christianity. By practicing their faith, they found it to be useful; by finding it to be useful, they found it to be true.

At the same time, the letter revealed the limits of Rickey's pragmatism. Rickey was hardly a stickler for theological specifics, but for him Christian faith could only have practical meaning for an individual if it was grounded in what Rickey viewed as core Christian doctrines about the deity of Christ and the reliability of the Bible. Rickey could not wholeheartedly follow a bishop who rejected those beliefs. And more than Rickey's own Methodist faith was at stake—the future of the country depended on the continuation of personal Christian commitment and belief. In Rickey's view, Bishop Wicke's liberal theology and intellectualism could undermine America's spiritual foundation and lead to communism.

Rickey's shaken faith made him eager to connect with Christians who shared his approach to religion. This background helps to explain Rickey's willingness to join the FCA cause. In July, as McClanen canvassed for supporters, Rickey sent word that he was "intensely interested" in the FCA idea and would be happy to discuss it.[97] When the two met in person the next month, Rickey enthusiastically endorsed the group and offered guidance and fundraising support. A few days after their meeting, Rickey sent a letter of encouragement, confirming his support for McClanen's plan "to bring together the Christian men in this country who happen to be more or less prominent in all sports" in order to "advance Christian thinking among the youth of America."[98]

Lest Rickey have any doubts about the shared sense among FCA leaders that they were embarking on an anticommunist crusade, Louis Evans put them to rest. Soon after hearing that Rickey had signed on, Evans sent the baseball executive a message to express his excitement. "So many signals in this great universal game are going snafu, and Christian democracy is being tackled for a loss in so many parts of the world, that it is time we got together under the Great Coach to make more yardage for His Cause," Evans wrote. "I am sure American youth is more than ready for this, and is poised to follow the right kind of leadership."[99]

* * *

Among FCA insiders, the story of the organization's founding, spearheaded as it was by a no-name junior college basketball coach, is nothing short of miraculous. Without question, it is a remarkable origin story. At the same time, one of the most striking features of the FCA's origins is the extent to which the organization rode the waves of popular culture. Images of religious athletes proliferated in the years after World War II, with both sports and religion viewed as essential elements of the American way. Creating an organization that mobilized pious athletes to inculcate religious values in American youth fit seamlessly with cultural trends that emerged in the 1930s and accelerated dramatically in the early Cold War era.

The mainstream nature of the FCA's origins is reflected, too, in its mainline Protestant roots. The sources of inspiration for McClanen came primarily from the middlebrow Protestant periodical *Guideposts* and from his connection to Presbyterian and ecumenical Protestant institutions. So, too, the endorsements of prominent churchmen like Louis Evans and James Stoner helped to legitimize the organization in the eyes of Protestant church leaders who otherwise would have been suspicious of the upstart movement. Because of these links, the FCA had an aura of respectability and ecumenicity that broadened its appeal. One did not need to be a zealous soul winner to join in with the FCA; one merely needed to believe that athletes and coaches had a responsibility to their country to encourage its youth to embrace religion.

The combination of mainline Protestant support, Cold War anxieties, and religious nationalism enabled McClanen to put together an impressive collection of famous athletes and coaches. By September 1954 he had stars like Otto Graham and Carl Erskine on the roster, as well as Branch Rickey. These early endorsements enabled the unknown McClanen to attract additional celebrity coaches and athletes, giving the FCA a foothold within big-time sports unprecedented among Christian organizations. Yet, the FCA's broad appeal proved both a blessing and a curse. On the one hand, it helped the FCA strengthen its cadre of athletes and coaches; on the other hand, as mainline Protestant leaders worked to keep the FCA from becoming yet another neoevangelical parachurch organization, clashes over the identity and mission of the new organization ensued.

4

To Be an Athlete Is Different

In 1961, five years after the Fellowship of Christian Athletes' (FCA's) inaugural summer conference at Estes Park, the group convened again in the Rocky Mountains for its annual week of "inspiration and perspiration." Signs of the organization's growth abounded, including a second summer conference at Lake Geneva, Wisconsin. Between Lake Geneva and Estes Park, more than twelve hundred boys and men attended the FCA's 1961 summer camps, quadrupling the number present at the original Estes Park event.[1] The roster of famous sports figures was impressive as well, featuring top coaches Paul Dietzel (football), Frank Broyles (football), and John Wooden (basketball), along with active and retired athletes Jesse Owens (track), Bob Feller (baseball), and Bob Pettit (basketball).[2]

Behind the scenes, however, FCA leaders faced an internal crisis over what to do with their leader and founder, Don McClanen. "It is obvious to all, I think, that we have been asking a good center, Don, to play quarterback for us," Tad Wieman, president of the FCA Board of Directors, explained to a fellow board member. "The results have not been good either for our team or for the miscast quarterback."[3] By the end of the 1961 Estes Park conference, the FCA demoted McClanen from his position as executive director. Two months later McClanen resigned from the organization he had founded.

The FCA's public image of stability and growth hid its private turmoil. The contrast reveals the tensions at the heart of the FCA undertaking. More than simply building a self-sustaining organization, the launch and development of the FCA initiated a movement and forged a new subculture within sports. In the process, the FCA faced difficult questions about its purpose and identity, particularly over its place within mainline Protestantism and its role in the sports industry.

Understanding how the FCA reached its fork-in-the-road moment in 1961— and why it chose to part ways with its founder—is crucial to understanding the shape and contours of the Christian athlete movement as it took its first, halting steps toward growth and maturity.

The Spirit of the Game. Paul Emory Putz, Oxford University Press. © Oxford University Press 2024.
DOI: 10.1093/9780190091095.003.0005

For Christ and His Church

The middlebrow, mainline ethos of the FCA, central to its origins, remained so throughout the 1950s. While the FCA featured a variety of theological perspectives, early ministerial leaders like Roe Johnston (Presbyterian), James Stoner (Disciples of Christ), and Dan Towler (Methodist) had strong connections to established Protestant institutions.[4] With committed churchmen providing direction, the FCA adopted a mainline mentality, a desire to "be all things to all Protestants," that embraced ecumenism and positioned itself at the responsible and respectable center of American society.[5]

These connections helped the FCA build trust with the National Council of Churches (NCC), mainline Protestantism's principal institution. In 1956 Albert Dimmock, Associate Secretary of the Board of Church Extension for the Presbyterian Church (USA), attended the FCA's inaugural summer conference and reported back to Berlyn Farris, executive director of the NCC's Joint Department of Evangelism. Dimmock endorsed the FCA's basic message, noting that FCA leaders encouraged conference attendees to get involved in their home churches and that the FCA seemed careful "not to create a growing number of little FCAs all over the country that would be in competition with church-sponsored programs."[6] Wary of the growing influence of neoevangelical parachurch ministries like Youth for Christ, Dimmock and Farris expressed hoped that "the large numbers of the Executive Committee who are solid Church men" would keep the FCA "in the right direction." They also invited Don McClanen to participate in the NCC's Joint Department of Evangelism's annual meeting. McClanen readily accepted.[7]

Throughout the 1950s and early 1960s, the friendly relationship between the FCA and the NCC continued. NCC leaders offered advice and guidance, and they reassured ministers that the FCA was not another Youth for Christ. The FCA played its part by distancing itself from the "undesirable and questionable tactics" of neoevangelical parachurch organizations and carefully guarding against signs that it was competing with churches.[8] In its literature and promotional materials, the FCA presented itself as a witnessing organization that used famous Christian athletes to channel sports-minded youth into "the church of their choice."

The FCA's links with the NCC influenced the organization's brand of religious nationalism as well. While public religion was rampant during the religious revival of the early Cold War era, there were variations on the theme. The NCC, at least in its rhetoric, tended toward an inclusive religious nationalism, presenting itself as a defender of American racial and religious pluralism and tolerance. To be sure, the NCC's support for religious pluralism was contradicted by its continued Protestant triumphalism, expressed in the 1950s through evangelistic campaigns that aimed toward the goal of "a Christian America in a Christian world." Even so, the NCC could not ignore the power of the tri-faith ideal in the postwar United States, with religious pluralism serving as a popular marker of American pride and identity.[9] To maintain its moral authority both at home and abroad, the NCC felt that it had to project its support for the ideals of religious and racial tolerance.

The FCA adopted this moderately inclusive approach. "There is no fatherhood of God without a brotherhood of man," Louis Evans declared at an early FCA conference. "You get out and call everybody in this world brother or somebody's gonna get there ahead of you and call every man comrade and then we're gonna have a heck of a mess."[10] Although dominated by white Protestants, in its early years the FCA included Black athletes. The organization could also point to the involvement of white Christians with a reputation for supporting racial inclusion, including Brooklyn Dodgers pitcher Carl Erskine and Branch Rickey. At the 1956 summer conference Rickey told attendees that the word "Christian" in the FCA name "doesn't have any discrimination" or "reference to color or nationality" and that "any man can be a member of this Fellowship of Christian Athletes."[11]

Like the NCC, however, the FCA's support for racial inclusion came on white terms and placed white concerns at the forefront. White football coaches at segregated Southern schools—men like Frank Broyles (Arkansas) and Paul Dietzel (Louisiana State)—were put forward as model Christian coaches, with no expectation that they speak out or challenge segregation.[12] The FCA did not reach out to Black churches and institutions, either, despite the fact that Christian leaders like John McLendon and Jake Gaither had operated in such spaces for years. In the 1950s the two Black men involved in FCA leadership, Dan Towler and Rafer Johnson, came from predominantly white religious institutions before joining the FCA.[13]

Because of the FCA's cautious approach, there was little controversy over its support for racial inclusion. Religious pluralism proved to be a topic of greater debate. In contrast to the NCC, an organization composed of Protestant denominations, the FCA was a loose collection of individuals linked together by involvement in athletics. And the FCA hoped to operate primarily in public schools and popular media, spaces in which a sense of Protestant exclusiveness ran counter to prevailing public sentiment favoring a tri-faith conception of American identity.[14] After hearing about the FCA movement, Ed Sullivan, a pioneering star in broadcast television and host of the popular *Ed Sullivan Show*, took the organization to task in a syndicated newspaper column. He urged the group to include Jewish athletes "along the inclusive lines of the National Conference on Christians and Jews" in order to protect against "unhealthy prejudices."[15]

Few FCA leaders were interested in heeding Sullivan's advice and creating another tri-faith organization. "I told [Sullivan] we felt that if we were too broad in our concept," McClanen reported to Branch Rickey, "we would have to water down our objectives to the point where we had practically nothing more than possibly a good sportsmanship program."[16] Louis Evans agreed: "If we water down this thing and keep it from being definitely Christocentric, I feel it will just go flat."[17] Yet, because of their concern for access and cultural respectability, Sullivan's criticism made FCA leaders take notice. By excluding Jews, the FCA faced criticism from national media and, as Don McClanen put it, was "running into some real problems getting into public schools," especially in the Northeast.[18]

James Stoner, a self-described "ecumaniac" who had spent nearly a decade navigating interfaith questions while working for the NCC's University Christian Mission, helped forge the FCA's strategy. In the 1930s and 1940s, UCM had developed a plan for Religious Emphasis Weeks in which it sponsored the Protestant part of the week while encouraging Catholics and Jews to sponsor their own programs. The FCA followed this precedent, with one notable change: although Jews were encouraged to form their own separate organization for athletes, the FCA decided to include Catholics, inviting them to join what Louis Evans called a "brave experiment in cooperation."[19]

Few Catholic leaders reciprocated the interest. They had confidence in their own institutions and had developed a strong sporting ideology through organizations like the Catholic Youth Organization and schools like Notre Dame.[20] The lone Catholic clergyman to join the FCA in its early years, Father Donald Cleary, was an outlier, shaped by his unique experience as the Catholic chaplain at Cornell University, which had a strong interfaith organization led by FCA Advisory Board member Glenn Olds.[21]

After attending the FCA's summer camp in 1956, Cleary wondered if he had made a mistake, expressing his concerns about the obvious Protestant bent of the organization. Still, FCA leaders pressed on with their "brave experiment," promising to address Cleary's complaints and asking him to accept the vice presidency of the FCA's Advisory Board. "I trust that we can convince the world as caustic critic of the churches," Louis Evans wrote to Cleary, "that those who love the Sign of the Cross can work together happily in the larger Christian function of such an effect."[22] While Cleary turned down the vice presidency, he stayed with the FCA in an advisory role throughout the 1960s.

The FCA also included members of the Church of Jesus Christ of Latter-day Saints (LDS), popularly called Mormons. Race car driver Ab Jenkins was among the initial batch of twenty athletes invited to join in 1954. Although he declined, Vernon Law, an LDS pitcher for the Pittsburgh Pirates, joined the FCA in 1955, serving as an important leader over the next decade. While neoevangelicals and

Southern Baptists criticized LDS theology as heretical, Roe Johnston and other mainline FCA leaders took a more open stance. Johnston recalled an early debate over Law's inclusion, in which the words of University of Denver athletic director Tad Wieman won the day: "Why don't we put the burden of proof on the person who wants to be part of us rather than set up rules people must conform to?"[23]

As with Catholics, LDS leaders had their own institutions and saw little reason to support the FCA.[24] Vernon Law spoke at FCA camps and contributed his testimony to FCA publications, but there was no collaboration with LDS institutions. Still, whatever the limits of the FCA's interfaith coalition, by including both Mormons and Catholics the FCA could project an ecumenical image that reflected the mainline Protestant character of the organization's early leadership and its support (at least symbolically) for a pluralistic and tolerant America.[25]

Given its ecumenical ethos, the FCA's early relationship with the neoevangelical movement was complicated. On the one hand, some early FCA leaders, including Donn Moomaw and Gary Demarest, had neoevangelical credentials through their connection to Henrietta Mears and Bill Bright.[26] Yet even if the FCA welcomed some neoevangelicals, it did not center their priorities, de-emphasizing the born-again conversion experience and also taking a more relaxed approach to the question of Sunday sports.[27] Two of the FCA's most prominent early spokesmen, Doak Walker and Otto Graham, earned fame in the National Football League, which, aside from Thanksgiving Day, played its games on Sundays. In contrast, Billy Graham represented the neoevangelical perspective in 1955 when he used his syndicated newspaper column to urge Christians not to "conform to the popular trend" by participating in Sunday recreation.[28] While neoevangelicals could join the FCA, the mainline Protestant leadership ensured that the organization was too broad to fulfill neoevangelical expectations of theological and moral purity.[29]

Despite the FCA's friendly association with mainline Protestant institutions and leaders and its self-conscious attempts to avoid the tactics of neoevangelical parachurch organizations, by the end of the 1950s the FCA began taking cautious steps to establish an independent identity. Try as it might to present itself as a useful ally to mainline Protestant churches, for the FCA to grow and thrive it needed to do more than simply mobilize famous athletes to present religious messages to the public; it needed to create its own constituency and foster a sense of connection and identity among its supporters.[30] FCA leaders began to focus more attention on ministering to the specific needs and life circumstances of college and professional athletes and coaches. As these shifts occurred, the FCA became increasingly enmeshed within the world of sports, forging an institutional home outside of existing Protestant structures.

The Subculture of Sports

Until the FCA, sports-specific ministries catering directly to the religious needs of athletes and coaches did not exist. The YMCA had long promoted a "muscular Christianity" in which athletics played a key role, but it never focused exclusively on sports, viewing athletics as one aspect of a complete, well-rounded life. And while neoevangelical organizations like Venture for Victory or middlebrow Protestant publications like *Guideposts* drew on the fame of athletes to preach a Christian message, their intended audience existed beyond the sports world.

The FCA started out like previous organizations, with a goal of mobilizing athletes to "sell" Christianity to a sports-friendly public. By 1955, however, as Don McClanen resigned from his junior college basketball coaching job and became the full-time director of the FCA, another vision for the organization emerged. Along with its stated goals of "serving Christ through the church" and "witnessing to other youth," the FCA aimed to help athletes and coaches "[find] fellowship for individual Christian growth."[31]

The FCA's sports-specific approach would not have been possible if the broader world of sports had not assumed a new level of popularity and institutional maturity in postwar American life. Amos Alonzo Stagg, who had lived through and contributed to the 1920s sports boom, noticed the trend right away. "Following World War I, there was a tremendous upsurge in interest in athletic sports and particularly in football," Stagg wrote to a student journalist in 1945. "In my opinion, the upsurge will be very much greater when this war is over."[32]

Stagg's words were prophetic. As servicemen returned home, interest in sports skyrocketed. Professional football and college basketball, only minor affairs during the 1920s, gained in prestige, and a new professional basketball league, the National Basketball Association (NBA) was formed. These all paled in comparison with Major League Baseball—which saw attendance double between 1945 and 1950—and college football. More than two million veterans took advantage of the GI Bill's higher education provisions, flooding colleges with war-hardened men who often ended up on the gridiron. Although the rapid spread of television cut into sports attendance in the early 1950s, by the end of the decade it was clear that television could be a boon to the prominence of sports in American life.[33]

The growing popularity of sports aided the expansion and development of professions like coaching and athletic administration. This process of professionalization dated back to the 1920s with the creation of the American Football Coaches Association (1921), the National Association of Basketball Coaches (1927), and the beginning of coaching trade journals including the *Athletic Journal* (1922) and *Scholastic Coach* (1931). The National Collegiate Athletic Association (NCAA), first formed in 1905 as an advisory organization, expanded its power in the 1940s by sponsoring tournaments and providing organization and oversight—efforts that were bolstered in 1952 when the NCAA hired a full-time director and established headquarters in Kansas City.[34] Writing in 1953, the editor of the *Athletic Journal* recognized the opportunity in front of his constituency. "If we in the field of athletics and physical education are ready for the indoctrination of the youth of the country into our sports philosophy," he wrote, "we can make this the most sports-minded nation in the world."[35]

Along with the maturing institutions and bureaucratic structures that bolstered sports-related professions, two national magazines devoted entirely to sports emerged after World War II. *Sport*, a monthly, began operations in 1946; *Sports Illustrated*, a weekly, launched in 1954, part of Henry Luce's Time Inc. enterprise.[36] The creation of national sports magazines reflected a paradoxical reality of post–World War II American life. On the one hand, there was a shift in corporate marketing strategies after World War II from a mass market approach to one that targeted market segments. This shift, historian Lizabeth Cohen notes, "recognized and reinforced subcultural identities" but also "contributed to a more fragmented America."[37] Yet, the distinct sports subculture that was being formed had a unique influence beyond its own borders, providing common ground and a sense of community identity for diverse constituencies.

Writing for the *Christian Century* in 1952, Ralph Cooper Hutchison, president of Lafayette College, took note of this, describing college football as "the emotionally integrating force of the American college" and "the symbol about which are gathered the loyalties of students, faculty, alumni, and friends."[38] And the unifying power of football was not confined to the college campus. In the Midwest and South in particular, university football teams could unite entire states or towns. Professional baseball and football teams served a similar role for their cities, as did high school sports in small towns and urban neighborhoods. And at a national level, the ideological battle between the Soviet Union and the United States intensified the stakes and sense of national belonging associated with the Olympics and other international sporting events.[39]

The FCA's leaders may not have fully understood these trends, but they capitalized on them. They catered to a specific, professionalized subculture that happened to be one of the most powerful integrating cultural forces in American society. And for the FCA, there was an added dimension: they hoped to create a subculture within the subculture of sports. More than anything else, this was the transformative aspect of the FCA's work. They gathered the scattered individual Christians involved in sports and encouraged them to identify as a group of "Christian athletes" with shared interests and goals. "I've been in major college athletic activities for more than a quarter-century," Denver athletic director Tad Wieman, a longtime football coach, explained in 1956. "It was only through the fellowship movement that I found out that some of the men with whom I had been dealing for years have deep Christian values."[40]

FCA leaders began to forge their new community of Christian athletes and coaches at their first public event, a series of speaking engagements in Oklahoma in January and February of 1955. When speaking at high schools, FCA leaders addressed a mass audience of all students. But at the colleges, they spoke directly to small groups of athletes. After one of these meetings at the University of Oklahoma, FCA leaders received a request: could the athletes form their own FCA group? FCA leaders hesitated, careful to guard against the perception of competition with the church. But they also recognized an unmet need for the college athletes. Striking a balance, they decided to allow small fellowship groups of college-aged Christian athletes and developed plans to publish a "special athletic daily devotional booklet" for use by the groups.[41]

Published in November 1955, the FCA's first devotional book was titled *The Christian Athlete Speaks: Daily Devotional Thought Provokers Written by and for Athletes*. It included eighteen entries from athletes and ex-athlete ministers, each featuring a Bible verse, a short inspirational message, and a concluding prayer. Most of the devotionals connected athletic experiences to religious life or used sports metaphors to encourage spiritual discipline. Methodist minister Glenn Olds, for example, wrote that "[t]o be an athlete—or religious—is different. Such life is open only to participants, to those who move . . . into the disciplined daring of the game." By framing the devotionals in this way, the contributors encouraged readers to identify with an imagined "Christian athlete" community defined by a shared experience in athletics and a commitment to "[keep] in training" through consistent religious habits that would help them win the "game of life" and develop Christian character.[42]

In 1956 the FCA expanded on its athlete devotionals by enlisting Methodist minister LeRoy King to serve as editor of the booklets. Titled *The Christian Athlete's Devotional: Meditations Written by and for Athletes*, the second version followed a similar format as the first but expanded to twenty-five testimonials.[43] In typical middlebrow fashion, the devotionals generally mirrored the aims of *Guideposts*, serving as an entry point for athletes to apply religion to their daily lives and learn to articulate religious ideas.

The FCA's ministerial leaders recognized the limitations of their devotional books. For men who had received seminary training, some of the entries seemed simplistic and shallow. Gary Demarest, a Presbyterian minister with a degree from the neoevangelical Fuller Theological Seminary, joined the FCA staff in 1958. Like Louis Evans, Demarest held evangelical convictions with ecumenical sensibilities, seeking to build bridges across Protestant communities. He also sought to deepen the faith of FCA members. "One of the great problems is directly related to the depth of expression of so many of our fellows," Demarest reported to an FCA-affiliated minister in 1959. "There are really so few of them who are able to express themselves with any great degree of depth in writing."[44]

In order to provide more spiritual depth and guidance to athletes and coaches, in 1959 Demarest helped the FCA expand its literature with the launch of a new magazine, the *Christian Athlete*.[45] Through the magazine, the FCA could encourage readers to identify with the movement and help them grow in spiritual maturity. In one 1960 issue of the magazine, readers were urged to "start a definite Christian reading program of your own" with suggested books from Elton Trueblood, J. B. Phillips, Samuel Shoemaker, and Dietrich Bonhoeffer—all of whom wrote for general audiences, but with more sophistication than Norman Vincent Peale and *Guideposts*.[46]

The athlete-focused devotional books, college fellowship groups, and *Christian Athlete* magazine constituted important elements in the FCA's developing ministry. The most significant initiative, however, was launched in the summer of 1956: an annual summer camp in Estes Park, Colorado. Christian summer camps were hardly an innovation, and they had long featured recreation and sports.[47] But the FCA's camp was different, with a centralized focus on sports and unprecedented athletic prestige among the camp's leadership. It attempted to bring together in one location the leading Christian athletes and coaches in the country, providing a point of contact for up-and-coming high school and college athletes. Not only could the young readers of the FCA's devotional and promotional materials imagine themselves as part of a nationwide Christian athlete movement; with the camp they could develop personal relationships and interactions with the heroes of their newfound community.

Plans for Estes Park began in the fall of 1955. McClanen hoped to bring three hundred college and 150 high school athletes to Colorado, where they could be trained and strengthened in their faith and then sent back to their communities as leaders.[48] FCA leaders sought national publicity as well. Louis Evans secured coverage in *Life* and *Newsweek* and telegrams of support from President Dwight Eisenhower and Secretary of State John Foster Dulles.[49]

In addition to connecting the FCA with the religious nationalism of the 1950s, McClanen used Estes Park to symbolically link his movement with the most prominent Christian sports leaders from the past. He successfully recruited Branch Rickey and Kansas basketball coach Phog Allen to the event, and he arranged a ceremony on the first night to honor the legacy of Amos Alonzo Stagg, whose health prevented him from attending. With leading muscular Christians from the past generation—representing each of the three major American team sports—the conference was set up as a "passing of the torch" moment.[50]

Despite McClanen's grand vision and the impressive roster, only 250 people attended, half of McClanen's estimate of 500. But while the conference did not meet expectations for attendance, it galvanized the FCA movement. In subsequent years, enrollment gradually increased. In 1959, the last year that the FCA held only one conference, attendance reached capacity at 607 people, with hundreds being turned away. A second summer camp was added in 1960, and enrollment grew throughout the decade, with powerful trickle-down effects. As young attendees matured into adults and took careers in sports, they often stayed connected and involved with the FCA. Future coaches like Tom Osborne and future pro athletes Bill Bradley, Fran Tarkenton, and Bill Curry all attended FCA camps before they gained fame.[51]

The FCA summer conference also had profound meaning for established sports figures. Clarence "Biggie" Munn, Michigan State football coach from 1947 to 1953 and Michigan State Athletic Director from 1954 until 1971, struck this note in a letter to McClanen one week after he attended the 1956 conference. Munn reflected on one particularly powerful evening, with a "big full moon" coming over the mountains, and a glowing campfire illuminating a cross in the distance. "As I sat there in the glorified spot," Munn told McClanen, "I couldn't help but thank the Lord for a fellow who has the vision like you to put such a thing across."[52]

Although the FCA had been created to reach youth, sports leaders who were mobilized for the task often felt a heightened sense of purpose and community. Many prized the feeling of camaraderie that came from working with their peers on a shared mission to Christianize America's youth, and the annual summer conferences allowed them to build relationships with the FCA's growing community. For Munn, the experience led him to re-engage with his local church (an ecumenical Protestant congregation), and to devote time and attention to building up the FCA movement over the next decade.[53]

As the FCA used its summer camps to build a network of Christian leaders in sports, those leaders began to carve out new spaces for the FCA to operate within the sports institutions they inhabited. College football was an especially important partner. While the sport had faced scrutiny and criticism from Protestant leaders throughout its history, it had also benefited from its close links with muscular Christianity, fostered by men like Amos Alonzo Stagg. The moral undertones and vigorous masculinity of the sport paired well with the FCA's aims.

FCA leaders first began to develop their alliance with college football by turning to their home base: Norman, Oklahoma, which served as FCA headquarters until 1956. In the mid-1950s the University of Oklahoma football team was in the middle of a forty-seven-game winning streak, and its coach, Bud Wilkinson, was a lifelong Episcopalian. After Branch Rickey endorsed the movement, Wilkinson agreed to join.[54]

Thanks to Wilkinson's support, the Sooners had a strong presence at the FCA's first summer conference, with football players Clendon Thomas and Bill Krisher serving on the staff. The two athletes also promoted the FCA throughout the 1956 season, linking the movement with the winning masculinity of the nation's best college football team. "It's hard to be a Christian witness when you're trying to knock somebody's head off on the football field," Krisher admitted. "But Christianity is not just for old ladies and children. . . . It takes a man to be a Christian."[55] By providing public support and access to his team, Wilkinson helped the FCA build credibility within the college football world.

Other coaches and teams soon followed thanks to the efforts of Biggie Munn. In January 1958, Munn hosted the FCA's first breakfast at the annual meeting of the American Football Coaches Association. The goal, as Munn explained, was to get the FCA "in contact directly with the High School and College coaches."[56] Twelve coaches showed up for the first breakfast, including Louisiana State's Paul Dietzel. That summer Dietzel brought several of his players to the FCA's summer camp, and when his team went on a championship run in the fall, he credited the Estes Park experience with providing the spark. "Things like that," he said about the conference, "wipe out the false notion you have to be a sissy to believe in God. People forget that probably the toughest person that ever lived was Jesus Christ."[57]

The impulse among FCA leaders to distance their Christian identity from the "sissy" label revealed ongoing anxieties about the compatibility of the Christian faith with popular notions of manhood. Football culture nurtured a masculinity associated with aggression, violence, and physical courage; despite the long history of muscular Christian participation in the sport, there was still a sense among some football insiders that a sincere commitment to the Christian life would soften the edge that athletes needed to excel. And more than a game was at stake. In the midst of the Cold War, the importance of forging disciplined men prepared for battle sharpened the national and civic importance that football had long possessed.[58]

Yet, the FCA's identification with vigorous manhood—overzealous though it may have been—was not simply a full-scale embrace of militant masculinity. Coupled with the desire to prove that Christians were "real men" was the desire to help "real men" see their need for the Christian faith—to help them cultivate a spirituality that could give them a moral compass and higher power to which they could submit. "We grow spiritually by learning to kneel," Dietzel liked to say.

He highlighted a similar theme in his poem "Sissy," which he wrote for his LSU team and presented at the FCA's summer conference in 1959 (as well as in talks and lectures for years to come). If it was "sissy" to be a Christian athlete, Dietzel suggested, then he wanted more sissies on his team: young men who gave their full effort, put the team first, refused to drink alcohol, taught Sunday school classes, worked hard in the classroom, and respected their parents. "If that's being a sissy," Dietzel's poem concluded, "I'm hunting for sissies. Because sissies, gentleman, are the timber from which champions are fashioned."[59]

With some of the top coaches in the country publicly supporting the FCA, the coaches' breakfast quickly expanded. Thirty-five men attended in 1959 and over fifty showed up in 1961. In 1959, too, Kansas State athletic director H. B. "Bebe" Lee launched an identical FCA breakfast for basketball coaches at their annual meeting, held every March during the NCAA basketball tournament. Both the football and basketball coaches' breakfasts became annual events, providing an ongoing path for the FCA to recruit coaches while helping them build intimacy and friendship with others who identified with the movement.[60]

The FCA also worked to develop inroads in the professional ranks. Football stars Otto Graham, Doak Walker, and Dan Towler all spoke on behalf of the FCA in 1955 and continued to stay involved after they retired from their sport later that year. Meanwhile, the FCA's growing college presence helped to replenish its professional football stock. Athletes like Bill Glass, who got connected with the FCA while he starred at Baylor University, continued to speak at FCA events and rallies during their pro career.[61] As for baseball, the FCA relied heavily on Branch Rickey. The veteran executive helped to win over Dodgers pitcher Carl Erskine and Pittsburgh Pirates pitcher Vernon Law; those two were joined by Philadelphia Phillies pitcher Robin Roberts, New York Giants shortstop Alvin Dark, and New York Yankees second baseman Bobby Richardson as the most prominent baseball spokespersons in the FCA's early years.[62]

Although the FCA could recruit professional athletes to speak at its events, it had a more difficult time building a ministry to serve them. A strategic plan, written by future Presbyterian pastor Richard Armstrong while he was a student at Princeton Theological Seminary, is helpful in showing the FCA's struggle. Armstrong—who would become an important advisor to the FCA—sent his paper, titled "Professional Sports: A Missionary Frontier," to Don McClanen in 1958; McClanen circulated it among FCA leaders, urging them to use it as a framework for extending the FCA's reach into the big leagues.[63]

Armstrong's plan centered on practical ways that a settled minister working from a local congregation could connect with professional athletes and minister to their needs. He focused on mainline Protestant structures and priorities: church membership, gradual spiritual growth, and civic duty. "The common objective would be to make better Christians of all players," Armstrong wrote, "bringing them into the active life of the church and teaching them their Christian responsibility as public figures." To coordinate this effort, Armstrong suggested turning to the NCC, with the ultimate goal of forming a "permanent inter-denominational committee" charged with a "far-reaching missionary program directed at professional athletes" and "an educational program" for pastors.[64]

The FCA never implemented Armstrong's plans. With games on Sundays and constant travel, the mainline Protestant emphasis on channeling athletes into established church structures was difficult to fully achieve. Meanwhile, entrepreneurial solutions were a step too far for many mainline leaders. To suggest that athletes were a special constituency in need of targeted spiritual support seemed to challenge the unity of the Christian message and the centrality of church traditions. Still, FCA leaders did experiment with new programs, holding several sparsely attended winter retreats for pro athletes from 1957 through 1961. The small attendance at these events portended future developments. The FCA never achieved an institutional presence in professional sports comparable to its place in high school and college sports, an opening which other sports ministry organizations would exploit in the 1960s.[65]

Along with cultivating its networks with coaches and athletes, the FCA placed a heavy emphasis on establishing links with sports media. Two sports-specific periodicals were especially helpful: *Scholastic Coach* and *Sports Illustrated*. The former, the leading trade journal for high school coaches, was founded in 1931 by G. Herbert McCracken, then a football coach at Lafayette College.[66] When McCracken began to serve as an FCA advisor in 1955, he used his magazine to promote the organization. "In this atomic age . . . [the FCA's] message comes like a huge cloud of fresh air," McCracken wrote in one 1956 editorial. "America is built on a spiritual foundation, and without a moral and religious awareness we cannot lead the full, Christian life."[67]

In 1956, *Sports Illustrated* featured the FCA in a laudatory article. Established two years prior, *Sports Illustrated* had not yet developed its reputation for critical and literary sports writing. It did, however, have a large subscriber base. In early 1956 Louis Evans worked with Henry Luce to arrange for *Sports Illustrated* to cover an FCA citywide event in Denver. The subsequent article was titled "Hero Worship Harnessed."[68]

The FCA also cultivated friendly viewpoints on the sports page. Two of its most prominent supporters were Fred Russell of the *Nashville Banner* and Ernie Mehl of the *Kansas City Star*. Russell, a Methodist, was well established in Tennessee, but he also had a national reputation thanks to his annual "Pigskin Preview" feature for the *Saturday Evening Post*. In 1957 his hometown sent thirty athletes to the FCA's Estes Park camp, leading Tad Wieman to write to Russell, asking him to discuss the returning campers in the *Nashville Banner* and give the FCA a boost. Over the next few years Russell published positive stories about the organization and helped make Nashville a hub of FCA activity.[69]

Mehl, also a Methodist, played a similar role for the FCA in Kansas City. Indeed, it was at Mehl's suggestion that the FCA moved its headquarters from Norman, Oklahoma, to Kansas City in 1956. Mehl's pitch to the FCA was based on the city's connection to big-time sports. While Norman had the University of Oklahoma, Kansas City was close to the University of Kansas and Kansas State University, it had a Major League Baseball team, and it housed the headquarters of the NCAA. FCA leaders saw the wisdom in Mehl's proposal, moving their organizational home to Kansas City in 1956.[70]

The FCA's move symbolized its evolving relationship with the world of sports. While the FCA attempted to cooperate with mainline Protestants, it did not develop a lasting home in their institutions. But the organization did work to embed itself within sports-based institutions. Its leaders planned events to fit into the rhythms and schedule of the sports calendar: breakfasts at the annual basketball and football coaching conventions, summer camps in August just before college football practices began, and a professional athletes' retreat in December for baseball players in their off-season. The FCA also published devotional literature aimed specifically at the needs of athletes and coaches, and it established headquarters in the same city as the leading college sports organization.

By the end of the 1950s, the FCA had taken its original reason for being—to mobilize Christian athletes to "sell" the faith to young people—and used it to create a ministry that also focused on ministering to and within the sports world.

Tensions and Departure

As the FCA developed during the 1950s, its focus on forging an identity based on the shared experience of athletic participation and on a broad, ecumenical vision of Christianity helped the organization carve out a place in the sports world. It also fostered a theological diversity rare among the Protestant parachurch organizations in the post–World War II years. The FCA, Don McClanen stated in 1958, was "not divided into groups such as Liberals and Fundamentalist, Progressives and Conservatives (although some of us are), but rather . . . we have been able to come together in a powerful united effort to work and witness as followers of the Lord Jesus Christ."[71]

But the FCA's broad vision also posed potential problems, not least conflict over the direction of its mission. As the FCA began to develop its own teaching and training materials, the question of what it meant to be a Christian athlete or coach—and who would set the boundaries and determine the priorities—became much more significant. Meanwhile, the FCA's founder was moving in new spiritual directions. When he launched the FCA in the early 1950s, McClanen was drawing on *Guideposts* and other popular inspirational religious literature. This literature emphasized the therapeutic value of religion to one's daily life, but it tended to be simplistic, and it made few demands on the lives of its readers. Its value for FCA leaders lay primarily in its potential as a witnessing tool, a way to get young people to embrace a religious identity and get involved within the institutional structures of the church. There, under the oversight of trained religious professionals, young athletes could grow and develop spiritually.

As the FCA began to take tentative steps toward involving itself in the spiritual training of athletes, McClanen's reading preferences matured. Two authors in particular influenced his evolving perspective: Elton Trueblood and Samuel Shoemaker. Trueblood held a doctorate in philosophy from Johns Hopkins University and worked as a professor of religion at Earlham College, a small Quaker school in Indiana. A prolific author, Trueblood sought to reach ordinary men and women with a style that blended the liberal mysticism of fellow Quaker Rufus Jones, the neo-orthodox sense of sin articulated by Reinhold Niebuhr, and the thoughtful "mere Christianity" of C. S. Lewis.[72]

Trueblood's central message, articulated in books like *Alternative to Futility* (1947), *Your Other Vocation* (1952), and *The Company of the Committed* (1961), focused on the need for small groups of intensely devoted Christians to join together in "an experiment in radical Christianity" for the renewal of Christianity and the redemption of society.[73] These small "spiritual cell groups"—later formalized as the Yokefellow movement—reflected Trueblood's insistence that the doctrine of the "priesthood of all believers" broke down the divides between the "secular" work of laypeople and "spiritual" work of clergy. In Trueblood's view, all Christians should see their vocations as a form of ministry. At the same time, Trueblood recognized that many churchgoers would not be open to the demands required of a "yokefellow." Thus, in an era marked by bigness—heightened public religiosity, a church-building boom, and ecumenical consolidation—Trueblood focused on devoted bands of believers, on cultivating within the broad churchgoing public "an order . . . devoted to the recovery and fulfillment of radical Christianity."[74]

Samuel Shoemaker stressed similar themes. An evangelical Episcopal priest, Shoemaker was the American leader of Frank Buchman's controversial Oxford Group movement of the 1920s and 1930s, which focused on forming and developing small cells of spiritually committed Christians. During World War II Shoemaker split with Buchman, in part because Buchman was taking the movement (by then christened Moral Re-Armament) away from an exclusively Christian identity.

After the war Shoemaker continued to use the methods and strategies pioneered by the Oxford Group, including personal evangelism, small-group sharing, confession of sin, private devotional times, and a focus on reaching social elites. But he did this without the baggage of his earlier association with Buchman. In the religion-friendly climate of the early Cold War era, Shoemaker had a renaissance as a national religious leader, earning positive profiles in national magazines and in 1955 being named by *Newsweek* as one of America's ten greatest preachers.[75]

In 1956 McClanen enthusiastically encouraged FCA leaders to read Trueblood's *Your Other Vocation*; two years later he purchased copies of

Trueblood's *The Yoke of Christ* for each member of the FCA's Advisory Board. By 1959 McClanen was not just reading Trueblood; he was turning to him for spiritual advice and recruiting him to speak at FCA summer conferences.[76]

The Pittsburgh-based Shoemaker, meanwhile, got involved with the FCA in 1958 because of its strong presence in his city. After serving as a speaker at the FCA's 1959 Estes Park conference, he came away thoroughly impressed. "I have not in years seen anything that heartened me more," he declared in a radio sermon in September 1959, "or so much made me feel I wanted to begin all over again in dedicating my own life to Christ and His work!" In the wake of Shoemaker's sermon, McClanen began turning to him for guidance and advice on how to lead the FCA movement.[77]

The serious-minded lay-focused ministries of Shoemaker and Trueblood had obvious appeal to FCA leaders who wanted to help athletes and coaches connect their faith with their vocations. Both men stressed the importance of spiritual discipline, which could resonate with athletes who were used to the demands of physical training. Both men preached an irenic inner-focused evangelical message that did not dwell on traditional vices (gambling, smoking, swearing, and breaking the Sabbath) or draw boundaries between secular and sacred life. This openness to "the world" provided a framework for Christians to inhabit the supposedly secular environment of sports without reservation. Meanwhile, their openness to the mystical elements of Christianity and their emphasis on private prayer and devotional life also had the potential to provide a religious antidote to the psychological stress and inner anxieties that athletes faced.[78]

But for all the ways that Trueblood and Shoemaker preached a message that could appeal to athletes and coaches, it was also a potentially divisive message. Both men tended to separate the truly committed from the nominal believers. And while both men consciously targeted ordinary laypeople as their audience, they carried with them a sense of sophistication that appealed to clergymen or intellectually minded laypeople and had less resonance for athletes and coaches who did not fit that mold.

A favorite story among early FCA leaders reveals this disconnect. On their way to an FCA summer camp in 1960, Gary Demarest picked up Biggie Munn from the airport. When Demarest told Munn that "Trueblood"—using only his last name—would be speaking at the event, Munn looked at him with surprise and confusion. Although Elton Trueblood was well known in Protestant circles and McClanen had frequently recommended his books, the only "Trueblood" Munn knew was a trout fishing expert named Ernie Trueblood.[79]

Munn was not alone in his naivety. Many of the athletes and coaches involved in the FCA could get behind an affirming and positive message about going to church, believing in God, following Jesus, and applying the Golden Rule, but they had little interest in the more challenging ideas of religious intellectuals, even those like Trueblood who sought to reach a popular audience. For FCA leaders like Gary Demarest, this came with the territory—he seemed to understand and accept that not all FCA members would share his deeper theological interests and commitments. But as McClanen grew more enthusiastic about the teachings of Shoemaker and Trueblood, he became increasingly frustrated with the lack of spiritual depth and commitment in the FCA.

One reason for McClanen's frustration stemmed from his intense personality. He did not need to read Trueblood and Shoemaker to believe that one should be wholeheartedly committed to the Christian cause. It was precisely because of McClanen's passion and drive that the FCA got off the ground. He had borrowed money, mortgaged his car, and driven across the country to make his FCA idea a reality. And he did this with little desire for self-promotion; he never presented himself as the public face of the FCA, preferring to operate in the background.

Yet while McClanen was humble in public, deferring praise to others, behind the scenes his zealous work ethic and protectiveness of the FCA made him difficult to work with. If someone rejected McClanen's fundraising appeals, he viewed it as a sure sign that the person lacked faith. When Bud Wilkinson informed McClanen that he was unsure if he could attend the 1958 Estes Park conference (in the end he did attend), McClanen fired off a letter to Biggie Munn declaring that he was "personally thoroughly disgusted" with Wilkinson.[80] Ruth Jobush, hired as the FCA's office manager in 1956, frequently expressed frustration about working with McClanen. "Don has really started a wonderful movement and accomplished a lot," she wrote to Biggie Munn, "but we aren't going to go ahead with one individual in control who won't accept counsel of men like you and Jim [Stoner] and Roe [Johnston] and Dr. [Louis] Evans." Munn agreed. "Don has wonderful ideas," he told Jobush, "however, if the organization is to exist on a big basis we must have more help."[81]

In the summer of 1958 more help arrived when Gary Demarest agreed to take a position as associate director. He lasted just a couple years. Even with Demarest on staff and the FCA Board attempting to provide more oversight, McClanen continued to operate independently, often making decisions about the FCA's future without consulting others.

This problem became especially acute after Samuel Shoemaker spoke at the FCA's 1959 summer conference. McClanen grew enamored with Shoemaker's call for a "world wide, sweeping movement of the Holy Spirit" and his warnings about the danger of independent religious movements growing too close to established church structures.[82] McClanen wrote to Shoemaker asking him to expand on his warnings, and Shoemaker obliged, turning to a somewhat unlikely source: liberal Protestant theologian Henry Van Dusen's book *Spirit, Son and Father: Christian Faith in the Light of the Holy Spirit.*

Van Dusen—who had a friendship with Shoemaker dating back to their time with the Oxford Group in the 1920s—had recently identified what he called a "third force" in Christianity. Alongside Catholics and Protestants there existed "fringe sects" that placed a great deal of emphasis on the Holy Spirit and on the experiential and emotional elements of the faith. Although these groups, usually associated with Pentecostalism, lacked the cultural respectability of established churches, they were growing rapidly. And, in an argument that previewed the coming charismatic movement, Van Dusen believed that established churches could learn from them.[83]

Shoemaker pointed McClanen to several passages in Van Dusen's book, including the following:

> The Holy Spirit has always been troublesome, disturbing because it has seemed to be unruly, radical, unpredictable. It is always embarrassing to ecclesiasticism and baffling to ethically-grounded, responsible durable Christian devotion.... But—the Spirit will not long be silenced. When neglected or denied by the prevailing "churchianity," it unfailingly reappears to reassert its powers, often with excesses and aberrations, beyond the bounds of conventional Church life.[84]

With Shoemaker's encouragement and guidance, McClanen began to think of the FCA as a movement of the Holy Spirit that challenged "the prevailing 'churchianity.'" Within a few weeks he had made plans to hold an "exploratory discussion" in Pittsburgh with leaders of like-minded "independent movements," including Elton Trueblood's Yokefellows and Samuel Shoemaker's Pittsburgh Experiment. These movements shared commonalities, with a focus on laypeople, an openness to spiritual experiences, and a respectable middle- and upper-class target audience. "I wonder if God is not trying to speak through these various independent movements of His," McClanen wrote in a letter to FCA leaders announcing his plans, "to help bring about the genuine Christian revolution that is needed in the world."[85]

McClanen's letter announcing the meeting reveals the new path he was attempting to chart for the FCA, particularly in its relationship with the Protestant establishment. He noted that the FCA was "primarily a witnessing or surface presentation program." It aimed to funnel youth into the churches, where they could develop into mature Christians. But McClanen expressed disappointment with the ability of mainline Protestant churches to fulfill that task. "Unless our Churches become literally saturated with mature Christians who have grown deep and strong," he wrote, "many a youngster who is inspired at an FCA rally or Conference will die on the vine as he turns to many churches where pastors are too busy and laymen are so inept that they can't help in spite of themselves."[86]

To aid churches in the task of developing mature Christians, McClanen believed that the FCA should partner with independent groups like Yokefellows, which, he noted, was "primarily a depth movement." While McClanen suggested that the FCA should continue to "work with [the Church], and they in turn with us," he clearly felt that the organizational structures of mainline Protestantism were deficient. He was hesitant to turn the FCA into a membership program— he wanted a fully formed Christian life to be the way one identified with the movement—but he felt new strategies were needed to ensure that the FCA's faith was "a force rather than a fashion."[87]

If McClanen's involvement with Shoemaker and Trueblood signaled a new direction for the FCA's relationship with mainline Protestantism, it also pointed toward a new relationship with the sports industry. In the letter announcing the Pittsburgh meeting, McClanen referred his fellow leaders to Trueblood's new book, *The Idea of a College*. In the book Trueblood spent a few pages discussing intercollegiate athletics. While Trueblood adamantly defended the value of sports, he also argued that college leaders must work to keep athletics "within reasonable limits."[88] For Trueblood, this meant no recruiting of athletes, limited travel for games, and coaching salaries that did not outpace those of professors. In short, Trueblood argued, athletics must not be overemphasized. "Winning a debate must be made as important as catching a forward pass," Trueblood declared.[89]

McClanen supported Trueblood's argument, praising "his [C]hristian approach and wisdom to the athletic situation as it exists in our colleges today."[90] But at the same time, the FCA had been formed precisely because of sports' outsized influence in American life. Its most prominent members were the college football and basketball coaches who benefited from and participated in the very excesses that Trueblood decried. While most FCA leaders would have agreed that sports should not be overemphasized, few believed that the drastic steps proposed by Trueblood were necessary. In fact, far from taking steps to rein in athletic excess, many of them believed the FCA should play a public relations role for sports, helping to "combat the negative sensational aspect of sports publicity" by providing a positive image to an American public supposedly inundated with newspaper accounts that "stress the scandal and rough play in athletics."[91]

As McClanen dreamed of aligning the FCA with the church renewal programs of Trueblood and Shoemaker, he and his wife Gloria experienced a personal tragedy when their twelve-year-old daughter Judy suddenly passed away in early 1960. McClanen grew even closer to Shoemaker and Trueblood in the wake of the tragedy. He purchased subscriptions of Shoemaker's *Faith at Work* magazine for FCA leaders, bought them all copies of Shoemaker's 1960 book *With the Holy Spirit and With Fire*, and expressed hope that he could bring Shoemaker,

Trueblood, and "others who are doing outstanding small group work" to an FCA national conference where they could conduct small group sessions with coaches and develop plans to project "this thinking to the church at large."[92]

McClanen embarked on this new path with the assumption that FCA leaders would follow along. He made his decisions to purchase magazine subscriptions, order books, and organize conferences without always consulting other FCA leaders. Meanwhile, the death of his daughter Judy likely exacerbated the problems with his intense personality. He seemed to become more frustrated with the apparent lack of commitment displayed by fellow FCA members when they did not enthusiastically endorse his plans. In his view, the only explanation for the hesitancy of FCA leaders to join his push for a Holy Spirit–led renewal of the church was their lack of faith and commitment. Frequent tension between McClanen and fellow FCA staff members resulted, often leading to emotional outbursts from McClanen.[93]

At Estes Park in 1961, when matters finally came to a head, the FCA Board of Directors finalized plans to reorganize the FCA home office, effectively demoting McClanen from his position as executive director to an associate director position of equal authority with two other staff members. The board members also encouraged McClanen to seek professional counseling and to take a three-month vacation with his wife Gloria, and they instituted new policies so that the FCA staff could not initiate new activities without the approval of the board.[94] McClanen was unwilling to accept his new role. In October 1961, seven years after he launched the FCA, McClanen announced his resignation and developed plans to move to Earlham, Indiana, where he could study under Elton Trueblood.[95]

In letters to Shoemaker written after his resignation, McClanen interpreted the actions of his fellow FCA leaders as a betrayal. He saw them as an attempt to assert clergy control and to stifle the "lay theological" and "evangelical emphasis" he believed he represented. He cast blame far and wide, expressing frustration with FCA leaders like Roe Johnston ("a very likeable fellow who is a typical contemporary pastor professing a vital message but actually very anti-evangelical") and Branch Rickey ("very naive on matters such as many clergy lacking evangelical fire").[96] In short, McClanen felt that the entire leadership of the FCA stood against him. Aside from Trueblood and Shoemaker, only LSU football coach Paul Dietzel seemed to take his side.[97]

But McClanen's tale of decline missed how his turn to Trueblood and Shoemaker represented a break from the FCA's original path. From its early years the FCA had been a broad and inclusive organization that worked closely with mainline Protestant churches and institutions. That aura of ecumenism and respectability allowed it to get a foothold within big-time sports and establish close connections with laymen athletes and coaches like Otto Graham, Biggie

Munn, and Doak Walker—men who were committed to the respectable faith of patriotic, churchgoing, middle-class Americans. With religion viewed as an antidote to communism in the early Cold War era, these men saw in the FCA an opportunity to serve their country by speaking up about their faith. Few shared McClanen's religious zeal; fewer still his belief, inspired by Shoemaker in the late 1950s, that the FCA should become a force for a radical Holy Spirit–led awakening.

As McClanen sought to conform the FCA to his newfound vision, the FCA's laymen athletes and mainline Protestant ministers pushed back. Many did not necessarily have a problem with Shoemaker or Trueblood; the FCA, after all, possessed a mainline Protestant sensibility that attempted to be "all things to all Protestants." Rather, the single-mindedness with which McClanen adopted and promoted the teachings of Shoemaker and Trueblood turned off some FCA leaders. They also worried that McClanen's focus on rigorous Christian living and his willingness to criticize sports would hamper their attempts to expand the FCA base and attract donor support. As FCA Board member and University of Kansas basketball coach Dick Harp put it, only with a broad and affirming attitude could the FCA recruit enough people to "impress foundations, press, etc."[98] While there was a place for the small-group "company of the committed" style within FCA, it could not dominate the agenda. And McClanen found it difficult, if not impossible, to accept this fact.

McClanen's intense personality and the tragedy of losing his daughter undoubtedly exacerbated these problems related to theology and identity. The FCA's leaders were coaches, ministers, and athletic directors, all men used to being in charge. They wanted stability in their leader, and they chafed at McClanen's emotional outbursts and his tendency to act on impulse rather than to chart a steady course.

At the same time, it was clear that the FCA would not exist but for the personal characteristics they now saw as a problem. "Administration may not be his forte, and public speaking is not his forte, but he is a 'hound of heaven' when it comes to winning people personally," Shoemaker wrote to Paul Dietzel after McClanen's resignation. "[A]nd it can never be forgotten that it was he who, under God, created FCA."[99]

* * *

After 1961, the FCA would develop without its founder. One of the first orders of business: ensuring that the FCA continued to work closely with the NCC. In 1962, Methodist minister LeRoy King, recently hired as a full-time FCA staff member, wrote to the NCC's Department of Evangelism to ask if he could continue the FCA tradition of sending a representative to the NCC's annual meeting of the Secretaries of Evangelism. King reminded the NCC that the FCA "is primarily a witnessing movement which seeks to reach persons primarily in the athletic world and guide them more actively into their local church."[100] Ralph Holdeman, director of the Department of Evangelism, warmly welcomed King.[101]

Despite this sign of continued cooperation with mainline Protestant institutions, it was clear that the FCA was increasingly taking on an independent identity. By the 1960s FCA leaders had developed plans to allow local communities to charter their own FCA groups, and they had created new ways—such as identification pins and covenant cards—for young people to feel connected to the FCA. Most importantly, they continued to enmesh themselves within the world of sports by fostering close relationships with prominent coaches, athletic directors, athletes, and sportswriters and by holding annual coaches' breakfasts and professional athletes' retreats. On top of that, by producing devotional books, a magazine, and sports-based summer conferences, they developed ways to provide spiritual guidance specifically targeted to those within the sports world.

In 1960, William Rogers, a college ministry leader with the NCC, recognized these developments. In a report on "the present campus situation" as it related to religion, Rogers lamented Protestants' fragmented approach. Denominational campus ministries, he noted, were physically and spiritually housed on the peripheries of the campus. And nondenominational groups were no better. "Such conservative groups as 'Intervarsity' or such specialized groups as 'The Fellowship of Christian Athletes,'" he argued, "by the very nature of their limited Gospel seem to attempt to evangelize fragmented areas of their converts' lives."[102]

While the FCA was not necessarily theologically conservative at the time, Rogers recognized that it had developed into a niche ministry within a specific subculture. For Rogers, this cut against his belief that campus ministry should minister to the whole person. But with American society moving toward market segmentation, specialized ministry among subcultural groups was the way of the future.[103] And sports, despite existing as a subculture, was unique in its ability to extend its reach across diverse constituencies.

As the institutions of big-time sports continued to expand in cultural influence and financial success during the 1960s and 1970s, they would bring the FCA—and a handful of newly created sports ministries—along with them.

5

Scoring Heavily in the South

The Fellowship of Christian Athletes (FCA) came to Atlanta on February 1, 1964. One week earlier, student protesters had staged sit-ins throughout the city, spotlighting the persistence of segregation and urging action against injustice.[1] Atlanta's white business and civic leaders—including the white moderates who famously proclaimed their community "the city too busy to hate"—recoiled at the confrontational tactics of the protesters and rejected their demands. The FCA, however, received a more welcoming response. From Friday through Sunday, FCA-affiliated athletes and coaches spoke at more than fifty high schools and eighty churches, reaching over 250,000 people.[2]

Focusing on Christian uplift and nonconfrontational cooperation, the FCA did not directly challenge segregation, instead presenting its blend of faith and sports as an antidote to social divisions. "Our hearts are sick over some of the problems in America . . . but sports teach the greatest lessons," FCA president and Army football coach Paul Dietzel declared. "No matter what your color, or what side of the track you come from, or how you comb your hair, everything's equal."[3]

Dietzel's message that "everything's equal" in sports tapped into a long-standing myth in which the country's athletic fields were harbingers of a more democratic future. It also reflected the boosterish vision of Atlanta's civic and business leaders. By embracing the positive spirit and economic opportunities of the emerging Sunbelt economy, city leaders believed racial conflict and divisions could be diminished. The FCA fit perfectly into these aims, offering an organized expression of the region's long-held interest in combining masculinity, faith, and sports, formulated to fit into a post–*Brown v. Board* age.

Although the FCA began under the leadership of Northern-based mainline Protestants, in the 1960s it swept through Atlanta and other communities across the South. By the end of the decade it had become a civic institution in the sporting life of the region—a prominent feature of Southern public life, particularly on the football field.

Importantly, the FCA's southward shift had national ramifications. First, it fostered connections among white Southern Protestants, neoevangelicals, and middlebrow mainliners, helping to form a coalition that would eventually unite under the "evangelical" banner. Second, it shaped the response of FCA leaders

The Spirit of the Game. Paul Emory Putz, Oxford University Press. © Oxford University Press 2024.
DOI: 10.1093/9780190091095.003.0006

to a wave of Black athlete activism that emerged at the end of the 1960s. By supporting the inclusion of Black athletes within white sports institutions while resisting calls for broader structural changes, the FCA helped to construct a colorblind consensus on race.

Buoyed by these twin developments, the Christian athlete movement forged ahead with a new geographical base and a message that combined Sunbelt optimism with an appeal to "traditional" religious values.

Southernization

By the end of the 1960s it was clear that the Sunbelt states of the South and West were economically ascendant. Federal government policies that supported defense industry jobs and the construction of sprawling suburbs combined with corporate-friendly antilabor laws and the expansion of the oil and tourism industries to position Sunbelt states as sites of economic opportunity. In the South this growth was concentrated in metropolitan areas and among middle- and upper-class whites, many of whom represented what scholar Matthew Lassiter has called the "Sunbelt Synthesis," a "booster vision" of the South that sidestepped the region's history of white supremacy and racial segregation by focusing on "the twin pillars of rapid economic development and enforced racial harmony."[4]

Sports played a pivotal role in this vision.[5] Even before World War II, the region had emerged as a hub for end-of-the-year football spectacles, developing several college football bowl games in the 1930s—the Sugar Bowl (New Orleans), Cotton Bowl (Dallas), and Orange Bowl (Miami). By the 1960s the Sun Bowl (El Paso), Gator Bowl (Jacksonville), Tangerine Bowl (Orlando), Bluebonnet Bowl (Houston), and Peach Bowl (Atlanta) had been added.[6]

The 1960s also witnessed the entrance of big-time pro sports into the region. Although there were teams on the Southern fringe (most notably in St. Louis and Washington, DC), until 1960 no major professional sports team resided in the South. Attracting big-league teams became an obsession for metropolitan Southerners who hoped to signal their newfound importance and influence in the national economy. In the 1960s, teams associated with the three major professional team sports were either created in or relocated to Houston, Dallas, Miami, Atlanta, and New Orleans. By 1968, Atlanta had teams in all three major sports; in the 1970s Houston and Dallas joined Atlanta as three-team cities.[7]

The FCA followed the influx. To be sure, from its 1954 inception in Oklahoma, the organization had a presence along the edges of the region. Baylor University in Texas was an especially important early partner. Former Baylor basketball player Jack Robinson served on the FCA's first Advisory Board, and four Baylor graduates—more than any other school—served on staff at the FCA's inaugural 1956 conference in Estes Park.[8]

But despite Southern involvement in the FCA, until the 1960s the organization's leadership remained dominated by Northern mainline Protestants. As of 1962 the FCA had hired four full-time staff members, none of whom were from the South and all of whom were connected to mainline denominations. Similarly, in 1962 only two members of the fifteen-person board of directors—the ultimate source of authority for the FCA—hailed from the South (James Jeffrey and Bob Taylor, from Texas and Tennessee, respectively).[9] And although the FCA had expanded to three summer conferences by 1963, they were located in Colorado, Wisconsin, and New York. With its mainline Protestant leadership, the FCA of the 1950s developed a broad, ecumenical, and racially inclusive approach that would not have been possible if the organization's early leadership had come from the South.

At the grassroots level, however, FCA leaders quickly recognized that white Southerners were especially drawn to their movement. In 1959 Don McClanen observed that "most of our City-Wide activity is conducted in the Southern half of the nation," and in 1962 an internal report noted that seventy percent of the attendees at the FCA's summer conferences came from the South.[10] This support was due in part to the pervasiveness of evangelical Protestantism in the public life of the region. Southern Baptists served as something like an unofficial church establishment, while Methodists and Presbyterians—as well as holiness groups and Pentecostals—had a strong presence.[11] The FCA had difficulty gaining access to public schools in the more cosmopolitan and religiously diverse Northeast, but in many Southern cities the FCA was welcomed into high schools and colleges with open arms and no strings attached.

The FCA also tapped into long-standing cultural support for blending sports with Christian manhood. From Morgan Blake to Billy Graham to the pages of the *Baptist Student*, Southern boys and men had linked together their religious and athletic identities long before the FCA came into existence. Elmin Howell, a Southern Baptist and early FCA supporter, recalled that the FCA seemed like a natural fit with his previous experiences. Even before he heard of the FCA, he had "dreamed of this kind of organized effort." As a result, he "fell right in line" after being introduced to the organization in Nashville in 1955.[12]

Of course, the FCA did not immediately take the whole of the South by storm. It received most of its early support from metropolitan areas outside of the Deep South. Most of these cities also had a major college athletic program: Waco (Baylor), Dallas (Southern Methodist), Nashville (Vanderbilt), Durham (Duke), Atlanta (Georgia Tech), and Chapel Hill (North Carolina) served as hotbeds of FCA support early on. In these communities, football was usually the sport driving FCA involvement. While there were exceptions—at North Carolina, FCA members Frank McGuire and Dean Smith tapped into the state's passion for basketball—the FCA became intertwined with Southern college football in a unique way.[13]

Baylor University and Duke University serve as prime examples. The head football coaches at both schools were early national FCA leaders: Bill Murray (Duke) and John Bridgers (Baylor). Both schools were among the first to create regular meetings for college FCA groups, and both found that football players were most likely to be involved. At Baylor, the FCA scheduled most of its activity after the football season, a nod to the sport that most of its members played.[14] Meanwhile, Duke assistant football coach Marty Pierson informed Don McClanen that "practically all of the [FCA] members [at Duke] are football players."[15] Branching out from Baylor and Duke, the FCA soon received a warm welcome across the Southern football landscape.[16]

City and state leaders in the South also saw the organization as a useful way to promote community spirit and provide young residents with positive role models. In the late 1950s, FCA city-wide rallies were held in Texas and Tennessee; by the early 1960s numerous other Southern cities clamored to do the same. In 1963, the mayor of Daytona Beach, Florida, disturbed by unruly college students who descended on his city during Easter break, invited the FCA to launch a mission aimed at reaching them. In 1965, an FCA staff member noted that the mayor of Montgomery, Alabama, "expressed an urgent plea for FCA in the Montgomery community."[17]

As the FCA gained Southern support in the early 1960s, the national office had difficulty keeping up. The rapidly proliferating FCA groups in cities and college campuses had little formal guidance on how to proceed or how to communicate with the FCA's national leadership. This decentralization was due in part to the hesitancy of the FCA's mainline leaders to create individual FCA units that would make the FCA "another group working outside the church," and also to the organization's fluctuating leadership in the early 1960s. Founder and executive director Don McClanen departed in 1961, and his successor, Bob Stoddard, died suddenly of a heart attack in 1963.[18]

Undeterred, Southern FCA boosters went about organizing themselves. In 1964, leaders from Nashville, Chattanooga, and Atlanta presented a plan that called for the creation of a Southeastern regional FCA office in Atlanta. It stipulated that the office would be funded by FCA leaders in the region and would be run by Loren Young, a Duke graduate and Methodist minister who had played a key role in forming Atlanta's FCA community. In return for Southern financial support, the proposal called on the FCA's national office to implement a chartering plan as soon as possible so that cities and communities launching local FCA units would have a template to follow.[19]

Discussion of the proposal among the FCA's Board of Directors focused primarily on timing, with some leaders skeptical that the FCA was ready to launch a new regional office. But the arguments of Paul Dietzel, then the head football coach at Army, and Bob Taylor, a Nashville-based lawyer, won the day. The two men emphasized the "great deal of interest and activity in the Southeastern region" and Atlanta's importance as a regional hub and strategic site for fundraising opportunities.[20] They also pointed out that "the entrance of professional football and major league baseball in the Southeastern Region" would create opportunities for special FCA events and promotions. By getting in on the ground floor of the Southernization of big-time sports, Dietzel and Taylor suggested, the FCA could set itself up for future success.[21]

The creation of a regional FCA office in Atlanta quickly paid dividends. Soon after the construction of Atlanta Stadium in 1965, the city attracted the Braves (Major League Baseball) and Falcons (National Football League), both of whom began play in 1966, with the Hawks (National Basketball Association) coming in 1968.[22] The FCA used its Atlanta office to take advantage of the city's new place of prominence in pro sports. In 1965, three hundred high school and college FCA members served as ushers for the first football game played in the new Atlanta Stadium, an exhibition matchup between the Minnesota Vikings and the Pittsburgh Steelers. The following year, before the Falcons' first home game, Loren Young delivered the invocation. "We are full of anticipation . . . for this opens a new era to our land," Young prayed. "We have become closely related to a new excitement and a new challenge. We are here because of our common bond and interest in the game."[23]

Young's prayer was not a one-off event; he frequently spoke at the Falcons' pregame chapel services and established a warm relationship with players and team officials. Young also got involved with the Atlanta Hawks booster club when the team came to town in 1968.[24] Given the direct connections between the FCA, sports, and Atlanta's civic boosterism, it is no wonder that in 1965 Atlanta mayor Ivan Allen Jr. and Georgia governor Carl Sanders issued a joint statement praising the FCA for "challenging our youth to live a moral, religious, and sober life by following Christ in the fellowship of the church." They also noted that the FCA was "especially effective in Atlanta, in Georgia, and in the Southeast and certainly deserve[s] everyone's support."[25]

The creation of the FCA's regional office in Atlanta and its cozy relationship with civic leaders and sports boosters signified a southward shift in the FCA's geographical orientation. While the FCA enjoyed support in cities like Indianapolis, Kansas City, and Pittsburgh, as well as in numerous small cities and towns in the Midwest and Great Plains, no region embraced the FCA with as much fervency as the South. And with the creation of the Southeastern regional office and the implementation of a chartering plan for local FCA units, Southern excitement for the FCA program was further unleashed: nine of the first four-teen communities to be awarded local FCA charters were located in the South.[26] Carl Walters, sportswriter for the *Clarion-Ledger* in Jackson, Mississippi, put it well in a 1964 article: "Fellowship of Christian Athletes Is Scoring Heavily in the South."[27]

The FCA and the Civil Rights Movement

Carl Walters's support highlighted the FCA's Southern popularity. Yet it also raised the question: How did FCA leaders approach the civil rights movement? Walters, like many white Southerners, supported segregation and believed it was sanctioned by Christianity—in 1959 he described a friend as a "true-blue Southerner, born and bred; a staunch segregationist, and a high-type Christian gentleman."[28] The FCA, however, had always been racially integrated. As it expanded in the South, the FCA's leaders sought to position themselves in a moderating role as an "above the fray" moral guardian.

The framework for the FCA's racial strategy was influenced by its middlebrow Protestant origins and the legacy of Branch Rickey. Taking a paternalistic ap-proach that resisted dramatic and immediate change, middlebrow Protestants sought to carefully guide the United States into a more inclusive future by in-viting and assimilating exemplary Black men into white spaces. At an FCA event in Houston in 1956 an audience member asked Philadelphia Phillies pitcher Robin Roberts, "What do you think of Negro baseball players?" Roberts prefaced his response with a nod to white segregationists—"my background is different from yours and I am sure we approach this from a little bit different angle"—but went on to declare "that color means absolutely nothing on a base-ball team." He continued, "A man hits a ball and runs to first, you don't stop to see what color he is."[29]

Deployed in a Southern state like Texas, this rhetoric contrasted sharply with the militant segregationist rallying cry of "massive resistance." Following the *Brown v. Board of Education* decision in 1954, white segregationists, particularly in the Deep South, advanced a defiant policy of opposition to integration, with sports as a key site of conflict. In 1955 when Georgia governor Marvin Griffin asked the Georgia Tech Board of Regents to refuse an invitation to play in the Sugar Bowl against an integrated Pittsburgh team, he framed his request with an apocalyptic tone. "The South stands at Armageddon," he warned. "There is no more difference in compromising the integrity of race on the playing field than in doing so in the classroom. One break in the dike and the relentless seas will rush in and destroy us."[30]

Ultimately, Georgia Tech did play the game against Pittsburgh. But for the next decade in the Deep South, segregationists sought to guard against any possible "break in the dike" by passing new laws banning integrated sports competition.[31]

Many white Southern Christians, like Carl Walters, supported these efforts to defend segregation. Most national FCA leaders, however, sided with white moderates in the region, upholding the principle of racial inclusion and working quietly to encourage interracial interaction among Southerners. In 1961, for example, FCA leaders introduced a new alphabetical system for housing assignments at its summer conferences (at that time, all camps were held outside the South) in order to keep Southern attendees from choosing their own racially segregated housing arrangements.[32] FCA conferences also featured messages encouraging interracial cooperation. At its 1962 camp in Lake Geneva, Wisconsin, attended by a strong contingent of white Southerners, former Olympic champion Jesse Owens told the dramatic story of his friendship with German athlete Luz Long, with whom he competed in 1936. "The brotherhood of man can be made known," Owens told campers, if "you will go out and do what must be done."[33]

As the FCA worked to launch its first Southern summer camp, it factored race into its selection of a camp site. In 1963 FCA leaders stipulated that "any camp must include all races" and rejected one possible Southern location because no information "relative to the inclusion of other races at this camp" was forthcoming.[34] Ultimately, the FCA chose a place near Black Mountain, North Carolina, because it permitted interracial groups to use the campgrounds. Through actions like these, the FCA felt it was capitalizing on the "great opportunity to be a creative influence with the general racial problem today."[35]

The FCA's first gathering at Black Mountain—held in 1964—featured several Black sports leaders, including pro football players Curtis McClinton and Prentice Gautt, and basketball coach John McLendon.[36] Dating back to the 1940s, McLendon had been a key leader among HBCU basketball coaches, where he cultivated a particular style of muscular Christianity that prioritized both Black pride and racial integration. Gautt, meanwhile, had been the first Black football player for Oklahoma in the late 1950s. The FCA was influential during his time with the Sooners, but Gautt did not get heavily involved with the FCA until the 1960s, when an injury during his pro career led to a spiritual reawakening.[37]

The final night of the 1964 conference included a small-group huddle session focused on racial problems. It apparently had a strong effect on some attendees. Earlier in the week, with Gautt in the room, a white boy had loudly proclaimed, "I'm at Mississippi State. If Negroes come there, you can look out for bloodshed." The boy's words stung Gautt, but he remained quiet. Then, after the Thursday night huddle session on race, Gautt received a knock on his door. When he opened it, Gautt saw the white student from Mississippi State. The two discussed racial issues until early the next morning, a conversation that attracted a crowd as more and more boys came to the room to listen and join in. For Gautt, the incident provided evidence that "face-to-face dialogue between Christian Negroes and whites produces better relations." It also provided evidence of the FCA's usefulness. "That's one value of the FCA. It's ecumenical and interracial," he explained. "When Christian athletes—and other people for that matter—play and live together in close fellowship, they come to know and understand one another."[38]

Yet, even if the FCA could legitimately claim that it was relatively progressive among white Southerners, there were clear limits. The same week that the FCA was holding its conference in the mountains of North Carolina, Black men and women were gathering at First African Baptist Church in Tuscaloosa, Alabama, to pray and prepare. They planned to march from the church to the courthouse to remove "whites-only" signs. Soon after starting their march on June 9, in what would become known as "Bloody Tuesday," Alabama law enforcement beat and tear-gassed the demonstrators, sending over thirty to the hospital and over ninety to prison.[39]

As an organization, the FCA steered clear of supporting these demonstrations or the legislation for which activists marched. While some individual FCA leaders, primarily Black Protestants like Prentice Gautt or mainline ministers like Roe Johnston, supported civil rights activism, this support was in the minority. Basketball standout and future United States Senator Bill Bradley, a prominent FCA spokesperson in the 1960s, recalled attending a 1964 FCA conference and noticing that, despite the FCA's support for symbolic racial inclusion, there were hardly any Black athletes present. He was also surprised to learn that his roommates opposed the Civil Rights Act. Over time, Bradley's uneasiness with the FCA's stance on racial issues played a role in his separation from the organization.[40]

Instead of actively supporting the civil rights movement, most FCA leaders embraced what Steven Miller describes as "a postwar elite evangelical consensus on race," viewing racism as an individual sin of the heart while remaining skeptical of efforts by the government to address racial injustice.[41] They felt uncomfortable with disruptive tactics like sit-ins and freedom rides, and their desire to be inclusive (even when it came to segregationists) and to focus on the positive rendered FCA leaders hesitant to wade too far into controversial social issues or to openly criticize racist systems. As a result, the FCA's basic approach reflected a belief that racism would disappear one person at a time. Sports would be an engine of that progress.

The small number of Black Protestants in the organization also tended to adopt a gradualist perspective, emphasizing interracial relationships. Following the logic of muscular assimilation, they entered into the predominantly white FCA space in hopes that their involvement would pave the way for a more equitable future. Writing in his autobiography, FCA member and Olympic track star Rafer Johnson drew on the example of sports to explain why he stayed in predominantly white Christian spaces. "I thought about men like Jackie [Robinson] and Jesse Owens and Ralph Bunche, and all the hearts and minds they had changed just by being themselves," Johnson wrote. "Maybe, in my own way, I could do the same by simply worshiping where I wanted to."[42]

Johnson's involvement in the FCA primarily involved delivering talks at conferences and city-wide events. There was, however, one Black man who had a voice among the FCA's decision makers in the 1960s: "Deacon" Dan Towler. A native of Donora, Pennsylvania, Towler starred as a running back on the football field in high school, graduating in 1946. He received attention from major colleges but chose to attend Washington & Jefferson College, a small predominantly white school in Pennsylvania, so that he could study for the ministry while continuing his playing career.[43]

The NFL's Los Angeles Rams selected Towler in the 1950 draft, where his religious reputation followed him. In his rookie season newspaper stories described Towler leading the team in pregame prayers, and a 1953 Hollywood movie about teammate Elroy "Crazylegs" Hirsch re-enacted one such scene, with Towler playing himself. He received attention for his play on the field, too, earning four Pro Bowl appearances as a fullback and twice leading the league in rushing touchdowns. After receiving his master's degree in theology, he retired from the sport in 1955, taking over as minister of an interracial Methodist congregation in Los Angeles. He also joined the fledgling FCA movement. For the next two decades Towler held key leadership positions with the FCA, often as the only Black voice in the room.[44]

Towler did not entirely reject civil rights demonstrations or the need for legislation. In 1964, he spoke up about housing discrimination, explaining to a *Los Angeles Times* reporter that segregated housing and limits on economic opportunities for Black people were like "the football coach telling his fullback to drive off tackle, but the guards won't block for him or open up a hole."[45] But Towler generally held back from insisting on immediate change. Years later he provided additional insight into his perspective when he was interviewed about the lack of Black head coaches in professional football. "In this business if you're aggressive, it destroys you," he said. "You've got to let somebody open the door and give you a chance. If you try to break it in, it will close tighter."[46]

Towler took a similar approach in the 1960s when it came to his work with the FCA. He was careful not to push too far or too fast. In 1964, a few months after Martin Luther King Jr. headlined the March on Washington, Towler published an article in the *Christian Athlete* titled "A March for Freedom." Towler's article struck a conciliatory note, writing that "God's judgment is on the Negro and Caucasian alike" and that the answer to the country's racial problems could be found in open and honest communication between people of different races. If churches could become sites for interracial interaction, cooperation, and communication, they could create "the March that lasts, the one that sets us free to love one another."[47]

The following year Towler expanded on this theme in an interview in the *Christian Athlete* titled "Love, Not Laws, Will End Race Difficulties." Towler again highlighted the need for Blacks and whites to get to know and interact with each other. "You can legislate all the integration you want," Towler declared, "but it's going to take real love of man toward man to solve our race problem."[48]

Although Towler, a mainline minister and strong supporter of the ecumenical movement, did not emphasize the need for born-again experiences, he did present a solution that focused on personal relationships rather than government intervention. His booster/builder disposition, emphasizing positivity and well-ordered gradual change, fit comfortably with the approach of the white-dominated FCA. Racism, in their view, was a problem that could be solved on a person-by-person basis, either through education and interaction (which appealed to middlebrow Protestants) or through a new birth in Christ (which appealed to Southern Baptists and neoevangelicals). The social activism of Black Christian civil rights leaders like Martin Luther King Jr., by contrast, was not welcomed or prioritized.[49]

By focusing on moderation and gradual change, the FCA framed racial views as a matter of personal preference rather than a moral imperative. Segregationists like Carl Walters could feel at home in the FCA. So could men like Alvin Dark, who accepted integration but spoke disparagingly about nonwhite racial groups. A prominent FCA spokesperson as a big-league shortstop in the 1950s, Dark became a manager in 1961. He appeared on the cover of the *Christian Athlete* in 1962 and was cited as an example of active Christian commitment in a 1963 article in the magazine. The next year, as manager of the San Francisco Giants, Dark made headlines when he complained to a New York sportswriter about the "Spanish-speaking and Negro players" on his team who "are just not able to perform up to the white ball players when it comes to mental alertness."[50]

Dark's comments were a reminder that desegregation did not eliminate racist perspectives. A white coach could have proximity to Black athletes without standing in solidarity with their concerns. Even so, many civil rights activists saw integration in sports as a moral issue, working to integrate athletic programs at white Southern colleges in the 1960s.

True to its hands-off approach, the FCA allowed for a variety of responses from its members. Frank Broyles, University of Arkansas football coach and a key FCA leader, was especially notable for dragging his feet. He did not recruit

Black players until 1969, making Arkansas the last Southwest Conference program (along with Texas) to desegregate on the playing field. In 1965, when a
Black walk-on named Darrell Brown attempted to make the Razorback team,
he received no support from Broyles. Instead, he endured vicious abuse from
other coaches and players—Brown recalled drills in which he was sent to return
a punt, only to have his blockers quit, allowing eleven white players to pummel
him as they shouted racial epithets. Brown never made the Arkansas varsity
team, leaving the abusive situation in 1966.[51]

Other Southern FCA-affiliated coaches, including Bill Yeoman at the
University of Houston and Hayden Fry at Southern Methodist, were more pro-
active when it came to racial integration.[52] At Baylor, the Alabama-born John
Bridgers, who coached football from 1959 through 1968, also advocated for
Black players. Writing in 1963 for the Christian Athlete, Bridgers explained that
Christian coaches had a great opportunity to shape the future of the nation and
to work for "progress, achievement, and a better world" by cultivating "high
moral values" among their athletes.[53] While this did not lead Bridgers to the
front lines of the civil rights movement, it did lead him to support a Black student
named John Westbrook who tried out for the Baylor team in 1965. In the spring
of 1966, Bridgers overruled his assistant coaches and gave Westbrook a football
scholarship. That fall, when Westbrook took a hand-off and darted nine yards
in a game against Syracuse, he became the first Black athlete to compete in the
Southwest Conference.[54]

At the University of North Carolina, basketball coach Dean Smith offered
the most pronounced support for the civil rights movement among the FCA's
Southern coaches. A Kansas native, Smith served on the FCA's Board of Directors
in the 1960s and was a member of Olin T. Brinkley Memorial Baptist Church, a
progressive, interracial congregation in Chapel Hill. Both Smith and his pastor,
Robert Seymour, identified with the small-group, "company of the committed"
style of spirituality that Don McClanen had embraced before his departure from
the FCA. Similar to McClanen, Smith read Elton Trueblood, developed a deep
inner spiritual life, and embraced the notion that all Christians—including
laypeople—should view their vocations as a sacred and spiritual calling.[55]

For Smith, this vocational calling extended into social issues. As an assistant
coach in 1959, he and Seymour took a Black theology student out to dinner at
a segregated restaurant in Chapel Hill, hoping this small gesture might help
break down the color line. But Smith was no revolutionary. While the restaurant
owners allowed the three to share a meal without incident, they did not change
their policy until after civil rights legislation in 1964, and Smith did not push
further or join with subsequent sit-ins.[56] Similarly, soon after Smith was named
head coach of North Carolina in 1961, Seymour encouraged him to "find a black
basketball player for the university" as part of his vocational calling.[57] Although

Smith began recruiting across the color line, it took a few years—until 1966—before he successfully signed Charlie Scott, the first Black scholarship athlete in any sport at the University of North Carolina.[58]

Scott came to the Tar Heels from Laurinburg Institute, a Black prep school whose program was led by Frank McDuffie. Like many Southern Black athletes and coaches, McDuffie and Scott had strong Christian commitments that had been nurtured in Black churches, schools, and athletic institutions.[59] This offered a theoretical point of connection as Black athletes entered into white sports programs in the South—and an opportunity for the FCA to expand its racial diversity. Yet a shared Christian faith could not easily transcend the realities of a culture shaped by white supremacy. A 1963 survey of Southern Baptists found that nearly ninety percent of its churches would not allow Black people as church members, while a poll conducted the following year by the *Christian Herald* found that well over half of its readers in the Deep South opposed integrated churches.[60]

The FCA did not turn away Black athletes or coaches, but as a predominantly white organization it was not always a welcoming place. In 1970, John Westbrook published an article in *Guideposts* about his experience at Baylor. Titled "I Was the Man Nobody Saw," Westbrook discussed the racism and loneliness he experienced, even revealing that he had attempted suicide—this, even though he was an FCA member playing for a generally supportive coach who was also an FCA member.[61]

A 1966 exchange in the pages of the *Atlanta Constitution* highlighted these ongoing tensions. After attending an FCA event in July, one local resident fired off a letter to the editor declaring his disappointment. "I went to the dinner to see a fellowship of Christian athletes of all races and creeds," he complained. "The only nonwhite athletes that were there were the game players." Within a week an FCA supporter wrote to the *Atlanta Constitution* defending the organization. "The FCA includes whites and Negroes and is interested only in furthering the cause of Christ in all races," the supporter declared. "Maybe our racial problems would be a little less difficult," the supporter concluded, if people "would quit trying so hard to find discrimination in every nook and corner."[62]

Converging White Protestant Communities

While the inclusion of Black athletes in the FCA remained limited in the 1960's, the organization's southward shift did help to unite a different set of constituencies: middlebrow mainliners, white Southern Protestants, and neoevangelicals.[63] The two men who took charge of the FCA in 1964 symbolized the FCA's converging religious communities.

At the helm stood executive director James Jeffrey, a Texas-based Southern Baptist layman and insurance salesman who had played football for Baylor in the early 1950s. While the incessantly positive Jeffrey was skilled at selling the organization, he had little interest in administrative details. To hold down the fort in Kansas City while Jeffrey flew across the country to meet with potential donors, the FCA brought in the Kansas-born Dick Harp, formerly head basketball coach at the University of Kansas, to serve as managing director.[64] Harp was affiliated with the Northern-based American Baptist Convention. Thus, the FCA had a practical Midwesterner operating in the background, much like the FCA's continued resonance among middlebrow Protestants, while it had a fast-talking Texas salesman and Sunbelt booster taking charge as the new face of the organization.[65]

Harp and Jeffrey were different in style and geography, but they shared a similar vision for the FCA's identity, focusing less on the rigorous development of mature Christians and more on including as many people—especially young people—as possible. In 1960 Harp wrote to his fellow FCA leaders to advocate for a "broad membership" plan instead of the "limited membership" that Don McClanen desired. A limited plan, Harp noted, "would stress the discipline required of members" and might be a turnoff for potential FCA recruits. But a "broad membership" program—one that did not ask much of FCA members—would build a larger base of financial support and "a statistic which might impress foundations, press, etc."[66]

Similarly, in 1963 the question of capping conference enrollment was discussed at an FCA committee meeting. Dan Towler, Gary Demarest, and Jim Stoner, all seminary-trained pastors, wanted to limit conference enrollment to four hundred people and initiate a training program to strengthen the maturity and depth of FCA huddle leaders. James Jeffrey disagreed. He did not believe, he said, that the "main purpose of the conference was to deepen the spiritual leadership of the boys." Rather, he suggested that the FCA should attempt to gather and reach "as large a group as possible" at their conferences.[67] In both the case of the membership plan and the conference enrollment caps, the perspective of Harp and Jeffrey won the day.

Jeffrey's desire to reach as many people as possible included support for mass evangelism, a common feature of Southern Baptist culture. The FCA conferences had originally been conceived as a way to reach and strengthen those who were already Christians. While young athletes were encouraged to make renewed commitments to Christ and to their home churches, the FCA's early conferences did not promote a born-again salvation experience, in part because of tensions between Northern-based mainline Protestants and neoevangelicals over the meanings and methods of evangelism. In the South, however, mass evangelism was an expected part of public life. Southern Baptist moderates and conservatives alike agreed on its importance.[68] As Jeffrey became the FCA's new leader and as the organization began to reflect its Southern constituency, evangelism that focused on born-again experiences became more common.[69]

So did collaboration with evangelist Billy Graham. Although Graham had featured sports stars in his crusades dating back to the 1940s, he had not worked closely with the FCA. In the 1960s, however, the FCA warmly embraced the evangelist.[70] Articles from Graham's *Decision* magazine were reprinted in the *Christian Athlete*, the FCA sent members to speak at Billy Graham events, and in 1965 Graham himself spoke at an FCA conference in North Carolina.[71]

The FCA's collaboration with Graham was not solely due to the organization's shift to the South. The evangelist was moving closer to the cultural space that mainline Protestants had long occupied, building a national ministry that, as historian Grant Wacker puts it, was "regionally inflected but not regionally limited."[72] As the popular face of the post–World War II neoevangelical movement—a movement that sought to distance itself from militant, separatist fundamentalists—Graham took steps in the 1950s to cooperate with and appeal to at least some mainline Protestants. He was a key figure in the launch of *Christianity Today*, a journal intended in part to reach mainline Protestants sympathetic to neoevangelical theology. He supported moderate racial inclusion. And he increasingly worked with local NCC-affiliated church councils when conducting his evangelistic crusades.[73]

As the Graham-led neoevangelical movement distanced itself from separatist fundamentalists, it adopted a more irenic tone toward Christian athletes who played on Sundays. Into the 1950s, to be a "Christian athlete" in the eyes of fundamentalists and neoevangelicals generally required one to sacrifice athletic fame and glory for the sake of evangelistic zeal and moral purity, including upholding the Sabbath. In the 1960s, however, evangelistic pragmatism won out. As long as athletes were willing to speak publicly about their Christian convictions and their born-again experiences, they were usually welcomed into Billy Graham's orbit.[74]

To be sure, the FCA maintained its ecumenical identity even as it welcomed neoevangelicals like Graham. In 1963 liberal Presbyterian minister Bob Meneilly attended an FCA conference and gushed about his experience: "A wondrous and amazing compatibility of fundamentalism, middle-of-the-road and liberal theological positions, I have never seen any place else or under any other circumstances."[75] This ecumenical diversity was a source of pride for some FCA mainline leaders. Yet it could be a liability among the growing number of Southern Protestants and neoevangelicals in the organization, for whom ecumenism was a mark of compromise or evidence of a watered-down faith.[76]

The clearest sign of this tension was the relationship between the FCA and Campus Crusade for Christ. Founded by Bill Bright in 1951, Campus Crusade overlapped with the FCA in several areas. For starters, Bright was profoundly shaped by Henrietta Mears and Hollywood Presbyterian, the church pastored by FCA founding father Louis Evans Sr. And Bright's organization first achieved widespread attention for its influence among UCLA football players, some of whom—like Donn Moomaw—later collaborated with the FCA.[77] Yet, while the FCA included evangelicals as one group among others, Campus Crusade was firmly rooted within neoevangelicalism.

Crusade's neoevangelical identity—which will be discussed more in the next chapter—was evident in its theology, which emphasized Keswick and premillennial themes and a zealous commitment to winning souls to Christ. While the FCA supported evangelism, it saw itself as a channel funneling people into the church of their choice. Crusade, on the other hand, had little interest in cooperating with mainline Protestant institutions or churches.[78] Instead, Bright encouraged converts to find a "Bible believing" church—one, he explained to his staff, where the preacher emphasized the need for personal conversion and did not talk about politics.[79]

While Crusade did not focus exclusively on sports, it strategically targeted college athletes, leading to turf wars with the FCA. Writing in 1964, soon after the creation of the FCA's regional office, Loren Young reported meeting with Georgia Tech football players to discuss "the FCA–Campus Crusade problem at Tech." The issue persisted over the next few years, most likely because some athletes sought to use Campus Crusade training material in their FCA work.[80] In 1966, FCA board members responded by clarifying that the FCA must maintain an identity distinct from Campus Crusade and other neoevangelical groups in order to focus on its "unique dialogue to the athlete."[81] In short, the FCA saw itself as the primary organizational force for the growing Christian subculture within sports. It was, as the name of its periodical implied, the representative voice of the *Christian Athlete.*

If the FCA was challenged on its right by the zealous soul winning of Campus Crusade, it was also challenged on the left by mainline Protestant intellectuals and activists. An example of this occurred in 1961 when University Christian Mission (UCM) was dissolved by the NCC. Since the 1930s, UCM had cultivated an ecumenical and socially aware evangelistic style—as we saw in Chapter 3, it was central to the formation of the FCA. But in 1961, NCC leaders felt that this type of college evangelism had run its course. In the wake of its dissolution, former UCM director Jim Stoner—by that time serving on the FCA Board of Directors—wrote to express his dismay. "I am saying, as a minister of the local church, able to observe criticism of the National Council," Stoner wrote, "that evangelism must be the primary work of the council."[82]

UCM's demise was a sign of a de-emphasis on evangelism among mainline Protestant leaders that continued throughout the 1960s. While UCM had combined evangelism with social concern, mainline intellectuals were no longer as committed to holding those two together. Instead, they concentrated their energy on what they saw as the more urgent need for serious social reform. Racism, war, and poverty: these were the pressing needs calling for the church's attention.[83] As an organization focused on evangelism, this made it difficult for the FCA to strengthen its partnership with mainline Protestant institutions.

FCA leaders also faced a growing divide in mainline denominations over religious nationalism, with Protestant intellectuals criticizing the public blending of faith and sports that the FCA promoted. Throughout the 1960s the *Christian Century* ran a satirical column titled "Pen-ultimate," written by religious historian Martin Marty, that lampooned "recent religious trends." At several points Marty took aim at FCA coaches and players. In 1962, for example, he blasted the "cheap exhortations to the moral life, couched in the terminology of athletics" that proliferated "ever since the sports world got religion a few years ago." As evidence, Marty pointed to a recent prayer written by a college football coach that read in part, "We hope to win like all the rest, But especially, help us, Lord, to do our best."[84]

Not all of the *Christian Century*'s readers were amused with Marty's satire. "Why is it that the 'praying pros' like yourself cannot appreciate the attempts of a layman to put into practice his religious beliefs?" one asked, while another complained that the sarcasm "was thoughtless and unfair" to the sincere piety of the coach.[85] Mainline Protestants like these were expressing the middlebrow sensibility that preferred to affirm rather than criticize. As in the 1920s, the key element to the middlebrow posture was the booster/builder ideal. Edgar Guest's 1929 poem "Builder or Wrecker"—republished by the *Christian Athlete* in 1966—put it succinctly: one could either be "a builder who works with care ... patiently doing the best I can," or one could be a "wrecker" who focuses on "tearing down."[86]

Guest's poem was not the only piece of 1920s middlebrow Protestant culture brought into the FCA in the 1960s. UCLA basketball coach John Wooden, who cited Amos Alonzo Stagg as a key coaching influence, served as a conduit for middlebrow ideas. In 1963, the *Christian Athlete* published an early copy of Wooden's "Pyramid of Success." The pyramid had been developed during Wooden's days as a high school coach in Indiana in the 1930s. It reflected the "true success" literature common in business-friendly middlebrow periodicals like *American Magazine*. Wooden's pyramid featured fifteen character traits—industriousness, loyalty, cooperation, self-control confidence, poise, and the like—that, if developed, would serve as building blocks for success, which was measured not by bottom-line results but, rather, by "self-satisfaction in knowing you gave the best you are capable of."[87]

Three years later, Wooden wrote a devotional entry for the FCA's second official book, *Courage to Conquer* (1966), where he took the connections to *American Magazine* one step further. Wooden's entry, titled "Success," claimed that when he graduated from eighth grade at a small country school in Indiana, his father gave him a plain white card on which he had written a seven-point creed to live by. The creed included the following points:

> Be true to yourself; Help others; Make each day your masterpiece; Drink deeply from good books, especially the Bible; Make friendship a fine art; Build a shelter against a rainy day; Pray for guidance and count and give thanks for your blessings every day.

Since the creed supposedly came from the mind of Wooden's father, an ordinary man from Indiana, it symbolized the continued relevance and usefulness of traditional small-town Midwestern values.[88]

But the creed had not been conceived by his father. It was first published as a six-point list in an *American Magazine* article in 1931 titled "Help Yourself to Happiness."[89] Wooden's father apparently liked the list enough to write it down on a notecard and give it to his son. When Wooden wrote of his father's creed in *Courage to Conquer*, he was unwittingly revealing the direct links between the middlebrow Protestant ideology of the 1920s and the FCA of the 1960s.

This booster/builder idea served as a unifying force for the FCA's neoevangelical, white Southern Protestant, and middlebrow mainline communities. It reflected the social status and aspirations of predominantly white middle-class men from Middle America. Although distant from the more sophisticated and cosmopolitan centers of American cultural power, they exerted considerable influence and authority within their local communities. Placing their faith in American individualism, capitalism, and carefully guided progress, they believed that they were the builders, the men who possessed the moral character, work ethic, and practical wisdom that had made the United States a great country in the past. Under their guidance, America could build upon and improve on its solid foundation. Meanwhile, the "wreckers" were those who challenged capitalism, criticized "traditional" moral values, or sought to change American society through disruption.

In the 1920s the booster mentality had been shaped by a popularized Protestant modernism associated with the Midwest. By the 1960s, however, the center of gravity for white middle-class booster culture had shifted to the sprawling suburbs of the Sunbelt. With it, the evangelistic impulse became more prominent—Southerners, after all, did not share the suspicion of revivalism maintained by some mainline Protestants. Instead, as historian Joel Carpenter put it, Southern Baptists were "immersed up to their Sunday School and Rotary pins in the main current of Southern civic life," all the while supporting evangelism as a positive community good.[90]

As this support for conversion-oriented evangelism filtered into the FCA in the 1960s, a few mainline FCA leaders raised the alarm. In the 1950s, liberal Presbyterian minister Roe Johnston had been one of the FCA's most important advocates. By 1967, he worried that the FCA was developing a reputation as "an ultra-conservative and rather meaningless organization" because of its growing tendency to favor "purely emotional" testimonies of faith rather than a "calculated and reasonable witness of an expression of faith and a response in service."[91] But Johnston was in the minority, even among his fellow mainliners. Middlebrow Protestants like John Wooden may not have possessed evangelistic zeal—"If you believe in a faith, if you feel in your heart it's right for you, then I think it's wonderful," he told a reporter.[92] They did, however, support the practical Christianity and positive messaging that white Southern FCA leaders promoted.

An insurance salesman turned FCA's executive director, James Jeffrey perfectly embodied this sentiment. A Florida-based newspaper columnist marveled at Jeffrey's positivity and how it took Jeffrey "about a minute to make a friend out of a total stranger."[93] Jeffrey's personal charms made him a popular speaker at city-boosting functions, where he linked his FCA work with the progress of local communities.[94]

Jeffrey's ability to sell the organization and his connections with Sunbelt businessmen helped the FCA expand over the course of the 1960s. The annual budget went from $101,000 in 1960 to $1,000,000 by 1969, and from two summer conferences and 1,200 attendees in 1961 to sixteen summer conferences with 7,550 delegates in 1969. When Jeffrey was hired in 1963 the FCA had only three full-time staff members; by 1969, there were twenty-two. And while the FCA maintained a strong presence in the Midwest and Great Plains, the Southern strength of the organization was much more apparent by the end of the decade. In 1963, only two members of the FCA's Board of Directors were from the South; by 1969, that number had grown to eight. Even more telling, a survey in 1967 found that fifty-seven percent of the FCA's local chapters were located in Southern states.[95]

Writing for the *New York Times* in 1971, West Virginia columnist L. T. Anderson took note of this geography. He wrote of how closely the FCA had become entwined with football and the South, claiming that Southern football coaches were "the circuit riders" of the FCA faith. As for the religious ethos of the FCA, Anderson declared that its members "look upon Billy Graham as a minor deity" and that "their doctrine owes much to Norman Vincent Peale's teaching that a vice-presidency and gobs of money await the devout sales executive."[96]

While Anderson's criticism extended into hyperbole, he did accurately connect the FCA to the booster ethos found at the confluence of neoevangelicalism, white Southern Protestantism, and middlebrow mainline Protestantism. By focusing on making faith relevant to the individual lives of its men—and linking that masculine faith with American identity—FCA leaders in the South and beyond helped the organization grow and expand. Their theology may have been diverse, but they could unite around a shared desire to preserve what they saw as the country's traditional values while maintaining an optimistic, success-oriented outlook on life.

Responding to the Black Athlete Revolt

Optimism may have abounded in the rhetoric of FCA boosters, but it came with a dark side. Running alongside visions of economic prosperity and gradual progress toward racial harmony was an undercurrent of fear that "wreckers" and "radicals" could destroy it all unless they were kept in check. Talk of positive mindsets could quickly turn to talk of punitive repression when boosters felt their authority challenged.

This dual impulse shaped the reaction of FCA leaders to the rising tide of Black athlete activism in the 1960s.[97] Led by figures like Muhammad Ali and Bill Russell, a growing number of athletes and activists, inspired by the Black Power movement, began to see that racism in sports was not simply a Southern problem tied to segregation; it was a national issue focused on structural inequalities within the sports establishment.[98] In 1967 a professor, activist, and former athlete named Harry Edwards sought to consolidate this activism into a unified effort, organizing the Olympic Project for Human Rights (OPHR) to explore a Black athlete boycott of the 1968 Olympic games.

Although the boycott did not occur, two Black athletes—Tommie Smith and John Carlos—won Olympic medals in Mexico City and then raised their gloved fists in solidarity with the Black freedom struggle. Meanwhile, in college athletic programs across the country, Black athletes increasingly spoke out against racial disparities and injustices they faced at predominantly white colleges.[99]

This flurry of activity in the late 1960s and early 1970s, dubbed the "revolt of the black athlete" by Edwards, directly challenged the logic of muscular assimilation long present among Black Christian athletes. The contrast with the beginning of the decade was striking. In 1960, FCA member Rafer Johnson had carried the American flag as he led the US delegation into the Olympic arena for the opening ceremonies in Rome, the first Black athlete to do so.[100] Johnson was breaking another racial barrier, opening a door (the logic went) through which other Black people could follow. The Black athlete revolt, by contrast, sought to use sports, including the stage of the Olympics, to directly confront white America's sense of innocence. The revolt's leaders saw little value in propping up Black athletes as symbols of racial progress when racism remained so persistent throughout American society.

The surge in Black athlete activism undermined the FCA's self-perception as a force for racial progress. The FCA preferred a slow and gradual approach, with white leaders operating as gatekeepers; the Black athlete revolt demanded immediate change. The FCA was a Christian, integrationist, and mostly white sports-boosting organization; most prominent leaders of the Black athlete movement criticized the sports establishment, were skeptical of prioritizing integration at the expense of Black institutions, and either rejected Christianity as a "white" religion (particularly those like Muhammad Ali who supported the Nation of Islam) or de-emphasized Christianity as a core aspect of their identity. "We don't catch hell because we're Christians," Lew Alcindor (later Kareem Abdul-Jabbar) told a reporter in 1967. "We catch hell because we're black."[101]

Within the FCA, several different responses developed. Some leaders took a reactionary tone, rejecting the demands of Black activists and rallying around a defense of "traditional" values and discipline. This group included some white men who had a strong track record of racial inclusion, including Biggie Munn, the athletic director at Michigan State, a school known in the 1960s for its racially inclusive roster.[102] When Michigan State's Black football players joined the revolt in 1968, demanding better treatment and more Black coaches, Munn responded with defiance. "I will resign my position as Director of Athletics when I am told who I have to hire and who my coaches must play by the athletes themselves," he declared. "In Athletics I have always been for fair play and equal rights no matter what color or creed."[103]

Munn's resistance extended to events beyond Michigan State. In 1969 Detroit-based sportswriter Roger Stanton penned an article titled "Blacks Are Ill-Advised" in which he denounced Black athlete-activists as prima donnas. "The greatest tragedy of the 1969 football season is the revolt of certain black football players," Stanton wrote. "They are hurting themselves, their schools, and the entire Negro race." Munn wrote to tell Stanton that the article was "fantastic."[104]

Another college football coach prominently involved with the FCA, Paul Dietzel, echoed Munn's concerns. The Ohio-born Dietzel had coached segregated teams at Louisiana State University (LSU) from 1955 to 1961, winning a national championship with an undefeated season in 1958. He moved from LSU to Army in 1961, and then to South Carolina in 1966, where he served as football coach and athletic director until 1974. At both Army (1965) and South Carolina (1969) Dietzel recruited the school's first Black football players. Yet in both cases Dietzel was a follower rather than a leader, lagging behind peer institutions.[105]

In a 1969 interview with the South Carolina student newspaper, the *Gamecock*, Dietzel warned that "Athletic departments throughout the country" were "being lampooned by different militant groups." Dietzel cited reports from friends in the coaching profession who had Black players on their teams. Those players, Dietzel claimed, regularly received phone calls "from highly militant groups" across the country who urged the Black athletes to take actions "of a disruptive nature."[106]

As president of the American Football Coaches Association in 1969, Dietzel had a prominent platform to air his concerns. He used the AFCA's official publication to urge his fellow coaches to "hold your ground" and maintain discipline.[107] One way to do this, he suggested, was through Christian commitment. Speaking to the annual AFCA convention in 1970, Dietzel recalled attending an FCA summer camp with his son, where the athletes in attendance modeled the disciplined approach that Dietzel desired. An FCA athlete, Dietzel claimed, was "the kind of man that I am very happy my son has picked as his hero."[108]

For Dietzel, Munn, and others in the reactionary camp, the problem with the Black athlete revolt was its apparent attack on authority. They lumped it in with the broader protest movements associated with college students in the 1960s, seeing their opposition to activism not as a racially motivated position but, rather, as a defense of traditional values. It shared affinities with Richard Nixon's cultivation of a "silent majority," with law-and-order themes that could be called "colorblind" while at the same time drawing on white backlash and racial resentment.[109]

The political and cultural resonance of these themes came through in 1969 during the "Game of the Century" football matchup between undefeated Arkansas and Texas—two teams with all-white active rosters. With prominent FCA advocate Frank Broyles pacing the Arkansas sidelines, Billy Graham delivering the pregame prayer, and Richard Nixon watching from the stands, television viewers witnessed a counterimage to scenes of student protests and social unrest. Here was a disciplined and orderly vision for society, one buttressed by Protestant faith and with white men at its center.[110] It was a vision that many mainline Protestant intellectuals and denominational leaders had turned against in the wake of the social changes of the 1960s, but one that middlebrow mainliners like Biggie Munn continued to embrace—even if it meant aligning themselves with Billy Graham and other neoevangelicals whose theology they did not necessarily share.[111]

A second approach within the FCA aimed for a path of moderation, with white leaders adopting the role of responsible and empathetic listeners. San Jose State football coach Dewey King served as one example. His school was an incubator of the Black athlete revolt—Harry Edwards, an alum, taught sociology classes and organized protests there in the late 1960s, and both Tommie Smith and John Carlos were graduates. Writing in the *Christian Athlete*, King recalled his first team meeting after arriving in 1970: he entered a room with seventy-five athletes, "half of them blacks, some of them militants."[112]

King's strategy in this environment was to connect with his players as individuals. He grounded it in the Christian doctrine of the *imago Dei*, telling his players: "God created each of you. He created you in his image and as such you are unique." This, he claimed, "struck a bell with our black athletes faster than anything." Whether or not his players felt the same way, it did free King to worry less about enforcing rules. He cited *The Awesome Power of the Listening Ear*—written by John Drakeford, a Southern Baptist seminary professor—as an especially helpful book. He also referenced advice he had heard from John Wooden at an FCA camp. "Athletes come from different backgrounds, have different temperaments and will therefore respond differently," Wooden had said. "Find out how to best approach each of your players."[113]

Wooden had experience with this need for adaptability. In the late 1960s he coached a team led by one of the leading voices in the Black athlete revolt, Kareem Abdul-Jabbar (then Lew Alcindor). Wooden's relationship with Abdul-Jabbar did not truly blossom until years later, but even during Abdul-Jabbar's time at UCLA, Wooden demonstrated a willingness to learn from the perspective and experiences of his Black players.[114] The desire by coaches like Wooden and King—and many others, including Dean Smith and Nebraska football coach Tom Osborne—to understand the cultural challenges posed by Black activism led the FCA to create a new summer conference for coaches, launched in 1969. It also showed that a middlebrow ethos defined by belief in gradual progress still resonated in the movement; reaction was not inevitable.[115]

Black leaders within the FCA, meanwhile, often found themselves pulled in competing directions. Asked to play a mediating role between a white-led movement claiming to speak for Christian athletes and a Black-led movement focused on galvanizing Black athletes for social change, Black FCA members had to carefully navigate a complex set of interests and affiliations. For some, like Dan Towler and Rafer Johnson, belief in the continued possibility of gradual change through interracial cooperation opened them up to scrutiny from activists. Writing in *The Revolt of the Black Athlete*, Edwards specifically named and criticized both Towler and Johnson for their refusal to support his movement.[116]

Edwards was more understanding when Florida A&M football coach Jake Gaither also opposed the Olympic boycott.[117] As an HBCU coach, Gaither had spent his entire adult life working with and mentoring Black men. But his belief in Black pride and the need for strong Black institutions was joined by his firm commitment to Christianity and, in the words of historian Derrick White, his "deeply held social conservatism."[118] He felt he had more in common with an organization committed to Christianity than Edward's movement. By the end of the 1960s, Gaither became prominently involved in the FCA, speaking frequently at rallies and conferences—at one event he described the FCA as "one of the greatest organizations in the world."[119]

Other Black FCAers took a more ambivalent perspective. In 1968, while he was still enrolled at Baylor, John Westbrook was interviewed by the *Christian Athlete* about America's racial crisis. "I don't know the answer—riot, push harder, wait, negotiate, march. It may take all of these things," Westbrook stated.[120] In 1969, Prentice Gautt was asked to speak for coaches, penning an article for the *Christian Athlete* on "The Coach and the Black Athlete." Recently retired from his NFL career and serving at Missouri as one of the first Black assistant coaches at a white school, Gautt addressed many of the issues that athletes engaged in the revolt were raising. He warned against insensitive racial jokes and "stacking" Black players into the same positions. He urged coaches not to crack down on expressions of identity, like hairstyles and celebrations after a great play. And while Gautt encouraged the hiring of more Black coaches, he warned against "token integration."[121]

In their public statements for white audiences, Gautt and Westbrook spoke clearly about the reality of racism. Yet, like Towler and Johnson, the two refrained from advocating for protest and disruption, aiming instead to find common ground through shared athletic identities and Christian commitments.[122] Speaking in 1970 at an FCA summer camp, Gautt displayed a positive outlook. "So many doors have been open to Negro athletes because of sports in America," he stated. "I am convinced that a Negro athlete, or a white athlete, has a great opportunity to help the race situation today, especially if he is a dedicated Christian."[123]

The eagerness with which the FCA sought out the voices of Black leaders like Prentice Gautt, Dan Towler, Rafer Johnson, and John Westbrook—as well as the flexible approaches adopted by white Christian coaches like John Wooden and Dewey King—showed that many in the movement desired to be sensitive to the concerns raised by Black athlete protesters. Even so, theirs was ultimately a vision with clear limits. It could include individual Black athletes and attempt to listen to their perspectives, but it could not adopt race-conscious remedies that deviated from an individualistic, colorblind ideology. John Westbrook, hired in 1969 as the first Black FCA staff member, found this out the hard way. He lasted only a year before he resigned, in part because FCA leaders censored the racial content of his talks.[124]

Bill Curry also ran up against the limits of the FCA's racial imagination. A white Atlanta native who played football at Georgia Tech and then in the NFL, Curry's FCA involvement dated back to 1962, when he attended a camp in Wisconsin and roomed with an African American—the first time he ever encountered a Black person as a peer. His racial views evolved in part because of his FCA experience. After Martin Luther King Jr's assassination in 1968, however, Curry realized how little things had changed. On a personal level, he was willing to accept Black people as friends and teammates; yet once he left the locker room he remained ensconced in white communities, doing nothing to support Black communities or the causes for which King stood.

Curry felt compelled to march in King's funeral, and he later spoke to a reporter about his frustrations and laments. "I had talked a good game but I never got in the game," Curry said.[125] Feeling that there was little support within the FCA for a faith that advocated for racial justice, Curry distanced himself from the organization over the next decade.[126]

If Westbrook and Curry represented FCAers who ran into racial boundaries, Jackie Robinson represented a Black Christian perspective that did not have a place in the movement to begin with. Despite his involvement with other Christian groups and his friendship with FCA founder Branch Rickey, Robinson never joined the organization. He found religious inspiration instead in the work of civil rights activists like Martin Luther King Jr. Following their lead, Robinson threw his support behind the Olympic protest movement in 1968, including publicly praising Smith and Carlos for their Black Power gesture.[127]

In a 1969 speech Robinson framed his support with reference to his faith, turning to the biblical figure of Job. "I translate [Job's] story into the story of the black man in America today," Robinson explained. "Like Job, we have advisors telling us if we are so mistreated it must be our own fault.... But like Job we answer, 'I am a man and therefore worthy. Though you slay me I will maintain my own ways before you.'"[128] While Robinson remained committed to the principle of interracial cooperation, he saw in the revolt an opportunity for Black athletes to take authorship of their own story rather than accepting their place, as he put it in his autobiography, as "a Black man in a white world."[129]

Robinson's perspective ran headlong into the growing backlash against civil rights activism. By 1968 the civil rights movement no longer focused primarily on ending laws that sanctioned white supremacy in the South; it sought to address the racial inequality built into systems and structures in communities across the nation. This, as Martin Luther King Jr. recognized in his final book, was a step too far for most white Americans. As white reaction to civil rights advances commenced, King noted, "it appeared that the white segregationist and the ordinary white citizen had more in common with one another than either had with the Negro."[130]

The FCA's response to the Black athlete revolt was an example of this solidarity across regional lines. With segregation no longer a dividing issue, middlebrow Protestants, white Southern Protestants, and booster-minded neoevangelicals could join together around a shared vision of American society that focused on maintaining social order, guarding traditional values, and achieving gradual progress. It was a vision that still centered white authority, even as it invited some Black Christians into the room, and it enabled the FCA to build a strong base of support in the communities and sports teams of the South while maintaining a national reach, particularly in Middle America. Similar to the process of racial integration within sports, it led, as historian Frank Guridy puts it, to "a realignment, rather than a demolition, of social hierarchies."[131]

The man who followed James Jeffrey as the FCA's president in 1972, John Erickson, embodied this vision. A former University of Wisconsin basketball coach and Milwaukee Bucks general manager, Erickson made a run for the U.S. Senate in 1970 because he wanted "to help save the country" from both "the Soviets outside and the revolutionaries at home." A Republican, he had a reputation as a moderate with views on race that fit comfortably within the new colorblind status quo embraced by many white Southerners and Northerners alike. "There has been great progress, especially in the South, with less trouble than expected," he said in 1970. As for other matters of racial justice, including housing discrimination, Erickson saw no need for government intervention or continued agitation. "We cannot change philosophies by law," he said. "If each of us will put our arms around each other, and call each other brother, it will be solved."[132]

* * *

As the 1970s dawned, the Black athlete revolt lost momentum. With television money beginning to flood into big-time sports, Black players had heightened economic incentives to set aside political positions that might cost them sponsorships and money. So, too, according to historian Simon Henderson, leaders of the sports establishment were able to maintain authority and stifle dissent with a combination of "strategic concessions" to the demands of Black activists and a reassertion of the cultural narrative that sports were an engine of racial progress.[133]

But despite its alignment with the sports establishment and its strength in the South, the FCA faced challenges both new and old. On its left, the criticism of sports launched by Harry Edwards and fellow Black activists expanded in new directions. Critics increasingly viewed sports as a weapon used to stifle dissent and promote racism, militarism, and sexism—and some FCA members began to listen. Meanwhile, on its right, neoevangelicals launched new sports ministries that challenged the FCA's place as the voice of the Christian subculture within sports. Out of these struggles and challenges, the Christian athlete movement would grow and expand beyond the guidance of the FCA, while at the same time remaining tethered to the FCA's boosterish vision for American society—a vision, after the 1960s, firmly rooted in the Sunbelt South.

6

Call It Sportianity

In April 1976 *Sports Illustrated* fired the "shot heard round the sports/faith world" when the magazine published Frank Deford's three-part series on "Religion in Sports."[1] Deford focused his aim on what he labeled "Sportianity," the growing network of evangelical ministries gaining prominence in big-time sports.[2] Had he written the article ten years earlier, there would have been one organization to discuss: the Fellowship of Christian Athletes (FCA). Now, an array of entrepreneurial ministers and three new ministries—Athletes in Action, Pro Athletes Outreach, and Baseball Chapel—joined the FCA as an organized Christian presence in major athletic institutions.

Mainstream media, including the *New York Times*, had taken note of the prevalence of evangelicals in athletics before Deford, but no major journalist had so thoroughly dissected the phenomenon. His series marked the moment at which the Christian athlete movement, launched in 1954 with the founding of the FCA, reached a point of wide public awareness.

The arrival of Sportianity on the national scene coincided with a growing interest in the evangelical movement. 1976 was dubbed "The Year of the Evangelical" by *Newsweek*, with pundits trying to make sense of the nebulous identity that seemed to be centered on the experience of being born again.[3] The Christian athlete subculture provided ample evidence of evangelicals' ascent to influence in American life. Instead of the mainline Protestant leadership that gave rise to the FCA in the 1950s, the major new sports ministry organizations all had roots in neoevangelical networks and organizations. And the FCA, too, continued down the path toward evangelicalism.

Yet, this evangelical identity could raise as many questions as it resolved. While neoevangelical leaders claimed to hold the keys to the kingdom, in truth the evangelicalism that emerged in the 1970s was diffuse and decentralized. Part political movement, part consumer subculture, part church renewal program, evangelicalism encompassed a variety of theological traditions and perspectives. As historian Molly Worthen points out, American evangelicalism "owes more to its fractures and clashes, its anxieties and doubts, than to any political pronouncement or point of doctrine."[4]

These tensions mapped onto the Christian athlete movement, with the new sports ministries clashing at times with the FCA, and with the FCA facing its

The Spirit of the Game. Paul Emory Putz, Oxford University Press. © Oxford University Press 2024.
DOI: 10.1093/9780190091095.003.0007

own internal tensions over direction and purpose. Differences, however, could not overpower the ties that bound the organizations of Sportianity together. Put simply, evangelicals successfully positioned themselves as the primary religious presence in big-time sports by adopting middlebrow strategies: they focused on the therapeutic benefits of one's personal faith, the defense of "traditional" American values, and the promotion of gradual American progress. At the same time, they turned to neoevangelical tools and theological frameworks to achieve those ends, drawing on a burgeoning evangelical consumer subculture for resources and support.

Sports Evangelism for the Big Time

Frank Deford's *Sports Illustrated* series came at a time when many cultural observers were fretting about America's insatiable appetite for sports.[5] It was impossible to ignore in the 1960s and 1970s, with television money flooding into the major spectator sports, transforming the industry. In 1962 the National Football League (NFL) received just under $5 million for the annual television rights to its games; by 1977 that figure had risen to over $160 million. Network television rights for Major League Baseball (MLB) grew from about $4 million in 1962 to $23 million in 1977, while the National Basketball Association (NBA) went from a mere $650,000 in 1964 to $10 million in 1977. In college sports, too, revenue for broadcast rights to football and basketball surged dramatically.[6]

The infusion of television money into big-time sports amplified the financial rewards for college coaches and professional athletes. While salaries for pro players did not truly explode until the 1980s, after hard-won battles for free agency, growth was apparent in the 1970s. Average salaries in the NFL went from $20,000 in 1963 to $55,000 in 1977 (adjusted for inflation, a 42 percent increase). In baseball, they increased from about $15,000 in 1963 to $75,000 in 1977, the year after free agency was instituted.[7] And the rise in average salaries told only part of the story; the seemingly extravagant money earned by the highest paid players probably did more to shape public perception. When baseball pitcher Catfish Hunter signed a five-year, $3.75 million contract in 1974, it shocked fans—one FCA staff member declared that he was "sick" over Hunter's "ridiculous" salary.[8]

Of course, back in the 1920s the national emergence of big-time sports had drawn both concern and awe at its power to hold public attention. Seen in this light, the television revolution was merely an extension of trends that had begun with newspapers, radio, and other forms of mass media. Even so, television intensified earlier developments, bringing unprecedented amounts of money and attention into the big-time sports landscape—and inspiring new sports ministries to get in the game.

Athletes in Action (AIA) was the most important of these new organizations. Founded in 1966 as a sports-specific subsidiary of Campus Crusade for Christ, AIA did not start out with the same reach or name recognition as the more ecumenical FCA. But it did have the advantage of clarity and coherence of message. AIA focused on a single mission: channeling the power of big-time sports for evangelism. Although it started small and lean, AIA quickly developed into both a cooperative partner with the FCA and a rival source of authority within the Christian athlete movement.

The rivalry could be traced to the years before AIA's founding, when the FCA and Campus Crusade jostled for position on college campuses in the South. AIA's emergence heightened that tension, helping to shape the ways the organizations positioned themselves. In a 1967 magazine article introducing AIA, Bill Bright described a visit to a college campus, where he met a stand-out college athlete. In high school, the athlete had listened to a Christian sports star deliver a talk at a school assembly. He was so inspired that he began attending church, and he had not missed a Sunday in two years. But when Bright asked the athlete if he was a Christian, the young man was not sure. "No one has told me how," he said. So, the Crusade founder led him through a born-again conversion experience, instructing him on the steps needed to receive Christ as his personal Savior and Lord.[9]

Although Bright did not mention the FCA, his critique would have been clear to anyone familiar with the FCA's mode of operation. While the FCA held events where it told young people to follow Christ and get involved in church, it did not always zero in on the born-again experience that neoevangelicals believed was essential to true Christianity. This was changing as the FCA moved more fully into the evangelical camp, but the ecumenical origins of the FCA continued to exert influence. "We provide a strengthening process, the identification of a peer group," one FCA executive explained. "We ought to understand that what the FCA does best is affirm, not evangelize."[10]

AIA, on the other hand, not only wholeheartedly emphasized soul-winning evangelism; it also provided a ready-made template for evangelism with Bright's "Four Spiritual Laws." Starting with a positive affirmation ("God loves you and offers a wonderful plan for your life") before moving to the problem of sin ("Man is sinful and separated from God") and then the solution ("Jesus Christ is God's only provision for man's sin"), the Crusade system ended with a call to action ("We must individually receive Jesus Christ as Savior and Lord; then we can know and experience God's love and plan for our lives").[11] For athletes and coaches unsure of their biblical knowledge or evangelistic abilities, the Four Spiritual Laws offered a helpful script to follow as well as a sense of clarity that the more theologically diverse FCA lacked.

Although Bright set the foundation for AIA, the organization's founding director, Dave Hannah—along with his wife, Elaine—gave it vision and momentum. Hannah had been a punter for the Oklahoma State football team when he had a born-again experience that brought him into Crusade's orbit. Quickly identified as a potential leader, influential Crusade figures Swede Anderson (then at the University of Colorado) and Hal Lindsey (then at the UCLA) mentored him. When the twenty-four-year-old Hannah launched AIA in 1966 as the sports wing of Campus Crusade, he had an ambitious global vision, aiming for the evangelization of the entire world through sport.[12]

Hannah's worldwide perspective was shaped in part by AIA's roots in fundamentalist and neoevangelical networks, where dispensationalism exerted influence. Hannah's mentor, Hal Lindsey, would go on to author the bestselling *The Late Great Planet Earth* (1970), a book arguing that Christ's return was imminent (accordingly to Lindsey, it would happen by 1988) and that the Bible offered the key for understanding current events and their relationship to the coming apocalypse. While Bill Bright was less enthusiastic about end times predictions, Hannah seemed to share Lindsey's interests, further sparking his zeal to evangelize the world through sports. In a 1971 editorial for *Athletes in Action*, Hannah connected developments in Israel and the Middle East with biblical prophecy—"events in our world are taking place just as the Bible predicted"—and concluded that Christians had a responsibility to "use all of our energy to tell others about Christ's love and forgiveness."[13]

This belief in Christ's imminent return had inspired fundamentalists of previous generations to leave behind their athletic pursuits and go into the mission field. For Hannah, it galvanized his desire to engage high-level athletes in the missionary enterprise through the formation of traveling teams. Although AIA also developed media operations and field ministry on college campuses and with professional teams, the centerpiece of its early ministry came from its evangelistic sports teams, particularly its basketball squad, originally named the Chargers. "My reoccurring dream was to fill the gymnasium with students and tell them about Christ," Hannah explained. "One day it dawned on me that you can fill gymnasiums with basketball games."[14]

It is unclear whether Hannah knew of the work of Venture for Victory/Sports Ambassadors, which had been sending teams of basketball missionaries on exhibition tours across the globe since 1952. But even if Hannah's idea was not new, his vision for AIA basketball was audacious. He wanted to create the best amateur basketball team in the world, populated entirely by former college athletes who were evangelical Christians, while developing a television network that could broadcast AIA games from coast to coast. In short, he wanted sports evangelism fit for the big time. "The better we are, the more people will watch us," he explained. "The more people who watch us, the more we reach for Christ."[15] In this way, Hannah carried on the paradox long present among premillennial fundamentalists and neoevangelicals, a paradox emphasized by scholars like

Matthew Sutton: belief in the coming apocalypse could inspire a zeal for action that shaped the present world.[16]

Hannah's ambitious plans required remarkable resilience. The AIA basketball team started with just one player: Larry Tregoning, a new Crusade staff member who had captained the University of Michigan basketball team in 1965. With Tregoning in tow, Hannah set off for the 1967 NCAA men's basketball coaching convention, where he shook hands and made his pitch, asking coaches to schedule his upstart team for an exhibition game. Thanks to Tregoning, whose presence provided legitimacy, AIA managed to put together a full schedule of games for the 1967–1968 season. But Hannah still needed a team and a coach. Those pieces trickled in during the months ahead. Former college players Ken Gustafson (University of Wisconsin), DeWayne Brewer (New Mexico State), and Bill Westphal (University of Southern California) joined Tregoning, as did head coach Fred Crowell, who had recently resigned from his position at the University of Alaska.[17]

AIA may have filled out its roster and put together a full schedule, but from 1967 until 1975 the Chargers struggled to reach the big time, with most of their wins coming against smaller colleges. Just as worrying for Hannah, the sports media seemed uninterested. AIA stood outside of both college and professional basketball, relying on a dying version of amateur basketball—the postcollege company teams of the Amateur Athletic Union (AAU)—that had peaked in the 1940s. AIA basketball struggled to break out of the liminal space between organized big-time basketball and novelty evangelism.[18]

At the end of the 1970s, however, AIA basketball came close to achieving Hannah's lofty goals. With new coach Bill Oates leading the way and a roster featuring legitimate NBA prospects like Bayard Forrest and Ralph Drollinger, AIA won the 1976 AAU title, defeated several ranked college teams, and represented the United States in the 1978 FIBA World Championships. Meanwhile, Hannah managed to cobble together a television network that broadcast AIA games on tape delay, with former UCLA coach John Wooden providing the color commentary. This surprising success finally earned the publicity Hannah had been seeking, with *Sports Illustrated* and the *New York Times* writing about AIA's exploits. "Hallelujah, What a Team," the *Sports Illustrated* headline declared.[19]

If AIA basketball's ascent to national relevance revealed the strength of the ministry's resolve, it also exemplified its desire to link born-again faith with the destiny of the American nation. In Bright's 1970 book *Come Help Change the World*, he described the basketball team's goals this way: "to present Jesus Christ and to call America back to a solid faith and the Christian principles upon which this country was founded."[20] An *Athletes in Action* article in 1968, meanwhile, described the team as a "positive answer for the swing to LSD, free sex and the contempt for authority so evident among students today."[21]

While both Bright and AIA leaders rejected charges that they were involved in politics, their solution to social problems—born-again faith in Christ—carried a strong political resonance because it rejected government intervention and social reform as a key to lasting change. Writing in *Revolution Now!* (1969), Bright contrasted his evangelical focus on individual conversion with "mob violence" and "well-motivated community renewal projects." The latter two, he said, dealt only with symptoms and not causes. Only the revolution of the "inner man," occurring through faith in Jesus Christ, could lead to true transformation.[22] This either/or proposition—one could either focus on introducing people to a personal relationship with Christ, or one could focus on community renewal and social activism—appealed to political conservatives who sought to limit government intervention and social reform.[23]

Bright's strategy had one key problem, however: the salience of race. For many Black Americans, the 1960s felt more like a decade of Christian advance than of retreat. Returning to a "Christian America" before the 1960s would have meant returning to a time when segregation was not only accepted but supported by the majority of white Christians. While Bright had not personally advocated for segregation—Campus Crusade counted Black athlete Rafer Johnson as one of its early converts at UCLA in the 1950s—he kept his distance from the civil rights movement. He warned Crusade staff members in the 1960s not to attend churches that discussed politics from the pulpit, and he barred staff members from getting involved in civil rights activism.[24]

The backlash to the gains of the civil rights movement, however, gave Bright an opening. Although he had played no part in securing or advocating for the historic civil rights laws of the 1960s, Bright stepped in after the fact to claim that his organization had the solution to racial unity. Since sports were one of the few prominent public spaces where racial integration was already visible— and where Black people were present in white spaces—AIA played a key role in Crusade's broader strategy. In 1971, for example, *Athletes in Action* profiled basketball player Clint Hooper. Describing him as "one black athlete who feels he knows the answers to some of today's pressing campus problems," the article contrasted civil rights activism with faith in Christ. "Passing new laws is not the answer" the article claimed, before quoting Hooper directly. "All a person has to do is trust and rely on Jesus Christ to change these attitudes as he receives Christ as his Savior and Lord," Hooper said.[25]

This simple solution to racial division fit within the contours of the color-blind ideal growing in popularity in the wake of the civil rights movement. For both Black and white Christians, the vision of a colorblind society could inspire friendships and relationships across the racial divide. Yet, in the hands of predominantly white organizations only recently awakened to the sin of segregation, it could also be used to maintain their own innocence. So long as Black people were allowed to assimilate into white evangelical organizations, how could racism be a problem? This logic, historian Jesse Curtis argues, enabled white evangelical organizations to use the color-blind ideal to silence concerns about continued racial disparities; white normativity could be "dethroned in name but not decentered in practice."[26] For AIA, this meant that white leaders continued to set the parameters through which interracial friendships took place, as well as determining which Black Christian voices and ideas would be included and promoted.

As AIA developed into a major sports ministry organization in the 1970s, its approach to race overlapped in some ways with that of the FCA. Like its older rival, AIA often linked its evangelistic efforts with the defense of "traditional" American values and colorblind racial progress. Yet, AIA's overall program was shaped by a slightly different cultural orientation. Broadly put, the FCA, rooted in college and high school sports within predominantly white Protestant communities in the Bible Belt, continued to possess an establishment mentality and a desire to nurture a big tent community of Christians. AIA, with a more global perspective and with a more demanding set of expectations for its adherents, viewed itself less like a moral guardian and more like a band of elite Christians infiltrating the sports world.

This ethos brought something distinct and new to the Christian athlete movement: a neoevangelical zeal that both carried on and transformed the fundamentalist tradition that prioritized missions and moral purity. With its basketball team, AIA encouraged a select group of Christian athletes to set themselves apart, to sacrifice the money and status that might come from joining the NBA, and to instead join a missionary organization. At the same time, AIA demonstrated a greater willingness than its fundamentalist predecessors to be "in the world" of big-time sports, encouraging its basketball players to fully engage in high-level competition and to actively cultivate the spotlight—not for self-serving purposes, but in order to use the platform of sports for soul-winning evangelism.

Breaking into Professional Sports

As AIA moved the Christian athlete movement in a more neoevangelical direction, its traveling sports teams were just one weapon in its arsenal. And the organization's influence extended beyond the bounds of its own initiatives, particularly in the realm of professional sports. Nowhere was this more evident than in the NFL.

Founded in 1920, the NFL spent its first three decades as a minor part of the American sports scene. It lacked the middle- and upper-class respectability of college football, and with games played on Sunday, it had a difficult time winning support from churchgoing Protestants. To the extent that there was a religious ethos in the early decades of the NFL, it was driven by Catholics, including owners and executives George Halas (Chicago Bears), Tim Mara (New York Giants), and Art Rooney (Pittsburgh Steelers), and unofficial team chaplains like Father Benedict Dudley, a Catholic priest who served with the New York Giants beginning in the 1930s. As historians Randy Roberts and James Olson explain, these leaders infused the NFL with elements of "immigrant Catholic culture" that set it apart from other professional sports leagues.[27]

As professional football rose in popularity throughout the 1950s, however, a committed contingent of Protestant football players began to emerge. Most were affiliated with the FCA. This developing subculture was represented at first by Los Angeles Rams running back Dan Towler and Cleveland Browns quarterback Otto Graham. Both men were Methodists—born in Pennsylvania and Illinois, respectively—and both became involved with the FCA soon after its founding. They embodied the ecumenical, middlebrow Protestant ethos that undergirded the organization in the 1950s.

The leading FCA-affiliated professional football players of the 1960s were different. They reflected a religious sensibility more in line with neoevangelical concerns. Baltimore Colts linebacker Don Shinnick, whose career stretched from 1957 to 1969, symbolized this change. A member of UCLA's famed "Eleven from Heaven"—so-named because the majority of the 1954 starting lineup was involved with Campus Crusade—Shinnick's teammates Donn Moomaw and Bob Davenport declined opportunities to play in the NFL. Following the old fundamentalist approach, Moomaw and Davenport saw Sunday football as a sin that undermined their Christian witness.[28] Shinnick took a different path. Drafted by the Baltimore Colts in 1957, he made it clear that playing football on Sunday was consistent with his religious commitments. "After all," he noted, "a farmer milks his cows on Sunday."[29] Shinnick's perspective quickly became the norm for a new generation of evangelical Protestant football players.

Following Shinnick into professional football, Bill Glass also influenced the growing Christian athlete network. The defensive end from Baylor University turned down the NFL after graduating in 1957, spending one year playing football in Canada where there were no Sunday games. But in 1958 he reversed course. "I just couldn't believe," Glass later wrote, "that God was willing for all pro sports to go without a witness just because of Sunday game days."[30]

In many ways, Glass embodied the Sunbelt shift. Born and raised in Texas, he grew up attending a Southern Baptist church. Glass subsequently enrolled at Baylor; there, he got involved with the FCA, attending the organization's first summer conference in 1956. After turning pro, Glass spent his first few offseasons studying theology at Southwestern Baptist Theological Seminary, where he honed his understanding of the Bible. Glass developed an admiration for Billy Graham, too, mirroring the famed preacher's perspective on evangelism and moderate racial inclusion. In his 1965 book *Get in the Game*—for which Graham wrote the foreword—Glass urged readers to "forget color and treat everyone alike."[31]

With his Southern Baptist and neoevangelical affiliations, Glass quickly became a galvanizing force among fellow Protestant athletes, helping to cultivate what he described as "a close fellowship of concern." Many of these athletes had developed relationships through their shared involvement in FCA activities. Glass expanded on this by initiating Bible studies, prayer services, and other forms of spiritual support.

It began in Detroit, where he played from 1958 through 1961. There, Glass struck up a friendship with sportswriter Watson Spoelstra of the *Detroit News*, who had recently experienced a dramatic evangelical conversion. Spoelstra turned to Glass for spiritual guidance—he later described Glass as his "spiritual daddy"—and the two began to hold Bible study and prayer meetings in hotels before games. Soon, they invited other players to join, and the group expanded. When Glass was later traded to Cleveland he launched a Bible study with his new team, with a simple and practical format: the players would read a chapter of the New Testament together, and then rewrite the chapter in their own words.[32]

Other professional football players expanded on Glass's efforts. In the early 1960s, Tony Romeo of the Boston Patriots, Prentice Gautt of the St. Louis Cardinals, and Shinnick with the Colts helped lead team Bible studies. Meanwhile, Buddy Dial, receiver for the Pittsburgh Steelers, noticed that Catholic players often had the opportunity to attend Mass before games, but Protestant players rarely had accessible religious services. In 1963 Dial arranged a plan with head coach Buddy Parker in which local Methodist minister Bob Messenger would hold a short devotional service for Protestant players before the team's Sunday breakfast. Dial, who grew up in an Assemblies of God church in Texas that frowned on Sunday sports, framed his initiative as proof that a Christian athlete could do "the Lord's work" even while playing on Sunday.[33]

Dial's idea caught on with several other teams in the league. With so much religious activity developing at a grassroots level, the FCA was poised to step in to provide structure, organization, and support. In 1964 the organization took a step in this direction when it hosted a Professional Athletes Conference in Tampa, sponsored by its longtime ally, *Guideposts*. Featuring both professional football and baseball players (around thirty in all) the athletes met for spiritual encouragement and shared tips on how to consciously bring their faith into the world of professional sports. Yet, although the athletes declared afterward that the gathering "should be repeated annually," it proved to be a one-time event.

With its limited resources, the FCA chose to prioritize its ministry to college and high school athletes and coaches.[34]

While the FCA de-emphasized its work in professional sports, an entrepreneurial minister named Ira Lee "Doc" Eshleman went the other way. A graduate of the fundamentalist Moody Bible College, in 1950 Eshleman made his way to Boca Raton, Florida, where he created what eventually became known as "Bibletown, USA," a combination of various ventures including a church, a real estate enterprise, a family-friendly vacation spot, and a Bible study conference center.[35] Although he had no sports background, Eshleman began to take an interest in professional football in 1964 after meeting several FCA athletes. Intrigued, he attended an FCA conference that summer, and in the fall Bill Glass invited him to worship with the Cleveland Browns in a devotional service before a game against the Philadelphia Eagles. "It was heartwarming," Eshleman told a reporter at the time. "There in the hotel room sat eight big, beefy professional football players. I was amazed to think there were that many on one pro team who would place such emphasis on the importance of prayer."[36]

Soon after that experience Eshleman retired from his work at Bibletown and began to formulate plans to "crash the ranks of the NFL."[37] Financially independent thanks to his real estate investments in Boca Raton, Eshleman could afford to pay his own travel expenses as he infiltrated pro football. However, he still needed to win the trust of coaches and players. To do that, he relied on the FCA's network and the pregame devotional services already in place in professional football, along with a carefully cultivated image of masculinity that he thought would appeal to the pros. As a 1969 hagiographic account of Eshleman's work put it, "Doc had to play the man. His talk had to be straightforward, direct. . . . In attire he had to have rapport with the men too." Wearing a white turtleneck sweater, red Bombay blazer, and blue Jaymar slacks, Eshleman made sure that his pregame services were "no goody-goody affair, punctuated by pious platitudes!" Instead, he presented players with the "very guts and core of Christianity": a personal relationship with Jesus Christ.[38]

Shrewd and pragmatic in his evangelism, Eshleman was careful not to come across as an overzealous outsider. He painstakingly deferred to the authority of coaches; in a list of tips for providing spiritual guidance to athletes, Eshleman's first eight suggestions involved how to interact with and gain the trust of the head coach.[39] Eshleman also worked to make himself useful. Along with personally conducting and coordinating pregame chapel services, he visited injured players in the hospital, providing encouragement and comfort. By the end of the 1967 season, Eshleman's first year serving as a full-time football chaplain, he had won the support from players and coaches on teams including the Los Angeles Rams, Cleveland Browns, Baltimore Colts, and Green Bay Packers.[40]

Thanks to his knack for self-promotion, Eshleman became a minor celebrity in the professional football world. He issued press releases about his activities and declared himself "The Unofficial Chaplain of the Sports World."[41] Not all players were impressed. In *North Dallas Forty* (1973), a semiautobiographical exposé of professional football culture, former Dallas Cowboys player Peter Gent poked fun at Eshleman, using him as a model for a character named "Doctor Tom Bennett." Bennett was a minister from Florida who "materialized in our training camp" wearing "cardigan sweaters and duck-billed golf hats" as he wandered around team headquarters acting like "everybody's pa."[42] His access to the team was secure, however, thanks to the support of the Cowboys head coach—"B.A" in the book, a character intended to evoke Tom Landry, a strong FCA supporter and the pro football coach most closely identified with the Christian athlete movement.

Gent's book highlighted a key paradox for the Christian athlete subculture in the NFL: it was marked by both access to power and a state of precarity. On the one hand, Eshleman and other would-be chaplains had a place in the Cowboys locker room because of their faith-based connections to Landry and star players like quarterback Roger Staubach, a Catholic FCA member. Landry and Staubach imbued the Cowboys of the 1970s with the imagery of "traditional" American values—strong, sturdy, and clean-living men willing to proclaim their faith in God. Yet, many other Cowboys had a reputation for drinking and partying that directly contradicted conservative Christian expectations. So, too, the majority of players did not identify with the Christian athlete movement at all, and some openly mocked it. The narrator in *North Dallas Forty* (presumably representing Gent) frequently registered his annoyance with the Eshleman character, gleefully declaring that he "always made it a point to talk as profanely as possible around the Doc."

If Eshleman wanted to maintain access in this environment, he had no choice but to develop strategies of accommodation. In both the novel and in real life Eshleman took the ridicule in stride, going about his self-appointed role as chaplain while he solidified and expanded the NFL's network of pregame chapels. By 1975, thanks in part to Eshleman's organizing influence, every single NFL team held these services. What had started in the 1960s with athletes like Bill Glass and Buddy Dial was now part of the rhythms and rituals of professional football.[43]

The system that took root in the NFL required a roster of potential chapel speakers ready to serve in each NFL city, as well as players and coaches who could advocate for and help organize their team's chapel program. Although Eshleman continued to position himself as *the* sports chaplain, in truth he was more of a transitional figure, a bridge between the scattered FCA-affiliated efforts of the

1960s and the more organized neoevangelical networks of the 1970s, which featured a new crop of entrepreneurial ministers and sports chaplains.

Tom Skinner, one of the few Black leaders in the 1960s to carve out a public role within the neoevangelical movement, was one. Known for his criticism of white Christian complicity in racism, in 1970 Skinner electrified the crowd at InterVarsity's Urbana Student Missions Conference with a blistering sermon entitled "The U.S. Racial Crisis and World Evangelism." His words directly challenged organizations like Campus Crusade that claimed to hold the solution to racial division. "The difficulty in coming to grips with the evangelical message of Jesus Christ in the black community," he told the audience, "is the fact that most evangelicals in this country who say that Christ is the answer will also go back to their suburban communities and vote for law-and-order candidates who will keep the system the way it is."[44]

Skinner's work in sports was less prophetic and more pastoral. In the late 1960s he began speaking at NFL chapel services and in 1971 started working primarily with the Washington Redskins (the team finally changed its racially insensitive name in 2020). His pregame chapel messages, emphasizing the sacredness of relationships and the importance of shared commitments to one another, won the approval of head coach George Allen. When Washington went to the Super Bowl in 1973, Skinner received substantial attention from the press, particularly after television cameras captured Skinner leading the team in prayer following their victory in the conference championship game.[45]

Billy Zeoli, president of evangelical media company Gospel Films, also got involved with football chaplaincy. Matching Eshleman's penchant for self-promotion, Zeoli called his chapel messages "God's Game Plan" and, like Eshleman, took a liking to the Dallas Cowboys, where Tom Landry once again provided a warm welcome. Players had mixed reviews. Cowboys defensive end Pat Toomay, writing in his autobiographical *The Crunch* (1975), described Zeoli as an overly eager "peripheral person" who was always "grinning and shaking hands, reeking of success, affluence, and good news."[46] Zeoli's desire to be around powerful and successful people carried over into politics, where he cultivated a close friendship with Gerald Ford. By 1976, when Deford wrote his *Sports Illustrated* series, Zeoli had overtaken Eshleman as the most recognizable sports chaplain.[47]

If Eshleman helped to carve a path in the NFL for other entrepreneurial ministers, he also helped to bring AIA more fully into the league. Eshleman had a strong affinity for the organization. He used the Four Spiritual Laws as the basis of his spiritual counseling program for athletes, and his son, Paul, was a staff member with Campus Crusade. As Doc built up his ministry he often recruited AIA staff members to speak at services.[48] But while Eshleman focused on providing teams with a rotating cast of guest speakers, in 1974 AIA leaders adopted a new strategy: they began to place staff members in key cities where they could serve as settled chaplains for professional teams in the area.

The new ministry had links to Eshleman's work; it was a "cooperative tie," one AIA staffer explained.[49] But it was also influenced by behind-the-scenes work done by AIA staffers on college campuses—men like Jim Stump, who arrived at Stanford in 1970 and began providing one-on-one mentoring for Cardinal athletes.[50] Unlike Eshleman, AIA ministers generally avoided the spotlight, preferring to minister behind the scenes to players and coaches. They carved out long-term roles in sports simply by being present and establishing trust, so much so that by the 1990s more than half of the NFL's chaplains were AIA staff members. In Pittsburgh, for example, Hollis Haff served as team chaplain for the Steelers for nearly two decades; in Cincinnati, Wendel Deyo occupied the same role with the Bengals.[51]

Another transformative offshoot from Eshleman's football ministry emerged in 1971 through a collaboration with AIA. It started out as a single event, a post-season spiritual training conference. The vision for the gathering came from Campus Crusade staff members Eddie Waxer and Paul Eshleman. Waxer, in particular, was a significant behind-the-scenes leader in Crusade's sports efforts, dating back even before AIA's founding to his time as a student at Michigan State in the 1960s. Similar to Don McClanen, Waxer defied the celebrity-focused stereotypes of sports ministry. He had little interest in personal promotion or fame, yet he had a gift for connecting with people in one-on-one settings and building collaborative relationships, making him one of the most respected and important evangelical sports ministry leaders of the 1970s and beyond.[52]

Waxer recognized, more clearly than most, that professional athletes needed and wanted opportunities for deeper spiritual growth. He and Paul approached the elder Eshleman about creating an event for athletes modeled after Campus Crusade's lay evangelism training institutes. NFL players who regularly attended their team's chapel services would be invited to the conference, where they would learn effective evangelism strategies and receive spiritual care and attention. Financed with the support of Phoenix businessman and Crusade board member Arlis Priest, the inaugural "Pro Players Christian Leadership Conference" took place in Dallas in the spring of 1971. Thirty-five players from sixteen NFL teams—with married players bringing their wives—gathered at a Holiday Inn where they participated in training sessions and small-group discussions taught and led by Eshleman and Crusade/AIA staff members.[53]

The 1971 conference was a smash hit among players—"nothing short of a miracle," according to Miami Dolphins offensive lineman Norm Evans, who emerged as the key leader of the new conference. In effect, it took what was significant about the 1964 pro athletes conference organized by the FCA—the desire for community—and added a specific training and teaching program.

A sympathetic reporter who interviewed several attendees found that they "seemed completely taken aback, even as Christians, with the power of the fellowship and the closeness to the Lord that was evident throughout the conference."[54] Word spread among the NFL's cohort of Christian athletes, and the next year the conference doubled in size, with eighty players attending. The player response made it clear: the annual off-season conference was here to stay.

Yet the conference also elevated the tension between the FCA and AIA. It was clearly aligned with AIA, with the speakers and training material coming directly from Campus Crusade. But many players at the conference had ministry ties and involvement with the FCA. Dave Hannah claimed that FCA staff members boycotted the conference; FCA staff claimed they were never invited. Frustrated with the bickering organizations, in 1974 pro football players led by Norm Evans decided to take control of the event and create their own organization, naming it Pro Athletes Outreach (PAO). They tapped Crusade board member Arlis Priest to provide business leadership. As an athlete-led ministry with Evans at the helm, PAO would focus on ministering to the unique needs of pro players by running the annual off-season conference and helping to facilitate chapel services and Bible studies. Athletes connected to PAO were then free to work with any and all sports ministry organizations and churches.[55]

As with AIA, PAO was a product of predominantly white neoevangelical networks, institutions, and ideas, with leaders occasionally linking their ministry efforts with the defense of conservative American values. "We've lost our perspective, turning to drugs, free sex," Arlis Priest lamented in 1976. "Do we really think we're that much smarter that we can turn away from God?" Priest continued by describing professional athletes as "the most disciplined group of people left in this country." Their dedication and willingness to sacrifice for the good of a team, Priest declared, "is what we need in America."[56]

Yet, PAO also allowed space for Black Christian perspectives that did not always align with the conservative "Christian America" rhetoric.[57] Tom Skinner's involvement is a case in point. Bill Pannell, a fellow Black evangelical who worked closely with Skinner, recalled that in the early 1970s "Crusade was never really that open to us." Bill Bright preferred politically conservative Black Christians, like Los Angeles pastor E. V. Hill, over Black leaders like Skinner and Pannell who directly challenged systemic racism.[58] Skinner's icy relationship with Crusade, however, did not entirely carry over into sports ministry. In the 1970s he was prominently involved with the NFL's chapel ministry and with the Crusade-inspired PAO, often serving as a featured speaker at the annual conferences, where his messages emphasized community and social responsibility.[59]

Skinner's involvement with PAO enhanced the organization's credibility among Black players. At the time, racial integration was rapidly accelerating in the NFL. From just 12 percent of the league in 1960, Black players comprised

28 percent at the end of the 1960s and more than 40 percent by 1975.[60] While there were plenty of churches and Christian leaders rooted in the Black church tradition, few had access to or involvement with the neoevangelical networks that emerged as gatekeepers to the NFL's religious subculture. With Skinner, PAO had the support of one of the few Black leaders involved in evangelical spaces.

PAO also invited several Black players into leadership roles on its player-led executive committee. These included Tom Graham, a journeyman linebacker; Ken Houston, a safety for Washington who was good friends with Skinner; and Calvin Jones, a cornerback for the Denver Broncos. Both Houston and Jones had deep Christian commitments that extended back to their upbringings within Black churches. With faith already a central part of their lives, it made sense that Black Christian players would connect with an organization like PAO.[61]

Still, fault lines remained below the surface. Calvin Jones, the son of a Black Baptist preacher, had participated in civil rights activism during his college days at the University of Washington, leaving the team in 1971 until the athletic department agreed to provide more support for Black players.[62] His involvement with PAO brought invitations to speak to white churches and organizations, where race would often come up. For Jones, this usually led to a dilemma: how to point out that racism still existed without offending white sensibilities. "I still have to check myself out when I'm speaking to white congregations about the racial problems," he explained in 1976, "to make sure I'm together in my thinking."[63]

In the middle of the 1970s, that tension was not as pronounced as it had been five years before. But it remained ever present, ready to emerge in the years ahead whenever racial issues became a matter of public debate and controversy. In the meantime, by bringing both white and Black players together, PAO ensured its survival and growth in a league where the percentage of Black players continued to grow.

The NFL's system of chapel services, team Bible Studies, and an off-season retreat sponsored by PAO took root in MLB as well. Throughout the 1960s there were several baseball teams that held pregame chapels. Yankees second baseman Bobby Richardson, one of the most prominent early spokespeople for the Christian athlete movement, helped to conduct services with a handful of his teammates early in the decade.[64] But there was nothing organized on a broad scale. In 1973, after retiring from his work as a sportswriter, Watson Spoelstra changed that, founding Baseball Chapel to organize and expand chapel services before baseball's Sunday games.

In contrast to Eshleman's team-by-team work in the NFL, Spoelstra went straight to the top for approval, securing the cooperation of MLB commissioner Bowie Kuhn, a Catholic. With the commissioner's endorsement, Spoelstra's enterprise quickly encompassed every big-league team (and eventually every minor league team). Neoevangelical influence and control remained central to the organization, particularly behind the scenes where Baseball Chapel eventually developed an evangelical doctrinal statement that all of its volunteer chaplains had to sign. At the same time, Kuhn's support and involvement gave Baseball Chapel a more ecumenical public image, as did Spoelstra's broadminded spirituality. "My beliefs," the Episcopalian Spoelstra explained, "are best expressed in a Breton fisherman's prayer: 'Dear God be good to me, The sea is so wide, And my boat is so small.'"[65]

Baseball Chapel remained closely intertwined with PAO. But instead of merging (which the two organizations discussed in the 1970s) they chose to maintain distinct identities, working behind the scenes to forge and maintain a collaborative network. Popular football chapel speakers Billy Zeoli and Tom Skinner served on Baseball Chapel's board, as did key figures in the development of PAO (Eddie Waxer and Arlis Priest), and Spoelstra's longtime friend, Bill Glass. Dave Swanson, who worked with PAO to coordinate chapel services for visiting teams until his retirement in 1995, also worked with Baseball Chapel, succeeding Spoelstra as its executive director in the 1980s.

The overlap existed at the ground level too. Baseball Chapel's roster of speakers often came from the same sources as the NFL's, with evangelical ministers and leaders, including FCA and AIA staff members, heavily featured. NFL players were often called upon to speak at MLB chapels and vice versa. Recognizing these shared connections, in 1975 PAO launched a new off-season spiritual training conference for baseball players that was cosponsored by Baseball Chapel.[66]

When Frank Deford wrote his *Sports Illustrated* series in 1976, it was this new sports ministry infrastructure within professional sports that captured his attention. In the two most popular professional sports leagues in the United States, neoevangelicals had developed an organized presence through AIA, PAO, and Baseball Chapel, all of which had been formed in a seven-year span between 1966 and 1973. "Now that religion in sport—call it Sportianity—is booming," Deford wrote, "all major league baseball and football teams have Sunday chapel service, home and away."[67] And the chapel services were just the entry point into the evangelical discipleship and training programs offered to pro athletes.

This model would grow and expand to other leagues, too, including the National Basketball Association and the National Hockey League, as well as pro tours in golf, tennis, and auto racing. In the process, professional sports were transformed into a prominent public platform for evangelical Christian witness—and, with Christian athletes sharing their testimonials in books, magazines, and television, linking Sportianity to an evangelical consumer subculture growing in prominence after the 1970s.[68]

The Neoevangelical Spirituality of Pro Sports Ministry

To some observers, including Frank Deford, the growth of the Christian athlete movement within pro sports was best understood as an example of manipulation. Leaders in the movement were "more devoted to exploiting sport than
to serving it," he argued.[69] The dynamics on the ground, however, were more
complex. Some athletes did indeed feel used, put on a platform and given a
script to read simply because of their fame. Others had positive experiences with
sports ministries, finding resources that helped meet their everyday needs. In
the neoevangelical ministries—especially AIA and PAO—those needs were met
through a particular spiritual framework developed by Campus Crusade that
claimed to offer a neglected key to the abundant Christian life: access to the
power of the Holy Spirit.

Arlis Priest believed in this power. When he began his role with PAO, he
insisted that teaching athletes the basics of "the Holy Spirit-filled life and sharing
their faith" had to be central to the program.[70] Unlike charismatic or Pentecostal
Christians, who associated the Spirit-filled life with ecstatic supernatural
experiences like speaking in tongues, Crusade leaders like Priest taught a version of Keswick spirituality that Bill Bright had adapted from his Hollywood
Presbyterian mentor, Henrietta Mears. It distinguished "carnal" Christians—
those for whom "Christ has *a* place in his heart but not *the* place of supremacy"—
from "spiritual" or "Spirit-filled" Christians. Spirit-filled Christians had not only
experienced a born-again conversion; they had also totally surrendered to Christ,
receiving spiritual power to live a life of complete Christian commitment.[71]

Bright's version of Keswick spirituality sought to bring order and efficiency to
the work of the Holy Spirit in the believer's life, but it came with contradictions.
On the one hand, it encouraged Christians to release control, to surrender themselves to Christ and receive the supernatural power of his Spirit working through
them. Yet this posture of surrender required constant vigilance. The Holy Spirit
was like a power source that was always on. At every moment, the Christian
could either "abide" in this power, or the Christian could block themselves off
from the power. While a Christian's salvation was not dependent on continually
abiding in the Spirit, everything else was. "God uses only those vessels which are
cleansed and filled," Crusade members were taught. "The smallest sin will break
fellowship with God and thus render us impotent and unfruitful for Christ." If,
however, Christians immediately confessed any known sin, they could quickly
tap back into the Holy Spirit's power, once again experiencing a "life of exquisite
and overflowing happiness" as well as the "power to witness."[72]

Functionally, this understanding of the Christian life separated Christians
into categories determined by their spiritual performance. Actively engaging in
evangelism and displaying enthusiasm and joy were markers of the Spirit-filled

life, while negativity or ineffectiveness in evangelism were considered evidence of unconfessed sin and carnal Christianity.[73] In this way, AIA, rooted in the fundamentalist soil of neoevangelicalism, sought to maintain a marked sense of difference from the world, including from worldly Christians. An early AIA training manual explained it this way to staffers: "Remember—most Christians are still sleeping and you are one of the very few who are awake."[74]

While this approach to spirituality could create tension with "sleeping" Christians outside the AIA fold, it was essential to the appeal of programs offered by AIA and PAO. For high-level athletes accustomed to the demands of elite performance, Keswick spirituality offered a way to attain an elite spiritual level as well. While the FCA avoided identifying with any particular theological framework for discipleship, Crusade's Keswick program offered specific answers to complex questions that had vexed Christians for centuries—like the mystery of the work of the Holy Spirit—as well as practical steps for spiritual growth. And it invited athletes to experience tangible here-and-now benefits of the Christian life. Norm Evans described the effects of his decision to surrender to Christ this way: "In the chaotic business of pro football, I claim God's word and find peace in my life—even in the midst of pressure from every side, both physically and mentally."[75]

By framing the act of surrendering to Christ as a practical tool that would bring happiness and peace, neoevangelical athletes articulated their own version of the positive and pragmatic approach to faith that had long been used by middlebrow Protestants.[76] Still, the evangelical desire to be "in the world but not of it" remained strong. Christians were supposed to be different, and this difference was supposed to extend to all of life. The goal, Atlanta Falcons linebacker and PAO member Greg Brezina explained, was to "be dependent on God 24 hours a day."[77] For athletes, a practical faith infused by Crusade's Keswick theology would necessarily need to speak to their ordinary, everyday lives.

Chief among a pro athlete's everyday concerns was their performance. Middlebrow Protestants had a long history of addressing this issue by connecting sports success with the development of Christian character. In the 1970s, coaches like John Wooden continued to draw on and advance this idea. In the 1960s, neoevangelical athlete Bill Glass took this a step further by working with pioneering sports psychologist William J. Beausay to develop mental visualization techniques for enhanced performance.[78] Glass viewed the methods he learned from Beausay within the framework of common grace—they were not distinct to Christianity but instead were available to all people because they involved a "psychological process, not a spiritual one." For Glass, it was precisely because everyone could practice performance visualization techniques that Christians had a responsibility to use them. "We must try to make these practical success ideas blend perfectly with our sincere Christian commitment," he urged.[79]

Because neither middlebrow "true success" ideas nor Glass's psychological techniques were distinctly Christian, AIA believed Christian athletes needed their own set of principles to help them abide in the Holy Spirit on the athletic field. Here, Keswick advocates were not entirely unique—as we have seen, Glenn Clark, working from a liberal Protestant framework in the 1920s, had developed techniques for tapping into the Holy Spirit on the field of play. Still, as AIA staff members worked to apply Crusade's Keswick teachings to the world of sports, they developed a new and distinct approach to athletic performance.

Wes Neal, an AIA weightlifter, pioneered in these efforts. Neal recognized that although he knew how to use the platform of sports to talk about Jesus, he had a difficult time seeing any difference in his approach to competition compared with that of a non-Christian. "How do I lift weights the way God wants me to lift them?" he asked.[80] To answer that question, Neal turned to his Bible and Crusade's training material on the Holy Spirit—particularly the pamphlet "Have You Made the Wonderful Discovery of the Spirit-Filled Life?"—and began to apply Crusade's Keswick teachings to a sports-specific audience. By 1972, Neal had compiled his work into a training manual, *The Making of an Athlete of God*, published by Campus Crusade. Fifteen of the sixteen lessons focused on the question "How can my relationship with Jesus improve my athletics?"[81]

Neal was careful to point out that Christian athletes would not always "win" by the world's standards (the scoreboard)—in fact, he believed a Christian perspective on winning would not consider the scoreboard at all but instead would focus on the extent to which an athlete conformed their attitudes and actions to Christ's teachings. At the same time, Neal claimed that born-again Christians had access to a spiritual dimension that could maximize their individual athletic potential. The key was to tap into the power of the Holy Spirit by surrendering completely to Christ. "When you are dead to yourself and alive to Him, He draws you to a level of efficiency beyond that which you could reach on your own power," Neal explained. "You are now potentially a more developed athlete than before you became a Christian!" Markers of a "total release performance" (as Neal called it) included a heightened level of intensity, a continuous sense of motivation and positivity, and a stable perspective that did not let negative circumstances determine one's attitude.[82]

Scholar Annie Blazer notes that Neal's theology of sports performance emerged simultaneously with a growing interest in sports psychology and mental visualization techniques.[83] The same year that Neal compiled *The Making of an Athlete of God*, a tennis pro named Timothy Gallwey was writing *The Inner Game of Tennis*, which became a go-to book for athletes and coaches seeking mental techniques to improve their concentration. Like Neal, Gallwey suggested that peak athletic performance came packaged in paradox: it required a form of surrender. For Gallwey, one had to set aside overthinking and overanalyzing and reach a state of relaxed concentration; for Neal, this came from the Keswick notion of total surrender to Christ.[84]

In the years to come, both AIA and Neal (who left AIA to launch the Institute for Athletic Perfection) continued to refine and adapt the basic principles and ideas developed in *The Making of an Athlete of God*. While it was not a finished product in 1972, it made a key intervention by blending Keswick principles with pop psychology and bringing them directly into the sphere of athletic competition. So, too, it provided a model of Christian maturity and growth that fit into the contours of big-time sports and the needs of elite athletes. Over time, it would help to forge a formula that became ubiquitous across evangelical sports ministries: by finding their identity in Christ, athletes could have a steady foundation to navigate the highs and lows of sports and unleash their full potential.

By the end of the 1970s, the influence of Neal's approach to sports performance was already apparent. In a 1979 book published by PAO, *One Way to Play Football*, New England Patriots offensive lineman John Hannah referenced a technique used by AIA and Neal in which athletes were encouraged to reflect on the death of Jesus and then respond with gratitude through the intensity of their performance. "Every time I see the goal posts they remind me of my Lord Jesus Christ and what He went through for me," Hannah said. "He experienced excruciating torture and died a horrible death in order that I might have forgiveness of sin. If He did all that for me, then I certainly can give everything I have for Him on the football field."[85]

In the same book, Seattle Seahawks wide receiver Steve Largent echoed a common AIA phrase as he encouraged Christian athletes to resist the pressures of big-time sports by focusing on God. "I'm really only playing for an audience of one," Largent explained. Meanwhile, New England Patriots kicker John Smith explained how memorizing Bible verses helped him concentrate on the field. After making a game-winning kick, he told reporters that he had visualized Philippians 4:13, "a verse in the Bible that says that I can do everything, including kick field goals, through Christ who strengthens me." For Smith, this technique affirmed the positive effects of the Christian faith. "I believe that I'm a much better kicker than I would have been had I not become a Christian."[86]

Joining with the emphasis on athletic performance, Keswick-influenced sports ministries also focused their attention on the marriage relationship. This was a crucial concern for pro athletes, where extensive travel made it difficult to maintain healthy family routines. So, too, as the salaries and celebrity status of pro athletes rose in the 1970s, interest and demands from the outside world increased, including—at least from the perspective of the male athletes—more sexual interest from women. Some athletes embraced the attention, with brash young stars like Joe Namath taking chauvinistic celebrations of heterosexual promiscuity that had long been a part of locker room culture and making it a form of personal branding. "Any clergyman who seeks employment in the pro locker room," Deford wrote, "better understand that the bulk of his counseling will involve sex."[87]

To counter Namath's brand of masculinity, the Christian athlete movement positioned itself as a space where athletes could form deep and meaningful marriage relationships as they embraced the responsibilities of being faithful husbands and fathers. This was central to the growth and allure of PAO. From the beginning, Norm Evans and PAO leaders saw the ministry as "a Christian training program for husbands and wives." Instead of an off-season conference in which players were whisked away from their families, PAO invited wives to join their husbands and scheduled sessions and panels focused on marriage, with topics like sexual temptation and effective communication.[88]

PAO's vision of the family, like Campus Crusade's, was undoubtedly conservative. Rejecting the feminist movement of the 1960s as a challenge to God-ordained roles for men and women, at PAO conferences men were encouraged to take responsibility as leaders within their homes. "The man has to be the leader and lover in marriage," Norm Evans argued. "That, to me, isn't chauvinism, just scriptural."[89]

Yet PAO leaders did not frame male leadership as primarily the assertion of dominance. Rather, they encouraged men to serve their wives and to be emotionally available, making their case on pragmatic grounds. "The Bible has formulas about marriage which we've applied to our lives, and they've worked beautifully," Evans wrote. "We're not only man and wife, but we're also friends."[90] This idea of friendship and emotional connection in marriage was reflected in PAO training sessions, where athletes were encouraged to get in touch with their feelings—even to cry—and to give themselves sacrificially to their wives.[91]

For players' wives, particularly those with a desire to embrace the "traditional" gendered roles of homemaker and primary caregiver, the vision of family offered by PAO could be attractive. While it reinforced conservative stereotypes about differences between men and women—the former were deemed more "rational," and the latter more "emotional"—it seemed to speak to their practical realities in a way that the feminist movement did not always recognize.[92]

Marabel Morgan, author of the bestselling *The Total Woman* (1973), recognized this disconnect. A Campus Crusade convert who lived in Miami, Morgan became a guru in a growing market for evangelical family advice. She started with small workshops for wives, where she encouraged them to adapt to their husbands, to treat a husband "like a king and cater to his needs."[93] This approach placed men at the center of the family structure, prioritizing their concerns. But Morgan made her case on pragmatic grounds, arguing that her methods would lead to greater personal fulfillment and increased emotional intimacy for women. Better sex was part of the equation, too. As scholar Emily

Johnson writes, Morgan believed that a "mutually satisfying sexual relationship was essential to marriage as God designed it."[94] In these ways, Morgan selectively adapted new cultural trends from the 1960s to fit the structures of conservative gender norms.

Morgan's book and teachings had a direct connection with PAO through her Miami neighbor, Bobbie Evans, the wife of Norm Evans. In *The Total Woman*, Morgan praised the Evans family as an example of a thriving Christian marriage operating on biblical principles. Bobbie Evans, in turn, championed Morgan's teachings, helping to organize "Total Woman" seminars for wives throughout the 1970s, beginning with several women married to Miami Dolphins players. That group met in 1971, learning from Morgan how "to put their husbands first and bring out the very best in them." (The next year, the Dolphins went unde-feated and won the Super Bowl.)[95]

The development of players' wives as a new constituency within sports min-istry occurred simultaneously with the growth of women's sports opportunities, spurred on by Title IX (1972) and the famed "Battle of the Sexes" tennis match between Billie Jean King and Bobby Riggs (1973). Sports ministry for women athletes, however, was slow to develop—a theme that will be discussed more in the next chapter. Within the masculine world of Sportianity, it was more common to see women first as wives (or potential wives) than as athletes. Still, for the players' wives in PAO, the opportunity to minister to and lead fellow women could be meaningful and empowering. "I have no argument with women's lib-eration if that's what makes a woman happy," Bobbie Evans explained. "But it didn't work for me."[96]

For men, the version of Christian masculinity and male leadership put for-ward by Crusade and PAO had obvious appeal. Yet, it did not exactly give them free rein to do as they pleased. Instead, following the Keswick framework, it expected them to surrender to the Holy Spirit, and it imposed expectations and responsibilities that contrasted with the alternative masculinities on display in professional football. PAO members were encouraged to be devoted husbands and fathers, investing time and emotional energy in their relationships with their wives and children. This vision of "soft patriarchy" would become associ-ated most closely with the Promise Keepers movement of the 1990s, but it was already being developed in the 1970s through neoevangelical forms of sports ministry.[97]

To be sure, aggressive physicality was expected too, with the faith commitments of Christian athletes meshing with the demands of football. "I guarantee you, Christ would be the toughest guy who ever played this game," Norm Evans argued. "Jesus was a real man, all right. . . . He would be an aggres-sive and tremendous competitor."[98] Such overzealous attempts to cast Jesus as a "man's man" received frequent ridicule, overshadowing Evans's emphasis on

Jesus's well-rounded qualities. "Under the toughness there would be a kind, understanding, patient nature," Evans continued. "All the good qualities would be woven in."[99]

Greg Brezina echoed this balance. "I want to play football like Christ would. With dedication and intensity," he said. This aggressiveness did not sanction unmitigated violence and force. Instead, it was tempered by a Holy Spirit–inspired concern for one's opponent. "I'd see a guy and I'd want to hurt him," Brezina explained of his mindset before his conversion. "After becoming a Christian, you start thinking, 'My attitude in my heart shouldn't be to hurt the guy.'"[100]

Brezina's posture illustrates the blend of accommodation and ambivalence that defined the Keswick spirituality of the Christian athlete movement. Although Keswick theology did not hold a monopoly on Christian approaches to sports, it served as the engine behind PAO's and AIA's new elite force of Christian athletes. Through their influence, a focus on a personal relationship with Christ renewed through continual moments of surrender became the central framework for the Christian life. A key selling point, for many Christian athletes, was that the Spirit-filled life doubled as a technique for success. The Bible, read and applied through a Keswick lens, was transformed into a middlebrow text, providing a method for achieving happiness and meeting one's desires and needs: maximized performance on the field, strengthened marriages and support systems off of it, and a sense of significance and meaning that came from participating in work that had eternal value.

Sports and War

The Keswick spirituality offered by AIA and PAO had another selling point: it offered an individualistic path to Christian maturity that sidestepped growing concern over the social and ethical dimensions of big-time sports. Building on the activism of Black athletes and inspired by opposition to the Vietnam War, in the early 1970s a new wave of critics challenged the long-standing myths regarding the character-building and democratic potential of athletics. They linked the athletic enterprise instead with authoritarianism, exploitation, and militarization. NFL player Dave Meggyesy's *Out of Their League* (1970) was among the most strident of these critiques. "I've come to see that football is one of the most dehumanizing experiences a person can face," Meggyesy wrote. "It is no accident that President Nixon, the most repressive President in American history, is a football freak."[101]

This sharp condemnation of sports caught the attention of Christian leaders. From the mainline Protestant side, the *Christian Century* devoted an entire issue to the topic in 1972. "You may think all this is out of place in a serious Christian journal," the introductory editorial admitted. "Yet it is because sports are so much more than simple amusements that they deserve serious attention."[102] Articles in the issue generally sided with the new wave of criticism. One author argued that sports had become a new American religion, used by politicians like Richard Nixon to consolidate power. Another suggested that football, in an argument that would be repeated by scholars and intellectuals in the years ahead, was built on a foundation of sexism, and that it cultivated tendencies toward "racism, colonialism, imperialism and other types of oppression."[103]

The preferred magazine of neoevangelical intellectuals, *Christianity Today*, did not go as far in its critique, but it attempted to think responsibly about the excesses of athletics with a 1972 editorial that asked, "Sports: Are We Overdoing It?" The editor warned that Christians had uncritically embraced the culture of sports, "as if this particular human activity were beyond discussion."[104] A 1975 editorial, "It's Time to Think Seriously about Sports," made a similar point. "Christians have given little thought to the place of sports in human affairs," the author claimed. "This is a mistake. We need to examine everything we do in light of good stewardship."[105]

These censures from Christian intellectuals carried little weight among Christian athletes and coaches. But they could not be ignored entirely within the Christian athlete movement, and debate over how Christians within sports should engage with calls for systemic reform led to three basic responses. Some—especially the new crop of neoevangelical sports ministries—mostly ignored the debate, instead doubling down on their efforts to save individual souls. "We try to concentrate on Christ and sharing Him," AIA director Dave Hannah explained when asked whether his organization sought to address ethical problems. "We're not committed to change the wrongs, but to change lives which we hope would have an effect on the whole system."[106]

Within the more ecumenical FCA, this viewpoint was present, too. But there was also support for a second, related perspective. Shaped by the FCA's establishment impulse, some sought to engage with the debate by actively defending the institution of sports even as they emphasized the need for individual conversion. Since athletics, in this view, were considered a key place for inculcating traditional American values, the potential good far outweighed the bad. Christians were expected to accept the status quo, focus on the positive, and highlight the primacy of the individual rather than the system.

The most developed version of this argument came from a book coauthored in 1972 by the recently retired Bill Glass and William Pinson Jr., a professor of Christian ethics at Southwestern Baptist Theological Seminary. The title made its argument clear: *Don't Blame the Game: An Answer to Super Star Swingers and a Look at What's Right with Sports*. Glass argued that sports, while not free of faults, were being used as a scapegoat for social problems. Rather than blame sports for brutality, militarism, racism, drug abuse, and dehumanization, Glass argued that those problems existed in sports only to the extent that individual athletes and coaches adopted those mentalities. "It's the person, not the game, that makes the difference," he wrote. People in sports needed to stop "blaming the game" and instead accept "personal responsibility" and "get busy setting things right" at an individual level.[107]

In many ways, Glass followed the path of the middlebrow Protestants who defended sports in the 1920s. Like them, Glass recognized flaws but also associated sports with his idea of traditional American values and gradual progress. However, there was a key difference: for Glass, the way to "get right" in sports was through a personal relationship with Christ. While Glass went deeper than most in engaging with the ideas and perspectives of the new wave of critics, he ultimately affirmed the culture of big-time sports and suggested that any problems could be addressed through individual changes of heart. "People won't treat others with love and concern until they've been changed spiritually by Christ," he argued.[108]

Glass's perspective resonated with both the newer neoevangelical sports ministries and Christian athletes like Dallas Cowboys quarterback Roger Staubach, a Catholic who had little interest in soul-winning evangelism. "I'm just not into the fundamentalist thing," he explained.[109] But he believed in Glass's conservative moral views and vision for American society. "Many people will call me a square. If loving my family and being a Christian are the traits, then I'm proud to be a square," Staubach wrote in the foreword to Don't Blame the Game. "We want our influence to count for good. We aren't self-righteous prudes, but we do believe in a God-centered morality."[110]

While Glass's blend of evangelism with a defense of the sports establishment stood at the center of the Christian athlete movement, there was a third perspective, located on the margins, that showed more sympathy for the concerns of critics. The most prominent advocate for this view was Gary Warner, editor of the FCA's magazine, the Christian Athlete. A former sportswriter, Warner joined the FCA staff in 1966 after working for Billy Graham's Decision magazine. He took over as editor of the Christian Athlete in 1968 and began to dream about a new vision for the magazine, one that did not focus only on inspirational testimonials.[111] Working with associate editor Skip Stogsdill, the two announced in 1971 that the Christian Athlete would expand to thirty-two pages and would embrace "healthy controversy" within its pages. "The status quo often needs jarring both within and outside the athletic world," they wrote. "Material will appear in the CA with which you disagree. If not we haven't done our job."[112]

Warner delivered on this promise with the January 1972 issue of the *Christian Athlete*. The cover article, written by University of Minnesota student Jerry Pyle, was entitled "Sports and War." Pyle questioned the outsized role that sports played in American life and its connection to a win-at-all-costs ideology that promoted militarism and denied the reality of social injustices. "To make co-operation secondary to victory," Pyle claimed, "is to worship competition and power and ignore love." Pyle argued that sports should be reorganized to lessen the emphasis on winning and to promote greater cooperation. A series of photo illustrations juxtaposing scenes from sports with scenes from the Vietnam War added visual weight to Pyle's arguments.[113]

Warner knew that the article would stir debate, and he penned an editor's note to distance himself from Pyle's perspective. He informed readers that he wanted to "editorially tightrope between extremes" of those who were excessively critical and excessively supportive of sports. In short, recognizing that the FCA was the leading organization for the Christian athlete movement, Warner hoped to use the magazine to provide a forum for serious reflection on contemporary issues, helping Christian athletes and coaches engage in difficult conversations, wrestle with complex problems, and consider possible solutions.[114]

Reader response to "Sports and War" was the largest in the history of the *Christian Athlete*. One letter, typical of the positive responses, praised the *Christian Athlete* for demonstrating "a new dimension of concern and sub-stance." Philip Yancey, then serving as editor of Youth for Christ's *Campus Life* and later a bestselling Christian author, called the issue "the most courageous piece of Christian journalism I've seen."[115]

Other readers were disturbed. The most strident response came from a Texas golf pro named Bob Goetz. "I am uninterested in a balanced viewpoint," Goetz declared. "I want dogmatic answers that I can use in a 'crisis situation': answers that I can give others seeking positive solutions; answers taught dogmatically in the Scriptures." In Goetz's view the *Christian Athlete* had fallen prey to liber-alism—"a great tool of Satan"—and as such he felt he had no choice but to sever his ties with the FCA.[116]

FCA leaders may not have gone as far as Goetz, but many felt a sense of unease, if not anger. They wanted the *Christian Athlete* to focus on the posi-tive and to build up the Christian athlete community through practical guid-ance and encouragement. They viewed "Sports and War" as a betrayal of the organization's mission. Bill Glass was particularly upset, firing off a series of angry letters to fellow FCA leaders. In response, the FCA's Board of Directors appointed Leonard LeSourd, editor of *Guideposts*, to serve as chairman of a new Publications Committee that would work to limit controversial material in the *Christian Athlete*.[117] "It is not up to FCA to try and be a judge and jury for all the concerns of the sports or educational world," FCA president John Erickson later explained. Instead, Erickson saw the FCA's role as that of "a 'perspective builder' and positive organization."[118]

The furor and fallout over "Sports and War" fit into a larger debate within the evangelical movement over American identity, Christian maturity, and social responsibility. On the one hand, Warner represented the FCA's evangelical turn. He had experienced a born-again conversion and worked for Billy Graham, and under his watch the *Christian Athlete* increasingly promoted neoevangelical authors and ideas. A reader in 1974 recognized this, thanking Warner for centering "the evangelical perspective that I have prayed for and felt the promise of in the FCA since my advent into it some 14 years ago."[119]

Yet, by the early 1970s, when the "Sports and War" issue was published, a small subset of younger evangelicals had grown disenchanted with the tendency to associate evangelical theology with conservative politics. Rather than uncritically affirm American institutions, these "progressive" evangelicals echoed mainline Protestant intellectuals by bringing what they regarded as a prophetic voice to such issues as racism, economic inequality, and American imperialism.[120] "You and I have common goals—to exalt Jesus Christ as Saviour and Lord," Warner wrote to Bill Glass in 1973. But that desire played out differently for the two men. While Glass focused on witnessing to the individual person within sports, Warner felt compelled to "speak out against what we sometimes do to sports and to its participants in the name of sport." In short, Warner shared the progressive evangelical belief that Christian maturity must involve not just a deeper individual piety, but also a growing concern for the social environment and cultural context in which one lived.[121]

Warner's approach stood outside the methods preferred by most leaders and individuals within the FCA and the broader Christian athlete community. "I like Gary a lot and he is a very capable editor," LeSourd wrote to Bill Glass, "but like so many young men, in my opinion he gets too wrapped up in the social action issues."[122] Most FCA leaders wanted practical resources formulated to meet the unique spiritual needs of athletes; challenging the social structures that provided them with salaries and meaningful employment required a level of time and sacrifice that would detract from the ever-increasing demands of big-time sports. Warner may have been an evangelical, but within the Christian athlete movement he was not the right type of evangelical.

In a 1975 interview, Warner and Skip Stogsdill talked openly about this conflict. When asked if they viewed the *Christian Athlete* as a medium for changing athletics, Warner replied,

> Skip and I would see that. The FCA board and officers would not see that. They
> would see our role as projecting Christ. If you get a man in touch with Christ
> and get enough people to become Christians in athletics, they say, the problems

will be done away with and everything will take care of itself.... We think to be realistic you have to deal with people and issues. You must be gut level honest and deal with the issues. Discuss them. Get both sides. But the board would rather have us not stir the waters. Just print the good story about the good ole' boy who does good things.[123]

Warner remained editor of the *Christian Athlete* through 1977, frequently clashing with FCA leadership. While he published traditional stories and testimonials of athletes and coaches whose lives had been changed by Christ, he also continued to take up controversial topics and urge FCA readers to confront problems, including drug use in sports and worrying trends from the increasingly organized world of youth sports.[124] One of his most ambitious efforts was a 1975 series that sought to articulate a Christian approach to competition. Warner wanted to go beyond "platitudes and cliches," encouraging Christian athletes, coaches, parents, and fans to "say 'no' to the pressures and inequities and fallacies around them and 'yes!' to their Christian conscience of competitiveness."[125]

FCA founder Don McClanen, who had reconciled with the organization after his stormy exit, cheered these developments from afar.[126] His opinion was undoubtedly shaped by his involvement with the Church of the Saviour in Washington, DC, an influential incubator for progressive evangelicalism. "You are doing the kind of thing I had always hoped and prayed would come off—not just witnessing boldly for Christ in ordinary ways but opening up new areas of growth and maturity," he wrote to Warner in 1975. McClanen compared the recent Watergate scandal and Richard Nixon's downfall with the ethical problems emanating from big-time sports. Just as the investigations exposed the "the false and cheap patriotism and nationalism of the President," McClanen hoped that Christians would be willing to do serious reflection about their relationship with sports and recognize the problems with "making athletics, and athletes and coaches, into a god."[127]

McClanen's opinion carried symbolic weight, but little else. The disconnect between the editors of the *Christian Athlete* and the FCA's leadership finally came to a head in 1977 when FCA board members stepped in to make drastic changes to a December issue of the magazine focused on violence in sports. In response, Warner resigned, citing "untenable personal and professional conditions."[128] Rather than Warner's vision, FCA leaders preferred the vision put forward by an Oklahoma FCA member: a "light, entertaining magazine chock-full of testimonies" that was not "controversial, complicated, difficult in form."[129]

Warner's departure did not end progressive evangelical involvement with the FCA, which continued to represent a broad constituency. His assistant editor and kindred spirit, Skip Stogsdill, took over as editor, serving through the next decade. Yet the conflict over Warner's goals for the *Christian Athlete* did help to mark the boundaries of what the FCA and other organizations within Sportianity would prioritize at a national level.

* * *

The momentum and growth of the Christian athlete movement was on full display at the White House on February 15, 1976. That Sunday morning, two months before Deford's *Sports Illustrated* series hit the stands, nearly two hundred guests from the world of pro sports—athletes, coaches, sports ministry leaders, and their spouses—gathered with President Gerald Ford for a Professional Athletes Prayer Brunch. The event was organized by Ford's friend and spiritual advisor, Billy Zeoli, and the invite list featured a "who's who" of Sportianity: AIA director Dave Hannah, FCA president John Erickson, PAO leaders Arlis Priest and Norm Evans, Baseball Chapel founder Watson Spoelstra, as well as Doc Eshleman, Bill Glass, Eddie Waxer, Calvin Jones, Tom Landry, Tom Skinner, and numerous others who had helped to create the thriving evangelical subculture within big-time sports.[130]

Gerald Ford, a former college football player, addressed the gathering with a message that connected the faith of the Christian athletes before him with the destiny of the American nation. Reprising themes he had developed in an essay written for *Sports Illustrated* in 1974, Ford lauded the discipline, competitive drive, and spiritual faith of Christian athletes. These were the qualities, he declared, that had made America great in the past; these were the qualities that could ensure that the country remained on the right path in the future.[131]

There was no particular political issue on the agenda, yet there were political implications. Ford, running for a second term, was in the middle of a primary campaign in which he had to hold off California governor Ronald Reagan, a darling of movement conservatives within the Republican Party. Then he had to pivot to the general election against the Democratic candidate, Georgia governor Jimmy Carter. A Southern Baptist, Carter spoke openly about his born-again faith, making evangelicalism a key theme of the 1976 presidential election.

With two candidates courting the evangelical population, Ford won just fifty-one percent of evangelical voters, not enough to defeat Carter, who maintained strong support among Southern Baptists. Soon after moving into the White House, however, it became clear that Carter's more progressive vision of faith and its implications for public life did not match the convictions of the majority of white evangelical voters. Like Gary Warner's, his was not the right type of evangelicalism—as the election of middlebrow Protestant Ronald Reagan in 1980, supported by two-thirds of the white evangelical vote, made clear.[132]

As the 1980s dawned, these political developments loomed large for evangelical sports ministries. The Christian athlete movement had always been driven by a desire to meet the practical needs of athletes and coaches and to promote a particular vision of American society. Never before, however, had that vision been so closely linked with an organized religious political movement lining up behind one political party.

7
Doing Sports God's Way

Frank Deford's 1976 *Sports Illustrated* series was the first major investigation of the Christian athlete movement, but it was far from the last. Every few years after Deford's series, another journalist from a media outlet would tackle the blending of sports and Christianity.

James Baker, a history professor and a frequent contributor to the *Christian Century*, told one such reporter in 1982 that he saw the infusion of evangelical religiosity within sports as a fad that "had a good decade run" but would not "be around much longer."[1] He was wrong. The organizational infrastructure of Sportianity, embedded within the sports industry through the Fellowship of Christian Athletes (FCA), Athletes in Action (AIA), Pro Athletes Outreach (PAO), and Baseball Chapel, ensured that evangelicalism maintained a steady presence in the lives of coaches and players long after Baker's prediction of decline. In many ways its influence grew. Pick any big game in college or professional football, baseball, and basketball after 1980, and there was sure to be a cadre of self-identified Christian athletes and coaches on both teams—and probably a team chaplain or sports minister, too.

At the same time, there were important changes within the Christian athlete movement, as well as jostling for leadership and influence—for the right to determine what it meant to be a "Christian athlete" or how to "do sports God's way." Leaders of the evangelical sports subculture constantly worked to set the boundaries for how those within their movement should interpret and understand Christian teachings in light of the cultural and social questions of the day. What to do about women in sports? How about gender roles and the growing movement for gay rights? What was the relationship between evangelical sports ministries and a predominantly white Christian Right political movement aligned with the Republican Party? How could athletes combat the worrisome trends evident among young people, who were supposedly veering out of control with an appetite for drugs and alcohol, sex and money, and rock and rap music?

Those questions hovered over the Christian athlete movement as it grew in strength in the 1980s and 1990s. Persecuted in its eyes, powerful in the eyes of critics, by the end of the twentieth century the Christian athlete movement often mirrored America's larger cultural trends—yet always with ambiguities, nuances, and dissidents from within.

The Spirit of the Game. Paul Emory Putz, Oxford University Press. © Oxford University Press 2024.
DOI: 10.1093/9780190091095.003.0008

Growth

The basic architecture of Sportianity, in place by the 1970s, was filled in throughout the 1980s and 1990s as players, coaches, chaplains, and sports ministry staff spread out into the nooks and crannies of the sports world. Much of this growth could be attributed to two simple strategies: presence and availability.

For AIA, this involved its field ministry on college campuses and its chaplaincy work in pro sports. By 1984 full-time AIA staffers served thirty-five college athletic programs and fourteen strategically selected pro cities, numbers that grew in the years ahead.[2] Like nearly all Campus Crusade staff members, they raised their own salaries through financial gifts from friends, family, and other supporters. This enabled them to provide their services free of charge, which in turn helped to secure and maintain their access within an increasingly guarded sports industry.

FCA leaders did not prioritize sports chaplaincy in the same way—at least not until the 1990s, when they began to train staff members to serve as "character coaches" on college sports teams.[3] Instead, FCA staffers tended to see themselves as representatives of a particular civic community or geographic area, with much of their work focused on leading and directing a robust system of volunteers. Because of the FCA's orientation toward civic identity and community leadership, it maintained a strong presence in the South and portions of the Midwest where public expressions of evangelical Protestant religiosity were prominent.

The heart of the FCA's ministry was focused on younger athletes and their coaches, and football remained king. The annual breakfast at the American Football Coaches Association (AFCA) convention served as an anchor point, with coaching conferences providing another important source of influence. Each year new generations of football players and coaches experienced the FCA and found meaningful connections between the high-stakes sport they played and their Christian faith. In 1994, when FCA member and recently retired Baylor football coach Grant Teaff was named executive director of the AFCA, the long-standing links between the FCA and the football coaching community were further enhanced.[4]

FCA coaches offered variations in style and approach even as they represented a broadly shared vision for American society. Tom Osborne, head coach at the University of Nebraska, exemplified the middlebrow mainline roots of the Christian athlete movement. A Methodist from the Midwest who attended his first FCA conference while he was a college athlete in 1957, Osborne possessed a thoughtful, irenic posture and published books like *More than Winning* (1985) that advanced "true success" ideas. Bobby Bowden at Florida State embodied the Southern Baptist ethos. Born and raised in Alabama, he got involved in the FCA in the 1960s and was a strong supporter of Billy Graham, seeing soul-winning evangelism as his central purpose. At Colorado, meanwhile, the Catholic-turned-evangelical Bill McCartney symbolized a more aggressive and militant evangelicalism shaped by the growing culture wars and a surging Pentecostal/charismatic movement.[5]

The ongoing success of the FCA's work with football coaches inspired similar efforts in other sports. The FCA hosted breakfasts at annual meetings for baseball and basketball coaches, and, as its women's ministry grew, softball and volleyball coaches as well. These events helped recruit new members and strengthen existing relationships among coaches who saw themselves as part of a shared Christian sports movement.[6]

Within pro sports, meanwhile, a series of annual events were tied to All-Star and championship games. In the 1970s, Baseball Chapel began hosting a gathering at the MLB All-Star game. In the NBA, an All-Star Chapel Service was launched in 1981, with Philadelphia 76ers executive Pat Williams—closely connected to all evangelical sports ministry happenings—providing early leadership.[7] AIA received approval from the NFL office to host a breakfast during Super Bowl week. They launched it in 1988 and in the following year began presenting the Bart Starr Award to a player who exemplified character and leadership (Seattle Seahawks wide receiver Steve Largent was the first recipient). In 1997, AIA replicated this model in men's college basketball, inaugurating a "Legends of the Hardwood" breakfast to be held in conjunction with the Final Four, where a John Wooden "Keys to Life" award was presented.[8]

Crucially, these events occurred *within* the structures of big-time sports. More than simply projecting a message of Christian faith out to the general public, they provided opportunities to strengthen relationships inside the sports industry and to build networks of mutual support and concern.

At the same time, the leaders of Sportianity did not ignore public displays of faith. Those increased through the 1980s and 1990s as well. The cable television wave and the launch of ESPN, with its around-the-clock sports coverage, brought more games and highlight packages to TV screens, helping to popularize new scripts for Christian witnessing.[9] Jerry Terrell, an infielder with the Kansas City Royals and a regular with Baseball Chapel and Pro Athletes Outreach, highlighted this strategy when he was interviewed after a game in 1979. "I don't get interviewed much, so I'd like to take this opportunity to give credit to Jesus Christ," Terrell told the reporters. "He is number one in my life." Variations of Terrell's comments became increasingly common in the years to come, with the phrase "I'd like to thank my Lord and Savior, Jesus Christ" emerging as a popular way for Christian athletes to begin an interview.[10]

Symbolic gestures increased as well. Two especially prominent examples in the 1970s came from Black athletes, highlighting the infusion of African Americans into Sportianity.[11] In 1977 Philadelphia Eagles running back Herb Lusk took off on a seventy-yard touchdown run and then knelt on one knee in the end zone. "You know what he's doing right now? Praying," the play-by-play announcer declared during the television broadcast.[12] In 1979, Baltimore Orioles outfielder Pat Kelly pointed his finger to the sky after hitting a home run in a playoff game against the California Angels. Reporters initially took his gesture as a sign of disrespect aimed at the fans. But Kelly set the record straight. "I'm a Christian and a child of God. I was pointing to my Savior in the sky," he explained.[13]

Building on symbolic in-game gestures, Christian athletes also developed collaborative postgame prayer rituals. In 1989, NFL players with Philadelphia, Washington, and San Diego began huddling on the field after games to pray, with players from both teams invited. While college football had featured interteam prayers before, they were not part of the culture of the NFL, which frowned on fraternization between opponents.[14]

The next year the practice continued with the New York Giants and San Francisco 49ers. Before a highly anticipated Monday Night Football matchup in December 1990, the chaplains for the two teams, AIA staffers Pat Richie and Dave Bratton, hatched a plan for a postgame prayer. After talking to their chapel regulars, Richie and Bratton found several players eager to participate. Following the game—a 7-3 defensive battle—two Giants players joined six 49ers in the prayer huddle. For the rest of the season, culminating in a Super Bowl win, Giants players gathered at midfield for prayer after their games, with opponents frequently joining them.[15]

NFL leaders did not seem particularly enthusiastic about the new ceremony. They briefly attempted to re-enforce their "no fraternization" rule following the 1990–1991 season, but to no avail. When the 49ers and Giants played once again in a Monday Night Football matchup to start the next season, a handful of players knelt together at midfield after the game, daring the NFL to enforce the rule. No fines or discipline came. The prayer huddles were here to stay.[16]

The NFL's ambivalence toward public prayer highlights the key paradox undergirding the Christian athlete movement. Alongside its claims of growth and momentum, many evangelical athletes and coaches nurtured a sense of marginalization. As much as the evangelical subculture of sports had grown since the 1950s, it remained just that—a subculture. The percentage of players who attended chapels on a given team could occasionally exceed fifty percent, but it varied by team—and far fewer regularly attended Bible studies or PAO conferences.

So, too, those outside the movement often expressed pointed criticism of evangelical athletes. In baseball, some scouts and managers accused born-again players of losing their competitive edge. "They're going to be the ruination of baseball" one scout declared in 1981.[17] The following year in the NFL, Chicago

Bears safety Gary Fencik complained to a reporter about outspoken Christian teammates like Mike Singletary and Vince Evans. "Certain players have a tendency that if you aren't receptive to their invitation to accept Christ, you become 'they' rather than 'us,'" Fencik said. He added a dig aimed at the Christian players' masculinity, poking fun at their pregame ritual in which they "go into the shower room, hold hands and pray."[18]

Sports ministries may not have liked these comments, but they recognized the need to cooperate with nonevangelical teammates, coaches, and league executives if they wanted continued access. Unlike other forms of evangelical popular culture, including music, books, and television, evangelicals could not simply create their own big-time sports league. Instead, the pluralistic nature of the sports industry meant that evangelicals had to participate within an industry whose boundaries and priorities they did not dictate.[19]

More often than directly challenging sports insiders, then, Christian athletes and coaches tended to blame mainstream sports media for their perceived persecution. "When I start talking about Jesus, some reporters walk away," Philadelphia Eagles defensive end Reggie White complained in 1989. Two years later, an FCA staff member suggested that "when a player kneels and give thanks to the Lord" the sports media responded with criticism that "prayer doesn't belong on the playing field."[20]

There was some truth to this perspective. Dating back to Frank Deford's 1976 *Sports Illustrated* series, media coverage of the evangelical sports subculture often took a critical or cynical tone. In 1979, Glenn Dickey, sportswriter for the *San Francisco Chronicle*, attributed the San Francisco Giants' struggles to the team's evangelical players. He suggested that the Giants should trade "one or two of the most obvious born-agains" in order to "break up that clique."[21] Meanwhile, in a blistering column following the 1991 Super Bowl, *Sports Illustrated* columnist Rick Reilly complained about "elaborately orchestrated 50-yard-line religious sales pitches," which he saw as an unwelcome intrusion "wholly inappropriate to a sporting event." He called on the NFL to ban the postgame prayers and urged television networks to ignore them.[22]

Rhetoric like this seemed to confirm evangelical fears. Yet, what sports ministries experienced as marginalization could also be understood as a thwarted desire to control the narrative. In the 1950s and 1960s the FCA found plenty of sportswriters willing to praise its clean-living Christian athletes as emblems of the American way. Men like Ernie Mehl in Kansas City and Watson Spoelstra in Detroit served as glorified PR agents. By the 1980s, sports media had changed. Some sportswriters and broadcasters continued to support the efforts of the Christian athlete movement, but journalists seemed more interested in asking hard questions or considering angles beyond the scope of sports ministry priorities.[23]

The leaders of the Christian athlete movement could complain about this—and many did. But some took another step. Recognizing that they could not drive the media narrative in the direction they preferred, they sought to develop new media spaces where they could center the conversation around evangelical concerns. Out of this desire came the most important evangelical sports media property of the late twentieth century: *Sports Spectrum* magazine.

Gurus

Sports Spectrum's origins can be traced back to one of Sportianity's rising stars of the 1980s: Ralph Drollinger. A backup center for UCLA from 1972 through 1976, Drollinger turned down the chance to play in the NBA after graduation and instead joined the AIA basketball team. The team was at the height of its influence, and Drollinger quickly emerged as one of AIA's most eager spokesmen. In 1978 he arranged for a press conference in New York City to announce that he had turned down a three-year, $400,000 contract offer from the New Jersey Nets and would instead stay with AIA, where his salary was just $7,500—an announcement that led to a flurry of sports columnists praising Drollinger and contrasting him with the supposedly greedy athletes taking advantage of free agency to negotiate higher salaries.[24]

Two years later Drollinger decided to make the NBA leap after all. The Dallas Mavericks won the sweepstakes, signing Drollinger in June to a guaranteed three-year, $450,000 contract.[25] An expansion franchise owned by evangelical businessman Don Carter and run by evangelical general manager Norm Sonju, the Mavericks seemed to be a perfect fit. Sonju, raised in Chicago, was efficient and detail oriented—a business executive trained in the latest corporate strategies and shaped by the evangelical business ethos of ServiceMaster, where he worked until his move into the NBA. He was also well acquainted with Sportianity, serving as a key behind-the-scenes leader alongside fellow basketball executives Pat Williams and Jerry Colangelo.[26] Carter, by contrast, was a Texas native who possessed more of a "wildcat Christianity" posture: willing to speculate, take risks, and rely on intuition.[27]

Despite their differences in style, the two men shared a hope that the Mavericks could become a conservative Christian model for the rest of the league, representing, in Sonju's words, "wholesomeness and goodness and respect for God and country."[28] Drollinger later recalled that the Mavericks "told me they were going to be the first Christian team in the NBA," confirming the suspicion of Dallas sportswriter Skip Bayless, who wondered if Sonju wanted a "born-again Boy Scout" team. But Drollinger helped to torpedo any efforts to build an evangelical roster. Hobbled by injuries, his NBA career lasted exactly six games and featured more personal fouls than points. For years to come the UCLA big man served as an important lesson for the Mavericks' leadership that born-again players did not guarantee on-court success. "It was one of the worst mistakes of my career," Sonju admitted.[29]

As the Mavericks moved forward, Sonju and Carter modified their vision, aiming less for a predominantly Christian roster and more for a "family friendly" basketball operation and environment. Meanwhile, Drollinger took his guaranteed salary and returned to AIA, where he initiated a new project that would dominate his interests for the rest of the 1980s: a television show centered on sports and Christian faith. Originally called *Athletes in Action Sports Magazine*, the show featured Christian athletes sharing their faith and discussing sports and life lessons. A glossy quarterly print magazine provided the backbone of the operation, with the cable television show building on the print magazine with recorded interviews.[30]

AIA's investment in sports media coincided with a transition in the media strategy of its chief competitor. The *Christian Athlete* had served for two decades as the de facto journal of record for the Christian sports movement. But the controversy over Gary Warner's editorial direction in the 1970s hemmed in his successor, Skip Stogsdill, a problem exacerbated by financial challenges faced by the FCA in the early 1980s (challenges resolved through a fundraising campaign tied to Dallas Cowboys coach Tom Landry).[31] No longer a magazine aiming to speak for the broader Christian athlete community, it became, in the words of the FCA's president, a "specialized ministry outreach for teenage athletes." Recognizing this shift, in 1982 FCA leaders changed the magazine's name to *Sharing the Victory*.[32]

AIA faced its own financial challenges, the result of the cost of breaking into cable television. By 1985 funding for Drollinger's project dried up, and the print magazine and television program were cut. Still, Drollinger did not give up. Using money from his NBA contract, he created his own media company, New Focus, and adopted the AIA strategy for himself: a print magazine combined with a faith-based sports show. He recruited NBA star Julius Erving to headline the effort and host the show. Called "Julius Erving's Sports Focus," it had a brief run on ESPN in 1985 before it was canceled. One issue of the magazine, *Sports Focus*, was published, too: it featured Erving on the cover and included a profile of retired basketball standout and recent evangelical convert Pete Maravich.[33]

Drollinger tried again in 1987 with a television show and magazine called *Second Look*. The television program once again did not stick, but the magazine had lasting success thanks to financial support and guidance provided by Radio Bible Class (RBC), a Michigan-based evangelical devotional ministry that eventually acquired the magazine. Renamed *Sports Spectrum* in the early 1990s, the magazine achieved a level of permanence with a subscriber base that stood at fifty-five thousand in 1993.[34]

Positioning itself as a positive and practical publication that focused on "the good in sports," *Second Look/Sports Spectrum* fused evangelical themes with the therapeutic values expressed in older middlebrow periodicals like *Guideposts*. A 1987 issue of *Second Look*, for example, featured a profile of John Wooden—the living embodiment of middlebrow Protestantism—as well as an interview with Dodgers pitcher Orel Hershiser that highlighted the connections between positivity, faith, and "inner success."[35] At the same time, the magazine centered theological perspectives rooted in the fundamentalist tradition, particularly during Ralph Drollinger's leadership, when the former center recruited neofundamentalist Bible expositor John MacArthur Jr. to write monthly columns for the magazine.[36]

Because *Sports Spectrum* was not tied directly to either the FCA or AIA, it featured athletes and coaches from both organizations (and the growing number of smaller sports ministries). Christian athletes from previous generations could be written into the movement, too. Eric Liddell, the Scottish runner who sat out his best event at the 1924 Olympics because it was held on a Sunday—and then won gold in a different event, the four hundred meters—captured the support of American fundamentalists back then with his Sabbath convictions. Yet, while he fit within British evangelicalism, he was not a fundamentalist; on the American side he was shaped more by Frank Buchman's Oxford Group and mainline Protestant ministers Harry Emerson Fosdick and E. Stanley Jones.[37] Even so, nearly four decades after his death, Liddell earned a place among the new generation of American evangelical athletes when the award-winning film *Chariots of Fire* (1981) told the dramatic story of his Olympic performance. According to a 1987 *Second Look* article, Liddell exemplified "running for an audience of One."[38]

For the Christian athlete movement, *Second Look/Sports Spectrum* served as the closest thing to a journal of record. Whether past or present, it provided readers with a roster of famous athletes and coaches who connected evangelical faith with their success at the highest levels of sport—in baseball (with cover athletes like Orel Hershiser, Joe Carter, Frank Tanana, and Dave Dravecky), basketball (Mark Price, Kevin Johnson, Avery Johnson, A. C. Green), and football (Steve Largent, Bobby Hebert, Reggie Williams), as well as individual sports like tennis (Michael Chang).

By the time *Sports Spectrum* adopted its new name and achieved a sense of stability, Drollinger had departed and turned his attention to leading Sports Outreach America (SOA), an umbrella organization that sought to connect sports evangelism with local churches. SOA was the North American branch of a larger network, the International Sports Coalition (ISC), developed in 1986 by sports ministry pioneer Eddie Waxer and evangelical pastor Dave Burnham to galvanize and nurture sports ministry on a global scale.[39]

Like *Sports Spectrum*, SOA's independence from the major sports ministries allowed it to provide a space where evangelical sports ministries could work together. Although this did not always happen—animosity and suspicion between the FCA and AIA remained high throughout the 1990s—SOA was able to build large-scale, event-based sports evangelism campaigns. In 1993, for example, SOA created an evangelistic Super Bowl kit for churches that included a video narrated by Tom Landry as well as testimonies from Emmitt Smith and other star football players.[40]

By developing what eventually became *Sports Spectrum* and then taking charge of SOA, Drollinger positioned himself at the top of the Sportianity hierarchy, using evangelistic events and sports media as a common cause around which the various sports ministries could unite.

While Drollinger focused on public outreach, former AIA staffer Wes Neal emphasized the behind-the-scenes development of training materials designed to help Christian athletes and coaches reach their "fullest athletic potential" by learning what Neal claimed was "God's way" of doing sports.[41] As we saw last chapter, Neal's signature product—*The Handbook on Athletic Perfection*—was first issued during his time at AIA, when it was published as *The Making of an Athlete of God*. After leaving AIA, Neal carved out a space as an independent expert who could help athletes apply biblical concepts directly to their sports performance.[42]

Neal's materials continued to influence AIA even after his departure. Wendel Deyo, who would eventually succeed Dave Hannah as AIA's president, expanded on what Neal started by helping to create AIA's "five principles" for developing the "total athlete" through the integration of Christian faith and athletic competition. AIA also launched a unique high-intensity camp (the Ultimate Training Camp) where athletes could practice and learn the principles.[43] Deyo's most eager disciple, Cincinnati Bengals offensive lineman Anthony Muñoz, served as an important spokesperson for AIA in the 1980s, speaking and writing about his improved results after he began to incorporate the practice of seeing the intensity of his athletic performance as a way of saying "thank you" to God.[44]

Neal's influence extended into the FCA, too, although his system was not embraced by everyone. Southern Baptists tended to prefer their own methods, and the middlebrow style, emphasizing the gradual development of Christian character, continued to have staying power. But Neal won over several FCA leaders, particularly in Nebraska, where the FCA had a strong presence and where staff member Gordon Thiessen and Cornhusker assistant football coach Ron Brown were especially strong advocates of Neal's teachings. Thiessen formed a publishing company, Cross Training, that released new editions of Neal's material, eventually rebranding Neal's ideas as "Doing Sports God's Way."[45]

For many athletes and coaches Neal provided a framework for elite performance that focused on process over results, offering a tangible way to integrate their faith commitments directly into the field of competition. As a 1982 *Athletes in Action* article review put it, Neal showed "that sports competition can glorify God and that the Christian athlete can develop spiritually through sports."[46] At the same time, part of Neal's appeal was that he offered definitive and unambiguous answers to complex questions. Although evangelicals—to say nothing of Christians from other traditions—had different interpretations on what the Bible meant on a wide variety of issues, Neal presented himself as an objective receiver and transmitter of timeless biblical principles, with little consideration for the theological and cultural influences that might shape his understanding of the Bible.

One example was the Keswick lens through which Neal understood the biblical texts. Another was his approach to the coach/player relationship. Neal focused on what he called the "chain-of-command," a "biblical concept designed by God" that helped "each person know his responsibility and function at the highest level of efficiency."[47] Yet the chain-of-command idea as Neal conceived it was not obvious in the biblical text; instead it was in the air of 1970s evangelicalism, popularized by Bill Gothard, who carved out an influential role in conservative evangelical circles through his Institute in Basic Youth Conflicts (later Institute in Basic Life Principles). Gothard's key teaching focused on hierarchies of authority that he called the "chain of command": each person, he said, had God-ordained authority figures to whom they were required to submit, as well as some over whom they had authority. In the family unit, this meant that God was the top authority, followed by the husband, and then the wife, and then the kids.[48]

Although Gothard's ideas about authority caused considerable debate and criticism in evangelical circles, Neal decided that the chain-of-command concept was indeed biblical and that it applied to the coach/player relationship. His proof text was 1 Peter 2:18–20, which reads, in part, "Slaves, in reverent fear of God submit yourselves to your masters, not only to those who are good and considerate, but also to those who are harsh. For it is commendable if someone bears up under the pain of unjust suffering because they are conscious of God."[49]

Referring to this text, Neal encouraged athletes to be what he called *doulos* athletes—a Greek word referring to a slave. Neal encouraged athletes to mentally prepare for this *doulos* posture of complete submission by picturing themselves chained to their coaches. A *doulos* athlete, Neal said, "is completely at the disposal of the person for whom he is a doulos"; by being obedient to his coach, he is "being obedient to God." While Neal recognized that coaches might be inept or insensitive, he believed that, with rare exceptions, Christian athletes should submit anyway. "When we take on responsibilities and concerns that God has not given us in the chain-of-command, our mind becomes encumbered with unnecessary weight," Neal explained.[50]

To make the master/slave relationship from the first century analogous to the coach/player relationship in the twentieth century was fraught with racialized dynamics, particularly as big-time sports leagues filled up with Black players while coaching staffs remained predominantly white.[51] This did not seem to cross Neal's mind. In his view, he had simply read the Bible and applied its plain meaning. Many Christian athletes and coaches agreed, finding in Neal's system what they regarded as a truly biblical approach to competition—one that went deeper than most other programs.

Shirl Hoffman, on the other hand, was not impressed. A former college basketball coach, Hoffman earned his doctorate in education and then in the 1970s launched an academic career in the emerging field of sport studies. From 1975, when he presented a conference paper (later published as an article) titled "The Athletae Dei: Missing the Meaning of Sport," to 2010, when he published *Good Game: Christianity and the Culture of Sports*, Hoffman analyzed what he called the "locker-room religion" of the Christian athlete movement. Writing in *Christianity Today* in 1986, he described the theology of the movement this way: "It is not so much orthodox evangelicalism as a hodgepodge of biblical truths, worn-out coaching slogans, Old Testament allusions to religious wars, and interpretations of Paul's metaphors that would drive the most straight-laced theologian to drink." Hoffman specifically highlighted Wes Neal's program as the "most popular doctrine in this locker-room religion."[52]

Hoffman was not merely a critic. He, too, sought to advance his own understanding of how to do sports God's way, with a perspective shaped by popular intellectual trends. Finding his foundation in the work of academic theologians like Jürgen Moltmann and Hugo Rahner, who developed a theology of play in the 1960s and 1970s, Hoffman argued that Christian athletes should approach sports "as an expression of the divine spark called play," and they should play for one reason: "to celebrate a joyous life, secure in Christ."[53]

In contrast to Neal, who presented Christianity as a tool for maximizing one's athletic potential, Hoffman believed Christian athletes should simply delight in the gift of sports, content in who they already were. In contrast to Drollinger, who wanted Christian athletes to use the platform of sports for evangelistic aims, Hoffman argued that instrumentalizing sports in this way led to an ethic that linked winning (and thus, a bigger platform) with Christian witness. To Hoffman, sports should be received and celebrated as a gift from God—there was no need to add anything more. "The integration of sport and genuine

Christianity is possible only when we recognize the potential for sport as a celebrative and worshipful act," Hoffman concluded.[54]

Reception to Hoffman's work within the ranks of Sportianity was understand-ably ambivalent. Some, like *Sharing the Victory* editor Skip Stogsdill, appreciated Hoffman's viewpoint and sought to promote some of his ideas.[55] Yet, in gen-eral, Hoffman's audience and support came primarily from fellow academics or Christian intellectuals. This made it easier for his ideas to be dismissed. When Watson Spoelstra, founder of Baseball Chapel, wrote to *Christianity Today* to comment on Hoffman's 1986 article, he made this clear. "If only Shirl Hoffman had encountered Andre Thornton or Norm Evans," he lamented. Spoelstra went on to list other famous Christian athletes who had inspired and encouraged him over the years, offering them as rebuttals to Hoffman's criticism. "The Lord has exciting people on his side in professional and college sports," Spoelstra concluded.[56]

By naming specific star athletes with whom he was friends, Spoelstra nodded to the key source of authority within Sportianity: the relationships its leaders and organizations had with high-level Christian athletes and coaches. Academics like Hoffman, following the incentives of their field of work, advanced their careers by writing for fellow intellectuals *about* sports. Leaders in the Christian athlete movement, on the other hand, did the same by building relationships *within* sports. When it came to popularizing and advancing a particular way of doing sports God's way, they had the advantage of presence and athletic prestige.

Culture Warriors

Academic criticism may have had little effect on the day-to-day operations of the Christian athlete movement. Yet, there was another way to challenge the existing sports ministry organizations: one could create new, rival groups. This was the path of Champions for Christ (CFC), created in 1985 by Greg Ball as the sports wing of the controversial Maranatha Campus Ministries.

Maranatha, launched in the early 1970s by Bob Weiner, was part of the charis-matic/Pentecostal wing of American Christianity. In the early twentieth century Pentecostals built a religious subculture around spiritual practices like divine healing and speaking in tongues, forming denominations that included the predominantly white Assemblies of God and predominantly Black Church of God in Christ. Initially a socially marginalized movement, by the middle of the twentieth century Pentecostal experiences and practices began to move into the mainstream, aided by a "charismatic renewal" movement that reached beyond Pentecostal denominations and into both mainline Protestant institutions and new independent charismatic networks like Maranatha.[57]

Within mainline denominations, the charismatic renewal could seem like an update on the middlebrow Protestantism of the 1920s, with the Holy Spirit serving as a source for a practical and therapeutic faith.[58] This was the perspective of Leonard LeSourd, the longtime editor of *Guideposts* and a trustee for the FCA, who became an advocate for the charismatic movement in Presbyterian circles. But while the FCA did not exclude Pentecostal perspectives, it privileged more subdued expressions of faith. AIA, meanwhile, had a more oppositional posture to Pentecostalism shaped by its distinctive Keswick teachings. Still, as long as Pentecostal athletes kept their focus on common evangelical territory, like the transforming power of faith in Christ, they could usually find a welcome space within Sportianity.

Maranatha and Champions for Christ, however, represented a more confident and militant Pentecostalism. Not interested in playing by the rules set by evangelical gatekeepers, CFC fully embraced charismatic teachings about the gifts of the Holy Spirit and made them central to its identity, with key leaders presenting themselves as "shepherds" who could interpret and discern God's will for those placed under their authority.[59] Greg Ball, a clean-cut white evangelist who looked like a college student, proved that this approach could work in 1981 when he won his most important disciple: Oregon State basketball player A. C. Green. Writing in his autobiography, Green described meeting Ball at a campus revival, where he was inspired by Ball's admonition not to be "just another Christian student on campus." Green recalled feeling "a power surge" like a "bolt of lightning" after Ball prayed for him. "It's one thing to know you're saved," Green marveled, "but another to be saved and have the power of God living inside you."[60]

Green's entrance in the NBA in 1985 marked the official beginning of CFC as an organization, and his rise to prominence with the Los Angeles Lakers gave CFC credibility, allowing it to overcome the failure of Maranatha, which disbanded as an organized network in 1989 following charges of authoritarianism and spiritual manipulation. CFC pressed on with Greg Ball in charge, joined by another former Maranatha leader, Rice Broocks, who launched a new charismatic network in the 1990s that went by the name Morning Star before rebranding as Every Nation.[61]

In the early 1990s CFC expanded its star power beyond Green, with Greg Ball playing a key role in the born-again conversions of Houston Rockets guard Dave Jamerson and San Antonio Spurs star David Robinson (Robinson quickly distanced himself from CFC, joining a more traditional evangelical church in San Antonio). It was in the NFL that CFC truly made its mark, however. There, Darrell Green of the Washington Redskins became an important early spokesman. His involvement with CFC came through his mentor and pastor Brett Fuller, one of the few Black leaders in the Maranatha movement of the

1980s. In the 1990s Mark Brunell and Tony Boselli of the Jacksonville Jaguars emerged as key leaders as well, with Greg Ball as their main influence.[62]

CFC's programming generally mimicked that of the other major sports ministries. It hosted off-season training conferences, provided opportunities for its athletes to evangelize, and worked to place its leaders as chaplains within sports teams. Sometimes this could lead to conflict. In 2004, John Feinstein documented religious turmoil on the Baltimore Ravens that involved a group of CFC-affiliated players who challenged the team's AIA chaplain, Rod Hairston, by trying to create their own team Bible study.[63] At the same time, CFC differentiated itself with its militancy and its shepherding strategy, presenting its leaders as divinely ordained with unique insight and access to God. That provided the foundation for CFC leaders to aggressively confront supposed sin in players' lives. "[CFC] is a ministry that just steps in and says: 'You know what? You may get offended, but here's how it is,'" Indianapolis Colts punter Hunter Smith said.[64]

CFC also seemed to rely on financial donations from its athletes to help fund its operations, something that the FCA and AIA had been careful to avoid. In 1998, the NFL opened an investigation into CFC's financial influence when Chicago Bears rookie Curtis Enis, recently recruited to CFC, fired his agent and hired Greg Ball's friend, an investor named Greg Feste, to represent him. CFC and Ball vehemently denied wrongdoing, framing the investigation as the result of spiritual warfare. Yet, there seemed to be not just smoke, but fire. After a run of prominence within the NFL that extended until the early 2000s, CFC's influence waned after 2004 when Greg Ball stepped down from ministry amid a new round of accusations over financial impropriety and other moral concerns.[65]

Although CFC eventually faded from the scene, its rise in the last two decades of the twentieth century highlighted two important trends in the Christian athlete movement. First, CFC made it clear that the charismatic movement could not be ignored. It became increasingly common for Christian athletes to speak of divine healing from injuries or to notice supernatural intervention of the Holy Spirit on the field of play. Some embraced the "health and wealth" teaching of the prosperity gospel movement as well.[66] Although these teachings about the Holy Spirit differed from what Wes Neal and AIA said about doing sports "God's way," sports ministries ignored Pentecostal expressions of faith at their own peril.

Second, CFC exemplified a more militant posture toward cultural engagement. While much of the work of evangelical sports ministry happened behind the scenes, through the ministry of presence developed by the established organizations, CFC turned up the dial on aggressive public activism. "We are called to bring the nation itself to Christ," Bob Weiner explained in his 1988 book *Take Dominion.*

And the nation is made up not only of the people who live there, but of the arts, the sciences, education, law, political systems, the media, business, and so on . . . our task is to bring every one of those areas of life under His influence and under biblical principles.[67]

Weiner's ideas reflected a form of dominion theology known as the "Seven Mountains Mandate." According to this view, Christians had a God-given responsibility to take "dominion" or rulership of key centers of influence in society—the "seven mountains" of religion, family, government, education, media, arts/entertainment, and business. "God has given this earth into our keeping, and it is our responsibility to rule it properly," Weiner claimed. "If we Christians don't rule, who will? Atheists and humanists and agnostics, that's who."[68] In the 1980s and 1990s, dominion theology gained influence among the loosely organized group that scholars have labeled "Independent Network Charismatic" (INC) Christianity, and of which Maranatha was a part.[69]

CFC took Maranatha's culture war approach and applied it to sports. "There have been many great sports ministries that have gone before and are out laboring," Greg Ball explained, "but very few people have ever asked God for the high places."[70] Ball's use of the phrase "high places" was a dominionist move. He was identifying sports as a place of worship in society—a peak on a cultural mountain that Christians needed to occupy—and presenting CFC as the band of soldiers who could claim it for Christ.

Bob Weiner saw CFC in a similar light. In *Take Dominion*, he cited CFC and its work with A. C. Green as an example of taking dominion in sports. Green, in turn, saw himself as part of a special group of Christians, set apart and filled with the Holy Spirit to confront wickedness in a sinful society. This involved not just personal holiness, but also public activism. In college, Green got his first taste of this when he crusaded to get Playboy magazine removed from area convenience stores. "We felt as though we had just stepped off the page of Acts," Green marveled. "We didn't just step on toes; we stomped them and mashed them into the ground."[71]

Green's reference to the book of Acts reflected the charismatic movement's desire to recover a first-generation Christianity, the kind described in the Bible, full of signs and wonders and miraculous events. The key point was that the Bible was not just a "playbook for life" or a set of principles to follow, as it was often framed by AIA and FCA; it offered a present reality into which modern Christians could enter. "God wants his people to be warriors," Green explained in a 1988 interview. "The Israelite warriors in the Bible were always ready to fight, to destroy their enemies and possess their land. It's that spirit that moves me." Through holy living, Spirit-filled prayer, and unashamed public advocacy, Green believed Christians could claim new ground for Christ.[72]

CFC's militant posture was not just a reflection of its Pentecostal dominion theology; it was also part of a broader evangelical culture war orientation. By the 1980s, many evangelicals had adopted a dualistic framework popularized by Francis Schaeffer (whose influential 1977 documentary film *How Should We Then Live?* was produced and distributed with the aid of Baseball Chapel leader Billy Zeoli). Schaeffer depicted American culture as a battleground between two incompatible forces. On one side stood secular humanism, offering a human-centered view of the world, where people set their own standards for morality. Christianity, by contrast, provided a God-centered view with a timeless and transcendent set of values and rules to which human beings were called to conform.[73] This perspective required a zero-sum mindset. There were two kingdoms at work in American culture, and neutrality was not an option.

Although conservative evangelicals believed they represented timeless and transcendent truths, they also sought to defend a particular understanding of Christianity's relationship with American society. Historian Andrew Hartman has labeled this vision "normative America," a set of cultural standards that achieved dominance in the 1950s only to be challenged by the revolutions of the 1960s. These included strict gender roles, opposition to sex outside of heterosexual marriage, and belief in American exceptionalism—the idea that the nation was uniquely rooted in Christian values.[74]

International Sport Coalition leader Dave Burnham captured this emphasis on "normative America" in a 1988 article for *Second Look.* "Back in the 1960s," he wrote, "we experienced what was called the sexual revolution." Since that time, he said, all hell had been unleashed: a rising divorce rate, increase in teen pregnancies and abortions, and the AIDS epidemic. All of this, in Burnham's view, came about because Americans had rejected "God's standards of morality."[75]

While the established sports ministries did not match CFC's militancy, their acceptance of this broader culture war framework marked a change in tone. Leaders had originally built the Christian athlete movement with a middlebrow emphasis on a practical, everyday faith and a vision of American society that combined tradition and progress, welcoming carefully guarded change. Accommodation and compromise were essential. Although these themes did not go away in the era of culture war, by the 1980s a distinctly confrontational posture toward mainstream American culture—one that sought to take back something that had been lost rather than carry forward traditional values into the future—began to rival the middlebrow approach at the foreground of the Christian athlete movement's public witness. "There are clearly two systems at work right now," FCA president John Erickson warned in 1982, "the world's system and God's system."[76]

While theological differences mattered and could lead to conflict as evangelical sports ministries advanced different approaches to doing sports God's way, there was also common ground built around a culture war narrative in which Christian athletes were enlisted in the battle against secular humanism in American culture.

Christian Athletes and the Christian Right

The culture wars were about much more than politics. Still, the voting booth mattered. And the rise of the Christian Right, which mobilized conservative white Christians as a Republican voting bloc, brought a partisan edge to the battle—with sports playing a key role in the imagery and ethos of this growing political movement.[77]

The most prominent Christian Right activist of the 1980s, Moral Majority founder and Liberty University president Jerry Falwell, had a strong interest in sports. A Baptist fundamentalist, Falwell had been an ardent segregationist in the early 1960s. When clergy marched in favor of civil rights for Black people, Falwell preached that it was not the place of ministers to get involved in politics. After the gains of the civil rights movement had been achieved, Falwell apologized for his earlier segregationist views. He also had a change of heart about politics, deciding that he had a moral duty to enter the fray. "For too long we have watched pornography, homosexuality and godless humanism corrupt America's families, its schools and its communities," he declared in a 1979 article announcing the formation of the Moral Majority.[78]

A lifelong sports fan, Falwell invested heavily in Liberty's football program soon after its founding in 1971, dreaming that one day it would become an evangelical Notre Dame and provide a greater platform to preach his militant brand of born-again faith and politics. To achieve his dream he turned to the Christian athlete movement, bringing in retired evangelical athletes to lead Liberty's sports programs. In 1973, he hired former MLB pitcher Al Worthington, an early supporter of the FCA, to serve as his baseball coach. When Worthington moved into the athletic director role at Liberty, he brought in former New York Yankees star Bobby Richardson, who was serving as president of Baseball Chapel at the time, to coach the team. In football, meanwhile, former NFL coach Sam Rutigliano, an FCA advocate, took charge of the Liberty program in 1988.[79]

Men like Worthington, Richardson, and Rutigliano embodied Falwell's vision for American society. They were strong Christian leaders whose success in the masculine domain of sports helped to link conservative Christianity with virile manhood and "traditional" values. By the end of the 1980s Falwell had not quite reached the big-time with Liberty athletics, but he did succeed in moving his football program up to the NCAA's second-highest division, I-AA (now known as the Football Championship Subdivision, or FCS).[80]

Falwell, however, needed Sportianity more than the other way around—in fact, Falwell's extremism could be a liability to the movement. He remained a relatively marginal figure in evangelical sports ministry spaces, where the affinity for Republican politics was driven less by new Christian Right firebrands and more by the long-standing conservative political preferences of its middle-class white Protestant constituencies in the Sunbelt and Midwest.

Ronald Reagan represented this more expansive conservative orientation. As California's governor in the 1960s, he had cited the FCA as an example of the "Creative Society" he sought to promote, a vision for building community without government intervention.[81] Reagan also attended a Presbyterian church pastored by former UCLA linebacker and FCA pioneer Donn Moomaw— a pastor who distanced himself from the Moral Majority, telling a reporter in 1980 that "we are more liberal in our ideas of the ways people can work out their faith."[82] In 1982, when FCA president John Erickson met with Reagan and offered the FCA's assistance to support the president's agenda, he was not someone recently awakened to Christian Right activism; instead, his entrance into politics came in 1970 when he ran for Congress as a moderate Republican.[83]

Former Buffalo Bills quarterback Jack Kemp, a New York congressman from 1971 until 1989, exemplified this broader conservative tradition, too. Fiercely optimistic, his belief in an American way defined by free-market capitalism and individualism hearkened back to the middlebrow Protestants of the 1920s. Writing in the *Christian Athlete* in 1973, Kemp linked his political philosophy to sports, suggesting that individual Americans could better themselves through competition and bring the rest of the country up with them. "We don't have to accept our circumstances; we can mold them. That's what it means to be a competitor," he wrote.[84] Focusing more on tax cuts and supply-side economics than on culture war issues, Kemp represented a more inclusive vision of conservatism than the militant rhetoric on offer by Falwell.[85]

Yet, the rise of the new Christian Right as a driving force within the Republican Party meant that Kemp and Erickson were closely linked with more militant right-wing leaders whose conservativism had emerged from the roots of Southern segregationist resistance to civil rights (like Jerry Falwell) or from the far-right conspiratorial imagination of the John Birch Society (JBS) (like Moral Majority cofounder Tim LaHaye).[86] These forms of conservatism may not have been dominant or prioritized within the Christian athlete movement, but they clearly had a place.

The example of Dave Dravecky is a case in point. In 1984 *Athletes in Action* magazine featured the San Diego Padres pitcher on its cover, with a profile titled "How Does a Nice Guy Like This Wind Up in the Majors?" A few months later Dravecky made national headlines and stirred debate for his membership in the John Birch Society, a political affiliation that Dravecky saw as the "natural outgrowth" of his born-again faith.[87] Stung by the media criticism, in future years Dravecky declined to speak about the controversy or the JBS. Meanwhile, his star rose within the Christian athlete movement for very different reasons: a courageous and heroic battle with cancer, which eventually ended his career and led to the amputation of his left arm.[88]

Dravecky was a prominent figure in Christian sports spaces because of his inspirational story of overcoming adversity, not his politics. Yet, his politics did help to reveal the boundaries and shape of the movement. While conservatives ranging from Kemp to Dravecky could feel at home, mainstream liberal political perspectives—to say nothing of the far left—often received pushback. Skip Stogsdill, the FCA magazine editor who continued to provide a space for progressive evangelical perspectives through the 1980s, resigned in 1989. He expressed frustration with what he saw as a tendency to create "cookie-cutter Christians" who conformed to conservative talking points instead of engaging in issues with complexity and nuance.[89] University of North Carolina basketball coach Dean Smith also stepped back from the movement and voiced alarm at the rise of the Christian Right.[90]

Roe Johnston, the liberal Presbyterian minister who helped launch and guide the FCA in the 1950s, expressed similar concerns. He wrote an article for *Sharing the Victory* in 1985 in which he reflected on his involvement in those early years and urged FCA leaders to "get into complex issues." He mentioned world peace, the economics of college athletics, and justice for the oppressed as issues of concern. And he encouraged the FCA to "become more ecumenical." "In the last decade we've become pretty confined to that portion of Christ's body called Evangelicals," Johnston pointed out. "I haven't seen the mainline denominations represented very well for a long time."[91]

Johnston's article sparked criticism from some readers. One complained about the notion that the FCA should "be devoted to social issues," urging the FCA to focus instead on the "eternal" goal of "the simple, clear, gospel message" and "saving knowledge of Jesus Christ." What the reader seemed to miss was that the FCA was already involved with social issues—it had simply selected social issues aligned with conservative politics.[92]

But while Johnston wanted more mainline Protestant influence, the disconnect went both ways. Although middlebrow mainliners remained involved, mainline intellectuals and institutional leaders had neglected the Christian athlete movement, particularly its emphasis on a ministry of presence and on evangelism. Evangelical sports ministries worked to place staff members in the field, strengthening connections within the sports industry; mainline leaders shied away from evangelism and generally preferred to engage in sports—if they did at all—by writing critical essays and articles. Just as significant, by the 1970s many mainline intellectuals and politically liberal leaders rejected the idea that the

United States had a uniquely Christian identity. They focused more on concerns about pluralism and respect for diverse religious viewpoints. As a result, sports ministry organizations—believing that a distinctly Christian perspective needed to be encouraged in the sports world—felt they had little in common with liberal mainline priorities.[93]

This became especially apparent with debates over the place of religion and prayer in public schools. In 1984, religious conservatives in Congress tried to pass an amendment that would enshrine school prayer as a constitutional right—a battle they had been fighting since the Supreme Court's *Engel v. Vitale* (1962) and *School District of Abington Township v. Schempp* (1963) decisions.[94] Many mainline leaders and organizations opposed the amendment, but several high-profile leaders in Sportianity, including Dallas Cowboys coach Tom Landry and Washington Redskins coach Joe Gibbs, offered their support. "The Supreme Court, in my opinion, took God out of every part of our life except church," Landry explained at a congressional forum. "Once God is taken out of the marketplace, I think humanism moves into the void."[95]

The school prayer amendment in 1984 fell short of the sixty-seven votes needed to advance in the Senate, yet debates continued over the boundaries of religious expression in public schools. As conservatives like Landry and Gibbs organized in support of school prayer, progressives in groups like the American Civil Liberties Union (ACLU) organized against it, seeking to limit the religious activities of coaches and sports ministry groups on public school campuses. In 1980, in one of the earliest high-profile cases involving prayer in school sports, the parents of a high school athlete in Oak Ridge, Tennessee, filed a complaint against head football coach Emory Hale, an FCA member who led his team in prayer before and after games. In college football, meanwhile, coaches like Bill McCartney (University of Colorado), Bobby Bowden (Florida State University), and Rey Dempsey (Memphis State) received scrutiny for encouraging Christianity within their programs.[96]

These skirmishes became an ongoing battle, with the threat of litigation curtailing some practices—at Colorado, McCartney had to make team prayers and chapel services optional. Yet, Christian coaches did not back down. They navigated new boundaries while developing other strategies to encourage Christianity within their teams. "Neither the ACLU nor any other group can keep me from sharing my beliefs with the world," Bill McCartney declared in his autobiography.[97] What liberals and progressives saw as a violation of the separation of church and state, leaders in the Christian athlete movement saw as essential to their ministry and a continuation of the nation's Christian heritage.

Still, for all the ways that a conservative political orientation shaped the Christian athlete movement, sports ministry organizations did not usually prioritize direct political activity. The example of Frank Pastore is instructive.

A professional baseball player with the Cincinnati Reds in the 1980s, Pastore converted to evangelical faith through the efforts of AIA leader Wendel Deyo. After his playing career, Pastore came on staff with AIA. Yet Pastore found himself losing interest in sports ministry work. As he explained in his autobiography, he conducted chapel services and worked with players on the Cincinnati Bengals and Reds but "found it pretty shallow." The players seemed to ask the same questions: they wanted help with their marriages, advice about life after sports, tips on how to handle money, and suggestions on how to relate their athletic performance to their Christian faith. "Those are valid questions," Pastore admitted. "But I wasn't a counselor, and I didn't like the hand-holding stuff."[98]

Instead of the "hand-holding stuff" that comprised the bulk of sports ministry work, Pastore wanted to get into the rough-and-tumble world of intellectual and political debate. So, in 1991, Pastore left his work with AIA, eventually becoming a conservative Christian radio host in Los Angeles, where he could defend his conservative Christian beliefs and talk more directly about politics.[99] Five years later, another former AIA member, Ralph Drollinger, took a similar path, leaving sports ministry for activist political ministry. Drollinger's new organization, Capitol Ministries, specialized in Bible studies for politicians that presented conservative talking points—from cracking down on undocumented immigrants to rejecting the science of climate change—as timeless biblical truths.[100]

That Drollinger and Pastore left sports ministry so they could pursue political influence underscores the continued middlebrow nature of sports ministry work. While some leaders in the Christian athlete movement understood their work through a culture war frame, for many people what mattered most was how Christian faith spoke to their everyday experiences. Sports ministry staff rarely had political activism at the forefront of their minds, focusing instead on meeting the practical concerns and pressures faced by athletes and coaches.

At the same time, there were political implications to sports ministry work. With ecumenical and liberal Protestant leaders like Roe Johnston pushed further to the margins and right-wing fundamentalist leaders like Jerry Falwell invited in, the political center of the Christian athlete movement shifted even more to the right. To be a Christian athlete, in the eyes of the public and within Sportianity, was to be politically conservative.[101]

Women as Christian Athletes

Because a conservative "family values" vision of gender was central to the rise of the Christian Right, the growth of women's sports after the 1972 passage of Title IX posed a challenge. Sportianity's infrastructure had been built precisely because sports seemed to provide a distinctly masculine space through which

Christian men could enhance their authority and shape the future direction of the country. The rise of women's sports, inspired in part by the feminist movement of the 1960s, could challenge this male-centered perspective. Yet sports ministries were continually looking for areas of growth. The infusion of women into athletics provided an opportunity to attract new members and supporters.[102]

This ambivalence was not confined to evangelical sports ministries. Women faced continued disparities in equity and opportunity across the American sports scene. The NCAA opposed Title IX implementation throughout the 1970s and did not offer intercollegiate sports for women until the 1980s. Instead, the Association for Intercollegiate Athletics for Women (AIAW), formed in 1971, sponsored championship tournaments and advocated for increased athletic opportunities. Meanwhile, efforts in the 1970s to launch professional team sports for women—a softball league in 1976 and a basketball league in 1979—fizzled after a few years. While some women starred in tennis, track, or golf, it was not until the creation of the Women's National Basketball Association (WNBA) in 1996 that women had a highly publicized, stable professional team sports league in the United States.[103]

Despite these continued challenges, rates of sports participation for women soared and sports ministries took notice. In fact, well before Title IX, women had been included in limited ways in the FCA's promotional materials. In July 1956 FCA founder Don McClanen announced that Patty Berg, one of the cofounders of the Ladies Professional Golf Association (LPGA), had joined the FCA. It appears that Berg offered her name and endorsement, but little else. In 1964, the *Christian Athlete* featured an article by former Wayland Baptist college basketball player Patsy Neal. Neal would go on to author several books and articles focused on themes of identity, play, and worship in sports.[104]

Occasional promotion of successful women athletes aside, the FCA did not move forward with plans for a women's program until 1972, when new FCA president John Erickson approved several experimental women's groups.[105] The following year the *Christian Athlete* published a story on one of these groups, titling it "Competition with a Feminine Touch." The article featured Julia Hoon, a physical education instructor, who led a "cuddle group," the girl's version of the FCA's high school "huddle group." Along with the "cuddle group" moniker, Hoon signaled the nonthreatening nature of the FCA's women's program by noting that she was personally "not gung-ho on women's lib."[106]

With women entering into the FCA, the organization moved to develop an institutional presence within women's sports organizations. Cindy Smith, hired in 1976 to serve as the first National Director for the FCA's Women's Program, led the charge.[107] In 1976 she wrote a letter to AIAW leaders, introducing herself and the FCA and suggesting that if the FCA could implement programs within women's college sports similar to those in men's college athletics, it could help the AIAW "expand the opportunities for women in sports." Two years later the AIAW allowed Smith to host an FCA coaches' breakfast at its annual convention; it did the same in 1979.[108]

Unlike the NCAA, which generally supported the FCA's attempts to embed itself within men's intercollegiate athletics, some AIAW leaders expressed concern with the FCA's motives. Margot Polivy, chief legal counsel for the AIAW, wrote to fellow organizational leaders after she noticed an invitation to an FCA breakfast in a 1979 AIAW mailing. "Has the question of why the Fellowship of Christian Athletes would want to sponsor (free of charge) a breakfast ever been seriously examined?" she asked, warning that the breakfast aimed to "establish a more positive climate for the Fellowship to pursue its missionary and proselytizing activities among collegiate athletes." In Polivy's view, by allowing the FCA to host a breakfast, the AIAW came dangerously close to violating the principle of separation of church and state. "I do not believe it is AIAW's role or place to assist them," she stated.[109]

Polivy's suspicions became a nonissue after the NCAA took over the administration of women's college sports in the early 1980s, driving the AIAW out of business.[110] The NCAA, which hired Cindy Smith to work in an administrative role in 1981, proved more amenable to FCA's presence.[111] Meanwhile, led by staffers like Marcia Burton, Cindy Nero, and Barb Bernlohr, in the 1980s AIA expanded its own women's ministry by hosting summer camps and sponsoring traveling teams of ex-collegians.[112]

Women were vital to the work of Ralph Drollinger's *Second Look/Sports Spectrum* project as well—especially his wife, Karen Rudolph Drollinger (after the two divorced, she dropped the Drollinger name). A former college basketball player, Rudolph served as a contributing author and editor for the magazine into the early 1990s, often writing profiles of women. Thanks to her efforts, prominent athletes and coaches like Lynette Woodard (basketball), Betsy King (golf), Madeline Manning Mims (track and field), and Kay Yow (basketball) were presented as models for Christian women, helping to inspire the growing ranks of young women athletes.[113]

The inclusion of women came with tensions and paradox. In an article for *Second Look* titled "Ladies of the Eighties," Rudolph discussed the influence of star women athletes who "are modeling a new style of toughness and femininity." Despite the success of a few prominent individuals, Rudolph believed that obstacles remained. "Can a woman be athletic and tough, yet remain feminine?" Rudolph asked.[114] For Christian men, participation in sports offered a way to prove their manhood, to establish masculine credentials. For women, sports could be viewed as transgressive, a potential threat to their womanhood. As scholar Annie Blazer has shown, Christian women athletes often felt pressured to perceive and present themselves in traditionally feminine ways and to keep their aggression and assertiveness as competitors in check.[115]

This dilemma was heightened by a growing debate in evangelical circles over a woman's place in the home, church, and society. Broadly, the debate took shape around two competing options. On one side stood the egalitarians. Galvanized in the 1970s by books like Nancy Hardesty and Letha Dawson Scanzoni's *All We're Meant to Be: Biblical Feminism for Today* (1974), egalitarians advanced their cause through the Evangelical Women's Caucus (EWC) and later Christians for Biblical Equality (CBE). Egalitarians argued that evangelical readings of the Bible were compatible with feminism and that the Bible sanctioned women's full participation in all aspects of church leadership as well as shared and equal authority between husband and wife in the home.[116]

On the other side were complementarians. With evangelical feminists organizing in the 1970s, some conservative evangelicals grew alarmed at the challenge to what they saw as the Bible's clear endorsement of a gendered hierarchy, with women submitting to male authority in the church and home (and, by extension, in society). Linking continued support for male headship with the authority of the Bible, in 1987 complementarians formed the Council on Biblical Manhood and Womanhood and issued the Danvers Statement to advance its cause. "Distinctions in masculine and feminine roles are ordained by God as part of the created order, and should find an echo in every human heart," the Danvers Statement declared.[117]

Because sports were associated with the development of confidence, strength, assertiveness, and courage—all traits that had been culturally linked with masculinity—one might assume that Christian women athletes would champion evangelical feminism. Yet, for several reasons, this did not occur. First, at the leadership level, the major evangelical sports ministries tended to support or privilege complementarian perspectives.[118] The FCA, with its history of ecumenism, likely had the greatest diversity of thought at the ground level. Because of its Southern orientation, however, many key FCA leaders were strongly influenced by the path of the Southern Baptist Convention (SBC), which embarked on a conservative turn in the 1980s that made complementarianism a test of biblical orthodoxy. In 1998, when the SBC codified a complementarian understanding of women's submission to male headship as a central tenet of the SBC faith, the two most powerful FCA leaders, Dal Shealy and Nelson Price, were Southern Baptists.[119]

In addition, coaches and athletes at the grassroots level often embraced complementarian perspectives as a common-sense view of traditional American values, an expression of "normative America." This involved a positive articulation of the therapeutic value of complementarianism, as well as more oppositional postures to cultural trends. In 1988, Houston Astros pitcher Bob Knepper, who had been converted through a Baseball Chapel service in 1978, expressed his disagreement when Pam Postema became the first woman to umpire an MLB game. "In my opinion, which I base on the Bible," he explained, "I believe that God's perspective is that women should not be in certain occupations."[120] In response to letters criticizing his comments, Knepper developed a three-page summary of complementarian talking points to defend his views, which emphasized that "men and women were equal" but that "God has created woman to be a special gift to man."[121]

Knepper's views about women umpires were not necessarily a mainstream perspective in the Christian athlete movement. Yet, complementarianism exerted a powerful pull. It existed easily within the world of sports because—despite the inclusion of a handful of women in men's sporting spaces—the American sports system was already organized around gender distinctions, with men and women competing on separate teams and in separate leagues. Even more, the sports industry as a whole remained deeply invested in men's sports. Despite the changes that emerged after Title IX, the vast disparity in time and money poured into televised men's sports compared with women's sports ensured that athletic competition would continue to be culturally linked with masculinity, even as women carved out more opportunities to participate.[122]

In this environment, the development of sports ministry programs for women remained compatible with complementarian ideas: women could simply confine their leadership and teaching roles to other women, with men overseeing the overall operation of ministry efforts. In 1987 women made up nearly half of the FCA's national membership, and yet there were only twelve women employed in full-time field staff roles, compared with 120 men.[123]

To be sure, there were some Christian athletes and coaches who advocated for egalitarian perspectives. In 1991, the University of Washington women's basketball coach Chris Gobrecht urged FCA leaders to treat women "as dynamic community leaders in the same way we minister to men" while also "ministering to men in the same ways we need to minister to women."[124] More often, however, women leaders in the Christian athlete movement either supported complementarian perspectives or agreed to operate within its boundaries.

In 1987, the FCA's director of women's ministry, Debbie Wall Larson, took this approach. Asked about the possibility that women on FCA's staff might have authority over men, she explained, "An FCA staff person is not in a position of Biblical authority over those they serve nor was it ever intended they should be." Recognizing the need to stay within the limits and boundaries prescribed for women, she noted that she tried not to "carry a chip on my shoulder or react negatively" to chauvinistic attitudes, focusing instead on cooperating within the system to gradually build opportunities for women.[125]

Put simply, the inclusion of women did not directly challenge the masculine ideals that undergirded Sportianity and gave it cultural resonance. Sports ministry organizations often served the dual roles of empowering women to identify as athletes and also encouraging them to accept the so-called traditional structure of American culture in which men were the ultimate leaders in the home, church, and society. "Men and women, although equal in their positions before God," Karen Rudolph wrote in *Grace and Glory*, "were created for different roles."[126]

Sexuality

While debates about complementarian and egalitarian perspectives loomed large over the acceptance of Christian women as athletes, another cultural issue proved just as significant. In a 1982 article for *Athletes in Action*, high school basketball star Cheryl Miller—on the cusp of a Hall of Fame career in the game—addressed it in a subtle way. Asked to explain how she maintained her faith and femininity while pursuing competitive excellence, she assured readers it was possible. "I can be ladylike," she insisted. "I'm not boy crazy, but I like boys a lot."[127]

Miller's comments highlighted fears about the links between women's sports and lesbianism. There was already a long history of women's involvement in sports being associated with "deviant" sexuality and "mannishness." Those insinuations became a topic of open conversation after 1981 when tennis stars Billie Jean King and Martina Navratilova were outed for same-sex romantic relationships.[128] With conservative ideas about the family and sexuality increasingly central to both evangelical identity and Christian Right activism, sports ministries felt compelled to speak. "The issue of homosexuality in women's athletics is one which can remain silenced no longer," Karen Rudolph claimed. "Whether through innuendo or direct accusation, women athletes and coaches are encompassed by this issue."[129]

For sports ministry leaders, as for many in the evangelical world, the issue seemed to be clear-cut. Drawing on a conservative understanding of biblical authority and New Testament passages like Romans 1:27, most evangelicals believed that sexual acts between members of the same sex were sinful.[130] A 1982 article in the *Christian Athlete*, titled "Lesbian Lust" and written by a college basketball player, illustrated the basic approach. "I think lesbianism is definitely a problem in women's sports today," the author explained. She recalled that she herself had "close calls" and that she had to "be alert" because "I still find certain girls attractive." "If you're susceptible to homosexuality, seek qualified Christian counseling and avoid situations where you'll be tempted," she encouraged. "But don't condemn gays as people. We need to love them as God does."[131]

In 1985, the FCA published "Homosexuality and the Female Athlete." Featuring interviews with two college women, it sought to strike a similar balance, on the one hand stating that "the Bible doesn't offer homosexuality as an acceptable lifestyle" but on the other hand encouraging Christians to be more empathetic. "The thing is to love them, not condemn them," one young woman explained. The 1985 article also encouraged people with "a problem with homosexuality" to seek help from two self-described "ex-gay ministries": Love in Action and Metanoia.[132]

While evangelical sports ministries sought to position themselves as loving and empathetic, their approach was not usually received that way by lesbian athletes. In her book *Strong Women, Deep Closets* (1998), Pat Griffin, a pioneering scholar and activist for LGBTQ college athletes, devoted a chapter to the conflict between evangelical sports ministries and lesbian athletes and coaches. Using research, interviews, and her own experiences, she argued that whatever the intentions of evangelical sports ministries, they created a hostile climate for gay and lesbian athletes.[133]

Along with the criticism from Pat Griffin and other LGBTQ advocates, the failures and controversies associated with ex-gay ministries posed a problem for the Christian athlete movement. Leaders with the two ministries recommended by the FCA in 1985, Love in Action and Metanoia, stepped down after confessing that they could not change their sexual orientation. In the coming years, ex-gay ministries would increasingly come under fire for their claims that gay people needed to—or even could—change their sexual orientation. For the Christian athlete movement, this was brought home through the example of Karen Rudolph. After serving as a leading voice for Christian women athletes in the 1980s, in the 1990s she quietly left the movement and divorced Ralph Drollinger; her former husband revealed this was because she had come out to him as a lesbian.[134]

By contrast, the presence of gay male athletes was rarely discussed. To Sportianity's leaders, gay men existed outside the structure of sports, a perception that fit with broader patterns in American culture. Although a couple of athletes, including Dave Kopay in the NFL (1964–1972) and Glenn Burke in MLB (1976–1979), were known by teammates and insiders to be gay during their playing days, they did not make any public announcements until after they retired. "It's harder to be a gay in sports than anywhere else," Burke said in 1982. "Only a superstar could come out and admit he was gay and hope to stay around."[135] As a result, the Christian athlete movement was almost entirely silent when it came to the possibility that gay men might be present in locker rooms.

That is not to say that the Christian athlete movement avoided the subject of gay sexuality. In the 1980s several leaders issued condemnations of homosexuality as a threat to American society and alluded to AIDS as evidence of the consequences of the sexual revolution.[136] This confrontational rhetoric intensified in the 1990s as the gay rights movement made gains in American society. In 1992, Colorado football coach Bill McCartney came under fire for speaking in support of a Colorado for Family Values campaign against gay rights ordinances. "I embrace what almighty God has said about these things to me when I read the Scriptures," McCartney explained. "Homosexuality is an abomination of Almighty God." While McCartney said he had no animosity toward gay people—he adopted the familiar line of rejecting the sin, but not the sinner—he argued that homosexuality was a "lifestyle" that did not deserve antidiscrimination protections.[137]

Six years later, Green Bay Packers defensive end Reggie White—arguably the most prominent Christian athlete at the time—caused an even greater stir when he took the floor of the Wisconsin state legislature and made his opposition to gay rights known. "Homosexuality is a decision, it's not a race," he said, claiming that many of America's problems could be traced back to the public's willingness to allow "this sin to run rampant in our nation."[138] His words ignited a firestorm that played out along culture war lines, with liberals denouncing his intolerance in mainstream news outlets and calling for Campbell's Soup and Nike to drop him from endorsement deals, while conservatives rallied to his support with an ad campaign and a book deal.[139]

The antigay pronouncements of White and McCartney increasingly defined the public image of Sportianity in the 1990s, as clashes between the Christian Right and gay rights advocates expanded. To its supporters, the Christian athlete movement was simply defending traditional values, teachings that came straight from the Bible and that were widely accepted in American culture before the revolutions of the 1960s. To its critics, the movement was embracing reactionary and outdated viewpoints, undermining the notions of progress and inclusion which had long been a part of the mythology of sports.[140]

Still, for as much attention as the public activism of McCartney and White received, those involved in the Christian athlete movement invested far less time speaking against gay rights than they did promoting a positive vision of heterosexual Christian life. This occurred behind the scenes, in the "hand-holding stuff" of college and pro sports ministry, where the work of sports ministers and chaplains often focused on helping athletes adhere to conservative sexual boundaries: faithfulness to one's spouse for married athletes and abstinence for single athletes. And it occurred in public, as Christian athletes and coaches helped to sell the joys and benefits of a conservative vision of marriage and sexuality.

One of the most prominent examples of this came from Promise Keepers (PK), a Christian men's organization founded by McCartney in 1990. McCartney developed the idea for PK while en route to an FCA event. The aim was simple: mobilize Christian men to dedicate themselves to God and to their roles as husbands and fathers. While it was not a sports-specific ministry, it drew heavily on sports imagery, holding rallies in sports stadiums. It reached a peak in 1997 when 1.2 million men attended PK events. Its vision for masculinity, building on themes that had been popularized in the 1970s with Pro Athletes Outreach, combined male leadership in the home with a call for men to love, serve, and be emotionally available to their wives and children.[141]

While McCartney and PK encouraged men to be devoted husbands and fathers, another leader in the Christian athlete movement, A. C. Green, focused on making sexual abstinence appealing. Green spoke proudly about his virginity and recruited a group of Christian athletes to participate in a collective he called "Athletes for Abstinence." Formed in 1992 in the wake of the shocking announcement that Green's teammate, Magic Johnson, had contracted the HIV virus, the group, which included David Robinson, Barry Sanders, and Darrell Green, produced a rap music video, "It Ain't Worth It," with the goal of linking their message of sexual purity with hip hop culture. "We believe in the Bible, not that you pass out condoms, but that you teach righteousness," Darrell Green explained. "And righteousness is to abstain."[142]

As scholar Scott Strednak Singer writes, the association of strong and fit Christian athletes with the sexual purity movement of the 1990s helped to make abstinence "sexy."[143] At the same time, the heavy emphasis on sexual purity as a defining feature of what it meant to be a Christian athlete raised the stakes for those associated with Sportianity. The pressure of performing—as a happily married Christian couple, or as a chaste single Christian—intensified, particularly with evangelicals arguing that their approach to sex, based on the Bible, offered the only sure way for happiness.

Barry Sanders became a prime example of these challenges. As a member of the Athletes for Abstinence collective, in 1992 Sanders participated in the group's rap song and music video. But two years later, when the music video was publicly released, word came out that the unmarried Sanders had fathered a child. "I never wanted to set myself up as the moral conscience for the sports world, but that role eventually became my identity," Sanders wrote in his autobiography. "It seemed more important to people that I be the person they needed me to be— the refreshing alternative to the modern, narcissistic athlete—than to be myself, an imperfect human being with flaws just like everyone else."[144]

Of course, alongside the public failures of evangelical athletes and coaches to live up to their standards for marriage and sexuality came many apparent success stories: David Robinson, Reggie White, and A. C. Green, who finally got married at age thirty-eight in 2002. Numerous others saw their marriages strengthened by the support they received from sports ministries like PAO. But since the model for marriage and sexuality put forward by the Christian athlete movement was based on a complementarian and heterosexual framework, athletes or coaches who fell outside that framework were unlikely to find the same support.

In the 1980s, when opposition to gay and lesbian sexuality remained strong across American culture, the movement's views did not receive sustained outside criticism. In many ways, the Christian athlete subculture simply reflected popular American sentiment. According to a Gallup Poll in 1986, just thirty-two percent of Americans agreed that gay or lesbian relations between consenting adults should be legal. By 1999, however, that had risen to fifty percent, and it would continue to grow. Similarly, support for same-sex marriage, at just twenty-seven percent in 1996 when Gallup first asked the question, crossed the fifty percent threshold in 2011. Meanwhile, the percentage of the population affirming that gay and lesbian relations were morally acceptable went from forty percent in 2001 to over fifty-two percent in 2010 before soaring past seventy percent.[145]

As support for gay and lesbian sexuality and same-sex marriage rose at the turn of the twenty-first century, evangelical sports ministries faced frequent charges of bigotry and homophobia; this became the main threat to their continued access within big-time sports. Yet, as the primary organized Christian presence within sports, their ability to define the boundaries and set the terms for what counted as God's way for athletes and coaches remained strong.

* * *

As the twentieth century drew to a close, reporter Chris Dufresne offered a glimpse into the growth and development of the Christian athlete movement with a feature story in the *Los Angeles Times*. Published a few weeks after the 1999 Super Bowl, it was the latest entry in the genre of journalistic investigations into the movement, confirming that Christian athletes were here to stay. "The number of religious athletes," Dufresne wrote, "appears to be rising faster than a Roger Clemens fastball."[146]

Dufresne captured many of the trends that had developed since Deford announced the arrival of Sportianity. He wrote about the rise and influence of television and the resulting growth of public displays of religion. "You can't channel-surf these days," he wrote, without encountering an "interview in which a player thanks God for a punt, pass, putt, rebound or right cross." He noted, too, the other side of celebrity: the recent examples of hypocrisy by prominent Christian athletes, including Atlanta Falcons safety Eugene Robinson, who in 1998 had been arrested for soliciting a prostitute just hours after receiving the Bart Starr Award from AIA. And he referenced the increasing presence of

Pentecostal spirituality, with quotes from athletes attributing success on the field to God's supernatural intervention.

Dufresne also described the ongoing ministry of presence by the FCA and AIA, with representatives from both organizations detailing the ways they helped athletes manage stress, deal with pressure, and apply Christian values to their athletic experience. The behind-the-scenes work of these organizations ensured that a steady stream of Christian athletes and coaches shaped by evangelical religiosity would populate the sports world. And he pointed to the culture war implications of the movement, making note of Reggie White's recent comments to the Wisconsin state legislature, as well as the hostility between Christian athletes and the media.

There were two aspects of Dufresne's story, however, in which what went unstated was just as revealing as what was said. First, despite the growth of women's sports, all of the athletes featured by Dufresne were men. To the public, Sportianity remained primarily a men's movement, focusing first and foremost on the cultivation of Christian manhood with women's involvement a secondary concern. Second, the majority of the athletes profiled by Defresne were Black. Although Defresne did not mention these racial dynamics, it highlighted a key contradiction at the heart of Sportianity. Here was a movement led by predominantly white evangelical leaders and organizations with an affinity for the predominantly white politics of the Christian Right. Yet, many of its most prominent public spokespeople were Black Christian men.

The racial tensions of this reality did not go without comment or action in the 1980s and 1990s. Rather, efforts to resolve and respond to this contradiction offered one more front in the ongoing struggle to define how to do sports God's way.

8

Jesse Jackson Has Reason to Be Concerned

One year before Reggie White stepped in front of the Wisconsin state assembly and became the subject of national controversy, he stepped in front of a group of high school students in Knoxville, Tennessee, and caused a smaller firestorm. Fresh off his 1997 Super Bowl victory with the Green Bay Packers, White returned to his home state as a conquering hero. But in his remarks, delivered at a predominantly Black high school and published by the *Knoxville News-Sentinel*, he did not preach the standard inspirational message of hard work and discipline. Instead, he acknowledged the reality that many of the students in his audience lived: the fact that young Black men were often targeted by police and disproportionally sent to prison.

"There's a lot of focus on you all and a lot of that focus is on putting you in jail," White reportedly said. "That's why police harass a bunch of you guys, because they want you to snap." He went on to highlight the financial incentives at play, with a focus on "building more prisons instead of creating opportunities for you." And he sought to connect the Christian savior to the experiences of his audience, describing Jesus as a poor man who grew up in the ghetto and became "the ultimate gang leader who went out and got twelve thugs to follow him."[1]

In Green Bay, shocked white readers of the *Press-Gazette* responded with dismay. A police officer wrote in to complain that White "has judged me by the color of my uniform. How hypocritical." Another reader told White that the policing was justified—if anything it was not enough. "A much better case could be made that this group [Black men] is underpoliced," he wrote, criticizing the "ghetto culture" that led to "perpetual wallowing in the slop of victimhood." Still another blasted "the racist, anti-police, stupid quotes by Reggie White, the self-proclaimed Christian Minister of Defense," which have "completely destroyed any respect that I had for this man."[2]

In Knoxville, too, readers chimed in. Rocky Ramsey, pastor of Corryton Baptist Church, concluded that "White is obviously a very bitter and suspicious person." Another minister, Presbyterian Mark Knisley, defended the police, the "brave men and women" who "put their lives on the line." He wondered whether

The Spirit of the Game. Paul Emory Putz, Oxford University Press. © Oxford University Press 2024.
DOI: 10.1093/9780190091095.003.0009

White had been misquoted. "It is incumbent upon people of all faiths to work to-gether for the reconciliation of, not the polarization of, our city."[3]

There were a handful of people who wrote in to support White. However, the consensus, when viewed through the letters and editorials published in the *Press-Gazette* and *News-Sentinel*, was that the Christian football star had hurt rather than helped his cause.

White's remarks and the response of his white fans revealed a tension that had been simmering below the surface of the Christian athlete movement since the 1970s. While its white leaders saw their racially inclusive movement as evidence that racism was mostly a relic of the past, Black athletes were more likely to see racism as an ongoing problem in the present. While white leaders believed racism, if it did exist, boiled down to individual attitudes from a few extremists, Black athletes were more likely to see its manifestations in social structures including policing, housing, school systems, employment opportunities, and more.

From the 1970s until the 1990s, as the Christian athlete movement expanded throughout big-time sports, those racial differences remained mostly in the background. In the 1990s, however, they came to the forefront in a dramatic way. Black Christian athletes and a handful of white Christian allies began to make opposition to racism a central moral concern. In their efforts, carried out in the midst of a broader evangelical movement for racial reconciliation, they pushed against the boundaries of the predominantly white Christian athlete movement. Yet Black Christian athletes often discovered—as Reggie White did—that to discuss racism as a present and systemic problem risked being cast as polarizing and militant.

Race and Politics

To understand the racial divides within Sportianity, a good place to start is with a person who embodied the fusion of racial uplift and social activism within both the Black church tradition and Black muscular Christianity: the Reverend Jesse Jackson. A former college football player, Jackson played quarterback at North Carolina A&T in the early 1960s, the same years that the sit-in movement took root at the school. Like several other Black Christian activists, including Medgar Evers and John Hurst Adams, his experience with college sports helped to prepare him for leadership in the civil rights struggle.[4]

As Jackson jumped into the protest movement, he found inspiration in Martin Luther King Jr.'s model of leadership. Accordingly, after college he attended seminary, became a Baptist minister, and expanded his activist work by joining King within the Southern Christian Leadership Conference (SCLC). Jackson set up shop in Chicago, overseeing the SCLC's Operation Breadbasket from 1966 until 1971, before stepping out and creating his own organization, People United to Save Humanity (PUSH). As Jackson biographer Marshall Frady put it, PUSH combined the economic equality focus of Operation Breadbasket with "a more general social ministry" and "an interracial popular movement" aimed at extending Martin Luther King Jr.'s "perspectives into all reaches of the nation's life."[5]

Jackson had support from star athletes. In the 1970s both Jackie Robinson and NFL standout Gale Sayers served in leadership roles within PUSH, and baseball stars Hank Aaron and Reggie Jackson counted Jackson as a friend. Writing in his autobiography, published in 1972, Jackie Robinson praised Jackson and offered his endorsement. "I think he offers the most viable leadership for blacks and op-pressed minorities in America and also for the salvation of our national decency," Robinson declared.[6]

As a minister and a former college athlete, Jackson technically had the markers of a "Christian athlete" identity. Yet, like Robinson, Jackson remained outside of the Christian athlete movement. One reason for this was his associ-ation with theological liberalism. Jackson was no radical and he had evangel-ical leanings—some observers saw him as theologically conservative—but his openness to the idea that Christianity did not offer the exclusive path to God made him suspect to evangelicals.[7] Of course, middlebrow Protestant members of Sportianity, including John Wooden, had expressed similar ideas.[8] But they remained comfortably within the movement in part because they did not have two other traits associated with Jackson: his roots in the social justice wing of the Black church tradition and his political progressivism. While Jackson had a reputation for cultivating connections with celebrities and social elites, his mes-saging highlighted the marginalized and the oppressed.

Jackson's engagement with sports followed this pattern. He developed friendships with athletes, but he focused his public declarations on matters of injustice. In 1973 Operation PUSH hosted a conference centered on racial ine-quality in athletics. "Virtually the entire sports establishment in this country is dependent on Black athletic excellence for its very existence," Jackson said. And yet, he noted, Black people continued to be barred from leadership positions, ranging from those on the field of play (like the quarterback position) to those off the field, including general managers and athletic directors. The theme of racial disparity in sports leadership remained a consistent part of Jackson's work in the years ahead.[9]

Although Jackson had considerable clout in the 1970s, he built a truly na-tional political profile in the 1980s, launching presidential campaigns in the 1984 and 1988 Democratic primaries around what he called the "Rainbow Coalition." Jackson's political campaigns, occurring during the same years in which the Christian athlete movement was growing closer to the Republican

Party, furthered his distance from Sportianity while also offering a different vision for Christian political engagement. In contrast to the Christian Right, which believed that Christians had a special relationship with the United States that needed protection, Jackson made pluralism and diversity central tenets of his creed.[10] He presented his Rainbow Coalition as a multicultural vision for American society comprised of "the white, the Hispanic, the black, the Arab, the Jew, the woman, the native American, the small farmer, the businessperson, the environmentalist, the peace activist, the young, the old, the lesbian, the gay, and the disabled."[11]

As Jackson moved into the realm of presidential politics, he kept his eye on the sports world. In 1987 he organized several panels focused on the absence of Black leaders in front office positions and suggested that Black baseball players should boycott games on July 4 to protest their lack of executive opportunities. In the early 1990s, Jackson organized the Rainbow Commission for Fairness in Athletics, which spent the next few years bringing attention to racial disparities in major sports leagues and organizations.[12] Yet, Jackson's stature as a political leader of international significance meant that his investment in sports was sporadic compared with his broader ambitions and activities. He did not establish a sustained ministry of presence within the sports industry that could offer an alternative to Sportianity rooted in Black Christian institutions and networks.

What Jackson represented for the Christian athlete movement, then, was not so much a direct challenge for control as a window into the ways racial identity could lead to different moral and political priorities for Christian athletes who otherwise attended the same chapel services and Bible studies. While white evangelicals viewed Jackson with alarm and suspicion, among Black Americans he was widely admired and respected—even though many Black church members held more theologically and socially conservative positions than did Jackson.[13]

Jackson also exemplified the strong Black support for the Democratic Party and the sense among Black Americans that the Republican Party seemed uninterested in their concerns. As historian Leah Wright Rigueur notes, in the 1980s and 1990s Black affiliation with the Republican Party was never higher than fifteen percent, and Black support for a Republican presidential candidate never exceeded twelve percent. A study in the late 1980s found that eighty-three percent of Black people—and a remarkable fifty percent of Black Republicans—believed that the Republican party did not care about African Americans' problems.[14]

The differences extended beyond political affiliation, reaching into the heart of the narratives that white and Black Christians told about their place in American society. While the Christian Right framed the 1960s as an attack on America's foundations, many Black Americans saw the decade as a time when freedom and righteousness advanced. While the Christian Right saw Ronald Reagan's presidency as a blessing from God, an opportunity to recover America's traditional values, for many Black communities the Reagan years brought little benefit, with Black poverty rates remaining over thirty percent, nearly three times higher than the rate among white Americans, and a white backlash against government support for the poor that trafficked in stereotypes depicting Black people as lazy and dependent.[15]

To be sure, Jackson's experience with the Democratic Party showed that it was not a fully welcoming place for Black Christian leadership either. Party insiders worked to thwart Jackson's presidential aspirations in 1984 and 1988, and in 1992 eventual president Bill Clinton cultivated white voters by publicly humiliating Jackson at a Rainbow Coalition event.[16] Even though Jackson's religious identity was central to his influence—Black churches served as the base of support for Jackson when he launched his voter registration and presidential campaigns—many white Democratic leaders preferred to de-emphasize distinctly Christian language. They also weeded out socially conservative religious convictions, like opposition to abortion, as the culture wars took shape. In 1977 Jackson declared his opposition to abortion on the grounds that life "is really a gift from God" that people do not "have the right to take away." By 1988, Jackson followed Democratic leaders in supporting abortion rights.[17]

Yet, even if white progressive leaders within the Democratic Party were more suspicious of Christian rhetoric than white leaders in the Republican Party—and even if some Black Christians could overlap with conservative white Christians on social issues—most Black Christians felt that the Democratic Party at least listened to their concerns. The Christian Right may have viewed the GOP as "God's Own Party," but for African Americans, the racial group with the highest rates of church attendance, Bible reading, and prayer, the Democratic Party better represented their constellation of moral priorities.[18]

When Black Christian athletes became involved with Sportianity, then, they were, on average, coming from religious families and communities that voted for or were sympathetic to the Democratic Party, and they were entering a world in which the Republican Party was viewed as the only choice for true Christians. They were coming from communities that saw the continued effects of systemic racism in society, and they were entering a world in which those effects were generally denied or ignored. But they were also entering into a space that desperately wanted them to be involved. The logic was simple. Sports ministries, built on the foundation of celebrity endorsements, needed major sports stars. And increasingly in the 1980s, the biggest sports stars were African Americans: over seventy-five percent of players in the NBA, over fifty percent in the NFL, and eighteen percent in MLB, up from twelve percent in the 1960s (although this would decline in the 1990s while the rate of Latino players would soar).[19]

These demographic shifts carried over into the world of sports ministry. While only a handful of Black athletes had been involved with the Christian athlete movement in its early years, by the 1980s it seemed as if they were front and center. With Andre Thornton, Madeline Manning Mims, Vince Evans, Mike Singletary, Julius Erving, Reggie White, A. C. Green, Darrell Green, and David Robinson—among many others—Sportianity became one of the few spaces in the world of evangelicalism in which Black people had substantial involvement.

In public, at least, the infusion of Black athletes into the Christian athlete movement brought few tensions. This was in part because Black athletes in the 1980s, regardless of their faith perspective, generally preferred not to prioritize social activism. Television money was flowing into sports and contracts were soaring; corporate sponsors were showing a greater willingness to sign Black athletes, at least those deemed noncontroversial. As Howard Bryant notes, these were the years when the model of the apolitical, corporate-friendly Black athlete took hold, with O. J. Simpson and Michael Jordan leading the way.[20]

But the apparent lack of tension was also a matter of who controlled the narrative. The donors, grassroots supporters, and leaders of sports ministries still came primarily from white evangelical networks. They could choose what voices to promote, what causes to prioritize, and what parts of an athlete's testimony to publicize. Probe deeper behind the official publications and pronouncements of sports ministry organizations, and it is clear that even in the doldrums of sports-focused racial activism, Black Christians affiliated with Sportianity were willing to speak about racism in ways that challenged the individualistic, colorblind approach preferred by white evangelicals.

Consider the example of Cleveland Indians slugger Andre Thornton. The first baseman received national attention in 1977 when his wife and daughter died in a tragic car accident. His steadfast faith earned the admiration and respect of fans and sports insiders, and he became a prominent leader in both Baseball Chapel and Pro Athletes Outreach, as well as one of the most recognizable Christian athletes of the early 1980s.[21]

In addition to proclaiming his faith in Jesus, Thornton went on record with his views about racism. In 1980 when an anonymous baseball executive suggested that Black and Latino players were more likely to use drugs than white players, Thornton called him out for unfairly profiling athletes of color. The following year, Thornton wondered aloud why he and other Black players on the team "have not been promoted by the Indians like some of the other ballplayers." In 1987, he agreed with Jesse Jackson that racism persisted in MLB, particularly in its hiring practices. "Jesse Jackson has reason to be concerned. It's not just the teams. It's the whole administrative arena of baseball," he declared.[22]

Henry Soles, an African Methodist Episcopal (AME) minister and one of the few nonathlete Black leaders in Sportianity, expressed similar concerns about politics. Soles had entered sports ministry work in the 1970s, eventually founding Intersports Associates to facilitate his efforts. He focused on the Chicago area, working with the Bears, Cubs, and White Sox. But it was with the NBA's Chicago Bulls that he had his greatest influence, serving as the team's chaplain for three decades with the help of associate chaplain Scott Bradley, a Church of God in Christ minister.[23]

Writing in 1985, Soles discussed the frustration among Black Christians with the moral priorities of the Christian Right. "At present, blacks are waiting to see if white evangelicals will use some of their zeal to vigorously fight racism and stand with the black church on behalf of the poor and the oppressed," he wrote. "The black community views the Moral Majority, and similar right-wing religio-political pressure groups, as weak in their application of biblical principles to the needs of oppressed people, in general, and blacks in particular."[24]

Neither Soles nor Thornton was a progressive activist in the vein of Jesse Jackson. Both had positive relationships with white leaders within Sportianity and generally worked as bridge-builders to connect Black and white Christians. And yet, white leaders within the Christian athlete movement paid little attention to their race-related concerns and certainly did not prioritize or amplify them. The presence of Black athletes in sports ministry spaces was considered progress enough.

Into the City

If leaders in Sportianity were hesitant to speak directly about racial injustice in the 1980s, they did address racial dynamics in more coded ways. They recognized, for example, that while famous Black athletes may have been on the front pages of their magazines, ordinary Black people were far less present in their camps and retreats. Leaders also began to acknowledge one reason for this: their base came primarily from white suburban areas.

Prentice Gautt, associate commissioner of the Big 8 conference, sounded the alarm in 1985. Asked to share his perspective as part of *Sharing the Victory's* "Sports Conscience" series, he told the Fellowship of Christian Athletes (FCA) that their message was not reaching urban residents. Too many FCA leaders, he felt, were more interested in presenting an image of clean-cut suburban conformity. "Young people, today, in my opinion, are looking for someone who's real," he declared.[25]

Gautt did not directly mention race, but in American culture more broadly the language of "urban" or "inner-city" often served as code for "Black."[26] While Black Americans existed across the economic spectrum and in rural, suburban, and urban areas, they were disproportionally represented in high-poverty areas in cities.[27] For many white Americans, poor Blacks, living in cities where entrenched racism, deindustrialization, and corporate disinvestment had hallowed out economic opportunities, came to serve as a stereotype for Black people as a whole. Widely publicized stories and images of rising crime rates and drug use in urban Black communities in the 1970s and 1980s made the Black person living in the inner city a composite figure of either pity, fear, or scorn. "Notions of black criminality," historian Elizabeth Hinton writes, "justified both structural and everyday racism."[28]

This played out in policing practices. As the War on Crime, launched by Lyndon Johnson in the 1960s, transitioned into Ronald Reagan's War on Drugs, government funding poured into police and prison systems—and with it, heightened surveillance of poor Black communities. The era of mass incarceration that ensued made the United States the worldwide leader in prisons and prisoners, with African American men disproportionally jailed.[29]

Leaders in the Christian athlete movement enthusiastically backed the War on Drugs, although they usually focused their efforts on the moral suasion of the "Just Say No" campaign.[30] This low-hanging fruit also had support from some Black leaders concerned with drug use in their communities. Jesse Jackson himself, after the death of college basketball star Len Bias from a cocaine overdose in 1986, urged Black communities and the federal government to do more in the battle against drug abuse.[31] Yet Jackson and other Black leaders did not focus simply on moral suasion and punitive policing. They also sought to address police brutality, economic inequality, and other forms of structural racism that created the conditions in which drug use and abuse often grew. Evangelical sports ministries, however, showed little interest in the specific challenges facing urban Black communities and had little to offer beyond antidrug campaigns.[32]

Despite this lack of organized support, some Black Christian athletes took matters into their own hands, attempting to link sports ministry to Black communities and neighborhoods. A prime example came in 1978 with the founding of Christian Family Outreach (CFO). Led by pioneering Black evangelical Howard Jones and his two famous sons-in-law, MLB players Andre Thornton and Pat Kelly, CFO aimed to reach inner-city youth and families in Baltimore and Cleveland with retreats, rallies, and events. It was literally a family operation: Thornton served as president, Jones as vice president, and Kelly as executive director.[33]

Another form of urban engagement came from former Black Christian athletes who entered the ministry after their playing days. Herb Lusk, the "praying tailback" with the Philadelphia Eagles, became a Baptist minister and took charge of Greater Exodus Baptist Church in Philadelphia in 1982, where he worked tirelessly to minister to his congregants and community. "The doorbell never stops ringing," he said in 1987. "People need food, they need clothing. Babies need milk. Where can they turn if not the church?" To help meet those needs, Lusk drew on his pro sports connections, with Reggie White (then with Philadelphia) and other Eagles players frequently attending services and participating in community outreach.[34]

The efforts of Lusk in Philadelphia, Kelly in Baltimore, and Thornton in Cleveland were mostly local in orientation, and they did not have the official endorsement of the major evangelical sports ministries. In Dallas, however, modest attempts to make urban ministry a priority for white evangelicals eventually reached a national audience through the influence of pastor Tony Evans, with sports ministry a key part of the process.

As the first Black student to receive a doctoral degree from Dallas Theological Seminary (DTS), a school closely associated with the fundamentalist/ neoevangelical movement, Evans had unique insight into white evangelical networks and relationships. In 1976 he planted Oak Cliff Bible Fellowship, eventually growing the congregation into the largest predominantly Black church in the Dallas area.[35] Meanwhile, his evangelical credentials helped him build local sports connections with Dallas Cowboys coach Tom Landry and Dallas Mavericks executive Norm Sonju. By the early 1980s he had been tabbed to serve as a chaplain for both teams. It helped that Evans had a background in sports and carried himself with the confidence of a standout athlete. "In football he was always the quarterback," Evans's father later explained. "He's a born leader, and lots of people listen to him."[36]

After six years of local ministry in Dallas, Evans expanded his work in 1982 with a program for national outreach aimed at predominantly Black communities. The name, Urban Alternative, codified Evans's vision. It reflected his belief that the church needed to offer a comprehensive vision for life that stood in contrast to the non-Christian world. Only then could the church be a force of renewal for the Black community.

In contrast to Jesse Jackson and other leaders from the social justice wing of the Black church tradition, who saw the mobilization of government resources to address racial and economic injustice as a matter of Christian concern, Evans argued that there was nothing distinctly Christian about this sort of social and political activism. Instead, he suggested, Christians should focus on building up the local church through evangelism and discipleship. From there, acts of mercy and justice could flow out into the community. While Evans recognized the need for social action, he believed this was best done at a local level through the work of the church, as a byproduct of a new life in Christ and as a "divine alternative" for the world to see.[37]

Evans applied this church-centered logic to the problem of racism. "It is obvious that American society has not successfully dealt with the problems of racism and prejudice," he wrote in 1991. The church could be the solution, he continued, if pastors would preach against racism from the pulpit; if church members would build interracial friendships; and if churches across the racial divide would work together on issues of community concern.[38]

With a localized vision for Christian social engagement that aligned with the conservative political orientation of white evangelicals, Evans found a ready audience and quickly expanded Urban Alternative's reach. "For the longest time I've wanted to do something for the black community," Norm Sonju gushed in an interview about Evans. "Now we can have an impact. Now we have a plan and direction."[39] Along with Landry and Sonju, Mavericks owner Don Carter and former Cowboys Roger Staubach and Bob Breunig served in advisory roles with Urban Alternative. Evans's support reached beyond Dallas, too. In 1986 Jerry Falwell's journal, The Fundamentalist, wrote a fawning profile of his work. James Dobson's Focus on the Family followed suit, recruiting Evans as the "black leader who would join forces with us—or us with him—in reaching out to inner city families."[40]

Support from white evangelical resources and media networks helped Evans expand his national ministry throughout the 1980s. At the same time, his church remained rooted in Dallas's Black community, and his success derived from the way he spoke to and ministered to the needs of the predominantly Black congregation that attended Oak Cliff every Sunday. Evans may have represented a new cadre of Black ministry leaders shaped by white evangelical institutions—future Senator Raphael Warnock, writing in The Divided Mind of the Black Church (2014), saw him as an example of "biblical fundamentalism" and its "rising influence within the culture of the black church."[41] But Evans also represented a longstanding Black Christian conservative tradition that focused on racial uplift and local community engagement while emphasizing evangelical doctrine.[42]

Evans also differed from white evangelicals in the seriousness with which he engaged with more progressive Black viewpoints. His doctoral dissertation offered a critical analysis of theologian James Cone, whose Black Theology and Black Power (1969) and A Black Theology of Liberation (1970) provided the foundation for the emergence and development of Black liberation theology.[43] Evans acknowledged that Cone offered important correctives to the American church. Black theology, he wrote, "justifiably called attention to a concern that is close to the heart of God," and it had much to teach evangelicals about the ways "racism and the 'American Way' has divided Christianity along racial lines." Yet Evans concluded that Black theology too often centered the situational experience of Black people rather than transcendent biblical revelation, thus running the risk of becoming "a sort of black social humanism with a theological label."[44]

This sort of perspective struck Raphael Warnock as a betrayal of "the black church's distinctive legacy and peculiar vocation as the conscience of the

American churches." Still, Warnock admitted that Black liberation theology seemed to have a stronger foothold in the halls of academia than in the pulpits of Black churches. Evans's perspective, Warnock wrote, may have been influenced by white evangelicalism, but it was "not much different from that of many pastors in the mainline black denominations."[45]

As Evans built connections with white evangelicals from his home base in Dallas, the FCA attempted to bring its ministry from the suburbs into the city, with Dallas as a test site.[46] FCA leaders tapped a staffer named Carey Casey for the task. Born and raised in small-town Salem, Virginia, Casey first got involved in the FCA as a high school athlete in the early 1970s, continuing his FCA af- filiation when he played football for the University of North Carolina. After completing his undergraduate work, he enrolled in seminary before taking the Dallas position in 1983. Casey moved to the FCA's national office in Kansas City in 1988 to serve as its Director of Urban Ministry, a position created by new FCA president Dick Abel and aimed at strengthening the FCA's work among predominantly Black communities in urban environments. It was the most im- portant leadership position ever given to a Black man in the Christian athlete movement.[47]

Casey, for his part, was willing to take on the challenge. "I've always wanted to do something of significance to help bridge the racial gap," Casey explained. And the FCA had a unique opportunity, because "sports, through Jesus Christ, are common ground."[48] Despite Casey's optimistic rhetoric, he also hinted at the depths of the challenge he faced. As a starting point, he needed to convince the predominantly white FCA to care about and invest in predominantly Black urban communities. At the same time, he needed to establish both his and the FCA's credibility with skeptical Black communities. "People say 'Where ya'll been the last 35 years? Who are you, working for the white man?'" he told one reporter in 1989. But he insisted that the FCA had his back. "I am not a token. I have the freedom to do what I need to do. Our commitment is for all staffers, white and black, to go into the urban areas."[49]

In January 1991 the FCA promoted Casey's work with a special "Urban Issue" of *Sharing the Victory.* In many ways it encapsulated the approach that had devel- oped over the course of the 1980s within the Christian athlete movement. On the one hand, there was a heavy dose of white paternalism. Editor John Dodderidge painted a picture of despondency in the "urban wastelands," while FCA pres- ident Dick Abel warned that in American culture there was "no battle zone as great as the urban area." None of the white FCA leaders specifically mentioned racism, policing, or economic conditions as a cause for urban problems; instead, they highlighted "drugs and alcohol, homelessness, a sense of being unloved, un- wanted" as issues that required an individual relationship with Jesus Christ and a "color-blind, nonpartisan, nondenominational" strategy.[50]

At the same time, the special issue showed that interracial relationships developed through sports had the potential to influence white leaders. "I have a burning zeal in my heart to make a difference in the area of urban ministry," Abel declared. The significance of Dallas hovered over the magazine issue as well, showcasing a specific community in which the FCA had made an intentional effort to connect with Black leaders. Along with an interview with Carey Casey, two other stories featured examples of Dallas-based Black athletes or coaches, and the issue also featured an article penned by Tony Evans.

If the 1991 "Urban Issue" summarized strategies that had developed during the 1980s, with a focus on identifying and collaborating with conservative Black Christian leaders, it also came at a time of transition. Later that year Rodney King would be brutally beaten by Los Angeles police; a video camera captured the scene, allowing the world to see policing practices that Black people had been calling out for decades. After the acquittal of the police officers in 1992, riots broke out in the streets of Los Angeles. In 1991, too, white supremacist former Ku Klux Klan leader David Duke ran for governor in Louisiana. Although he lost his bid, he won fifty-five percent of the white vote. Other events in the 1990s—from the O. J. Simpson trial, to the Million Man March, to the arson of Black churches in the South, to debates and controversy over multiculturalism and affirmative action—made racism a topic of national conversation in a way it had not been since the 1960s.

In response to these developments, some white Christians doubled down on racial conservatism, refusing to consider racism as a persistent problem in American society. But another response came from an evangelical racial reconciliation movement emerging as a national force, making waves for the willingness of its white advocates to speak about racism as a problem in the present. Suddenly it was not just Jesse Jackson and Black church leaders pointing out the continued prevalence of racism in American society; a growing number of white evangelicals, including several prominent figures in sports, agreed with the premise, if not always with the solutions.

Racial Reconciliation and Sports

The evangelical racial reconciliation movement of the 1990s had its roots in the work of Black evangelical leaders in the 1960s. Tom Skinner, a leader in PAO and Baseball Chapel in the 1970s, was an early advocate from his base in New York City. E. V. Hill, a Black Baptist pastor closely connected with Bill Bright and Campus Crusade, developed his own conservative approach through his leadership of Mount Zion Missionary Baptist Church in Los Angeles. Another key architect was John Perkins. From his ministry home in Jackson, Mississippi,

Perkins developed a holistic strategy for reconciliation that included attention to economic and social conditions and identification with the poor and marginalized. Inspired in part by Jesse Jackson's Operation PUSH in Chicago, Perkins's program emphasized the "three Rs" of relocation, reconciliation, and redistribution.[51]

Throughout the 1980s Perkins worked tirelessly in evangelical spaces to advance his vision of reconciliation and community development. He eventually captured the attention of the key leader in the Christian athlete movement doing that work, Carey Casey. After spending nearly a decade with the FCA seeking to build bridges between Black and white people, Casey felt called to do more, to follow the second "R" in Perkins's model: relocation. So, in 1992 he left his job at the FCA's national headquarters (he remained involved with the organization) and moved to a neighborhood in Chicago's West Side, where he became senior pastor of Lawndale Community Church, a predominantly Black congregation founded in 1978 by a white teacher and football coach named Wayne Gordon.[52]

Casey's arrival brought national attention to Lawndale. With its tutoring services, medical clinic, and thrift store, Lawndale received praise from *Christianity Today*, John Perkins, and others as a model for interracial Christian ministry and holistic community development. Casey's move showed, too, the potential for sports ministries to foster greater engagement in addressing the economic challenges faced by predominantly Black urban communities.[53]

Another sign of this potential came from Joe Ehrmann, a former defensive lineman with the Baltimore Colts. A white evangelical, Ehrmann became a Christian in 1978 after attending a team Bible study led by Colts chaplain Larry Moody. In the years ahead, as he finished his career, Ehrmann completed seminary and became an ordained Presbyterian minister. In 1986, a year after his playing days ended, he launched The Door, a ministry focused on meeting the needs and challenges of inner-city Baltimore. Described in one newspaper article as an organization "that blends a conservative biblical faith with social activism," Ehrmann connected The Door with his experience in football. "You could bring in 45 men, black and white, rich and poor, from every background, and have them totally come together for one purpose," Ehrmann said. "That's the goal of this ministry, to see all of society come together, focusing on an urban agenda."[54]

Over the next two decades Ehrmann worked with Baltimore church leaders to connect white and Black Christians and to address "issues of poverty and systemic racism and family disintegration."[55] His willingness to name racism as a systemic issue made him stand out among white evangelicals, many of whom preferred to view it as a matter of the heart. Even so, Ehrmann's work ultimately focused on relationships across racial and cultural divides. He remained connected to Sportianity, too, taking on the role of chaplain to the Baltimore Ravens when the team came to the city in 1996.[56]

While Ehrmann received some attention for his work, with scholars Michael Emerson and Christian Smith citing him as an important voice for racial reconciliation in their groundbreaking book *Divided by Faith*, the white Christian most closely associated with racial reconciliation in the 1990s was Colorado football coach Bill McCartney, the founder of Promise Keepers (PK). Writing in his 1990 autobiography, the same year he launched PK, McCartney identified racism as an issue "that demands my attention." Citing Bill Russell and Harry Edwards, two Black leaders from the heyday of 1960s activism, he noted that they helped him see the struggles his Black players faced as they entered into predominantly white settings like the University of Colorado. "There are people in the community who see the black or minority athlete as an invasive force," McCartney wrote.[57]

When McCartney founded PK, he brought that same burden with him. Horrified by the almost entirely white demographics of his early rallies—it "sent a chill down my spine"—McCartney vowed to build a racially inclusive movement that addressed racism head on. Along with insisting that racial reconciliation be included as one of the seven principles of his organization, he urged white Christians to "seek forgiveness for the sins of our fathers and for the same racial oppression that continues to this day." He also built a racially diverse board of directors and invited racially diverse speakers to address the men congregating in football stadiums across the country. For McCartney, who embraced the charismatic movement, the stakes were high: only if Christians repented of racism and took steps to repair the harm, he believed, would God bring revival to American churches.[58]

By simply acknowledging the continued reality of racism in American society and encouraging white men to recognize and repent of it, he took a step beyond the colorblind, urban-focused interracial work that the FCA engaged with in the 1980s. To Henry Soles, the AME minister and Chicago Bulls chaplain, it represented a meaningful and important change. Soles described attending a PK event in Chicago where white attendees were urged to recognize the ways they had benefited from racism. "It was real—I sense a real sense of reconciliation now," Soles said. "And it's something that needed to be highlighted."[59]

Like Soles, many prominent Black men involved with PK had connections with evangelical sports ministries: Ken Hutcherson, a former NFL player and PAO supporter who led a multiracial congregation in Seattle; Crawford Loritts, a Campus Crusade staff member who often worked with AIA; Tony Evans; Carey Casey. Athletes like Mike Singletary and Reggie White spoke on behalf of PK as well.[60] PK could draw on this more diverse set of speakers in part because of its roots in sports ministry and in part because its conservative approach to

Christian manhood had considerable overlap with the concerns of conservative Black Christian leaders.[61] With common ground around which white and Black men could unite, PK became one of the most public and prominent examples of the racial reconciliation movement.[62]

The reconciliation that PK promoted reached into Republican politics as well. In the 1990s, former New York congressman Jack Kemp, a Buffalo Bills quarterback and FCA member in the 1960s, and Oklahoma congressman J. C. Watts, a University of Oklahoma quarterback and FCA member in the late 1970s, became leading Republican advocates for a more racially inclusive party. In 1997, at the height of PK's influence, the two men wrote an editorial for the *Washington Post* connecting the idea of racial reconciliation with conservative economic policies. While they argued that "real reconciliation" takes place "person to person, one heart at a time," they also said that policies needed to be enacted to address the "still-present barriers to African Americans and other minorities." For Kemp and Watts, drawing on a long-standing tradition of Black capitalism as well as supply-side Reaganomics, expansion of business opportunities through "access to capital" was the solution.[63]

Kemp and Watts offered a more inclusive vision for the Republican Party, serving as harbingers of a "compassionate conservatism" that sought to pay greater attention to the problems of racism and to Black concerns. Yet they also exemplified the limits of evangelical racial reconciliation. When compared with the broader landscape of American Christianity, the movement remained bound to a conservative orientation, working with Black evangelicals like Tony Evans and with GOP politicians but not building strong connections with more progressive Black Christians.

Even that modest work proved challenging. Kemp and Watts experienced frequent frustration and setbacks in their attempts to broaden the Republican tent.[64] Similarly, McCartney's focus on racism as a present problem often alienated the white rank and file of the movement, who tended to downplay that aspect of the ministry. Writing in 1997, McCartney noted the "pressure to de-emphasize or soften the racial message" and reported that nearly forty percent of the attendees at PK's 1996 conference "reacted negatively to the reconciliation theme."[65]

At the same time, despite McCartney's emphasis on overcoming racial divides, he ultimately viewed racism as an individual spiritual problem in need of an individual spiritual cure. "Relationships are the only thing that truly 'work' in repairing the division in the church," McCartney noted.[66] To be sure, for McCartney relationships were not the end goal, but rather a starting point for Christians to work together to enact justice in society. In his 2003 book *Blind Spots*, he urged Christians to uphold both "personal righteousness" and "public justice" as equally important.[67] But while McCartney believed relationships could lead to action for change, for many white evangelicals interracial relationships functioned as the final goal and finish line—the evidence that racism had been vanquished. As a result, historian Jesse Curtis explains, the evangelical racial reconciliation movement ended up "less a turning point and more an appropriation" in which addressing racism moved into the realm of "consciousness and emotion" instead of the material conditions of a society shaped by racism.[68]

John Hurst Adams, an AME bishop in South Carolina and a representative of Black muscular Christianity—he had played sports in college before developing into a church leader and civil rights activist—had this in mind when he shared his perspective on the limitations of PK. It reached Black evangelicals, he noted, but was barely noticed within his denomination or among many others connected to the historic Black church tradition. "I don't think there can be any sense of reconciliation without a sense of justice, and they skip the justice part," he argued. "They want to ignore history and current conditions and leap over that into some sort of wonderful reconciliation, but what African-Americans want is a just society."[69]

For all the ways that evangelical sports ministries helped to support the rise of the racial reconciliation movement in the 1990s, limitations apparent since the 1960s remained. The presence of racism could be acknowledged, but the remedy rarely extended beyond a call for person-by-person change, fostered through the avenue of sports or a shared religious identity. It focused primarily on individual heart attitudes and interracial friendship, rather than the structural and redistributive elements of reconciliation championed by John Perkins and other Black Christian leaders. It could lead conservative Republicans to project a more inclusive tone, but it generally ignored the policies and ideas championed by Black Christian leaders outside of evangelical networks.

A sermon delivered by John MacArthur in 1992 highlighted the depth of these limits. As one of Ralph Drollinger's mentors, MacArthur had developed into a go-to Bible guru within some circles of the Christian athlete movement—this included writing a regular column for Second Look/Sports Spectrum in the late 1980s and winning the support of several AIA and FCA staffers.[70] MacArthur also represented the possibility for change in racial perspectives. A student at the fiercely segregationist and fundamentalist Bob Jones University in the 1950s, in the late 1960s MacArthur collaborated with John Perkins on interracial evangelistic events in Mississippi. "For a black man and a white man to share Christ together in Mississippi was a mighty witness to the gospel's power," Perkins would later write.[71]

On May 3, 1992, however, just days after Los Angeles erupted in flames following the acquittal of the police officers who beat Rodney King, MacArthur took the pulpit at his Grace Community Church in Los Angeles to deliver a sermon titled "The Los Angeles Riots: A Biblical Perspective." His sermon fiercely repudiated attempts to address systemic racism and inequality, arguing that sin was solely a problem of the individual heart. He blasted Black and mainline church leaders—"these reverends with no churches, and these churches with no gospel"—for trying to focus on educational and economic causes to social problems. He also took aim at a Black athlete, Muhammad Ali. "This tragic man did more to legitimize selfishness and legitimize pride than any other person in American history, maybe in the history of the world," he intoned. And (citing Tony Evans) he blamed the sexual revolution of the 1960s and rap music for promoting sexual promiscuity, thereby destroying Black families.

While MacArthur found plenty to criticize in modern culture, there was one institution he fiercely defended: the police department. Police, he said, were agents of law and order who had been unfairly maligned in a "concerted effort" by media and activists. Not only that, police were "ministers of God," and Christians had a duty to submit to their authority. Opposing police was opposing "almighty, holy God."[72]

MacArthur's support for police was standard fare among white evangelicals, drawing on biblical interpretations that had been popular since the 1960s, when the War on Crime began. Like other evangelical advocates of law and order, MacArthur used the Bible to sanctify what the majority of white Americans already took for granted about the role police played in maintaining the status quo. There may have been rhetorical flourishes in MacArthur's passion for the police, but many white evangelicals would not have known that serious Christians could land with starkly different conclusions about the matter.[73]

Yet, different conclusions were indeed possible. Standing in contrast to MacArthur's advocacy of law and order was another minister connected to the Christian athlete movement: Chicago Bulls associate chaplain Scott Bradley. A pastor with the Church of God in Christ, Bradley saw the Rodney King beating, trial, and riots as evidence of racist systems and structures that continued to plague American society. "When Rodney King was beaten mercilessly by white policemen in view of all the world, and the policemen were found not guilty by an all-white jury, this proved that society is still behind the times," he wrote in *The Black Man: Cursed or Blessed?* (1993).[74]

Bradley also called out the hypocrisy of the "War on Drugs" campaign and a criminal justice system that imprisoned Black people at disproportionally higher rates than white people. Where MacArthur saw immoral individual choices as the cause of the supposed breakdown in Black families, Bradley noted the effect of racialized policing practices and economic inequality. "The American system is set up to bring [Black men] down and put them away," he wrote. Instead of a Jesus who upheld the status quo, Bradley argued that "the biggest trouble maker who ever lived was our Lord and Savior Jesus Christ. . . . He came to break down the barriers. He came to set the captives free."[75]

Bradley extended his analysis to the sports world. Drawing on his intimate understanding of the NBA, he discussed the ways that racial inequality persisted in big-time athletics. Black athletes could make plenty of money, he admitted, but this did not eliminate exploitation. Instead, white owners and executives expected Black athletes to put their bodies on the line while giving them few opportunities to move into leadership positions when their careers ended. Meanwhile, fans expected Black athletes to be grateful for their personal fame and fortune. "The Black athlete," Bradley wrote, "is not to speak out on certain issues or else he is discredited and tabbed by the media as 'outspoken.'"[76]

Bradley's viewpoints barely made a ripple in the Christian athlete movement, in part because they were never promoted. In a *Sports Spectrum* article published in 1993, following the publication of Bradley's book, the magazine profiled Bradley's work with the Chicago Bulls and told the story of Bradley's nationally televised prayer immediately following the 1991 NBA finals. There was no mention of Bradley's book, his views on racial inequality, or the existence of any racial tensions in American society at all. Black Christians like Bradley could be included, but white evangelical leaders of the movement would determine what was prioritized and promoted.[77]

Tom Skinner, well acquainted with Sportianity from his time as a sports chaplain, recognized this. Speaking to a reporter in 1991, he explained what he had seen from his decades of work in white Christian spaces. "When integration occurred, the black leaders of the black community integrated into the white community. But they were never allowed to hold the same positions of leadership and power that they held in the black community," Skinner said. "Integration has always been on white people's terms. It is black folks integrating into white churches, white schools, and white neighborhoods. It is never whites attending black colleges, joining black churches, and moving into black neighborhoods, except to move blacks out."[78]

Race and Ministry in Professional Sports

As Black Christian athletes navigated an integration "on white people's terms" in the midst of the racial tension of the 1990s, the context of the sports leagues in which they operated shaped their possible responses. In college sports, the activism of the 1960s was a distant memory. Athletes usually had little say, with coaches holding the authority—and those coaches were usually white. Division I football programs hired just three Black head coaches between 1981 and 1993, even though more than fifty percent of the players were Black. Some white coaches, like Bill McCartney, expressed a sincere concern for the challenges faced by Black athletes at predominantly white campuses. But in general, at the highest levels of college sport, Black athletes participated in a system led primarily by white coaches, administrators, and sports ministry staff.[79]

In pro sports a similar disparity between leadership and players existed, but, depending on the league, with greater room for athlete autonomy. In the NBA, Black players had the greatest level of influence. The league had moved from a fifty-fifty split between white and Black players in the 1960s to one in which Black players comprised over seventy percent of league rosters by the 1970s. White resentment from fans simmered, while stories of drug use among high-profile players tapped into racist stereotypes about Black cultural pathology. Historian Theresa Runstedtler has shown that the media exaggerated and distorted this narrative, and yet it carried explanatory power for many white leaders.[80] "Our problem," NBA commissioner David Stern said in 1984, "was that sponsors were flocking out of the NBA because it was perceived as a bunch of high-salaried, drug-sniffing black guys."[81]

Within this cultural milieu the Christian athlete movement worked to extend its influence into pro basketball. In the late 1970s, individual chaplains started team services in Houston (John Tolson), Washington (Joel Freeman), Chicago (Henry Soles), and Boston (Bill Alexson). In 1977, too, forward Bobby Jones attended a PAO conference and returned determined to bring something similar into the NBA. When he joined the Philadelphia 76ers in 1978, he collaborated with the team's general manager, Pat Williams, to launch a pre-game chapel system for the team.[82] In Dallas, meanwhile, as we saw last chapter, Don Carter and Norm Sonu landed an expansion franchise in 1980 that they hoped could become a bastion of evangelical Christianity within the league.

To organize this growing evangelical presence, Sonju, Williams, and Phoenix Suns executive Jerry Colangelo worked with others to form a new organization, Pro Basketball Fellowship (PBF). Following the model of PAO and Baseball Chapel, PBF sought to oversee the league's pre-game chapel services, turning them into a feeder system for team Bible studies and post-season training conferences.[83]

Along with its support from high-level NBA executives, PBF benefited from the involvement of Julius Erving. The star forward known as "Doctor J" attended the first Philadelphia chapel meeting organized by Bobby Jones in 1978 and participated in the Christian athlete movement over the next decade.[84] Erving's star power was essential, but his racial identity mattered, too. PBF leaders recognized their need to get Black leaders involved, and they recruited several Black pastors and chaplains, including Tony Evans in Dallas and Henry Soles in Chicago, to provide leadership and guidance.[85] Still, even if PBF was more racially diverse than other sports ministry organizations, its overall leadership and networks remained under white authority. Claude Terry, a retired white player, provided operational leadership for PBF in the 1980s and 1990s, with white executives Williams, Sonju, and Colangelo continuing to help support the organization behind the scenes.[86]

With white evangelicals functioning as the gatekeepers for religious leadership within the NBA, cultural divides could limit the effectiveness of their ministry. Former AIA basketball player Ralph Drollinger, who came to the Dallas Mavericks in 1980 to support Sonju's mission of extending evangelical ministry throughout the league, ended up embittered by his experience. After his six-game career ended, he criticized the league's culture, drawing on coded racial stereotypes. "There's just a lot of drugs, kind of a bad image. I think the thing that bothered me most was the individualism at that level," he complained. "Unless they make it a team sport once again, it'll continue to go down and down."[87]

The rise of hip hop music and its connection with urban Black culture and a new generation of NBA stars in the 1990s also vexed evangelical leaders. At best, they might support efforts to use rap as a tool for evangelism and moral uplift, as with A. C. Green and his abstinence anthem, "It Ain't Worth It." More often, they saw rap music as a negative influence that reflected the supposed cultural pathologies of Black urban communities, as John MacArthur had implied in his 1992 sermon. During their time leading the Mavericks from 1980 until 1996, Sonju and Carter did not allow rap music at the arena.[88] A sense of paternalism also seemed to be the impetus for Sonju's policy, instituted in 1980, requiring Mavericks players to stand in formation and at attention during the playing of "God Bless America" before each Mavericks game. His reasoning, he later explained, was that he wanted to protect the team's Black players from the potentially racist perceptions of Dallas's white fans.[89]

The fact that the Christian athlete movement never achieved the same level of depth and commitment in the NBA as it did in the NFL and MLB is telling, and undoubtedly shaped, at least in part, by the racial dynamics and disconnect between a predominantly Black league and a predominantly white sports ministry network. While pregame chapels and team chaplains became a staple of NBA life, the Bible studies and off-season training conferences that formed the heart of the evangelical subculture in baseball and football had a limited reach in the NBA.

This ambivalence contrasted sharply with baseball. There, Baseball Chapel was entrenched, buttressed by the official approval of the commissioner's office. By the 1980s Baseball Chapel oversaw a system of volunteer chaplains who had been placed with every major and minor league team—all of whom signed a document affirming Baseball Chapel's evangelical doctrinal statement. In this way, Baseball Chapel exerted more centralized control over religious access to

sports teams than any other sports ministry organization in any other professional league.[90]

On top of that, the racial demographics of baseball were different, with white
players still in the majority, comprising nearly two-thirds of the league into the
1990s. American-born Black players never reached more than twenty percent of
league roster spots and began a slow and steady decline in numbers in the 1990s.
The percentage of Latino layers, however, grew rapidly. After hovering around
12 percent for much of the 1980s, their proportion of league rosters doubled by
2000, hitting nearly 25 percent.[91] The racial demographics of the league did not
translate to Baseball Chapel. A 1992 book of testimonials by Christian baseball
players, written by Sports Spectrum's Dave Brannon, provided a snapshot of the
Christian athlete movement in baseball. Written with the support of Baseball
Chapel, it featured twenty-nine profiles: twenty-five white men, four Black men,
and no Latino men.[92]

Recognizing this disparity, Baseball Chapel leaders in the 1990s focused their
attention less on African American concerns and more on taking steps to reach
the influx of Latino players—many of whom were Spanish-speaking Catholics.
In decades past, only a handful of Latino players had joined the Christian athlete
movement. Felipe Alou—who converted from Catholicism to evangelicalism
when a friend from the Dominican Republic gave him a Spanish Bible—served
as a lonely trailblazer in that regard.[93] By the start of the 2000s, however, Baseball
Chapel began incorporating Spanish-speaking chaplains and recruiting Latino
pastors into its ranks. A new group of evangelical Latino players slowly emerged,
including Mariano Rivera, Tony Fernández, Carlos Beltrán, and Albert Pujols,
helping to expand the racial diversity of the Christian athlete movement in baseball even as the number of African Americans dwindled.[94]

In the NFL, meanwhile, the racial dynamics of the 1980s and 1990s began
to resemble those of the NBA, with a predominantly white Christian network
providing chaplains and serving in a gatekeeping role for the spiritual services
provided to a majority-Black league. There were differences, of course. In football, evangelical sports ministries had already established a strong foothold by
the 1980s. So, too, the rhythms of the NFL calendar were far more conducive to
building a stable religious ecosystem: one game a week, regular weekly practices,
limited travel, and a lengthier off-season. Yet the racial disparity between the
players and the sports ministries serving them became more conspicuous in
the 1990s. AIA, for example, had only one Black chaplain out of sixteen staffers
serving in the league.[95]

For Black Christians in the NFL seeking to foster a greater sense of solidarity
and racial advancement, there were at least three basic strategies. One model can
be found in the example of Tony Dungy. Born and raised in a middle-class environment in a midsized Michigan town, Dungy went on to star as a quarterback

for the University of Minnesota. Playing the position in the NFL was not an option when he graduated in 1976, because most coaches and general managers considered Black players less capable of handling demanding leadership roles. After being drafted by the Pittsburgh Steelers, Dungy switched to defensive back, where he spent three seasons primarily in a reserve role.[96]

While Dungy's time as a player in Pittsburgh did not last, it helped to set the stage for his lifelong involvement with the Christian athlete movement. He developed a friendship with team chaplain and AIA staff member Hollis Haff, as well as with a cohort of players including Larry Brown, Jon Kolb, Donnie Shell, and John Stallworth—men who "worked hard to put God first," as Dungy put it. Although Dungy was already a Christian, attending Bible study with the Steelers players deepened and transformed his faith. "I had never fully engaged God and let Him direct my life moment by moment until I saw those guys doing it," he explained in his autobiography.[97]

The language of "moment by moment" direction was a hallmark of Keswick spirituality. In that sense, Dungy was simply like hundreds of other pro athletes who found meaning and spiritual strength through AIA and PAO. Yet the thoroughness with which Dungy embraced his faith commitments set him apart. So did his career path. Soon after his playing career ended in 1980, he accepted a position as a defensive backs coach with the Minnesota Vikings. From there Dungy began a slow climb up the coaching ranks, eventually landing a head coaching role with the Tampa Bay Buccaneers in 1996. At the time he was just the fifth Black head coach in NFL history. Eleven years later, with the Indianapolis Colts, he became the first Black head coach to win a Super Bowl (defeating another Black head coach, Lovie Smith of the Chicago Bears). Through it all, Dungy maintained a strong presence within the evangelical subculture of the NFL, particularly among AIA and its chaplains.[98]

Dungy's support for and involvement with the Christian athlete movement came alongside the struggles and challenges he faced as a Black leader in the NFL. Denied the opportunity to play quarterback and overlooked for head coaching jobs, Dungy personally experienced injustice, and he spoke openly about the pain of those events. Yet his response focused less on prophetic calls for reform and instead on taking on a mediating role, a strategy that had been pioneered by early Black leaders in the Christian athlete movement, men like Dan Towler and Prentice Gautt, who saw their careers through a narrative of gradual racial progress.[99]

At the same time, Dungy worked quietly in his own way to encourage and nurture Black leadership within predominantly white spaces. He developed strong friendships with fellow Black head coaches like Lovie Smith, Denny Green, and Herm Edwards, and he made it a point to hire at least one Black assistant coach when putting together a staff. After winning the Super Bowl in

2007 he connected his historic achievement with "those who had gone before me in other walks of life" and who "paved the way for me and for those who will come after me."[100]

If Dungy represented attempts to gradually create opportunities for Black people in predominantly white spaces, another model for Black support came from standout cornerback Aeneas Williams, who played for the Arizona Cardinals from 1991 until 2000. At first glance, Williams might not seem much different from Dungy. Both held to conservative viewpoints on the Bible, marriage, and sexuality. Both generally preferred not to rock the boat when it came to organized protest against racial injustice. And yet, there was one key difference: Williams adopted his views within an almost entirely Black context, with little involvement or interaction with white evangelicals. He represented a Black Christian conservative tradition that could find common cause across racial divides even as it focused attention on Black pride and uplift.

Williams developed his religious sensibilities in New Orleans, where he was born and raised. His father and mother had both graduated from Southern University, a prominent HBCU in the city. Williams enrolled at the same school in 1987 and eventually walked onto the football team. During his junior year he ended up attending revival services held at Greater St. Stephen Full Gospel Baptist Church, a New Orleans congregation pastored by Paul S. Morton. There, Williams came to understand and accept the personal reality of a faith in Christ.[101]

Paul Morton was not just any Baptist preacher. Historian Kate Bowler identifies him as a key figure in an emerging network of Black church leaders who were "synthesizing black Baptist and Pentecostal traditions." At the time Williams came under his influence, Morton was on the cusp of launching a new denomination, the Full Gospel Baptist Church Fellowship (FGBCF)—with the "full gospel" signifying a belief in the continued possibility of supernatural spiritual gifts like speaking in tongues. As a predominantly Black church network, the FGBCF operated primarily through megachurches in urban areas, with Black gospel music playing a key role in its growth and popularity. Like Rev. James M. Gates, who blended traditional religious sensibilities with mass media and popular culture in the 1920s, Morton and the FGBCF packaged the old-time religion with modern Black cultural expressions.[102]

For Aeneas Williams, his religious transformation through Morton and the FGBCF carried over into all of his life, including the football field. He applied a common FGBCF tagline—the "spirit of excellence"—to his vocation. "No matter what I'm doing," he explained, "I'm doing it as for God." This was similar to the language that AIA and PAO converts used. For Williams, however, it came not from white evangelical spaces but from a Black religious leader and church network.[103]

By the time Williams entered the NFL in 1991, he had been immersed in Black spaces for his entire life. From his family to his college to his new church home, Black leaders had mentored and shaped him. He still cooperated with leaders in the Christian athlete movement, but unlike Dungy, Williams opted to work in a more independent mode, launching his own team Bible study in 1994. He also sought out older Black Christian players like Gill Byrd and Ken Houston to mentor him, and as his career developed he became a key mentor for numerous younger Black Christians in the NFL. In short, although Williams rarely discussed or prioritized racial justice issues in public, he modeled a style of Black mentorship built from and for Black men that hearkened back to the work of leaders like Florida A&M coach Jake Gaither.[104]

In different ways, Dungy and Williams offered nonconfrontational approaches to prioritizing and serving Black spiritual needs within the NFL. As the racial tensions of the 1990s mounted, however, some Black Christian athletes felt that more needed to be done. The discovery that white Christians, including their chaplains, teammates, and coaches, had entirely different reactions to issues like police brutality caused some to wonder if the racial reconciliation movement was enough. Could religious organizations formed and led by white Christians truly understand and meet the needs of Black Christian athletes? Did Black Christians need to create new sports ministry spaces that could prioritize Black experiences and concerns?

The challenges to creating a stable and lasting organization like this were immense. The white-led organizations of the Christian athlete movement had a forty-year head start, with strategic partnerships enmeshing their ministries within the major sports leagues and organizations. So too, many white sports ministry leaders had demonstrated a willingness to listen, learn, and adapt when it came to race. They were often more progressive on racial issues than other white evangelical groups, and the presence of numerous Black Christians who found meaning and significance within the movement made it a generally multiracial place, especially at the professional level. Black Christian athletes and coaches could legitimately point to signs of progress when it came to racial inclusion, as well as to shared interests when it came to social conservatism on other matters.

Even so, for a handful of Black Christians involved in the movement, events in the 1990s made it clear that there was a need for another option. The most significant attempt to respond to this impulse and create a Black-led sports ministry organization came from Minnesota, where Minnesota Vikings receiver Cris Carter and team chaplain Rev. Keith Johnson joined forces.

Johnson had been on the front lines of the racial reconciliation movement as a co-pastor for a prominent interracial Methodist congregation in urban Minneapolis.[105] In the early 1990s he also began delivering chapel messages for the Vikings, a team coached by Dennis Green, one of just two Black head coaches in the NFL at the time. The Vikings already had a white chaplain, an AIA staff member named Tom Lamphere who had been involved with the team since 1984. Lamphere had an especially close relationship with Tony Dungy, who joined the Vikings staff as an assistant coach in 1992. But there were other Black members of the team who did not connect with Lamphere in the same way, or who felt that a Black religious presence was important. As Johnson began spending more time around the team, he grew closer to both Green and Carter; by 1994 he was functionally serving as a co-chaplain along with Lamphere.[106]

At the same time that Johnson's involvement with the Vikings expanded, he began developing a conviction that integration into white spaces had diluted Black solidarity. In 1995 he caused a stir within his church community when he attended the Million Man March, a gathering of Black men in Washington, DC, called by Nation of Islam leader Louis Farrakhan. The aim of the event was to inspire and encourage Black men to invest in their families and communities as they continued to fight the challenge of racism. Though faith leaders from several traditions were present, including Jesse Jackson, Farrakhan's association with antisemitism and racial separatism made the event controversial. Some Black Christians felt that attending would legitimize Farrakhan's teachings; for others, it offered a chance to connect with Black men from a variety of religious backgrounds and traditions.[107]

Johnson was one of the Black Christians who chose to attend. "I stood with hundreds of thousands of African-American men who were inspired, encouraged, challenged, and lifted up and loved," he wrote. "We have pledged with hundreds of thousands of African-American men that we will stand together for God, for each other, our families and our communities."[108] After returning to his Minnesota church, Johnson attempted to foster that same solidarity by forming a small group of Black men who met regularly to study and address the unique issues facing the Black community in Minneapolis. Although he continued to work across racial lines, supporting a Billy Graham crusade that came to Minneapolis in 1996, for some white members of Johnson's church the creation of a small group specifically for Black men was too much. Claiming that Johnson was promoting separatism and division, they forced Johnson to shut down the meetings.[109]

Johnson did not lose interest in promoting Black solidarity. After serving as a chaplain at the 1996 Olympic Games in Atlanta, he left his pastoral position and entered sports ministry full time, joining with Cris Carter in launching Christian Athletes United for Spiritual Empowerment (CAUSE).[110] The men hoped to foster and encourage Black leadership in spaces where most of the players being served were Black. In his 2000 autobiography, Born to Believe, Carter devoted a chapter to the problem of racism. "I find it stunning that only two of the 31 head coaches are black," he wrote. "It seems we're good enough to play the game, but not good enough to coach." A similar logic undergirded Carter's support for Johnson and for a Black-led ministry like CAUSE.[111]

As Johnson co-founded CAUSE and ascended to greater responsibility with the Vikings, Tom Lamphere found his role shrinking. After the 1997 season he stepped away from the Vikings and Johnson became the team's lone chaplain.[112] At the same time, Johnson and Carter began inviting other athletes into the CAUSE fold. NFL players Reggie White, Randall Cunningham, Keith Jackson, Brian Dawkins, Troy Vincent, and Hardy Nickerson joined, as well as NBA players Allan Houston and Charlie Ward.

With retreats and events that featured Black gospel musicians like Kirk Franklin and pastors like T. D. Jakes, CAUSE focused on outreach and uplift efforts within predominantly Black communities. Political activism was not the goal, but instead Black-led spiritual care and community involvement developed in an environment that embraced Black cultural expressions. "Our goal is to spearhead these spiritual changes in America and to invigorate the black faithful," Reggie White explained when discussing CAUSE in 1999.[113]

White's involvement with CAUSE highlighted the potential allure of a Black-led sports ministry, particularly in the NFL and NBA. White had grown up with Sportianity and experienced all that it had to offer. He participated in the FCA during his high school and college years in Tennessee. In the late 1980s and early 1990s, after turning pro, he attended team chapel services, participated in PAO conferences, won AIA's Bart Starr award, and was featured several times in *Sports Spectrum* magazine. But as White's involvement in Sportianity deepened and as he accepted frequent speaking engagements across the country, he began to notice, as he put it, "that the majority of the people I preached to were white." By the early 1990s, White grew more interested in engagement with Black communities.[114]

White's participation with CAUSE also came as he was becoming more outspoken in his public criticism of racism. His 1997 remarks in Knoxville about policing were one example of this. So was his autobiography, *In the Trenches*, published earlier that year. "Blacks in America are hurt and angry because the laws of America seem to be rigged against us," he wrote. Highlighting both the historical realities of racism in the United States and ongoing inequalities expressed in housing, employment, wealth, and the criminal justice system, White urged Black and white Christians to work together for "complete healing" that included "spiritual healing, economic healing, racial and relational healing."[115]

White's perspective did not necessarily align him with politically liberal Black Christians. No fan of Jesse Jackson, White claimed that he was neither a conservative nor a liberal. In his proposed solutions to on-going racial inequalities, he leaned more toward the "compassionate conservatism" articulated by Black

Republicans like J. C. Watts, emphasizing economic development and growth.[116] Still, his attention to systemic racism and issues like police brutality placed him at odds with many rank-and-file white evangelicals. Although White continued to work with white evangelical groups through the end of his playing career, he found in CAUSE a spiritual space that valued and promoted Black leadership and cultural expression.

Even with White's involvement and CAUSE's initial success, the organization did not last. Its dependence on the individual personalities of Keith Johnson and Cris Carter made it difficult for CAUSE to build a wide base of support. When the Vikings fired Dennis Green in 2001 and Carter retired the following year, Johnson lost his allies in Minnesota and also his position as team chaplain. Soon after, CAUSE lost much of its relevance among athletes. Johnson also turned to a new interest in the Hebrew Roots movement, an amorphous network of groups and individuals who believed that the key to true Christianity came from rediscovering the Jewish foundations and context of Jesus's life and ministry. Reggie White joined Johnson in his new endeavor. In 2004, when White died suddenly, he had begun making frequent trips to Israel and was busy teaching himself Hebrew.[117]

The same year that White died, Tom Lamphere returned to the Vikings as team chaplain, a return that exemplified the staying power of the established evangelical sports ministry organizations. Their sports industry connections, built up over decades, helped them maintain their place of influence and outlast challenges from new sports ministry organizations. Lamphere may have taken a hiatus as the Vikings chaplain, but he still had plenty of work to do during those seven years, serving with the Minnesota Twins and with the University of Minnesota and also helping Tony Dungy launch a new ministry effort for NFL coaches. When the Vikings chaplain position reopened, he was present and available.[118]

The staying power of evangelical sports ministries came, too, from their recognition that they needed to be flexible and adaptable. When it came to racial diversity in pro sports, they realized that if they wanted to stay relevant, they needed to be more inclusive and welcoming to athletes of color. This was a tricky proposition for organizations whose donor and consumer base was primarily white and conservative. Still, they responded to the racial tensions of the 1990s and the challenge of new ministries like CAUSE by taking gradual steps toward greater inclusion.

At the end of the 1990s PAO hired James Mitchell, formerly involved in inner-city work in Nashville for the FCA, as its Director of Outreach. AIA took steps to diversify by recruiting Black chaplains to join its NFL staff and incorporating racial reconciliation work into its pro football ministry. In 1996 a reporter profiled the reconciliation efforts of Mike Bunkley, a Black AIA staffer who had worked with UCLA in the 1980s before beginning a chaplaincy role with the Carolina Panthers in 1995. "We're laying a foundation," Bunkley explained. "There's a lot of things that have to be built and even torn down before there's going to be unity."[119]

In 1998 AIA also launched a new program in Chicago that it called the Urban Project. Led by a staffer named Paul Curtis, he turned it over in 2000 to Michael Sylvester, a Black AIA leader who worked at the University of Southern California. Sylvester brought the Urban Project to Los Angeles where he developed a unique summer program for college athletes that combined AIA's Ultimate Training Camp principles with engagement in matters of race, justice, and poverty. Sylvester incorporated John Perkins's work directly into the structure of his program, using the racial justice activist's book, *With Justice for All*, and making the three "Rs" of Relocation, Reconciliation, and Redistribution a central part of the curriculum. With AIA staff members across the country spending part of their summers going through the Urban Project (and later a shortened and more adaptable off-shoot, the Lenses Institute), it became arguably the most substantial racial justice initiative developed by a sports ministry organization.[120]

In the FCA, attempts to include Black voices also expanded. Carey Casey, who left the national headquarters in 1992 to serve at Lawndale Community Church in Chicago, returned in 1997 in an executive role. Meanwhile, Ron Brown, assistant football coach for the University of Nebraska, came on as a regular columnist for *Sharing the Victory*. Brown's conservative theology adhered closely to Tony Evans's approach, which emphasized the work of the church and the centrality of relationships rather than systemic issues. "Racial prejudice and division in the Body of Christ," Brown wrote, "is a horrible witness to a world which doesn't have a clue about God's love except what it sees in Christians."[121]

These steps toward greater racial inclusion reflected the tenor of the times and the popularity of the evangelical racial reconciliation movement, as well as the efforts of Black Christian athletes to demand and create change. Still, like the responses to the Black athlete revolt in the late 1960s, there remained limits and boundaries within sports ministries. Bringing Black and white athletes together around a shared vision of Christian manhood was encouraged. Portraying sports as a site for interracial cooperation was supported, too. But the tradition of civil rights activism that Jesse Jackson represented, rooted in the historic Black church, remained marginalized, confined to isolated individuals.

* * *

As a new century dawned, racial tensions were not necessarily at the forefront of the Christian athlete movement. With CAUSE fading from the scene and with evangelical sports ministries seeking to involve more Black voices, the Christian athlete movement strengthened its position as the primary gatekeeper for defining and developing what it meant to be a Christian athlete. Its presence within big-time sports allowed it to nurture a public image as one of the most racially and ethnically diverse spaces within the world of American evangelicalism.

In the coming years, however, the image of unity promoted by sports ministries would run into challenges. The election of America's first Black president and the rise of a new era of Black athlete activism led to a backlash among white evangelicals, with passion for racial reconciliation receding and a fierce counter-offensive emerging, labeling attention to racial justice as a distraction from the gospel. These developments would push and pull evangelical sports ministries in new ways, surfacing tensions that had always been present between a predominantly white Christian Right that wed conservative politics to the Christian faith and an increasingly multiracial constituency of Christian athletes who took a broader view of the political implications and possibilities of their faith.

Epilogue

Two Quarterbacks Who Knelt

In 2007, a new poster boy for the Christian athlete movement appeared in the form of University of Florida quarterback Tim Tebow, who won the Heisman Trophy as college football's best player. The chiseled left-hander continued to star at Florida for two more years before getting drafted by the NFL's Denver Broncos in 2010. Through it all, he made public displays of his faith central to his football identity, drawing a Bible verse on his eye black before games and frequently kneeling in prayer on the sidelines and field—a practice that became known as "Tebowing" after it was turned into a social media meme.

For as much attention as Tebow had received before 2011, his star rose to unprecedented heights that year. Five games into the NFL season, Tebow took over as Denver's starting quarterback, proceeding to lead the Broncos to the playoffs and a dramatic upset win in the first round over the Pittsburgh Steelers. The statistics were clear: Tebow was not a great NFL quarterback. In 2011 he was dead last among thirty-four qualifying players in completion percentage, and he was ranked twenty-eighth in total quarterback rating. Yet it was equally clear that he seemed to rise to the occasion under pressure. He led the Broncos to six comeback wins, orchestrating several game-winning drives. National media covered the Tebow phenomenon relentlessly, with constant ESPN coverage as well as high-profile articles in the *New York Times* and other major publications. Was there a higher power at work in his success? Was Tebow being unfairly criticized because of his outspoken Christian faith?

Those were questions his fans would never fully resolve. After his improbable run to the playoffs in 2011, he was out of an NFL job. But his career as an evangelical celebrity and spokesperson for the Christian athlete movement was just beginning, with books, documentaries, speaking appearances, an ESPN job, and a stint in minor league baseball keeping him at the forefront of conversations about Christians in sports.[1]

In some ways, Tebow was simply a product of an established infrastructure, the next in a long line of athletes who had been shaped and then promoted by Sportianity. He seemed to symbolize the direction the Christian athlete movement had taken over the course of its history. In the 1920s, white mainline Protestants like Branch Rickey and Amos Alonzo Stagg received most of the

The Spirit of the Game. Paul Emory Putz, Oxford University Press. © Oxford University Press 2024.
DOI: 10.1093/9780190091095.003.0010

public attention when it came to Christian witness in big-time sports. Tebow, on the other hand, grew up in Florida as the homeschooled son of Southern Baptist missionaries. He highlighted the evangelical and Southern turn of the new "mainstream" when it came to both the Christian athlete movement and American Protestantism. So, too, did his public advocacy for conservative social causes, including sexual abstinence before marriage and opposition to abortion, which served as central organizing causes for evangelical engagement in public life.

But critics also seemed especially invested in Tebow—in portraying outspoken Christian athletes as part of a white, right-wing movement. Better to focus on a figure who supposedly matched the stereotype than to highlight the sports stars making the Christian athlete subculture an increasingly diverse space. There was Maya Moore, who led Connecticut's basketball team to back-to-back national championships in 2009 and 2010 before getting selected first overall by the WNBA's Minnesota Lynx in 2011; Stephen Curry, the three-point shooter extraordinaire who transformed the NBA after his arrival in 2009; Jeremy Lin, the Asian American point guard who made "Linsanity" a global phenomenon with the New York Knicks in 2012; Albert Pujols, the Dominican American first baseman who won three MVPs between 2005 and 2009; and many others. Was Tebow really the center of the story, the epitome of the Christian athlete?

In 2016 that question became more pronounced when another quarterback knelt and controversy erupted. Colin Kaepernick had been a Fellowship of Christian Athletes (FCA) member when he played college football for the University of Nevada. He also spoke about his Christian faith after launching his NFL career with the San Francisco 49ers in 2011. By 2016, however, Kaepernick seemed to have little involvement with the Christian athlete movement. His focus turned to the ongoing problems of police brutality and racial inequality in America, problems punctuated by the killing of unarmed Black men Trayvon Martin, Michael Brown, Philando Castile, and others—events that led to the rise of the Black Lives Matter movement and a new wave of Black athlete activism.

Kaepernick joined that growing activism in August 2016 when he began sitting on the bench rather than standing during the national anthem. After reporters noticed and asked why, Kaepernick made it plain. "I am not going to stand up to show pride in a flag for a country that oppresses black people and people of color," he said. "To me, this is bigger than football and it would be selfish on my part to look the other way. There are bodies in the street and people getting paid leave and getting away with murder."[2]

The backlash was immediate and intense. In response, Kaepernick spoke with Nate Boyer, an NFL player who had been a former Green Beret. Boyer suggested kneeling, rather than sitting, as a middle-ground position that could demonstrate both respect and discontentment with the status quo. Before a preseason game on September 1, Kaepernick followed Boyer's advice, and, with teammate Eric Reid joining him, deployed his now-famous protest for the first time.

Kaepernick was not the first high-profile athlete to use the national anthem to protest injustice. In 1968, Olympians Tommie Smith and John Carlos had raised their fists on the medal stand while the anthem played. In 1996, Denver Nuggets guard Mahmoud Abdul-Rauf sat during the anthem, causing an uproar that led to his suspension from the NBA.[3] Jackie Robinson, the very symbol of racial progress through sports, had advocated for sitting out the anthem, too. Writing in his 1972 autobiography, he reflected back on a moment from his playing days, right before a World Series game. "As I write this twenty years later, I cannot stand and sing the anthem. I cannot salute the flag; I know that I am a black man in a white world," he wrote. "In 1972, in 1947, at my birth in 1919, I know that I never had it made."[4]

For Smith, Carlos, Robinson, Abdul-Rauf, and Kaepernick, the American story may have included promise and potential, but it also included oppression and injustice—slavery, segregation, violence, and continued racial disparities. The symbolic power of the national anthem provided an opportunity to use the attention directed at sports for the purpose of social reform and change. It was a logic that mirrored the impulse that had led to the founding of the Christian athlete movement in the first place: using sports to assert a claim about American identity and possibility.

Many Black Christian athletes understood Kaepernick's frustrations. The first NFL player to join Kaepernick's protest, Eric Reid, had been involved with Athletes in Action (AIA) in college, and he continued to publicize his faith as an NFL player. In an essay for the New York Times, he credited scripture with inspiring him to kneel with his teammate. "My faith moved me to take action," he wrote. "I looked to James 2:17, which states, 'Faith by itself, if it does not have works, is dead.' I knew I needed to stand up for what is right."[5]

Other early supporters included Philadelphia Eagles safety Malcolm Jenkins, another spokesperson for evangelical faith. In the second week of the 2016 season, Jenkins began raising his fist during the national anthem in solidarity with Kaepernick. While Black Christians within Sportianity expressed a variety of perspectives, ranging from unqualified support (Eric Reid) to open opposition (Jonathan Isaac), as a general rule the majority expressed sympathy for Kaepernick's aims, if not always his method.[6]

This contrasted sharply with the direction the broader evangelical movement was taking. In 2016, eighty-one percent of white evangelical voters opted for Donald Trump—a president who, the following year, would declare Kaepernick and other protesting athletes "sons of bitches" who deserved to be fired.[7] Over the next few years, through the course of Trump's presidency and the protests following the killing of George Floyd in 2020, an "antiwoke" backlash to racial justice activism took root among white evangelicals. Driven by figures like John MacArthur, who had engaged in similar dismissals of racial justice concerns after the beating of Rodney King, the antiwoke evangelicals labeled attempts to address America's history of racial injustice as evidence of critical race theory (CRT) and a threat to Christian unity.[8]

Their efforts had mixed results among evangelicals within sports. NBA player Kyle Korver and NFL head coach Frank Reich, both white Christians, took strong stands on behalf of the protests for racial justice. For sports ministry staff members and chaplains, particularly those working within spaces with a high number of Black athletes, genuine relationships and heartfelt conversations across racial lines often led to empathy and a desire to understand. Yet the antiwoke activists did manage to shut down one of the most significant evangelical racial justice initiatives in the history of the Christian athlete movement, the Lenses Institute. AIA president Mark Householder and many AIA staff members had been strong supporters of the Lenses Institute and its leader, Michael Sylvester. When a group of conservative Campus Crusade staff members targeted Lenses as an example of CRT in their midst, however, Lenses closed its American operations.[9]

Kaepernick may not have directly connected his protests with his faith, but the discussion and debate that resulted from his activism laid bare the dual impulses at the heart of the Christian athlete movement. On the one hand, it was a network focusing most of its attention on practical concerns, showing athletes and coaches how Christian faith could speak to their everyday needs. For issues like performance, motivation, setbacks, and personal relationships, sports ministries sought to offer something meaningful that spoke to these individual and ordinary experiences. In that sense it reflected tendencies that could be traced back to the middlebrow Protestants of the 1920s. "I want to live the ideals of Christ every day, in business and on the athletic field," Branch Rickey told an interviewer in 1931. To him, the Christian faith needed to be applied in practical ways; it required "laboratory demonstration" in real life.[10]

At the same time, the Christian athlete movement was also a cultural and political project that privileged and promoted certain ideas about America and Christianity over others. Recall Amos Alonzo Stagg's line when asked by a reporter in 1931 about America's ongoing obsession with football: "The fellows who play and the men who coach them must realize that, in no small way, by their actions they are preaching sermons and laying down rules of conduct for the coming generation."[11]

For Stagg and for the Christian sports leaders who followed, sports continued to hold special value as a site for moral formation and for broadcasting Protestant values to the nation. There was little room within this view for a faith that sought to critique rather than affirm or that challenged structures rather than worked within them. At the end of the day, it did not matter what Bible verse or Christian convictions Kaepernick and his allies cited. They may have been carrying on the "prophetic fire" of the social justice wing of the Black church tradition, but they violated the cultural sensibility at the heart of the Christian athlete movement: instead of builders and boosters, they were deemed knockers and wreckers.[12]

As the organizations and leaders of the Christian athlete movement move deeper into the twenty-first century and adapt to a changing sports landscape, there are key differences from Stagg's and Rickey's day. The middlebrow Protestantism associated with the mainline is no longer at the center of Protestant engagement with big-time sports. Neoevangelicals and white Southern Protestants, operating primarily through parachurch organizations and informal networks, have assumed leadership of the Christian athlete movement, with mainline Protestants receding to the background and with a growing number of Black Christians entering—so long as they are not too radical in their pursuit of racial justice.

New theological perspectives have made headway as well: the evangelical Calvinism associated with the "young, restless, reformed" movement; the charismatic and Pentecostal perspectives that can range from a health-and-wealth prosperity gospel to the Instagram influencer aesthetic of Hillsong to the politically engaged vision of seven-mountains dominionism. The sense of progress and optimism, long present in the Christian athlete movement, has been challenged by the darker and more violent rhetoric of Make America Great Again (MAGA) politics within the Christian Right. So, too, new issues, especially those related to gender and sexuality, have become primary markers of identity and flashpoints of controversy as the Christian athlete movement seeks to maintain its access within the pluralistic corporate structures of big-time sports.

Yet, despite the shifts in theological priorities and constituencies, two ideas advanced by Rickey and Stagg remain central to the Christian athlete movement's ongoing vitality. Its leaders continue to insist that Christian faith can be practically and meaningfully applied to the lives and experiences of coaches and athletes. And they continue to believe that Christian coaches and athletes can and should use their platform within sports to influence and shape the direction of American life.

The challenge for the movement and its organizations, when faced with growing divides and diversity, is this: Whose Christianity? And whose America?

Notes

Abbreviations for Manuscript Collections

AASP   Amos Alonzo Stagg Papers, Special Collections Research Center, University of Chicago Library

AIAW   Association for Intercollegiate Athletics for Women Papers, Special Collections, University of Maryland Libraries

BGEA   Billy Graham Evangelistic Association Records, Billy Graham Center Archives, Wheaton College

BRP   Branch Rickey Papers, Manuscript Division, Library of Congress

CBMP   Clarence L. "Biggie" Munn papers, Michigan State University Archives & Historical Collections

CFLP   Champions for Life Papers, Billy Graham Center Archives, Wheaton College

DUFCA   Fellowship of Christian Athletes, Duke University Chapter Records, Duke University Archives, David M. Rubenstein Rare Book & Manuscript Library, Duke University

LNBP   L. Nelson Bell Papers, Evangelism & Missions Archives, Wheaton College

NCC   National Council of the Churches of Christ in the United States of America Records, Presbyterian Historical Society, Philadelphia, PA

NPBP   N. Peggy Burke Papers, Iowa Women's Archives, The University of Iowa Libraries

PCUSA   United Presbyterian Church in the U.S.A. Records, Presbyterian Historical Society, Philadelphia, PA

SSP   Samuel Shoemaker Papers, Archives of the Episcopal Church, Austin, TX

Acknowledgments

1. John Fea, *Why Study History? Reflecting on the Importance of the Past* (Grand Rapids, MI: Baker Academic, 2013), 54.

Introduction

* Grantland Rice, "The Great Competitor," *Collier's*, February 28, 1925, 13.
1. For context on the sports boom of the 1920s, see Benjamin G. Rader, "Compensatory Sport Heroes: Ruth, Grange and Dempsey," *Journal of Popular Culture* 16, no. 4 (Spring 1983): 11–22; Mark Dyreson, "The Emergence of Consumer Culture and the Transformation of Physical Culture: American Sport in the 1920s," *Journal of Sport History* 16, no. 3 (Winter 1989): 261–281; Michael Oriard, *King Football: Sport and Spectacle in the Golden Age of Radio and Newsreels, Moves and Magazines, The Weekly and the Daily Press* (Chapel Hill: University of North Carolina Press, 2001).
2. On American "muscular Christianity," see Gail Bederman, *Manliness & Civilization: A Cultural History of Gender and Race in the United States, 1880–1917* (Chicago: University of Chicago Press, 1995); Clifford Putney, *Muscular Christianity: Manhood and Sports in Protestant America, 1880–1920* (Cambridge, MA: Harvard University Press, 2001); David P. Setran, "Following the Broad-Shouldered Jesus: The College YMCA and the Culture of Muscular Christianity in American Campus Life, 1890–1914," *American Education History Journal* 32, no. 1 (2005): 59–66; Andrea L. Turpin, *A New Moral Vision: Gender, Religion, and the*

Changing Purposes of American Higher Education, 1837–1917 (Ithaca, NY: Cornell University Press, 2016). On Black muscular Christianity, see Nina Mjagkij, *Light in the Darkness: African Americans and the YMCA, 1852–1946* (Lexington: University Press of Kentucky, 1994); Paul Emory Putz, "Tracing the Historical Contours of Black Muscular Christianity and American Sport," *The International Journal of the History of Sport* 39, no. 4 (2022): 404–424.

3. Tony Ladd and James A. Mathisen, *Muscular Christianity: Evangelical Protestants and the Development of American Sport* (Grand Rapids, MI: Baker Books, 1999), 22–94; William J. Baker, *Playing with God: Religion and Modern Sport* (Cambridge, MA: Harvard University Press, 2007), 23–128; Putney, *Muscular Christianity*, 45–72.

4. Ladd and Mathisen, *Muscular Christianity*, 79–94; Putney, *Muscular Christianity*, 7, 10.

5. On middlebrow culture, see Joan Shelley Rubin, *The Making of Middlebrow Culture* (Chapel Hill: University of North Carolina Press, 1992). My interpretation contrasts with Brian Ingrassia, whose excellent work has otherwise been formative to my thinking. Ingrassia argues in *The Rise of Gridiron University: Higher Education's Uneasy Alliance with Big-Time Football* (Lawrence: University Press of Kansas, 2012), 198, that by the 1920s big-time college football became "a lowbrow cultural activity that helped highbrow intellectual culture stay elevated." I argue that by linking religion with sports, Protestants used big-time college athletics as a middlebrow space, attempting to provide both moral education and wholesome entertainment.

6. Frank Deford, "Religion in Sport," *Sports Illustrated*, April 19, 1976, 88–102. I use the term "Christian athlete movement" because those within the sports ministry organizations that gave it direction viewed themselves simply as Christians rather than evangelicals or Protestants. Other self-identified Christian communities (including Catholics and Latter-day Saints) remained on the margins of the movement even though they also engaged in sports in important ways.

7. Catholics and Latter-day Saints are not a major focus of this book, except when they intersect with the Protestants I am studying. Important books on American sports and those religious groups include Murray A. Sperber, *Shake Down the Thunder: The Creation of Notre Dame Football* (Bloomington: University of Indiana Press, 1993); Julie Byrne, *O God of Players: The Story of the Immaculata Mighty Macs* (New York: Columbia University Press, 2003); Timothy B. Neary, *Crossing Parish Boundaries: Race, Sports, and Catholic Youth in Chicago, 1914–1954* (Chicago: University of Chicago Press, 2016); Richard Ian Kimball, *Sports in Zion: Mormon Recreation, 1890–1940* (Urbana: University of Illinois Press, 2003).

8. Major exceptions to this by academic historians are Baker, *Playing with God*, which is an exemplary historical overview of religion and sports in the United States, and Putney's *Muscular Christianity*, which is foundational for understanding muscular Christianity. More recently, religious historian Randall Balmer turned his attention to sports with *Passion Plays: How Religion Shaped Sports in North America* (Chapel Hill: University of North Carolina Press, 2022). His excellent book is primarily a work of synthesis. Art Remillard's forthcoming *Bodies in Motion: A Religious History of Sports in America* (Oxford University Press) brilliantly combines history and religious studies to examine the sacred meanings Americans have assigned to sports. Those outside the discipline of history, in such fields as religious studies and sociology, have created a thriving interdisciplinary subfield focused on religion and sports in which American Protestants receive attention. Two important interdisciplinary anthologies are Rebecca Alpert and Arthur Remillard, eds., *Gods, Games, and Globalization: New Perspectives on Religion and Sport* (Macon, GA: Mercer University Press, 2019); Jeffrey Scholes and Randall Balmer, eds., *Religion and Sport in North America: Critical Essays for the Twenty-First Century* (New York: Routledge, 2022). In addition, Nick Watson and Andy Parker have been catalysts for the interdisciplinary study of sports and Christianity. They have edited important collections like *Sports and Christianity: Historical and Contemporary Perspectives* (New York: Routledge, 2015).

9. Important works by those trained outside the discipline of history include literature professor Robert Higgs's *God in the Stadium: Sports and Religion in America* (Lexington: University Press of Kentucky, 1995); religious studies scholar Joseph L. Price's *Rounding the Bases: Baseball and Religion in America* (Macon, GA: Mercer University Press, 2006); kinesiology professor Tony Ladd's and sociologist James Mathisen's *Muscular Christianity*; kinesiology professor and pioneering sport studies scholar Shirl Hoffman's *Good Game: Christianity and the Culture of Sports* (Waco, TX: Baylor University Press, 2010); journalist Tom Krattenmaker's *Onward Christian Athletes: Turning Ballparks into Pulpits and Players into Preachers* (New York: Rowman & Littlefield, 2010); and religious studies scholar Annie Blazer's excellent historical and ethnographic study, *Playing for God: Evangelical Women and the Unintended Consequences of Sports Ministry* (New York: New York University Press, 2015).

10. By "mainline" I am referring to the people and networks connected to the predominantly white, predominantly Northern Protestant denominations that were involved with the Federal/National Council of Churches and other ecumenical Protestant endeavors and that—at least until the 1960s—viewed themselves as the nation's primary guardians of morality. My understanding of mainline/ecumenical Protestantism is drawn especially from William R. Hutchison, ed., *Between the Times: The Travail of the Protestant Establishment in America, 1900–1960* (New York: Cambridge University Press, 1989); Elesha Coffman, *The Christian Century and the Rise of the Protestant Mainline* (New York: Oxford University Press, 2013); Margaret Bendroth, *The Last Puritans: Mainline Protestants and the Power of the Past* (Chapel Hill: University of North Carolina Press, 2015); David Mislin, *Saving Faith: Making Religious Pluralism an American Value at the Dawn of the Secular Age* (Ithaca, NY: Cornell University Press, 2015); Nicholas T. Pruitt, *Open Hearts, Closed Doors: Immigration Reform and the Waning of Mainline Protestantism* (New York: New York University Press, 2021); Gene Zubovich, *Before the Religious Right: Liberal Protestants, Human Rights, and the Polarization of the United States* (Philadelphia: University of Pennsylvania Press, 2022); and everything David Hollinger writes, most recently *Christianity's American Fate: How Religion Became More Conservative and Society More Secular* (Princeton, NJ: Princeton University Press, 2022).

11. There are important exceptions to this. Three that stand out are Douglas Jacobsen and William Vance Trollinger Jr., eds., *Re-Forming the Center: American Protestantism, 1900 to the Present* (Grand Rapids, MI: Eerdmans, 1998); Matthew Bowman, *The Urban Pulpit: New York City and the Fate of Liberal Evangelicalism* (New York: Oxford University Press, 2014); and Lerone Martin, *The Gospel of J. Edgar Hoover: How the FBI Aided and Abetted the Rise of White Christian Nationalism* (Princeton, NJ: Princeton University Press, 2023).

12. An earlier generation of scholarship on post–World War II evangelicalism focused on the "re-engaged" fundamentalists of neoevangelicalism as the centerpiece of the movement. Examples of this narrative include George Marsden, *Reforming Fundamentalism: Fuller Seminary and the New Evangelicalism* (Grand Rapids, MI: Eerdmans, 1987) and Joel A. Carpenter, *Revive Us Again: The Reawakening of American Fundamentalism* (New York: Oxford University Press, 1997). Recent books on American evangelicalism have modified this narrative. Several have highlighted the importance of business networks to evangelicalism's development: Darren Dochuk's *From Bible Belt to Sunbelt: Plain-Folk Religion, Grassroots Politics, and the Rise of Evangelical Conservatism* (New York: W.W. Norton, 2010); Darren Dochuk's *Anointed with Oil: How Christianity and Crude Made Modern America* (New York: Basic Books, 2019); Timothy E. W. Gloege's *Guaranteed Pure: The Moody Bible Institute, Business, and the Making of Modern Evangelicalism* (Chapel Hill: University of North Carolina Press, 2015); and Darren Grem's *The Blessings of Business: How Corporations Shaped Conservative Christianity* (New York: Oxford University Press, 2016). Others have focused on the contested nature of evangelical authority and identity, including Molly Worthen's *Apostles of Reason: The Crisis of Authority in American Evangelicalism* (New York: Oxford University Press, 2013), Matthew Avery Sutton's *American Apocalypse: A History of Modern Evangelicalism* (Cambridge, MA: Harvard University Press, 2014), and Isaac Sharp's *The Other Evangelicals: A Story of Liberal, Black, Progressive, Feminist, and Gay Christians—and the Movement That Pushed Them Out* (Grand Rapids, MI: Eerdmans, 2023). Still others emphasize the centrality of an evangelical consumer subculture to the formation of modern evangelicalism: Daniel Silliman's *Reading Evangelicals: How Christian Fiction Shaped a Culture and a Faith* (Grand Rapids, MI: Eerdmans, 2021); Kristin Kobes Du Mez's *Jesus and John Wayne: How White Evangelicals Corrupted a Faith and Fractured a Nation* (New York: Liveright, 2020); and Daniel Vaca's *Evangelicals Incorporated: Books and the Business of Religion in America* (Cambridge, MA: Harvard University Press, 2019). My book adds to this conversation by bringing mainline, neoevangelical, white Southern, and Black Protestants into a shared narrative, highlighting the ways that a subset of mainline/ecumenical Protestants influenced and eventually joined the evangelicalism of post-1970s America.

13. Ladd and Mathisen, *Muscular Christianity*; Baker, *Playing with God.*

14. Matthew Hedstrom, *The Rise of Liberal Religion: Book Culture and American Spirituality in the Twentieth Century* (New York: Oxford University Press, 2013). See also Erin Smith, *What Would Jesus Read? Popular Religious Books and Everyday Life in Twentieth-Century America* (Chapel Hill: University of North Carolina Press, 2015).

15. Hedstrom's book argues that the "religious middlebrow" of the mainline ultimately moved away from an exclusive identification with Protestantism, paving the way for more

cosmopolitan and seeker-sensitive forms of spirituality after the 1960s. Stephen Prothero's book, *God the Bestseller: How One Editor Transformed American Religion a Book at a Time* (New York: HarperOne 2023), makes this case too. I am suggesting that, in addition to the paths charted by Hedstrom and Prothero, there was another route for the middlebrow segment of the mainline: connection to the growing evangelical consumer subculture.

16. I am sympathetic to David Bebbington's definition of evangelicalism in *Evangelicalism in Modern Britain: A History from the 1730s to the 1980s* (New York: Routledge, 1989), 2–3, which centers on conversionism, biblicism, activism, and crucicentrism as essential features. I am also influenced by Thomas Kidd, *Who Is an Evangelical? The History of a Movement in Crisis* (New Haven, CT: Yale University Press, 2019). Kidd simplifies Bebbington, putting the born-again experience, a deep commitment to the Bible, and belief in God's active and personal presence as defining features of evangelicalism. Yet, while the traits Bebbington and Kidd highlight may have been near the center of post-1970s American evangelicalism, consumer habits and political and cultural affinities also played a crucial role in shaping its boundaries and contours.

17. While Du Mez highlights more militant forms of masculinity, her nuanced book also explores the softer versions of masculinity that were common within the Christian athlete movement. On gender and evangelical Protestantism, see also Seth Dowland, *Family Values and the Rise of the Christian Right* (Philadelphia: University of Pennsylvania Press, 2015); R. Marie Griffith, *Moral Combat: How Sex Divided American Christians and Fractured American Politics* (New York: Basic Books, 2017); Blazer, *Playing for God.*

18. Two important books for understanding women's sports history are Pamela Grundy and Susan Shackelford, *Shattering the Glass: The Remarkable History of Women's Basketball* (New York: The New Press, 2005); and Susan K. Cahn, *Coming on Strong: Gender and Sexuality in Women's Sport*, 2nd edition (Urbana: University of Illinois Press, 2015). Annie Blazer's *Playing for God* is one of the few books to analyze evangelical women and sports.

19. An excellent recent example is Balmer, *Passion Plays.* My focus on American religious nationalism builds on scholarship including Kevin M. Schultz, *Tri-Faith America: How Catholics and Jews Held Postwar America to Its Protestant Promise* (New York: Oxford University Press, 2011); Jonathan P. Herzog, *The Spiritual-Industrial Complex: America's Religious Battle against Communism in the Early Cold War* (New York: Oxford University Press, 2011); Daniel K. Williams, *God's Own Party: The Making of the Christian Right* (New York: Oxford University Press, 2010); Kevin M. Kruse, *One Nation under God: How Corporate America Invented Christian America* (New York: Basic Books, 2015); and Andrew Hartman, *A War for the Soul of America: A History of the Culture Wars* (Chicago: University of Chicago Press, 2015). Meanwhile, my focus on sports as a form of national identity builds on the work of many scholars, including Steven W. Pope, *Patriotic Games: Sporting Traditions in the American Imagination, 1876–1926* (New York: Oxford University Press, 1997); Mark Dyreson, *Making the American Team: Sport, Culture, and the Olympic Experience* (Urbana: University of Illinois Press, 1997); Amy Bass, *Not the Triumph but the Struggle: The 1968 Olympics and the Making of the Black Athlete* (Minneapolis: University of Minnesota Press, 2002); Damion L. Thomas, *Globetrotting: African American Athletes and Cold War Politics* (Urbana: University of Illinois Press, 2012); Toby Rider and Kevin Witherspoon, eds., *Defending the American Way of Life: Sport, Culture, and the Cold War* (Fayetteville: University of Arkansas Press, 2018); Cat M. Ariail, *Passing the Baton: Black Women Track Stars and American Identity* (Urbana: University of Illinois Press, 2020).

20. There is a vast amount of literature on race and sports, which will be cited throughout this book. Two excellent anthologies are Patrick B. Miller and David K. Wiggins, eds., *Sport and the Color Line: Black Athletes and Race Relations in Twentieth-Century America* (New York: Routledge, 2004); and Michael E. Lomax and Kenneth L. Shropshire, eds., *Sports and the Racial Divide: African American and Latino Experience in an Era of Change* (Jackson: University Press of Mississippi, 2011). Christianity and Black athletic engagement is an understudied topic for historians, although Jeffrey Scholes has written an important recent book, *Christianity, Race, and Sport* (New York: Routledge, 2021). I am also indebted to recent historical scholarship on evangelicalism and race, including J. Russell Hawkins and Philip Luke Sinitiere, eds., *Christians and the Color Line: Race and Religion after Divided by Faith* (New York: Oxford University Press, 2013); Jemar Tisby, *The Color of Compromise: The Truth about the American Church's Complicity in Racism* (Grand Rapids, MI: Zondervan, 2019); J. Russell Hawkins, *The Bible Told Them So: How Southern Evangelicals Fought to Preserve White Supremacy* (New York: Oxford University Press, 2021); Jesse Curtis, *The Myth of Colorblind Christians: Evangelicals and White Supremacy in the Civil Rights Era* (New York: New York University Press, 2021); Anthea Butler,

White Evangelical Racism: The Politics of Morality in America (Chapel Hill: University of North Carolina Press, 2021); and Helen Jin Kim, *Race for Revival: How Cold War South Korea Shaped the American Evangelical Empire* (New York: Oxford University Press, 2022). Nearly everything Paul Harvey writes is worth mentioning, too, including *Christianity and Race in the American South: A History* (Chicago: University of Chicago Press, 2016).

Chapter 1

1. John R. Tunis, *$port$: Heroics and Hysterics* (New York: The John Day Company, 1928), 34.
2. Robert T. Handy, "The American Religious Depression, 1925-1935," *Church History* 29, no. 1 (March 1960): 3-16; Grant Wacker, "The Demise of Biblical Civilization," in *The Bible in America: Essays in Cultural History*, ed. Nathan O. Hatch and Mark A. Noll (New York: Oxford University Press, 1982), 121-138; Paula Fass, *The Damned and the Beautiful: American Young in the 1920s* (New York: Oxford University Press, 1977), 42-46, 136-139; David P. Setran, *The College "Y": Student Religion in the Era of Secularization* (New York: Palgrave Macmillan, 2007), 182-183.
3. Charles Sheldon, "Body and Spirit," *Christian Herald*, December 28, 1929, 8.
4. Ladd and Mathisen, *Muscular Christianity*, 79-94; Putney, *Muscular Christianity*, 7, 10.
5. See the introduction for scholarship on mainline Protestantism from which I am drawing. Especially useful for the 1920s: Coffman, *The Christian Century and the Rise of the Protestant Mainline*; Hutchison, *Between the Times*; Pruitt, *Open Hearts, Closed Doors*.
6. See the introduction for scholarship on muscular Christianity. For context on Stagg's place in college football and the "Big Three," see Ronald A. Smith, *Sports & Freedom: The Rise of Big-Time College Athletics* (New York: Oxford University Press, 1888), 52-98; Julie Des Jardins, *Walter Camp: Football and the Modern Man* (New York: Oxford University Press, 2015), 16-25; Robin Lester, *Stagg's University: The Rise, Decline and Fall of Big-Time Football at Chicago* (Urbana: University of Illinois Press, 1995), 8-12.
7. Luther Gulick, "Our New Gymnastics," in *Proceedings of the Twenty-Eighth International Convention of Young Men's Christian Associations* (New York: 1889), 100; Thomas Aiello, *Hoops: A Cultural History of Basketball in America* (Lanham, MD: Rowman & Littlefield, 2022), 1-16.
8. Setran, *The College "Y"*; William R. Hutchison, *The Modernist Impulse in American Protestantism* (New York: Oxford University Press, 1976); Gary Dorrien, *The Making of American Liberal Theology: Idealism, Realism, & Modernity* (Louisville, KY: Westminster John Knox Press, 2003).
9. "Yale's Pitcher," *Brooklyn Daily Eagle*, October 29, 1888, 1. On the connections between race, nation, and masculinity at the time, see Bederman, *Manliness & Civilization*.
10. Baker, *Playing with God*, 42-63; Putney, *Muscular Christianity*, 45-72.
11. Amos Alonzo Stagg with Wesley Winans Stout, *Touchdown!* (New York: Longmans, Green and Co., 1927), 130.
12. Stagg to Walter Davenport, July 2, 1926, AASP, Box 1a, Folder 15. See Lester, *Stagg's University*, for an overview of Stagg's college football leadership.
13. Baker, *Playing with God*, 64-84, 104-128; Putney, *Muscular Christianity*, 45-72; Robert Francis Martin, *Hero of the Heartland: Billy Sunday and the Transformation of American Society, 1862-1935* (Bloomington: Indiana University Press, 2002), 65-79; Susan Curtis, *A Consuming Faith: The Social Gospel and Modern American Culture* (Baltimore: Johns Hopkins University Press, 1991), 56.
14. Richard Henry Edwards, *Christianity and Amusements* (New York: Association Press, 1915), 82-97.
15. Pope, *Patriotic Games*, 139-156; Des Jardins, *Walter Camp*, 288-310. See also the endnote on sports in the 1920s from the introduction.
16. Erin Ann McCarthy, "Making Men: The Life and Career of Amos Alonzo Stagg, 1862-1933" (PhD diss., Loyola University of Chicago, 1994), 284-297.
17. Lester, *Stagg's University*, 101-124.
18. Oriard, *King Football*, 134; John Sayle Watterson, *College Football: History, Spectacle, Controversy* (Baltimore: Johns Hopkins University Press, 2000), 146-147. On Rockne during the 1920s, see Sperber, *Shake Down the Thunder*, 84-346.
19. On amateurism as an ideology, see R. Smith, *Sports and Freedom*, 62-66, 162-174; Pope, *Patriotic Games*, 18-36.
20. A. J. "Dad" Elliott to Stagg, February 12, 1921, AASP, Box 2, Folder 3.

21. Stagg, *Touchdown!*, 57.
22. Stagg, *Touchdown!*, 176–177; Untitled address, November 18, 1931, AASP, Box 111, Folder 1.
23. J. B. Griswold, "You Don't Have to Be Born with It," *American Magazine*, November 1931, 135.
24. Lester, *Stagg's University*, 117–119.
25. The following year Stagg compiled and edited the articles and published them in book form as *Touchdown!* See Box 106 of the Stagg Papers (AASP) for details on the writing and publication of the articles and book. On the significance of Stagg's serialized autobiography, see Oriard, *King Football*, 129, 135.
26. Oriard, *King Football*, 101.
27. Knute Rockne, for example, dismissed attempts to make college football adhere to the amateur ideal. Sperber, *Shake Down the Thunder*, 310.
28. "Amusement and Recreation," *The Presbyterian*, September 25, 1930, 4–5. See also Silas Bent, "Idol Worship: 1927," *Christian Advocate*, December 8, 1927, 1498.
29. See, for example, "The New Hall of Fame," *Christian Advocate*, April 1, 1926, 391.
30. Quotation from "The Making of Men," AASP, Box 110, Folder 4. See also "Modern Living Makes Softies, Says Stagg," *Great Falls Tribune*, February 16, 1925, 1.
31. Griswold, "You Don't Have to Be Born with It," 135.
32. Scholars have long noted the ambivalent traditional/modern cultural space occupied by athletic heroes in the 1920s. See, for example, Lynn Dumenil, *The Modern Temper: American Culture and Society in the 1920s* (New York: Hill and Wang, 1995), 77–78; Warren I. Susman, "Culture Heroes: Ford, Barton, Ruth," in *Culture as History: The Transformation of American Society in the Twentieth Century* (New York: Pantheon Books, 1984), 141–149. Similarly, Stagg's biographers show how he championed the preservation of Victorian values during the 1920s. See McCarthy, "Making Men," 317; Peter I. Berg, "A Mission on the Midway: Amos Alonzo Stagg and the Gospel of Football" (PhD diss., Michigan State University, 1996), 222–223. Missing in their analysis is the extent to which Stagg's message remained connected with Protestantism.
33. Arthur H. Steinhaus to Stagg, March 13, 1957, AASP, Box 6, Folder 6. The "strongly fundamentalist" quotation comes from a letter Stagg wrote to Hargrave A. Long, October 21, 1956, AASP, Box 5, Folder 2.
34. On the continued affinities among Protestants in the era of the fundamentalist/modernist controversy, see Jacobsen and Trollinger Jr., eds., *Re-Forming the Center*.
35. Sydney Ahlstrom, *A Religious History of the American People*, 2nd ed. (New Haven, CT: Yale University Press, 2004), 901; Barry Hankins, *Jesus and Gin: Evangelicalism, the Roaring Twenties and Today's Culture Wars* (New York: Palgrave Macmillan, 2010), 21–40.
36. Stagg's congressional testimony was subsequently published in brochure form under the title "A Fair Start in Life for Young People." See AASP, Box 107, Folder 1.
37. Henry T. Fowler to Stagg, October 3, 1926, AASP, Box 106, Folder 3.
38. For a few examples of Stagg's stand for clean living, see Stagg, "Sand," November 4, 1931, AASP, Box 111, Folder 2; Stagg to Henry M. Spickler, May 19, 1923, AASP, Box 2, Folder 15; Stagg, *Touchdown!*, 302.
39. On prayer as a unifying feature among Protestants in the 1920s, see Rick Ostrander, *The Life of Prayer in a World of Science: Protestants, Prayer, and American Culture, 1870–1930* (New York: Oxford University Press, 2000), 111–115.
40. Sperber, *Shake Down the Thunder*, 157–158; Baker, *Playing with God*, 138–141.
41. Frank G. Weaver, "Come On, You Praying Kentuckians," *Association Men*, March 1920, 416–418; "The Praying Football Team," *Literary Digest*, December 11, 1920, 39.
42. Robert F. Kelley, "It Makes a Difference," *Association Men*, June 1925, 440; "The Praying Football Hero," *Literary Digest*, June 27, 1925, 32–33.
43. "Stagg Kneels in Prayer before His Team Plays," *Ohio State Journal*, October 4, 1927, clipping located in AASP, Football Scrapbook, June–October 1927, Box 227.
44. "Praying Athletes," *Indianapolis Sunday Star*, October 3, 1926, 10.
45. Kelley, "It Makes a Difference," 440.
46. "Honor Stagg as Character-Builder," *Christian Century*, October 28, 1931, 1350.
47. "The Gospel for the College Student," *The Presbyterian*, August 20, 1931, 6.
48. Although "Major League Baseball" did not become the official name until 2000, I will be using it throughout the book to refer to the professional baseball played and organized by the National League and American League.
49. The definitive biography of Rickey is Lee Lowenfish, *Branch Rickey: Baseball's Ferocious Gentleman* (Lincoln: University of Nebraska Press, 2007). For a useful summary of Rickey's faith, see Michael G. Long and Chris Lamb, *Jackie Robinson: A Spiritual Biography* (Louisville, KY: Westminster John Knox Press, 2017), 51–67.

50. "Personal," *Christian Advocate*, January 22, 1931, 112; Loren M. Edwards, "Methodist Personalities," *Christian Advocate*, June 17, 1937, 573.

51. "Churchmen Defend Hoover Stand," *Cincinnati Enquirer*, December 19, 1930, 8; "Meeting to Make Plans for Preaching Mission," *St. Louis Post-Dispatch*, June 12, 1936, 3E.

52. "Billy Sunday, Opening Revival, Talks to 14,000," *St. Louis Post-Dispatch*, January 9, 1928, 3; William L. Stidger, "Introducing Branch Rickey," *Christian Herald*, October 1931, 45.

53. Lowenfish, *Branch Rickey*, 89–90; Stidger, "Introducing Branch Rickey," 15.

54. Norman Beasley, "Sticking in the 'Big League,'" *Association Men*, March 1924, 303–304, 326–327.

55. John Sheridan (a St. Louis sportswriter), quoted in Lowenfish, *Branch Rickey*, 85.

56. George Marsden, *Fundamentalism and American Culture*, 2nd ed. (New York: Oxford University Press, 2006), 13.

57. Presbyterian Church in the U.S. General Assembly, *Minutes of the General Assembly of the Presbyterian Church in the United States of America, 1920* (Philadelphia: 1920), 40.

58. Alexis McCrossen, *Holy Day, Holiday: The American Sunday* (Ithaca, NY: Cornell University Press, 2000), 100–105; Craig Harline, *Sunday: A History of the First Day from Babylonia to the Super Bowl* (New Haven, CT: Yale University Press, 2007), 332–356.

59. Baker, *Playing with God*, 162–164; "Should Christians Play on Sunday?," *Literary Digest*, January 30, 1926, 27–28, 57, 59.

60. W. A. Phelon, "Cincinnati Expert Sees Success for Rickey in New Double Role," *St. Louis Star*, February 1, 1919; Charlie Bevis, *Sunday Baseball: The Major Leagues' Struggle to Play Baseball on the Lord's Day, 1876–1934* (Jefferson, NC: McFarland & Co., 2003).

61. Lowenfish, *Branch Rickey*, 26–28; Long and Lamb, *Jackie Robinson*, 52; Damon Runyon, "Cardinals Respect Great Moral Courage of Manager Rickey," *St. Louis Star*, January 26, 1923, 16.

62. Robert S. Lynd and Helen Merrell Lynd, *Middletown: A Study in Modern American Culture* (New York: Harcourt Brace & Company, 1929), 341.

63. Stagg to Ben Sweeney, December 3, 1954, AASP, Box 6, Folder 5.

64. Branch Rickey, "Religious Education as Viewed from the Field of Sport," *Christian Advocate*, September 24, 1931, 1155.

65. Stidger, "Introducing Branch Rickey," 45.

66. Stephen Prothero, *American Jesus: How the Son of God Became a National Icon* (New York: Farrar, Straus, and Giroux, 2003), 87–115; Putney, *Muscular Christianity*, 98.

67. Branch Rickey, "A Losing Play," *Association Men*, July 1916, 554; Harry Emerson Fosdick, *The Manhood of the Master* (New York: Association Press, 1913), 52.

68. Lowenfish, *Branch Rickey*, 375.

69. Giovanni Papini, *Life of Christ*, trans. Dorothy Canfield Fisher (New York: Harcourt, Brace and Company, 1923), 10.

70. Rickey, "Religious Education as Viewed from the Field of Sport," 1155. Rickey's emphasis on "empirical knowledge" grounded in experience was shaped by William James. See Lowenfish, *Branch Rickey*, 375. On James's influence on the development of liberal Protestantism in the early twentieth century see Dorrien, *The Making of American Liberal Theology*, 218–226.

71. Prothero makes this point in *American Jesus*, 108–111. The classic formulation of this shift is Warren I. Susman, "'Personality' and the Making of Twentieth-Century Culture," in *Culture as History: The Transformation of American Society in the Twentieth Century* (New York: Pantheon Books, 1984), 271–285. See also T. J. Jackson Lears, "From Salvation to Self-Realization: Advertising and the Therapeutic Roots of the Consumer Culture, 1880–1930," in *The Culture of Consumption: Critical Essays in American History, 1880–1980*, ed. Richard Wightman Fox and T. J. Jackson Lears (New York: Pantheon Books, 1983), 1–38.

72. For a similar claim about the way "character" and "personality" blended together, see Richard Wightman Fox, "The Culture of Liberal Protestant Progressivism, 1875–1925," *Journal of Interdisciplinary History* 23, no. 3 (Winter 1993): 647–649.

73. Ingrassia, *The Rise of Gridiron University*, 171–199; Oriard, *King Football*, 108–110; Dyreson, *Making the American Team*, 199–207.

74. "When Does Sport Cease to Be Sport?," *Christian Century*, July 15, 1926, 885; "Sportsmanship Is Not Enough," *Christian Century*, September 22, 1927, 1096–1098.

75. "Honesty Is More Important than Amateurism," *Christian Century*, September 4, 1929, 1076; "Honesty in College Athletics," *Christian Century*, October 23, 1929, 1315. On the Carnegie Report, see Ronald A. Smith, *Pay for Play: A History of Big-Time College Athletics Reform* (Urbana: University of Illinois Press, 2011), 59–71.

76. "Athletics in Higher Institutions of Learning," *The Presbyterian*, August 27, 1925, 5.

77. "These Four," *The Presbyterian*, October 1, 1931, 3–4; "The Sporting World," *The Presbyterian*, October 8, 1931, 1.
78. On the construction of distinctions between "highbrow" and "lowbrow" culture, see Lawrence W. Levine, *Highbrow/Lowbrow: The Emergence of Cultural Hierarchy in America* (Cambridge, MA: Harvard University Press, 1988).
79. Rubin, *The Making of Middlebrow Culture*, xvii–xviii, 2–5.
80. Hedstrom, *The Rise of Liberal Religion*, 40.
81. E. Smith, *What Would Jesus Read?*, 11. Middlebrow Protestantism had nineteenth-century antecedents in the Chautauqua movement. See Andrew Chamberlin Rieser, *The Chautauqua Moment: Protestants, Progressives, and the Culture of Modern Liberalism, 1874–1920* (New York: Columbia University Press, 2003). It also continued trends from popular nineteenth-century ministers like Henry Ward Beecher and Russell Conwell, although it incorporated more recent insights from psychology. What Kate Bowler says of the proponents of positive thinking is an apt description of many leading middlebrow Protestants: "its prophets were not typically systematizers or intellectuals, but popularizers and doers." See Bowler, *Blessed: A History of the American Prosperity Gospel* (New York: Oxford University Press, 2013), 31.
82. Hedstrom, *The Rise of Liberal Religion*, 24–28, 39–46.
83. Hedstrom, *The Rise of Liberal Religion*, 80; Grem, *The Blessings of Business*, 14–19; Jeffrey Charles, *Service Clubs in American Society: Rotary, Kiwanis, and Lions* (Urbana: University of Illinois Press, 1993); Rolf Lunden, *Business and Religion in the American 1920s* (Westport, CT: Greenwood Press, 1988).
84. Richard M. Fried, *The Man Everybody Knew: Bruce Barton and the Making of Modern America* (Chicago: Ivan R. Dee, 2005), 84–107; Hedstrom, *The Rise of Liberal Religion*, 25–27; E. Smith, *What Would Jesus Read?*, 106–132; Charles H. Lippy, *Do Real Men Pray? Images of the Christian Man and Male Spirituality in White Protestant America* (Knoxville: University of Tennessee Press, 2005), 113–142.
85. Hedstrom, *The Rise of Liberal Religion*, 35.
86. Daniel Poling, *Mine Eyes Have Seen* (New York: McGraw-Hill, 1959). Poling's *Christian Herald* was a self-described "interdenominational Protestant" monthly magazine with a subscriber base of over two hundred thousand that championed "Evangelical Christian Faith . . . World Peace . . . Church Unity . . . [and] Prohibition" and had an editorial board that included the theologically conservative Poling and theological liberals Charles Sheldon and S. Parkes Cadman. On Fosdick, see Robert Moats Miller, *Harry Emerson Fosdick: Preacher, Pastor, Prophet* (New York: Oxford University Press, 1985), 418–440; Bowman, *The Urban Pulpit*.
87. Edgar Guest, "Wreckers," *Des Moines Tribune*, February 22, 1929, 10. On Guest see Joan Shelley Rubin, *Songs of Ourselves: The Uses of Poetry in America* (Cambridge, MA: Harvard University Press), 66–74.
88. James H. Hutchisson, *The Rise of Sinclair Lewis, 1920–1930* (University Park: Pennsylvania State University Press, 1996).
89. Schultz, *Tri-Faith America*, 15–42; Mislin, *Saving Faith*, 140–162.
90. Stagg to Sol Butler, May 10, 1926, AASP, Box 1a, Folder 12.
91. Mainline Protestants generally mirrored this approach when it came to race. See James F. Findlay Jr., *Church People in the Struggle: The National Council of Churches and the Black Freedom Movement, 1950–1970* (New York: Oxford University Press, 1993), 18–19; David W. Wills, "The Enduring Distance: Black Americans and the Establishment," in Hutchison, ed., *Between the Times*, 168–192. However, as Curtis J. Evans shows in *A Theology of Brotherhood: The Federal Council of Churches and the Problem of Race* (New York: NYU Press, 2024), the "theology of brotherhood" that some mainline leaders helped to forge played an important role in challenging theologies of segregation. On the "gentleman's agreement" that limited Black participation in baseball and interregional college football, see Charles H. Martin, *Benching Jim Crow: The Rise and Fall of the Color Line in Southern College Sports, 1890–1980* (Urbana: University of Illinois Press, 2010), 1–52; Chris Lamb, *Conspiracy of Silence: Sportswriters and the Long Campaign to Desegregate Baseball* (Lincoln: University of Nebraska Press, 2012).
92. "Religious Books of the Month," *Publishers Weekly*, October 29, 1927, 1641–1642. On Cadman as a middlebrow figure, see Francis J. McConnell, "S. Parkes Cadman," *Religion in Life* 5, no. 4 (Autumn 1936): 483–493; Bendroth, *The Last Puritans*, 136–139.
93. William L. Stidger, "Developing the Homiletic Mind," *Methodist Review*, May 1929, 391.

94. Barbara J. Keys, *Globalizing Sport: National Rivalry and International Community in the 1930s* (Cambridge, MA: Harvard University Press, 2006), 83.

95. Materials on the Sportsmanship Brotherhood are found in AASP, Box 6, Folder 10. See also A. E. Hamilton, *Sportsmanship: A Bridge of Understanding between the Nations of the World* (New York: 1926).

96. "War and Sport," *Sportsmanship*, December 1928, 1.

97. On the YMCA's theologically liberal but business-friendly approach in the 1920s, see Clifford Putney, "Character Building in the YMCA, 1880–1930," *Mid-America* 73, no. 1 (January 1991): 49–70; Setran, *The College "Y,"* 179–243.

98. Norman Beasley, "Sportsmanship," *Association Men*, December 1926, 151–152, 179.

99. Norman Beasley, "Are Athletes Good Business Risks?," *Association Men*, May 1927, 399–400. See also Robert F. Kelley, "How They Got That Way," *Association Men*, November 1924, 113–114. Kelley published a regular column on moral lessons from the world of sports.

100. "John M. Siddall," *Association Men*, August 1923, 567. Barton wrote forty-three articles for the magazine between 1920 and 1930, and from the late 1920s until 1932 he published a monthly column. On *American Magazine's* cultural approach, see Tom Pendergrast, *Creating the Modern Man: American Magazines and Consumer Culture, 1900–1950* (Columbia: University of Missouri Press, 2000), 111–166.

101. For analysis of the "true success" ideology of *American Magazine* and also the use of sports celebrities, see Charles L. Ponce de Leon, *Self-Exposure: Human-Interest Journalism and the Emergence of Celebrity in America, 1890–1940* (Chapel Hill: University of North Carolina Press, 2002), 113–138, 241–273. For a few specific examples, see Bo McMillin, "Fighting for Old Centre," *American Magazine*, February 1922, 53, 116–120; Grantland Rice, "Do Your Stuff," *American Magazine*, July 1924, 45, 169–171; William S. Dutton, "The House That Mack Built over Seven Cellars," *American Magazine*, June 1930, 42–43, 84, 86.

102. Hedstrom, *The Rise of Liberal Religion*, 105; Glenn Clark, "The Soul's Sincere Desire," *Atlantic Monthly*, August 1924, 167–172; Glenn Clark, *The Soul's Sincere Desire* (Boston: Little, Brown, and Company, 1925).

103. Glenn Clark, *A Man's Reach: The Autobiography of Glenn Clark* (New York: Harper & Brothers, 1949), 100, 158–160; Hedstrom, *The Rise of Liberal Religion*, 104–106; Jeanne Halgren Kilde, *Nature and Revelation: A History of Macalester College* (Minneapolis: University of Minnesota Press, 2010), 138–140.

104. Clark, "The Soul's Sincere Desire," 168. Clark discussed his involvement in athletics in his autobiography. See Clark, *A Man's Reach*, 81, 94–99, 119–122, 173–185.

105. Glenn Clark, "A Lost Art of Jesus," *Atlantic Monthly*, March 1925, 316–325; Glenn Clark, "Shall We Pray for Athletic Victory?," *The Intercollegian*, October 1925, 3–4.

106. Glenn Clark, *Power of the Spirit on the Athletic Field* (St. Paul, MN: 1929). The "in tune" phrase was popular in New Thought circles, especially after the publication of Ralph Waldo Trine's *In Tune with the Infinite* (1897).

107. Stagg to Paul Stagg, May 17, 1931, AASP, Box 2, Folder 15.

108. "Dr. Depew as Missionary," *New York Times*, October 31, 1887, 5.

Chapter 2

1. "Thousands Throng to Pay Last Tribute to 'Tiger' as Funeral Services Are Held at City Auditorium," *Atlanta Constitution*, November 22, 1927, 9; Morgan Blake, *A Sports Editor Finds Christ* (Hapeville, GA: Hale Publishing, 1952), 129.

2. The literature on fundamentalism is extensive. Especially important for my interpretation is Marsden, *Fundamentalism and American Culture*, and Gloege, *Guaranteed Pure*. Both Marsden and Gloege conclude their analysis in the 1920s. The best accounts of fundamentalism in the interwar years are Sutton, *American Apocalypse*, 80–262, and Carpenter, *Revive Us Again*, 13–140. Daniel Hummel's *The Rise and Fall of Dispensationalism: How the Evangelical Battle over the End Times Shaped a Nation* (Grand Rapids, MI: Eerdmans, 2023) is crucial for understanding the premillennial theologies embraced by fundamentalists.

3. My interpretation of Keswick spirituality is drawn from Marsden, *Fundamentalism and American Culture*, 77–80, 94–101; Carpenter, *Revive Us Again*, 80–85; and Gloege, *Guaranteed Pure*, 145–148.

4. They were summarized as five "fundamentals" by the Presbyterian General Assembly in 1910. See Marsden, *Fundamentalism and American Culture*, 117.

5. The "antimodernist evangelical" and "churchly conservative" descriptors are from Sutton, *American Apocalypse*, 80.

6. Bradley J. Longfield, *The Presbyterian Controversy: Fundamentalism, Modernists, and Moderates* (New York: Oxford University Press, 1991); Barry Hankins and Thomas Kidd, *Baptists in America: A History* (New York: Oxford University Press, 2015), 183–195.
7. Marsden, *Fundamentalism and American Culture*, 185–193.
8. Sutton, *American Apocalypse*, 147. On fundamentalists' continued engagement with mainstream American culture, see Sutton, *American Apocalypse*, 116–262; Douglas Carl Abrams, *Old-Time Religion: Embracing Modernist Culture* (Lanham, MD: Lexington Books, 2017); Douglas Carl Abrams, *Selling the Old-Time Religion: American Fundamentalists and Mass Culture, 1920–1940* (Athens: University of Georgia Press, 2001). There were Black Protestants who identified themselves as fundamentalists and shared similar theological emphases to those of white fundamentalists. However, they operated within Black denominations and remained outside the fundamentalist networks. See Daniel R. Bare, *Black Fundamentalists: Conservative Christianity and Racial Identity in the Segregation Era* (New York: NYU Press, 2021); Mary Beth Swetnam Mathews, *Doctrine and Race: African American Evangelicals and Fundamentalism between the Wars* (Tuscaloosa: University of Alabama Press, 2017).
9. Carpenter, *Revive Us Again*, 13–141; Grem, *The Blessings of Business*, 13–48.
10. Carpenter, *Revive Us Again*, 43.
11. Ladd and Mathisen, *Muscular Christianity*, 80–83; Martin, *Hero of the Heartland.*
12. On Liddell, see Duncan Hamilton, *For the Glory: Eric Liddell's Journey from Olympic Champion to Modern Martyr* (New York: Penguin Press, 2016), 97–112; "The One Day in Seven," *The Alliance Weekly*, April 27, 1929, 260. On Buker, see Charles E. Parker, "How Many Athletes to Follow Eric?," *Pittsburgh Gazette Times*, March 31, 1924, 9; Eric S. Fife, *Against the Clock: The Story of Ray Buker, Sr., Olympic Runner and Missionary Statesman* (Grand Rapids, MI: Zondervan, 1981).
13. Mrs. Howard [Geraldine] Taylor, *Borden of Yale '09: The Life That Counts* (Philadelphia: China Inland Missions, 1926), 123, 285.
14. The "missionary idealism" line comes from Carpenter, *Revive Us Again*, 83.
15. Carpenter, *Revive Us Again*, 57–63.
16. Joseph Britan, "Religious Foundations of National Life," *Moody Bible Institute Monthly*, November 1921, 564.
17. "The One Day in Seven," 260.
18. Abrams, *Selling the Old-Time Religion*, 76, 87; Michael S. Hamilton, "The Fundamentalist Harvard: Wheaton College and the Continuing Vitality of American Evangelicalism, 1919–1965," (PhD diss., University of Notre Dame, 1994), 195–196.
19. "Clergymen and Base Ball," *Moody Bible Institute Monthly*, August 1922, 1155.
20. Ladd and Mathisen, *Muscular Christianity*, 85; Abrams, *Selling the Old-Time Religion*, 76; Sutton, *American Apocalypse*, 119–120.
21. John Roach Straton, *Fighting the Devil in Modern Babylon* (Boston: Alpine Press, 1929), 129.
22. Margaret Lamberts Bendroth, *Fundamentalism and Gender: 1875 to the Present* (New Haven, CT: Yale University Press, 1993), 54–80; Betty A. DeBerg, *Ungodly Women: Gender and the First Wave of American Fundamentalism* (Minneapolis: Fortress Press, 1990), 75–117.
23. Martin, *Hero of the Heartland*, 65–79; Hankins, *Jesus and Gin*, 41–62.
24. Mark Sumner Still, "'Fighting Bob' Shuler: Fundamentalist and Reformer," (PhD diss., Claremont Graduate School, 1988), 37; Bendroth, *Fundamentalism and Gender*, 77; Barry Hankins, *God's Rascal: J. Frank Norris and the Beginnings of Southern Fundamentalism* (Lexington: The University Press of Kentucky, 1996), 14–15.
25. J. Elwin Wright, *The Old Fashioned Revival Hour and the Broadcasters* (Boston: The Fellowship Press, 1940), 33–34, 45–46.
26. For background on Rader, see Larry K. Eskridge, "Only Believe: Paul Rader and the Chicago Gospel Tabernacle, 1922–1933" (master's thesis, University of Maryland, 1985); Hankins, *Jesus and Gin*, 41–62; Tona J. Hangen, *Redeeming the Dial: Radio, Religion and Popular Culture in America* (Chapel Hill: University of North Carolina Press, 2002), 37–56.
27. Paul Rader, "The Offensive Defense," *The Alliance Weekly*, September 30, 1920, 450.
28. "This Week's Illustration," *The Alliance Weekly*, October 23, 1920, 475. See also "Lessons from Great Athletes," *The Alliance Weekly*, October 9, 1926, 661.
29. Paul Rader, "I Sent You to Reap," *The Alliance Weekly*, January 6, 1923, 678.
30. John C. Page, "Better Recreation," *Moody Bible Institute Monthly*, August 1922, 1154.
31. Hunter M. Hampton, "Salvation on the Gridiron: Fundamentalism, Football, and Christian Manhood at Wheaton College, 1900–1949," *International Journal of the History of Sport*

39, no. 4 (2022): 425–441; Mark Taylor Dalhouse, *An Island in the Lake of Fire: Bob Jones University, Fundamentalism, and the Separatist Movement* (Athens: University of Georgia Press, 1996), 136.

32. Statistics from Harvey, *Christianity and Race in the American South*, 121. Scholarship on religion in the South is an entire discipline unto itself. I am focusing here on the established Protestant denominations, mostly the Methodists and Baptists. For background on "mainline" Southern Protestantism, see Wayne Flynt's collected essays in *Southern Religion and Christian Diversity in the Twentieth Century* (Tuscaloosa: University of Alabama Press, 2016); Paul Harvey, *Freedom's Coming: Religious Culture and the Shaping of the South from the Civil War Era through the Civil Rights Era* (Chapel Hill: University of North Carolina Press, 2005); Alison Collis Greene, *No Depression in Heaven: The Great Depression, the New Deal, and the Transformation of Religion in the Delta* (New York: Oxford University Press, 2016). Although some fundamentalists operated in the South, the fundamentalist movement was centered in the North, Midwest, and West. See William R. Glass, *Strangers in Zion: Fundamentalism in the South, 1900–1950* (Macon, GA: Mercer University Press, 2001).

33. Benjamin Rader, *Baseball: A History of America's Game*, 3rd ed. (Urbana: University of Illinois Press, 2008), 154; Marshall D. Wright, *The Southern Association in Baseball, 1885–1961* (Jefferson, NC: McFarland, 2002).

34. Blake, *A Sports Editor Finds Christ*, 113–114; Floyd Chaffin, "'Pepper' Martin: An Interview," *Baptist Student*, November 1933, 23.

35. Andrew Doyle, "Foolish and Useless Sport: The Southern Evangelical Crusade against Intercollegiate Football," *Journal of Sport History* 24, no. 3 (Fall 1997): 336. See also Baker, *Playing with God*, 85–107. On the importance of sports to the civic culture of the South, see Patrick B. Miller, ed., *The Sporting World of the Modern South* (Urbana: University of Illinois Press, 2002), and Pamela Grundy, *Learning to Win: Sports, Education, and Social Change in Twentieth-Century North Carolina* (Chapel Hill: University of North Carolina Press, 2001).

36. George Biggers, "Centre Now Ranks alongside of Best Football Teams in the Country," *Danville Daily Messenger* (Danville, KY), November 13, 1919, 3; "'Miracle Man' of Football," *Danville Daily Messenger* (Danville, KY), November 15, 1919, 2; Watterson, *College Football*, 149.

37. See, for example, Fred Turbyville, "Centre College Prays and Cries, Then Goes Out and Wins," *New Castle Herald* (New Castle, PA), November 21, 1919, 14. For local stories that discussed Centre College's pregame prayer, see "Great Game," *Kentucky Advocate*, November 5, 1917, 2; "For Centre and Kentucky," *Danville Daily Messenger* (Danville, KY), November 14, 1919, 4.

38. Frank G. Weaver, "Come On, You Praying Kentuckians," *Association Men*, March 1920, 416–418. See also "Banquet for Football Team," *Danville Daily Messenger* (Danville, KY), November 24, 1919, 1.

39. Oriard, *King Football*, 75.

40. "When Centre Sinks Her Cleats into Harvard Gridiron Next Fall," *Danville Daily Messenger* (Danville, KY), December 17, 1919, 3.

41. Oriard, *King Football*, 75–78.

42. On the creation of Lost Cause mythology, see Charles Reagan Wilson, *Baptized in Blood: The Religion of the Lost Cause, 1865–1920* (Athens: University of Georgia Press, 1980); Arthur Remillard, *Southern Civil Religions: Imagining the Good Society in the Post-Reconstruction Era* (Athens: University of Georgia Press, 2011).

43. On the way that the sports press deployed Old South and Lost Cause themes when covering Southern football teams, see Oriard, *King Football*, 88–93. For more recent manifestations of the links between Lost Cause mythology and Southern college football, see Eric Bain-Selbo, *Game Day and God: Football, Faith, and Politics in the American South* (Macon, GA: Mercer University Press, 2009), 86–173.

44. Ralph D. Paine, *First Down, Kentucky!* (Boston: Houghton Mifflin, 1921), 314.

45. Paine, *First Down, Kentucky!*, 332.

46. Bentley Sloane, *The Glory Years of Football: Centenary College of Louisiana, 1922–1942* (Shreveport, LA: Centenary College, 2000), 6–7.

47. *Bulletin of Centenary College of Louisiana* 89, no. 4 (1922); Sloane, *The Glory Years of Football*, 8.

48. "'Bo' McMillin's Philosophy of Life," *New Orleans Christian Advocate*, February 2, 1922, 8.

49. Sloane, *The Glory Years of Football*, 6–14; "The Greater Centenary College," *New Orleans Christian Advocate*, September 20, 1923, 8.

50. Watterson, *College Football*, 147–149; Sloane, *The Glory Years of Football*, 12–14.

51. "Athletics as Advertisements," *Daily Lariat*, February 26, 1930, 2; Oriard, *King Football*, 78–83, 93–99.

52. Warren A. Candler, "Defeating Culture for Unworthy Advertising," *New Orleans Christian Advocate*, April 6, 1922, 4–5; Warren A. Candler, "A Direful Dilemma," *New Orleans Christian Advocate*, February 28, 1924, 23.

53. Andrew Doyle, "'Fighting Whiskey and Immorality' at Auburn: The Politics of Southern Football, 1919–1927," *Southern Cultures* 10, no. 3 (Fall 2004): 6–30; Dwayne Cox, *The Village on the Plain: Auburn University, 1856–2006* (Tuscaloosa: The University of Alabama Press, 2016), 82–87.

54. Jeff D. Ray, "Inter-Collegiate Football," *Baptist Standard*, December 19, 1929, 14–15; E. P. West, "Why I Am Not a Football Enthusiast," *Baptist Standard*, January 2, 1930, 3.

55. On rural and holiness movement groups suspicious of football, see Grant Wacker, *Heaven Below: Early Pentecostals and American Culture* (Cambridge, MA: Harvard University Press, 2001), 128, 134, 152; Ted Ownby, *Subduing Satan: Religion, Recreation, and Manhood in the Rural South, 1865–1920* (Chapel Hill: University of North Carolina Press, 1990), 194–211; Randall J. Stephens, *The Fire Spreads: Holiness and Pentecostalism in the American South* (Cambridge, MA: Harvard University Press, 2008), 69–71, 122–123. On the rural/urban divide among early twentieth-century Southern Baptists, see Paul Harvey, *Redeeming the South: Religious Cultures and Racial Identities among Southern Baptists, 1865–1925* (Chapel Hill: University of North Carolina Press, 1997), 197–226.

56. Andrew Doyle, "'Causes Won, Not Lost': College Football and the Modernization of the American South," *International Journal of the History of Sport* 11, no. 2 (August 1994): 231–251; Doyle, "'Fighting Whiskey and Immorality,'" 22–28.

57. Untitled editorial, *Baptist Standard*, March 12, 1931, 5.

58. Claude U. Broach, *Dr. Frank: An Informal Biography of Frank H. Leavell, Leader of Baptist Youth* (Nashville, TN: Broadman Press, 1950), 73. On the BSU, see also Joseph P. Boone, *It Came to Pass: The Birth, Growth, and Evaluation of the Baptist Student Union and the Baptist Chairs of Bible* (Ann Arbor, MI: Edwards Brothers, 1953). On the SBC's post–World War I expansion, see Hankins and Kidd, *Baptists in America*, 176–182.

59. See, for example, "Football and Religion," *Baptist Student*, September–October 1926, 21; "Falling Champions," *Baptist Student*, December 1926, 9; "Athletics and Religion—Their Relationship," *Baptist Student*, September–October 1931, 14–15; T. B. Maston, "Playing the Game," *Baptist Student*, November 1931, 4, 7.

60. The best account of Blake's life is his autobiography, *A Sports Editor Finds Christ*. On Blake's 1922 conversion and early evangelistic work, see Morgan Blake, "A Striking Testimony," *Christian Index*, November 9, 1922, 6.

61. An advertisement of Blake's and Barron's revival service can be found in the *Atlanta Constitution*, April 7, 1923, 20. See also Blake, *A Sports Editor Finds Christ*, 53. For Blake's 1929 Bible class in Nashville, see "Morgan Blake to Be Bible Class Speaker," *Nashville Tennessean*, November 10, 1929, 12.

62. *New Georgia Encyclopedia*, s.v., "Atlanta Journal-Constitution," by Chuck Perry, January 5, 2004, http://www.georgiaencyclopedia.org/articles/arts-culture/atlanta-journal-constitution.

63. "Hoover Says Bible Is Nation's Guide," *Baltimore Sun*, May 6, 1929, 3.

64. Blake, *A Sports Editor Finds Christ*, 112–113. Billy Sunday, Billy Graham, and the biblical figures of Moses and Paul made the cut as well.

65. Blake, *A Sports Editor Finds Christ*, 166–167. For background on Barnhouse, see C. Allyn Russell, "Donald Grey Barnhouse: Fundamentalist Who Changed," *Journal of Presbyterian History* 59, no. 1 (Spring 1981): 33–57. On the Baptist Tabernacle's links with Northern fundamentalists, see Glass, *Strangers in Zion*, 33–51.

66. Carter Latimer, "Morgan Blake on 'Sunday Baseball,'" *Greenville News* (Greenville, SC), August 6, 1942, 11.

67. Blake, *A Sports Editor Finds Christ*, 72–86.

68. Martin, *Benching Jim Crow*, 1–52.

69. Douglas Hudgins, "Christian Students Looking at the Problem of Race Relations," *Baptist Student*, March 1935, 10. See also "The Race Problem," *Baptist Student*, March 1927, 10.

70. On the "black Protestant establishment," see Wills, "The Enduring Distance," 170. Important books for understanding Black Protestantism in the early twentieth century include Carter G. Woodson's landmark *The History of the Negro Church* (Washington, DC: Associated Publishers, 1921); Evelyn Brooks Higginbotham, *Righteous Discontent: The Women's Movement in the Black Baptist Church, 1880–1920* (Cambridge, MA: Harvard University

Press, 1993); Dennis C. Dickerson, *The African Methodist Episcopal Church: A History* (New York: Cambridge University Press, 2020); Anthea Butler, *Women in the Church of God in Christ: Making a Sanctified World* (Chapel Hill: University of North Carolina Press, 2007); Lerone A. Martin, *Preaching on Wax: The Phonograph and the Shaping of Modern African American Religion* (New York: New York University Press, 2014); Gary Dorrien, *The New Abolition: W. E. B. Du Bois and the Black Social Gospel* (New Haven, CT: Yale University Press, 2015); Wallace D. Best, *Passionately Human, No Less Divine: Religion and Culture in Black Chicago, 1915–1952* (Princeton, NJ: Princeton University Press, 2005); Mathews, *Doctrine and Race*; Bare, *Black Fundamentalists*.

71. Derrick White, *Blood, Sweat, & Tears: Jake Gaither, Florida A&M, and the History of Black College Football* (Chapel Hill: University of North Carolina Press, 2019), 22–39. See also David K. Wiggins and Ryan A. Swanson, eds., *Separate Games: African American Sport behind the Walls of Segregation* (Fayetteville: University of Arkansas Press, 2016); Edwin Bancroft Henderson, *The Negro in Sports* (Washington, DC: Associated Publishers, 1939).

72. The "muscular assimilation" phrase comes from Patrick B. Miller, "To 'Bring the Race along Rapidly': Sport, Student Culture, and Educational Mission at Historically Black Colleges during the Interwar Years," in Miller, *Sporting World of the Modern South*, 130. For more on Black muscular Christianity, see Putz, "Tracing the Historical Contours of Black Muscular Christianity and American Sport."

73. Mjagkij, *Light in the Darkness*.

74. Edwin B. Henderson and Garnet C. Wilkinson, "Amateur Athletics," in *Official Handbook of the Interscholastic Athletic Association of Middle Atlantic States* (1912), 13. On the early growth of basketball in the Black community, see Bob Kuska, *Hot Potato: How Washington and New York Gave Birth to Black Basketball and Changed America's Game Forever* (Charlottesville: University of Virginia Press, 2004); Claude Johnson, *The Black Fives: The Epic Story of Basketball's Forgotten Era* (New York: Adams Press, 2021). For background on Henderson, see Edwin Bancroft Henderson II, *The Grandfather of Black Basketball: The Life and Times of Dr. E. B. Henderson* (Lanham, MD: Rowman & Littlefield, 2024); David K. Wiggins, "Edwin Bancroft Henderson: Physical Educator, Civil Rights Activist, and Chronicler of African American Athletes," *Research Quarterly for Exercise and Sport* 70, no. 2 (1999): 91–112.

75. White, *Blood, Sweat, & Tears*, 25. See also Miller, "To 'Bring the Race Along Rapidly,'" 129–152.

76. S. H. Archer, "Football in Our Colleges," *The Voice of the Negro*, March 1906, 200–201.

77. George E. Curry, *Jake Gaither: America's Most Famous Black Coach* (New York: Dodd, Mead & Company, 1977), 13–14, 81. See also White, *Blood, Sweat, & Tears*, 33–39, 90–91; Roosevelt Wilson, *Agile, Mobile, Hostile: The Biography of Alonzo S. "Jake" Gaither*, ed. Yanela G. McLeod (Tallahassee, FL: CreateSpace, 2017), 156–164.

78. Edwin B. Henderson, "The Colored College Athlete," *The Crisis* (July 1911), 115–119.

79. Onaje X. O. Woodbine, *Black Gods of the Asphalt: Religion, Hip-Hop, and Street Basketball* (New York: Columbia University Press, 2016), 38; Conrad V. Norman, "Athletics in New York and New Jersey," in *Official Handbook*, 93; Johnson, *The Black Fives*.

80. "Columbia University Basket Ball Star," *Chicago Defender*, April 2, 10.

81. Susan J. Rayl, "Robert L. 'Bob' Douglas: Aristocracy on the Court, and Architect of Men," in *Before Jackie Robinson: The Transcendent Role of Black Sporting Pioneers*, ed. Gerald R. Gems (Lincoln: University of Nebraska Press, 2017), 156; Lawrence H. Rushing, "A Black Woman and Proud: Effa Manley and Racial Self-Identification," *Black Ball* 4, no. 2 (Fall 2011): 26–27.

82. J. Le Count Chestnut, "Yale Best Sports," *Afro-American*, March 10, 1928, 13.

83. On Yost's refusal to recruit Black football players, see John Behee, *Hail to the Victors! Black Athletes at the University of Michigan* (Ann Arbor, MI: Ulrich's Books, 1974), 33.

84. Behee, *Hail to the Victors!*, 12–16; Mjagkij, *Light in the Darkness*, 131.

85. Roscoe Simmons, "The Week," *Chicago Defender*, July 19, 1924, 13.

86. "Kids Wild about Earl and Hubbard," *Afro-American*, August 15, 1924, A16.

87. De Hart Hubbard, "DeHart Hubbard's Sport Review," *New Journal and Guide*, December 5, 1925, 5.

88. William DeHart Hubbard interview with John Behee, September 26, 1970, John Richard Behee Sound Recordings, Bentley Historical Library, University of Michigan. Hubbard's newspaper columns ran in several Black newspapers in the 1920s, and his post-Olympics work was documented by the Black press. See, for example, "DeHart Hubbard, Famous Athlete, Has Quintet Which Ranks with Best," *Pittsburgh Courier*, February 15, 1930, 14.

89. Chestnut, "Yale Best Sports."

90. DeHart Hubbard, "DeHart Hubbard's Sports Review," *Norfolk Journal & Guide*, December 26, 1925, 4.

91. Although he does not focus on religion, Daniel Anderson's *The Culture of Sports in the Harlem Renaissance* (Jefferson, NC: McFarland, 2017) offers a thorough analysis of the debates about sports among Black intellectuals in the 1920s.

92. See, for example, "A.M.E. Preachers Go on Record," *New Journal and Guide*, December 22, 1928, 7.

93. Edwin Henderson, "Sports for Masses Essential," *Afro-American*, December 29, 1928, 12.

94. Charles H. Williams, "The Negro Church and Recreation," *Southern Workman*, February 1926, 59–69. As Gary Dorrien notes in *The New Abolition*, 10–12, full-fledged support for social gospel activism was a minority position for Black churches. However, concern for meeting practical needs and opposition to racism were central features of many Black churches even if they were conservative on other issues. On "mainline" Black Protestant support for sports, see also Clarence Taylor, *The Black Churches of Brooklyn* (New York: Columbia University Press, 1994), 84–85; Rob Ruck, *Sandlot Seasons: Sport in Black Pittsburgh* (Urbana: University of Illinois Press, 1993), 19–23.

95. Williams, "The Negro Church and Recreation," 61.

96. Martin, *Preaching on Wax*, 101.

97. Rev J. M. Gates, "The Ball Game of Life," recorded February 1928, streaming audio, accessed July 1, 2021, https://open.spotify.com/track/0TD4hfMoNFUaVZAlZ7tfQM?si=069c610900a044bd.

98. Rev J. M. Gates, "Tiger Flowers' Last Fight," recorded February 1928, streaming audio, accessed July 1, 2021, https://open.spotify.com/track/4OVWzQLSRacdJG3pmProDI?si=45b08fb896974ea5.

99. Randy Roberts, *Papa Jack: Jack Johnson and the Era of White Hopes* (New York: Free Press, 1983); Louis Moore, *I Fight for a Living: Boxing and the Battle for Black Manhood, 1880–1915* (Urbana: University of Illinois Press, 2017), 138–172.

100. Tiger Flowers "Tiger Flowers Finds That Christianity Doesn't Bar Boxing," *Chicago Defender*, February 14, 1925, 10. For background on Flowers, see Andrew M. Kaye, *The Pussycat of Prizefighting: Tiger Flowers and the Politics of Black Celebrity* (Athens: University of Georgia Press, 2004).

101. "Tiger Flowers Credit to Race Clean Liver," *Indianapolis Recorder*, March 13, 1926, 6.

102. Lester Walton, "Press and Public Accept Flowers' Victory over Greb with Grace and Equanimity," *New Journal and Guide*, March 20, 1926, 5.

103. Dick Hawkins, "Tiger Flowers," *Atlanta Constitution*, November 21, 1927, 7.

104. Kaye, *The Pussycat of Prizefighting*, 145.

Chapter 3

1. "Speech by Branch Rickey before the Fellowship of Christian Athletes" (1956). I thank Michael McClanen for providing a copy of the speech transcript. Stagg could not attend the conference for health reasons. See Don McClanen to Amos Alonzo Stagg, August 7, 1956, AASP, Box 108, Folder 4.

2. Wayne Atcheson, *Impact for Christ: How FCA Has Influenced the Sports World* (Grand Island, NE: Cross Training Publishing, 1994), 148–156. Atcheston's book is an indispensable source for understanding the FCA's history. See also Joe Murchison, *Caution to the Wind: Faith Lessons from the Life of Don McClanen* (Grand Island, NE: Cross Training Publishing, 2008), 29–39.

3. Leo P. Ribuffo, *The Old Christian Right: The Protestant Far Right from the Great Depression to the Cold War* (Philadelphia: Temple University Press, 1983).

4. George Shane, "Bob Feller Still an Iowa Farm Boy," *Des Moines Register*, October 4, 1938, 3; David Vaught, *The Farmer's Game: Baseball in Rural America* (Baltimore: Johns Hopkins University Press, 2013), 76–103.

5. Wendy L. Wall, *Inventing the "American Way": The Politics of Consensus from the New Deal to the Civil Rights Movement* (New York: Oxford University Press, 2008), 63–100.

6. On the goodwill movement see Mislin, *Saving Faith*, 140–162; Schultz, *Tri-Faith America*, 15–67. On white Protestants and pluralism in the 1930s, see Pruitt, *Open Hearts, Closed Doors*, 57–90.

7. Matthew Lindaman, *Fit for America: Major John L. Griffith and the Quest for Athletics & Fitness* (Syracuse, NY: Syracuse University Press, 2018), 121–152; Brad Austin, *Democratic Sports: Men's and Women's College Athletics during the Great Depression* (Fayetteville: University of Arkansas Press, 2015), 96–102.

8. "Here Below," *Scholastic Coach*, April 1934, 6.

9. Elmer Berry, "School Athletics and the Changing Times," *Scholastic Coach*, September 1934, 30.

10. Lowenfish, *Branch Rickey*, 222, 273; Amos Alonzo Stagg to Richard Hurd, February 26, 1941, AASP, Box 4, Folder 4.

11. Otto Nall, ed., *Vital Religion: A Crusading Church Faces Its Third Century* (New York: The Methodist Book Concern, 1938), 82–84.

12. See, for example, "Athletic Deflation," *The Intercollegian* (October 1933), 2; "To Investigate College Football Again," *Christian Century*, December 2, 1936, 1595.

13. Nall, *Vital Religion*, 74–77. For background on Downs, see Long and Lamb, *Jackie Robinson*, 27–38; Randal Maurice Jelks, "A Methodist Life," in *42 Today: Jackie Robinson and His Legacy*, ed. Michal G. Long (New York: New York University Press, 2021), 15–28.

14. Martin, *Benching Jim Crow*, 1–52.

15. The best sources on Willis Ward and the 1934 game are Tyran Kai Steward, "In the Shadow of Jim Crow: The Benching and Betrayal of Willis Ward" (PhD diss., The Ohio State University, 2013), and John Behee, *Hail to the Victors!* (Ann Arbor, MI: Ulrich's Books, 1974), 18–30.

16. Steward, "In the Shadow of Jim Crow," 191; "'Hurry-Up' Yost on Alcohol and Athletics," *Christian Advocate*, January 28, 1926, 111–112; John Richard Behee, *Fielding Yost's Legacy to the University of Michigan* (Ann Arbor, MI: Uhlrich Books, 1971), 46–47.

17. Behee, *Hail to the Victors!*, 33.

18. Steward, "In the Shadow of Jim Crow," 142–155.

19. Quoted in Behee, *Hail to the Victors!*, 26–27.

20. "Michigan Fans Irked as Ward Sits on Bench," *Hammond Times*, October 20, 1934, 10; Steward, "In the Shadow of Jim Crow," 152–153.

21. "What Is a Radical?," *Chicago Defender*, October 27, 1934, 4.

22. Ted Talbert, "Moments They'd Like to Forget," *Detroit Free Press*, September 11, 1983, 24.

23. "Here Below," *Scholastic Coach*, December 1934, 5.

24. E.A. Abbott, "What The People Say," *Chicago Defender*, July 23, 1938, 16.

25. Henderson, *The Negro in Sports*, 310–311.

26. William J. Baker, *Jesse Owens: An American Life* (New York: Free Press, 1986), 73–128; Dominic J. Capeci Jr. and Martha Wilkerson, "Multifarious Hero: Joe Louis, American Society and Race Relations during World Crisis, 1935–1945," *Journal of Sport History* 10, no. 3 (Winter 1983): 5–25; Randy Roberts, *Joe Louis: Hard Times Man* (New Haven, CT: Yale University Press, 2010), 142–171.

27. Joe Kelly, "That Fight Again," *Emporia Gazette*, June 30, 1938, 11.

28. "Our World's Champion," *Atlanta Daily World*, June 24, 1937, 6.

29. William H. Wiggins Jr., "Joe Louis: American Folk Hero," in Miller and Wiggins, eds., *Sport and the Color Line*, 134; Roberts, *Joe Louis*, 108.

30. Lauren Rebecca Sklaroff, *Black Culture and the New Deal: The Quest for Civil Rights in the Roosevelt Era* (Chapel Hill: University of North Carolina Press, 2009), 123–157.

31. White, *Blood, Sweat, & Tears*, 40–57.

32. James Overmyer, *Effa Manley and the Newark Eagles* (Lanham, MD: Scarecrow Press, 1993), 19–21; John Howard Johnson, "Don't Buy Where You Can't Work," *Harlem: The War and Other Addresses* (New York: Wendell Malliet and Company, 1942), 60–68; John H. Johnson, *Harlem from the Rectory Window* (New York: St. Johann Press, 2009), 58–68.

33. Jackie Robinson, *I Never Had It Made: An Autobiography of Jackie Robinson* (New York: Putnam, 1972), 8.

34. "Pasadena Jaysee News," *California Eagle*, May 23, 1940, 7-B; J. Cullen Fentress, "Athletic Club Formed in Pasadena," *California Eagle*, May 30, 1940, 3-B.

35. Karl Downs, *Meet the Negro* (Pasadena, CA: Login Press, 1943).

36. "Another Revolution in Race Relations Brewing," *Christian Century*, September 2, 1942, 1045–1046. See Evans, *A Theology of Brotherhood*, and Zubovich, *Before the Religious Right*, 120–173, for context on broader mainline Protestant support for racial integration.

37. On Naismith, see Bernice Larson Webb, *The Basketball Man: James Naismith* (Lawrence: The University Press of Kansas, 1973); Rob Rains, *James Naismith: The Man Who Invented Basketball* (Philadelphia: Temple University Press, 2009). On Allen, see Scott Morrow Johnson, *Phog: The Most Influential Man in Basketball* (Lincoln: University of Nebraska Press, 2016); Robert A. Hunt, "Methodist Personalities," *Christian Advocate*, February 17, 1938, 157.

38. Milton S. Katz, *Breaking Through: John B. McLendon, Basketball Legend and Civil Rights Pioneer* (Fayetteville: University of Arkansas Press, 2007), 11–23; Gary Warner, "Head Scout on the Olympic Trail," *Christian Athlete*, February 1969, 10; Kurt Edward Kemper, *Before March Madness: The Wars for the Soul of College Basketball* (Urbana: University of Illinois Press, 2020), 214–252.

39. "Baseball's Color Bar Broken," *Christian Century*, April 23, 1947, 517; Douglas Wood Gibson, "Jackie Robinson: All-American Youth," *Christian Herald*, May 1948, 37–39. On Robinson's faith, see Long and Lamb, *Jackie Robinson*; Gary Scott Smith, *Strength for the Fight: The Life and Faith of Jackie Robinson* (Grand Rapids, MI: Eerdmans, 2022).

40. Rob Ruck, *Raceball: How the Major Leagues Colonized the Black and Latin Game* (Boston: Beacon Press, 2012), 72–117; Carmen Nanko-Fernández, "Turning Those Others' Cheeks: Racial Martyrdom and the Re-Integration of Major League Baseball," in *Gods, Games, & Globalization*, 239–262.

41. Lowenfish, *Branch Rickey*, 349–361; Long and Lamb, *Jackie Robinson*, 51–67. On the campaigns for desegregation before Rickey, see Lamb, *Conspiracy of Silence*.

42. Robinson, *I Never Had It Made*, 81–86; Thomas, *Globetrotting*, 13–40.

43. Peter Eisenstadt, *Against the Hounds of Hell: A Life of Howard Thurman* (Charlottesville: University of Virginia Press, 2021), 261–262.

44. U.S. Congress, House Committee on Un-American Activities, *Hearings Regarding Communist Infiltration of Minority Groups, July 13–18, 1949, Part I* (Washington, DC: US Government Printing Office, 1949), 482.

45. There is a vast literature on the way sports were used to project an image of American identity during the Cold War. However, scholars rarely give serious attention to religion. See, for example, Thomas, *Globetrotting*; Ariail, *Passing the Baton*; Rider and Witherspoon, eds., *Defending the American Way of Life*. One exception is Baker, *Playing with God*, 193–201, who offers a discussion of the FCA's connection to Cold War religious nationalism.

46. "Pencilings," *Christian Advocate* (Pacific ed.), February 24, 1938, 24; "Only Missed Three Sundays," *Los Angeles Times*, February 6, 1938, 17.

47. Nall, *Vital Religion*, 83.

48. Carol V. R. George, *God's Salesman: Norman Vincent Peale and the Power of Positive Thinking* (New York: Oxford University Press, 1993), 84–88, 93–94; Kruse, *One Nation under God*, 3–15.

49. "Do You Wish You Could Do Something?," *Guideposts*, July 1952, 2; George, *God's Salesman*, 104; Norman Vincent Peale to Branch Rickey, January 25, 1947, BRP, Box 58, Folder 5.

50. Quote taken from the masthead of *Guideposts* in 1951. See also George, *God's Salesman*, 103–127.

51. Smith, *What Would Jesus Read?*, 135–156; Hedstrom, *The Rise of Liberal Religion*, 222–223.

52. "Brutus Hamilton," *Christian Century*, March 28, 1951, 397–398; "The Basketball Scandals," *Christian Century*, May 7, 1951, 291; "Games Corruption Hits West Point," *Christian Century*, August 15, 1951, 931.

53. Raymond Thornburg to Branch Rickey, October 3, 1951, BRP, Box 58, Folder 6.

54. Jackie Robinson, "Trouble Ahead Needn't Bother You," in *Faith Made Them Champions*, ed. Norman Vincent Peale (New York: 1954), 241. Of the 20 athletes featured in *Faith Made Them Champions*, 10 would get involved with the FCA.

55. Subscriber numbers are from George, *God's Salesman*, 114–115.

56. Herzog, *The Spiritual-Industrial Complex*. See also Kruse, *One Nation under God*, 127–161; Wall, *Inventing the "American Way,"* 168–187; Schultz, *Tri-Faith America*, 68–73.

57. Mel Larson, *Gil Dodds: The Flying Parson* (Chicago: The Evangelical Beacon, 1945); James A. Mathisen, "Reviving 'Muscular Christianity': Gil Dodds and the Institutionalization of Sport Evangelism," *Sociological Focus* 23, no. 3 (August 1990): 233–249; Thomas E. Bergler, "Youth, Christianity, and the Crisis of Civilization, 1930–1945," *Religion and American Culture: A Journal of Interpretation* 24, no. 2 (2014): 260.

58. For background on the NAE and YFC, see Carpenter, *Revive Us Again*, 141–176; Grem, *The Blessings of Business*, 36–48.

59. John G. Turner, *Bill Bright & Campus Crusade for Christ: The Renewal of Evangelicalism in Postwar America* (Chapel Hill: University of North Carolina Press, 2008), 45–49.

60. Ladd and Mathisen, *Muscular Christianity*, 115–116, 127–129; David Beryl Towner, "The History of Venture for Victory/Sports Ambassadors: The First Christian Sports Group to Evangelize Overseas" (master's thesis, California State University, Chico, 1990).

61. Quoted in Turner, *Bill Bright & Campus Crusade for Christ*, 41.

62. Donald J. Odle, "Venture for Victory," in Peale, ed., *Faith Made Them Champions*, 251.

63. Baker, *Playing with God*, 195–196; Ladd and Mathisen, *Muscular Christianity*, 103–122; Grant Wacker, "Billy Graham, Christian Manliness, and the Shaping of the Evangelical Subculture," in *Religion and the Marketplace in the United States*, ed. Jan Stievermann, Philip Goff, and Detlef Junker (New York: Oxford University Press, 2015), 79–101.

64. Grant Wacker, *America's Pastor: Billy Graham and the Shaping of a Nation* (Cambridge, MA: Harvard University Press, 2014), 112–115.

65. Blake, *A Sports Editor Finds Christ*, 173–176; "Go to Bat for Jesus," *Atlanta Constitution*, November 18, 1950, 16.

66. Bill Pitts, "Leadership in the Youth-Led Revival Movement," *Texas Baptist History* 32 (2012): 39–68; Bruce McIver, *Riding the Wind of God: A Personal History of the Youth Revival Movement* (Macon, GA: Smyth & Helwys, 2002).

67. Frank Leavell, "The Editor's Outlook," *Baptist Student*, November 1948, 19; Frank Leavell, "The Olympic Games -1948," *Baptist Student*, February 1949, 16–17; Ned Root, "Footnote to the Olympics," *Christian Herald*, August 1948, 23, 62.

68. See, for example, Dean Stone, "Bob Bodenhamer-Triple-Threat for Christ," *Baptist Student*, November 1947, 18; James L. Spangenberg, "He Always Follows Through," *Baptist Student*, March 1948, 16; Frank Leavell, "Christian First," *Baptist Student*, April 1950, 19.

69. Bria Bolton, "Founding Father," *State Magazine*, Spring 2009, 40–42.

70. The story of the FCA's origins from the previous two paragraphs is summarized from Atcheson, *Impact for Christ*, 148–155; Murchison, *Caution to the Wind*, 29–39; and the letters Don McClanen sent to potential FCA leaders in 1954, located in BRP, Box 57, Folder 7.

71. E. Stanley Jones, "The University Christian Mission," *Christian Century*, January 4, 1939, 11.

72. "Billy Sunday, the Last of His Line," *Christian Century*, November 20, 1935, 1476.

73. Richard V. Pierard, "Evangelical and Ecumenical: Missionary Leaders in Mainline Protestantism, 1900–1950," in Jacobsen and Trollinger, eds., *Re-Forming the Center*, 150–171; Thomas C. Berg, "'Proclaiming Together'? Convergence and Divergence in Mainline and Evangelical Evangelism, 1945–1967," *Religion and American Culture: A Journal of Interpretation* 5, no. 1 (Winter 1995): 49–76.

74. Sources explaining the purpose and history of the UCM can be found in NCC RG 9, Box 77, Folder 48, and NCC RG 6, Box 58, Folder 16. The "personal and the social gospel in a living blend" quote comes from the Minutes of the Committee on the Mission to Schools, Colleges and Universities, March 15, 1937. See also Douglas Sloan, *Faith and Knowledge: Mainline Protestantism and American Higher Education* (Louisville, KY: Westminster John Knox Press, 1994), 24–25.

75. For descriptions of early UCM events, see Hayden Hall, "Do College Men Want Religion at Illinois?," *Christian Herald*, May 1939, 22, 47; Frank S. Mead, "Do College Men Want Religion at Pennsylvania?," *Christian Herald*, May 1939, 23, 57.

76. "Stoner to Visit Campus to Aid Religious Week," *Daily O'Collegian*, January 4, 1949, 1; Owen Armbruster, "R.E. Week Is Annual Observance," *Daily O'Collegian*, March 3, 1951, 1; "Top Presbyterian Minister Speaks Here during REW," *Daily O'Collegian*, March 4, 1954, 8.

77. "Great Churches of America," *Christian Century*, September 20, 1950, 1098–1105; "Presbyterian in Hollywood," *Time*, August 25, 1947, 58–59; "Minister at Large," *Time*, January 12, 1953, 55.

78. For examples of these themes in Evans's message, see Louis H. Evans, *Youth Seeks a Master* (Westwood, NJ: Fleming H. Revell, 1941); Louis H. Evans, *The Kingdom Is Yours* (Westwood, NJ: Fleming H. Revell, 1952); Louis H. Evans, *Make Your Faith Work* (Westwood, NJ: Fleming H. Revell, 1957).

79. C. B. Seay, "Sporting Writer Picks All-Star Football Team for Occidental," *The Occidental*, December 11, 1917, 1; "New Minister to Preach at Third Church," *Pittsburgh Post-Gazette*, December 12, 1931, 12; "Great Preachers," *Life*, April 6, 1953, 127.

80. Evans, *The Kingdom Is Yours*, 9.

81. In 1962 Evans wrote a summary of his nine years as minister-at-large. See "The Ministry at Large" (1962), PCUSA, RG301.1, Box 7, Folder 13.

82. H. N. Morse to Louis H. Evans, October 27, 1952, PCUSA, RG300.1, Box 16, Folder 10.

83. Louis H. Evans to Hermann Morse, March 2, 1953, PCUSA, RG300.1, Box 16, Folder 10.

84. Marsden, *Reforming Fundamentalism*, 19; Michael H. Hamilton, "The Interdenominational Evangelicalism of D.L. Moody and the Problem of Fundamentalism," in *American Evangelicalism: George Marsden and the State of American Religious History*, ed. Darren Dochuk, Thomas S. Kidd, and Kurt W. Peterson (South Bend, IN: University of Notre Dame Press, 2014), 230–282.

85. Arlin C. Migliazzo, *Mother of Modern Evangelicalism: The Life & Legacy of Henrietta Mears* (Grand Rapids, MI: Eerdmans, 2020); John G. Turner, "The Power behind the Throne: Henrietta Mears and Post-World War II Evangelicalism," *The Journal of Presbyterian History* 83, no. 2 (Fall/Winter 2005): 141–157.

86. Atcheson, *Impact for Christ*, 153–156.

87. "Dr. Louis Evans Challenges to Let Great Coach Referee Life's Game," *Canyon News* (Canyon, TX), March 24, 1954, 10.

88. FCA publications would later put the initial list of invitees at nineteen, but the original letter shows twenty recipients: Doak Walker; Bob Mathias; Otto Graham; Carl Erskine; Branch Rickey; Pepper Martin; Chuck Mather; Phog Allen; Lynn Waldorf; Amos Alonzo Stagg; Ab Jenkins; Glenn Olds; Gil Dodds; Glenn Cunningham; Louis Zamperini; Donn Moomaw; Bud Wilkinson; Charlie Dowell; Merrill Green; Bob Bodenhamer.

89. Don McClanen to Branch Rickey, April 20, 1954, BRP, Box 57, Folder 7.

90. Murchison, *Caution to the Wind*, 42–43.

91. Murchison, *Caution to the Wind*, 40–45; Atcheson, *Impact for Christ*, 159–162; Joseph Dunn, *Sharing the Victory: The Twenty-Five Years of the Fellowship of Christian Athletes* (New York: Quick Fox, 1980), 16–21.

92. Don McClanen, "Tentative Project as of July 19, 1954," and "Form Letter #2," July 19, 1954, BRP, Box 57, Folder 7.

93. Rickey's papers include anticommunist pamphlets written by Kaub and McIntire. On Kaub and McIntire's campaign, see Markku Ruotsila, *Fighting Fundamentalist: Carl McIntire and the Politicization of American Fundamentalism* (New York: Oxford University Press, 2016), 118–125.

94. Branch Rickey to Robert G. Mayfield, June 20, 1953, BRP, Box 59, Folder 6.

95. Branch Rickey to Robert C. Howe, November 26, 1953, BRP, Box 59, Folder 6. Rickey drafted three different letters, all of which are included in his papers.

96. Branch Rickey to Harold E. McCamey, January 21, 1954, BRP, Box 59, Folder 6.

97. Rosey Roswell to Don McClanen, July 28, 1954, BRP, Box 57, Folder 7; Don McClanen to Branch Rickey, July 31, 1954, BRP, Box 57, Folder 7.

98. Branch Rickey to Don McClanen, August 18, 1954, BRP, Box 57, Folder 7.

99. Louis H. Evans to Branch Rickey, undated, BRP, Box 57, Folder 7.

Chapter 4

1. *Annual Report of the Fellowship of Christian Athletes* (1962), 11, CBMP, Box 445, Folder 62.

2. "FCA Administrative Assignments" (1961), CBMP, Box 445, Folder 61.

3. Tad Wieman to James Stoner, August 23, 1961, CBMP, Box 445, Folder 61.

4. In the 1950s all of the FCA's main clergy leaders were connected to mainline Protestant institutions: Glenn Olds (Methodist), Roe Johnston (Presbyterian), James Stoner (Disciples of Christ), Dan Towler (Methodist), Louis Evans (Presbyterian), Gary Demarest (Presbyterian), Donn Moomaw (Presbyterian), LeRoy King (Methodist), and Dick Armstrong (Presbyterian). Of those nine, only three (Evans, Demarest, and Moomaw) were also connected to neoevangelicalism.

5. Robert A. Schneider, "Voice of Many Waters: Church Federation in the Twentieth Century," in Hutchison, ed., *Between the Times*, 107.

6. Albert Dimmock to Berlyn Farris, September 4, 1956, NCC RG 6, Box 57, Folder 23.

7. Berlyn Farris to Albert Dimmock, September 12, 1956; Albert Dimmock to Berlyn Farris, September 24, 1956; Berlyn Farris to Don McClanen, October 4, 1956; Don McClanen to Berlyn Farris, December 5, 1956. All in NCC RG 6, Box 57, Folder 23.

8. "For Christ and His Church: The Fellowship of Christian Athletes" (1955), BRP, Box 58, Folder 1; "News from the Fellowship of Christian Athletes," March 22, 1956, BRP, Box 58, Folder 1.

9. Schneider, "Voice of Many Waters," 117; Schultz, *Tri-Faith America*.

10. *Under the Master Coach*, Word Records, 1962, LP.

11. "Speech by Branch Rickey before the Fellowship of Christian Athletes" (1956).

12. "A Report of Progress," *Christian Athlete*, May 1959, 1.

13. Rafer Johnson with Philip Goldberg, *The Best That I Can Be: An Autobiography* (New York: Doubleday, 1998), 46–48; Edward Drewry Jervey, *The History of Methodism in Southern California and Arizona* (Nashville, TN: Parthenon Press, 1960), 182.

14. On 1950s debates over religion in public schools, see Neil J. Young, *We Gather Together: The Religious Right and the Problem of Interfaith Politics* (New York: Oxford University Press, 2015), 68–78; Schultz, *Tri-Faith America*, 118–137; Kruse, *One Nation under God*, 165–201.

15. Ed Sullivan, "Little Old New York," *Daily News*, May 16, 1955, 46.

16. Don McClanen to Branch Rickey, May 11, 1955, BRP, Box 57, Folder 8.

17. Don McClanen to Branch Rickey, May 29, 1955, BRP, Box 57, Folder 8.

18. Fellowship of Christian Athletes Newsletter, November 1955, BRP, Box 57, Folder 8.

19. James Stoner to Don McClanen, September 16, 1955, BRP, Box 57, Folder 8; Louis Evans to Branch Rickey, September 3, 1956, BRP, Box 58, Folder 2.

20. "The Fellowship of Christian Athletes and the Catholic Church," *Christian Athlete*, December 1965, 9; Schultz, *Tri-Faith America*, 99–117; Neary, *Crossing Parish Boundaries*; Sperber, *Shake Down the Thunder*; Byrne, *O God of Players*.

21. W. W. Mendenhall, "A Quarter Century of Cooperative Religion at Cornell University," *Religious Education* 41, no. 2 (1946): 114–119.

22. Louis H. Evans to Donald Cleary, September 3, 1956, BRP, Box 58, Folder 2; Branch Rickey to Louis H. Evans, September 5, 1956, BRP, Box 58, Folder 2.

23. Roe Johnston, "No Challenge, No Adventure," *Sharing the Victory*, May/June 1985, 16. On neoevangelical and Southern Baptist opposition to Mormons in the 1950s, see Young, *We Gather Together*, 87–93. On Mormon acceptance in American culture, see Cristine Hutchison-Jones, "Reviling and Revering the Mormons: Defining American Values, 1890–2008," (PhD diss., Boston University, 2011); Benjamin Park, *American Zion: A New History of Mormonism* (New York: W.W. Norton, 2024).

24. Kimball, *Sports in Zion*.

25. Non-Protestant athletes were featured in the FCA's official publication, the *Christian Athlete*, the FCA's first film, *More than Champions*, and the FCA's first published book: Ted Simonson, ed., *The Goal and the Glory: America's Athletes Speak Their Faith* (Grand Rapids, MI: Fleming H. Revell Company, 1962).

26. Marsden, *Reforming Fundamentalism*, 90; Turner, *Bill Bright and Campus Crusade for Christ*, 29–31.

27. On neoevangelical opposition to ecumenism, see Young, *We Gather Together*, 93–96, 138–139.

28. Billy Graham, "My Answer," *Asheville Citizen-Times*, March 21, 1955, 16. See also "Academic Responsibility and Subversion of the Gridiron," *Christianity Today*, April 11, 1960, 22–23; L. Nelson Bell to Gary Demarest, June 9, 1960, LNBP, CN 318, Box 18, Folder 20.

29. See, for example, Mel Larson, *Ten Famous Christian Athletes* (Wheaton, IL: Miracle Books, 1958), in which Larson—a neoevangelical—ignored the FCA entirely even though three of the athletes featured in his book were FCA members.

30. Minutes of the Annual Meeting of the Board of Directors, Fellowship of Christian Athletes, CBMP, Box 445, Folder 60; "Identification with F.C.A.," *Christian Athlete*, October 1960, 1.

31. McClanen, *Guidebook for the Fellowship of Christian Athletes* (Norman, OK: Fellowship of Christian Athletes, 1955), 1.

32. Amos Alonzo Stagg to Jack Marcum, February 9, 1945, AASP, Box 5, Folder 3.

33. Rader, *Baseball*, 206–207; Kathryn Jay, *More than Just a Game: Sports in American Life since 1945* (New York: Columbia University Press, 2004), 9–78; Randy Roberts and James S. Olson, *Winning Is the Only Thing: Sports in America since 1945* (Baltimore: The Johns Hopkins University Press, 1989), 1–111; Kurt Edward Kemper, *College Football and American Culture in the Cold War Era* (Urbana: University of Illinois Press, 2009).

34. Robert Pruter, *The Rise of American High School Sports and the Search for Control, 1880–1930* (Syracuse, NY: Syracuse University Press, 2013); Murray Sperber, *Onward to Victory: The Crises That Shaped College Sports* (New York: Henry Holt and Company, 1998); Smith, *Pay for*

Play; Kemper, *Before March Madness*; Chad Carlson, *Making March Madness: The Early Years of the NCAA, NIT, and College Basketball Championships, 1922–1951* (Fayetteville: University of Arkansas Press, 2017).

35. "Preparing for the Future," *Athletic Journal*, January 1953, 55.
36. Michael MacCambridge, *The Franchise: A History of Sports Illustrated Magazine* (New York: Hyperion, 1997), 11–76.
37. Lizabeth Cohen, *A Consumers' Republic: The Politics of Mass Consumption in Postwar America* (New York: Vintage Books, 2003), 330–331.
38. Ralph Cooper Hutchison, "Football: Symbol of College Unity," *Christian Century*, April 16, 1952, 461–463.
39. Oriard, *King Football*; Jay, *More than Just a Game*, 45–78; Thomas, *Globetrotting*; Ariail, *Passing the Baton*.
40. Wieman's quote is from "Aid to Christianity," a *Denver Post* article covering the FCA's Estes Park conference held between August 19–23, 1956. The clipping was part of a page of reprinted *Denver Post* articles located in AASP, Box 108, Folder 10. Wieman coached at Michigan, Minnesota, and Princeton from 1927 through 1942 before becoming an athletic director.
41. McClanen, *Program Guidebook of the Fellowship of Christian Athletes* (1955), 4.
42. Don McClanen, ed., *The Christian Athlete Speaks: Daily Devotional Thought Provokers Written by and for Athletes* (1955), AASP, Box 108, Folder 4. The devotional was unpaginated.
43. Leroy King, ed., *The Christian Athlete's Devotional: Meditations Written by and for Athletes* (Kansas City, MO: [1957?]), AASP, Box 108, Folder 10.
44. Gary Demarest to Samuel Shoemaker, September 25, 1959, SSP, Folder RG101-32-37. Demarest would spend most of his life as a pastor and denominational leader within the mainline Presbyterian Church (USA).
45. Fellowship of Christian Athletes Annual Report, Fiscal Year 1958–1959, AASP, Box 108, Folder 4.
46. "Have You Read?," *Christian Athlete*, May 1960, 3. See also "Mature Christian Living," *Christian Athlete*, February 1960, 1.
47. Ladd and Mathisen, *Muscular Christianity*, 51–57; Rebecca A. Koerselman, "'Invading Vacationland for Christ': The Construction of Evangelical Identity through Summer Camps in the Postwar Era," (PhD diss., Michigan State University, 2013).
48. FCA Athletes Summer Conference Information, February 20, 1956, BRP, Box 58, Folder 1; Don McClanen to Amos Alonzo Stagg, April 2, 1956, AASP, Box 108, Folder 4; "First Annual Summer Conference, Fellowship of Christian Athletes," (1956), pamphlet in BRP, Box 58, Folder 1.
49. Don McClanen to Biggie Munn, January 20, 1956, CBMP, Box 133, Folder 36; "Christians in Sport," *Newsweek*, September 3, 1956; "A Muscular Boost for Christian Doctrine," *Life*, September 17, 1956, 67–68.
50. Don McClanen to Amos Alonzo Stagg, December 9, 1955, AASP, Box 108, Folder 4; FCA Athletes Summer Conference Information, February 20, 1956, BRP, Box 58, Folder 1.
51. Atcheson, *Impact for Christ*, 180–191.
52. Biggie Munn to Don McClanen, August 28, 1956, CBMP, Box 133, Folder 36.
53. Munn attended the People's Church, which was formed as a joint effort led by multiple mainline Protestant congregations.
54. Atcheson, *Impact for Christ*, 172.
55. Ernest Mehl, "Sporting Comment," *Kansas City Star*, November 25, 1956, 2b.
56. McClanen to G. Herbert McCracken, December 17, 1957, Box 354, Folder 65; Don McClanen to Biggie Munn, December 2, 1958; Biggie Munn to Jim Jeffrey, December 23, 1963, CBMP, Box 507, Folder 58.
57. "Christian Athletes Group an Inspiration for LSU," Associated Press story excerpted in "News from the Fellowship of Christian Athletes," January 1, 1959, AASP, Box 108, Folder 4.
58. Jeffrey Montez de Oca, *Discipline and Indulgence: College Football, Media, and the American Way of Life during the Cold War* (New Brunswick, NJ: Rutgers University Press, 2013); Kemper, *College Football and American Culture in the Cold War Era*; Du Mez, *Jesus and John Wayne*, 25–32.
59. Estes Park Newsletter, August 17, 1959, CBMP, Box 413, Folder 13.
60. Biggie Munn to Don McClanen, December 3, 1958, CBMP, Box 354, Folder 55; Don McClanen to Biggie Munn, December 2, 1958, CBMP, Box 354, Folder 67; Bebe Lee to Biggie Munn, January 20, 1959, CBMP, Box 413, Folder 14; Dunn, *Sharing the Victory*, 79–93.

61. Fellowship of Christian Athletes Newsletter, April 17, 1956, BRP, Box 58, Folder 1; Atcheson, *Impact for Christ*, 92–97.
62. Atcheson, *Impact for Christ*, 94–96; Otto Graham letter to Pittsburgh-area athletes, November 8, 1955, BRP, Box 57, Folder 9.
63. Richard S. Armstrong, "Professional Sports: A Missionary Frontier" (1956), 27, AASP, Box 108, Folder 10.
64. Armstrong, "Professional Sports: A Missionary Frontier."
65. Don McClanen to Biggie Munn, November 29, 1957, CBMP, Box 354, Folder 64; FCA Newsletter, September 29, 1958, AASP, Box 108, Folder 4; "Here and There," *Christian Athlete*, January 1960, 4; "Annual Professional Athletes Winter Retreat," *Christian Athlete*, February 1961, 5.
66. Herman L. Masin, "Herb McCracken, Our Head Coach," *Scholastic Coach & Athletic Director*, May 1995, 10. Jack Lippert, the New Deal supporter who had edited the magazine in the 1930s, was no longer in that role in the 1950s.
67. "Team of the Year," *Scholastic Coach*, April 1956; Don McClanen to G. Herbert McCracken, December 17, 1957, CBMP, Box 354, Folder 65.
68. Louis H. Evans to Branch Rickey, January 9, 1956, BRP, Box 57, Folder 8; FCA Athletes Summer Conference Information, February 20, 1956, BRP, Box 58, Folder 1; Gerald Holland to Branch Rickey, May 25, 1956, BRP, Box 58, Folder 1.
69. Tad Wieman to Fred Russell, August 23, 1957, CBMP, Box 354, Folder 65; Don McClanen to Biggie Munn, December 2, 1958, CBMP, Box 354, Folder 67.
70. Atcheson, *Impact for Christ*, 194–195; FCA Newsletter, July 30, 1956, BRP, Box 58, Folder 2; Ernest Mehl, "Sporting Comment," *Kansas City Star*, December 25, 1958, 18; "F.C.A. Personality You Should Know," *Christian Athlete*, March 1962, 3.
71. FCA Newsletter, September 29, 1958, AASP, Box 108, Folder 4.
72. James R. Newby, *Elton Trueblood: Believer, Teacher, and Friend* (New York: Harper & Row, 1990); Elton Trueblood, *While It Is Day: An Autobiography* (New York: Harper & Row, 1974).
73. Newby, *Elton Trueblood*, 89.
74. Newby, *Elton Trueblood*, 89–92, 114–116; Trueblood, *While It Is Day*, 104–124.
75. Daniel Sack, "Reaching the 'Up-and-Outers': Sam Shoemaker and Modern Evangelicalism," *Anglican and Episcopal History* 64, no. 1 (March 1995): 37–57; Daniel Sack, *Moral Re-Armament: The Reinventions of an American Religious Movement* (New York: Palgrave Macmillan, 2009); Helen Shoemaker, *I Stand by the Door: The Life of Sam Shoemaker* (New York: Harper & Row, 1967); "God and Steel in Pittsburgh," *Time*, March 21, 1955, 51.
76. Don McClanen to Biggie Munn, April 1, 1956, CBMP, Box 133, Folder 36; Don McClanen to FCA Advisory Board, December 19, 1958, CBMP, Box 354, Folder 67; Don McClanen to Branch Rickey, October 7, 1959, BRP, Box 58, Folder 3.
77. "Fellowship of Christian Athletes: Answer to America's Youth," BRP, Box 58, Folder 3. There is extensive correspondence between McClanen and Shoemaker that begins in late 1958 and extends through 1962.
78. See David W. Miller, *God at Work: The History and Promise of the Faith at Work Movement* (New York: Oxford University Press, 2006), 48–51, for a discussion of Trueblood's and Shoemaker's involvement in the "faith and work" movement.
79. Biggie Munn to Roe Johnston, September 14, 1963, CBMP, Box 507, Folder 58.
80. Don McClanen to Biggie Munn, February 17, 1958, CBMP, Box 354, Folder 68.
81. Ruth Jobush to Biggie Munn, November 17, 1957, CBMP, Box 354, Folder 64; Biggie Munn to Ruth Jobush, December 16, 1957, CBMP, Box 354, Folder 64; Ruth Jobush to Biggie Munn, May 15, 1962, CBMP, Box 445, Folder 61.
82. Don McClanen to Samuel Shoemaker, September 5, 1959, SSP, Folder RG101-32-37; Don McClanen to Branch Rickey, October 7, 1959, BRP, Box 58, Folder 3.
83. Henry P. Van Dusen, "Force's Lessons for Others," *Life*, June 9, 1958, 122–124; Henry P. Van Dusen, *Spirit, Son and Father: Christian Faith in the Light of the Holy Spirit* (New York: Scribner's, 1958); Shoemaker, *I Stand by the Door*, 142.
84. Excerpt from Van Dusen, *Spirit, Son and Father*, 126. It was included in Sam Shoemaker to Don McClanen, September 30, 1959, SSP, Folder RG101-32-37.
85. Don McClanen to Branch Rickey, October 7, 1959, BRP, Box 58, Folder 3.
86. Don McClanen to Branch Rickey, October 7, 1959, BRP, Box 58, Folder 3.

87. Don McClanen to Branch Rickey, October 7, 1959, BRP, Box 58, Folder 3; Murchison, *Caution to the Wind*, 73.
88. Elton Trueblood, *The Idea of a College* (New York: Harper & Brothers, 1959), 149.
89. Trueblood, *The Idea of a College*, 147.
90. Don McClanen to Branch Rickey, October 1, 1959, BRP, Box 58, Folder 3.
91. Armstrong, "Professional Sports: A Missionary Frontier"; "Hero Worship Harnessed," *Sports Illustrated*, February 6, 1956, 1.
92. Don McClanen to FCA Board of Directors, September 27, 1960, CBMP, Box 439, Folder 15; Don McClanen to Sam Shoemaker, March 29, 1961, SSP, RG101-36-19.
93. Don McClanen to Sam Shoemaker, December 2, 1960, SSP, RG101-34-35; Murchison, *Caution to the Wind*, 70–76.
94. Minutes of the Annual Meeting of the Board of Directors, Fellowship of Christian Athletes, August 14–17, 1961, CBMP, Box 445, Folder 61; Tad Wieman to James Stoner, August 23, 1961, CBMP, Box 445, Folder 61.
95. Don McClanen to FCA Board of Directors, October 19, 1961, CBMP, Box 445, Folder 61; Don McClanen to Sam Shoemaker, November 1, 1961, SSP, RG101-36-20.
96. Don McClanen to Sam Shoemaker, October 3, 1961, SSP, Folder RG101-36-20; Don McClanen to Sam Shoemaker, January 4, 1962, SSP, Folder RG101-36-20; Don McClanen to Sam Shoemaker, October 22, 1962, SSP, Folder RG101-36-20.
97. Don McClanen to Sam Shoemaker, November 9, 1961, SSP, Folder RG101-36-20; Paul Dietzel to Tad Wieman, January 22, 1962, CBMP, Box 445, Folder 59.
98. Dick Harp to Biggie Munn, July 13, 1960, CBMP, Box 439, Folder 15.
99. Sam Shoemaker to Paul Dietzel, October 24, 1961, SSP, Folder RG101-36-20.
100. LeRoy King to Quinter Miller, April 3, 1962, NCC RG 6, Box 57, Folder 23.
101. Ralph Holdeman to LeRoy King, April 25, 1962, NCC RG 6, Box 57, Folder 23.
102. William B. Rogers, "University Evangelism," July 5, 1961, meeting of Policy and Strategy Committee of the Department of Evangelism, NCC RG6, Box 57, Folder 1.
103. Robert Wuthnow, *The Restructuring of American Religion: Society and Faith since World War II* (Princeton, NJ: Princeton University Press, 1988), 100–131.

Chapter 5

1. Kevin M. Kruse, *White Flight: Atlanta and the Making of Modern Conservatism* (Princeton, NJ: Princeton University Press, 2005), 215.
2. Bill Blodgett, "'Rally Success' Voices Krisher," *Atlanta Constitution*, February 4, 1964, 16; "Atlanta City-Wide Program," *Christian Athlete*, March 1964, 10–11.
3. "FCA Presents Real Challenge to Citizens of Metro Atlanta," *Atlanta Daily World*, April 2, 1964, 8.
4. Matthew D. Lassiter, *The Silent Majority: Suburban Politics in the Sunbelt South* (Princeton, NJ: Princeton University Press, 2006), 11. My understanding of the Sunbelt and its connection to religion is strongly shaped by Steven P. Miller, *Billy Graham and the Rise of the Republican South* (Philadelphia: University of Pennsylvania Press, 2009), and Darren Dochuk, *From Bible Belt to Sunbelt: Plain-Folk Religion, Grassroots Politics, and the Rise of Evangelical Conservatism* (New York: W.W. Norton, 2011).
5. On the culture of sports in the South, see Miller, ed., *The Sporting World of the Modern South*.
6. Oriard, *King Football*, 7, 83–84, 183–185; Charles H. Martin, "Integrating New Year's Day: The Racial Politics of College Bowl Games in the American South," in *The Sporting World of the Modern South*, 175–199.
7. For historical background, see Frank Andre Guridy, *The Sports Revolution: How Texas Changed the Culture of American Athletics* (Austin: University of Texas Press, 2021); Clayton Trutor, *Loserville: How Professional Sports Remade Atlanta—and How Atlanta Remade Professional Sports* (Lincoln: University of Nebraska Press, 2022).
8. Those four were Jack Robinson, James Jeffrey, Ralph Langley, and Bill Glass.
9. The staff members included Don McClanen, Gary Demarest, Bob Stoddard, and Leroy King. The fifteen members of the board were Otto Graham; Tad Wieman; Dick Armstrong; Paul Dietzel; Dick Harp; James Jeffrey; Roe Johnston; H. B. "Bebe" Lee; Don McClanen; Donn Moomaw; Gary Demarest; Biggie Munn; James Stoner; Bob Taylor; and Dan Towler.
10. Don McClanen to Donn Moomaw, July 20, 1959, CBMP, Box 445, Folder 62; Minutes of the Annual Meeting of the Board of Directors, June 14 and 15, 1962, CBMP, Box 445, Folder 62.

11. On Southern Protestantism, see David Edwin Harrell Jr., ed., *Varieties of Southern Evangelicalism* (Macon, GA: Mercer University Press, 1981); Barry Hankins, *Uneasy in Babylon: Southern Baptist Conservatives and American Culture* (Tuscaloosa: University of Alabama Press, 2002), 14–40; Harvey, *Freedom's Coming*, 107–250; Elizabeth H. Flowers, *Into the Pulpit: Southern Baptist Women and Power since World War II* (Chapel Hill: University of North Carolina Press, 2012), 1–49; Stephens, *The Fire Spreads*.

12. Elmin Kimboll Howell Jr. with William Lee Pitts Jr., *Oral Memoirs of Elmin Kimboll Howell, Jr.*, Vol. 1 (Waco, TX: Baylor University Institute for Oral History, 1988), 71–73.

13. On North Carolina's basketball culture, see Grundy, *Learning to Win*, 190–225.

14. Jim Evans to Ted Youngling, November 29, 1961, DUFCA, Box 1, Folder 1.

15. Marty Pierson to Don McClanen, September 20, 1961, DUFCA, Box 1, Folder 1.

16. Bill Beall to Bill Murray, March 30, 1965, DUFCA, Box 1, Folder 3; Atcheson, *Impact for Christ*, 78–80.

17. "Daytona Beach Mission Conducted by Athletes," *Shreveport Times*, February 23, 1964, 5-B.

18. Minutes of the Annual Meeting of the FCA's Board of Directors, June 14 and 15, 1962, CBMP, Box 445, Folder 62.

19. The plan for the regional office was outlined in a letter from William T. Teas Jr. to James Jeffrey, April 26, 1964, CBMP, Box 507, Folder 59. Teas had been a star running back for Georgia Tech in the early 1950s.

20. Minutes of Annual Meeting of the FCA Board of Directors, May 11–13, 1964, CBMP, Box 507, Folder 60.

21. William T. Teas Jr. to James Jeffrey, April 26, 1964, CBMP, Box 507, Folder 59.

22. Lassiter, *The Silent Majority*, 110.

23. "Fellowship in Action," *Christian Athlete*, October 1965, 13; "Prayers at the Game," *Christian Athlete*, November 1966, 8.

24. Loren Young, Southeast Region Report, October 1968, CBMP, Box 792, Folder 36; Loren Young, Southeast Region Report, November 1968, CBMP, Box 792, Folder 36.

25. The comments from Allen and Sanders were printed on an FCA promotional brochure, located in CBMP, Box 769, Folder 33.

26. Paul Dietzel, Memo on Cities Interested in Chartering, June 19, 1964, CBMP, Box 520, Folder 47; "Identification" memo, 1965, CBMP, Box 520, Folder 46.

27. Carl Walters, "Fellowship of Christian Athletes Is Scoring Heavily in the South," *Clarion-Ledger*, January 31, 1964, 21.

28. Carl Walters, "Bisher Is True-Blue Southerner," *Clarion-Ledger*, February 29, 1959, 3. On Walters' support for segregation, see Jason A. Peterson, *Full Court Press: Mississippi State University, the Press, and the Battle to Integrate College Basketball* (Jackson: University Press of Mississippi, 2016). On white Southern Christian support for segregation, see Hawkins, *The Bible Told Them So*; Carolyn Renee Dupont, *Mississippi Praying: Southern White Evangelicals and the Civil Rights Movement, 1945–1975* (New York: New York University Press, 2013); Mark Newman, *Getting Right with God: Southern Baptists and Desegregation, 1945–1995* (Tuscaloosa: University of Alabama Press, 2001).

29. Robin Roberts, Talk to Houston Youth, n.d. (likely 1956), AASP, Box 108, Folder 10.

30. Quoted in Martin, *Benching Jim Crow*, 81.

31. Kemper, *College Football and American Culture in the Cold War Era*, 80–115.

32. Minutes of a Meeting of the National Conference Committee of the Fellowship of Christian Athletes, October 12 and 13, 1961, DUFCA, Box 1, Folder 13.

33. "More than Trophies," *Geneva Gems*, August 8, 1962, DUFCA, Box 1, Folder 13.

34. Minutes of a Special Meeting of the Board of Directors of the FCA, September 16, 1963, CBMP, Box 507, Folder 58; Minutes of the Conference Committee of the Fellowship of Christian Athletes, October 28, 1963, DUFCA, Box 1, Folder 13.

35. Minutes of the FCA's Board of Directors Meeting, May 24–25, 1965, CBMP, Box 769, Folder 34.

36. Details on the conference derived from the *Blue Ridge Athlete*, June 10–12, 1964, CBMP, Box 520, Folder 44; "Mountain-Top Experience," *Christian Athlete*, August/September 1964, 4–5; Wayne Atcheson, "A Report on the First National Fellowship of Christian Athletes Conference Held at the Blue Ridge YMCA Assembly" (1994).

37. Prentice Gautt, "Frustrations," in *Courage to Conquer: America's Athletes Speak Their Faith*, ed. Leroy King (Westwood, NJ: Fleming H. Revell, 1966), 98–100.

38. James C. Hefley, *Sports Alive!* (Grand Rapids, MI: Zondervan, 1966), 55; Atcheson, "A Report on the First National Fellowship of Christian Athletes Conference."

39. B. J. Hollars, *Opening the Doors: The Desegregation of the University of Alabama and the Fight for Civil Rights in Tuscaloosa* (Tuscaloosa: University of Alabama Press, 2013), 151–165.
40. Bill Bradley, *Time Present, Time Past: A Memoir* (Cambridge: Knopf, 1996), 421.
41. Miller, "The Persistence of Antiliberalism: Evangelicals and the Race Problem," in *American Evangelicals and the 1960s*, ed. Axel R. Schafer (Madison: University of Wisconsin Press, 2013), 81–96. See also Curtis J. Evans, "White Evangelical Responses to the Civil Rights Movement," *Harvard Theological Review* 102, no. 2 (April 2009): 245–273; Jesse Curtis, *The Myth of Colorblind Christians: Evangelicals and White Supremacy in the Civil Rights Era* (New York: New York University Press, 2021).
42. Johnson, *The Best That I Can Be*, 84.
43. Wendell Smith, "Deacon Dan Towler's Terrific," *Pittsburgh Courier*, November 6, 1948, 10.
44. "Rams Face Browns Today," *Los Angeles Times*, December 24, 1950, II-9; Dan Towler, "What's the Real Score?," in *Faith Made Them Champions*, 230–232; "Daniel Lee Towler," *Journal of the California-Pacific Annual Conference of the United Methodist Church* (2002), J-8.
45. Jerry Doernberg, "Former Grid Great Faces Rougher Battle," *Los Angeles Times*, November 2, 1964, 8. See also Dan L. Thrapp, "Deacon Dan Finds Home, Fading Bias," *Los Angeles Times*, November 6, 1966, H-11.
46. Hal Bock, "NFL Blacks Call Signals, but Not Plays," Associated Press, November 29, 1987.
47. Dan Towler, "A March for Freedom," *Christian Athlete*, January 1964, 4.
48. "Love, Not Laws, Will End Race Difficulties," *Christian Athlete*, October 1965, 2.
49. For theological context on Martin Luther King Jr.'s social Christianity, see Gary Dorrien, *Breaking White Supremacy: Martin Luther King Jr. and the Black Social Gospel* (New Haven, CT: Yale University Press, 2018). On the centrality of the Black church in the civil rights movement, see David L. Chappell, *A Stone of Hope: Prophetic Religion and the Death of Jim Crow* (Chapel Hill: University of North Carolina Press, 2004); Henry Louis Gates Jr., *The Black Church: This Is Our Story, This Is Our Song* (New York: Penguin Books, 2021), 109–148.
50. Stan Isaacs, "Out of Left Field," *Newsday*, July 23, 1964, 38c; "Are You an Armchair Christian?," *Christian Athlete*, September 1963, 23; Adrian Burgos Jr., *Playing America's Game: Baseball, Latinos, and the Color Line* (Berkeley: University of California Press, 2007), 210–211.
51. Martin, *Benching Jim Crow*, 212–213. Darrell Brown's account of the racism he encountered is described in Rus Bradburd, *Forty Minutes of Hell: The Extraordinary Life of Nolan Richardson* (New York: HarperCollins, 2010).
52. Guridy, *The Sports Revolution*, 87–93, 106–108.
53. John Bridgers, "Christian Obligations as a Coach," *Christian Athlete*, September 1963, 20–21.
54. John Hill Westbrook with Thomas Lee Charlton and Rufus B. Spain, *Oral Memoirs of John Hill Westbrook* (Waco, TX: Baylor University Institute for Oral History, 1973), 104.
55. Dean Smith with John Kilgo and Sally Jenkins, *A Coach's Life: My 40 Years in College Basketball* (New York: Random House, 1999), 78–80; Dean Smith, "Coaching - A Sacred Calling," *Christian Athlete*, January 1965, 14; Robert Seymour, *"White's Only": A Pastor's Retrospective on Signs of the New South* (Valley Forge, PA: Judson Press, 1991).
56. Art Chansky, *Game Changers: Dean Smith, Charlie Scott, and the Era That Transformed a Southern College Town* (Chapel Hill: University of North Carolina Press, 2016), 33–34.
57. Smith, *A Coach's Life*, 97.
58. On Scott's time at North Carolina, see Gregory J. Kaliss, *Men's College Athletics and the Politics of Racial Equality: Five Pioneer Stories of Black Manliness, White Citizenship, and American Democracy* (Philadelphia: Temple University Press, 2012), 109–137.
59. Chansky, *Game Changers*, 68–69.
60. Newman, *Getting Right with God*, 182; "Integration and You," *Christian Herald*, February 1965, 23; Randall J. Stephens, "'It Has to Come from the Hearts of the People': Evangelicals, Fundamentalists, Race, and the 1964 Civil Rights Act," *Journal of American Studies*, 50, no. 3 (2016): 559–585. See also the experience of Perry Wallace, described in Andrew Maraniss's *Strong Inside: Perry Wallace and the Collision of Race and Sports in the South* (Nashville, TN: Vanderbilt University Press, 2014), 112–113.
61. John Westbrook, "I Was the Man Nobody Saw," *Guideposts*, November 1970, 12–15. John Hill Westbrook with Thomas Lee Charlton and Rufus B. Spain, *Oral Memoirs of John Hill Westbrook* (Waco, TX: Baylor University Institute for Oral History, 1972), 74–75.
62. "Really Goofed," *Atlanta Constitution*, July 15, 1966, 4; "Athletic Dinner," *Atlanta Constitution*, July 22, 1966, 4.

63. Scholars have already noted that white Southern Protestantism shaped evangelicalism on a national level. See, for example, Dochuk, *From Bible Belt to Sunbelt*. I'm suggesting that a subset of mainline Protestants was part of this informal coalition as well.

64. Roe Johnston to Biggie Munn, May 7, 1964, CBMP, Box 507, Folder 59; Minutes of Annual Meeting of the FCA Board of Directors, May 11–13, 1964, CBMP, Box 507, Folder 60.

65. Atcheson, *Impact for Christ*, 218–227; Derek Oakley Coleman, "The Evangelistic Strategy of the Fellowship of Christian Athletes, 1963–1971" (PhD diss., Southern Baptist Theological Seminary, 1999), 76–79, 211–213; Dunn, *Sharing the Victory*, 79–81.

66. Dick Harp to Biggie Munn, July 13, 1960, CBMP, Box 439, Folder 15.

67. Minutes of the Conference Committee of the Fellowship of Christian Athletes, October 28, 1963, DUFCA, Box 1, Folder 13.

68. Hankins, *Uneasy in Babylon*, 34; David Stricklin, *A Genealogy of Dissent: Southern Baptist Protest in the Twentieth Century* (Lexington: University Press of Kentucky, 1999), 2–3.

69. *Oral Memoirs of Elmin Kimboll Howell, Jr.*, 71–73; Coleman, "The Evangelistic Strategy of the Fellowship of Christian Athletes, 1963–1971."

70. On Graham's place within the "southern evangelical mainstream," see Wacker, *America's Pastor*, 112–115; Darren Dochuk, "'Heavenly Houston': Billy Graham and Corporate Civil Rights in Sunbelt Evangelicalism's 'Golden Buckle,'" in *Billy Graham: American Pilgrim*, ed. Andrew Finstuen, Anne Blue Wills, and Grant Wacker (New York: Oxford University Press, 2017), 164–166.

71. Forrest Layman to James Jeffrey, June 9, 1966, BGEAC 13, Box 2, Folder 9; "North Carolina Conference," *Christian Athlete*, September 1965, 5.

72. Wacker, *America's Pastor*, 109.

73. Wacker, *America's Pastor*, 179–184; Marsden, *Reforming Fundamentalism*, 157–166; Curtis Evans, "A Politics of Conversion: Billy Graham's Political and Social Vision," in Finstuen, Wills, and Wacker, eds., *Billy Graham*, 143–160.

74. As an example of this shift, see L. Nelson Bell to C. Weston Jones, June 22, 1971, LNBP, CN 318, Box 18, Folder 20.

75. Leroy King to Branch Rickey, September 11, 1963, BRP, Box 58, Folder 3.

76. Young, *We Gather Together*, 93–96, 138–139.

77. Turner, *Bill Bright & Campus Crusade for Christ*, 45–49.

78. Turner, *Bill Bright & Campus Crusade for Christ*, 41–44; 84–89; William R. Bright, ed., *Teacher's Manual: Ten Basic Steps Towards Christian Maturity* (San Bernardino, CA: 1965), 106–107.

79. Bright, *Teacher's Manual*, 139, 142.

80. Loren Young, Southeast Region Report, September 1965, CBMP, Box 769, Folder 33; Loren Young, Southeast Region Report, January 1966, CBMP, Box 769, Folder 35.

81. Fellowship of Christian Athletes Board of Directors, Special Meeting Agenda, January 14, 1966, CBMP, Box 769, Folder 36.

82. James Stoner to Ralph Holdeman, March 31, 1961, NCC RG 6, Box 58.

83. Berg, "'Proclaiming Together,'" 49–76; Hollinger, *Christianity's American Fate*.

84. "Rickety Ree," *Christian Century*, January 31, 1962, 151; "Chamber of Horrors," *Christian Century*, December 27, 1967, 1671; "Time Out for Sports," *Christian Century*, March 12, 1969, 359.

85. "Touchdown!," *Christian Century*, February 28, 1962, 278; Untitled letters to the editor, *Christian Century*, March 14, 1962, 329.

86. "Builder or Wrecker," *Christian Athlete*, March 1966, 14. Guest's poem was discussed in Chapter 1.

87. "Success," *Christian Athlete*, March 1963, 9. For a historical assessment of Wooden's Pyramid of Success, see John Matthew Smith, *The Sons of Westwood: John Wooden, UCLA, and the Dynasty That Changed College Basketball* (Urbana: University of Illinois Press, 2013), 17–20.

88. John Wooden, "Success," in *Courage to Conquer: America's Athletes Speak Their Faith*, ed. Leroy King (Westwood, NJ: Fleming H. Revell, 1966), 36–39.

89. Merle Crowell, "Help Yourself to Happiness," *American Magazine*, January 1931, 1.

90. Carpenter, "Is 'Evangelical' a Yankee Word?," 82; Grem, *The Blessings of Business*, 13–81; Dochuk, "'Heavenly Houston,'" 161–194; Charles, *Service Clubs in American Society*, 149.

91. Johnston's letter quoted in Gerald David Ramey, "The Organization and Development of the Administration, Membership, and Program of the Fellowship of Christian Athletes Movement From 1954 to 1967" (master's thesis, University of Washington, 1968), 48.

92. Leslie Nudelman, "He Blinks and Breathes and Beats 'em All," *Christian Athlete*, February 1974, 10.

93. Fred Brown, "Special Strength," *Pensacola News* (Pensacola, FL), December 3, 1969, 15.

94. Tom English, "Faith, Positive Attitude Necessary, Florence Chamber Banquet Group Told," *Florence Morning News* (Florence, SC), January 27, 1970, 1; Coleman, "The Evangelistic Strategy of the Fellowship of Christian Athletes, 1963–1971," 76–79.

95. *Fellowship of Christian Athletes 1969 Annual Report*, CBMP, Box 797, Folder 4; Ramey, "The Organization and Development of the Administration, Membership, and Program of the Fellowship of Christian Athletes Movement from 1954 to 1967," 48.

96. L. T. Anderson, "They Said Their Prayers on First and Ten," *New York Times*, November 13, 1971, 33.

97. An adapted version of the section that follows is in Paul Emory Putz, "'There Is Talk of Black Power': Christian Athletes and the Revolt of the Black Athlete," in *Religion and Sport in North America: Critical Essays for the Twenty-First Century*, ed. Jeffrey Scholes and Randall Balmer (New York: Routledge, 2022), 13–34.

98. Jack Olsen, "The Cruel Deception," *Sports Illustrated*, July 1, 1968, 15.

99. There is an extensive literature on the "Black athlete revolt." See especially Harry Edwards, *The Revolt of the Black Athlete*, 50th anniv. ed. (Urbana: University of Illinois Press, 2017); Bass, *Not the Triumph but the Struggle*; Douglas Hartmann, *Race, Culture, and the Revolt of the Black Athlete: The 1968 Olympic Protests and Their Aftermath* (Chicago: University of Chicago Press, 2004); Louis Moore, *We Will Win the Day: The Civil Rights Movement, the Black Athlete, and the Quest for Equality* (Santa Barbara, CA: Praeger, 2017).

100. Thomas, *Globetrotting*, 115.

101. Quoted in Johnathan Rodgers, "A Step to an Olympics Boycott," *Sports Illustrated*, December 4, 1967. See also Aram Goudsouzian, "From Lew Alcindor to Kareem Adbul-Jabbar: Race, Religion, and Representation in Basketball, 1968–1975," *Journal of American Studies* 51, no. 2 (2017): 437–470; Maureen Smith, "*Muhammad Speaks* and Muhammad Ali: Intersections of the Nation of Islam and Sport in the 1960s," in *With God on Their Side: Sport in the Service of Religion*, ed. Tara Magdalinski and Timothy J. L. Chandler (New York: Routledge, 2002), 177–196; Randy Roberts and Johnny Smith, *Blood Brothers: The Fatal Friendship between Muhammad Ali and Malcolm X* (New York: Basic Books, 2016).

102. John Matthew Smith, "'Breaking the Plane': Integration and Black Protest in Michigan State University Football during the 1960s," *Michigan Historical Review* 33, no. 2 (Fall 2007): 101–129.

103. Quotation from untitled memorandum (likely April 1968), CBMP, Box 790, Folder 50. See also Don Edwin Coleman, "The Status of the Black Student Aide Program and the Black Student Movement at Michigan State University" (PhD diss., Michigan State University, 1971), 31–35.

104. Biggie Munn to Roger Stanton, November 24, 1969, CBMP, Box 797, Folder 58.

105. Martin, *Benching Jim Crow*, 139–143.

106. "Dietzel Gives His Opinion on Problems Concerning Recruiting of Black Athletes," *The Gamecock*, April 25, 1969, 6.

107. Paul Dietzel, "Open Letter to American Football Coaches," June 10, 1969, *American Football Coaches Association Summer Manual 1969* (1969), 2–3.

108. "Address by President Dietzel," *Proceedings of the Forty-Seventh Annual Meeting of the American Football Coaches Association* (Washington, D.C.: American Football Coaches Association, 1970), 7.

109. In 1970 Nixon invited the FCA to lead a prayer service at the White House. See "Erickson to Lead Prayer at Service," *Oshkosh Northwestern*, October 13, 1970, 2. See also Jesse Berrett, *Pigskin Nation: How the NFL Remade American Politics* (Urbana: University of Illinois Press, 2018), 108–132, on Nixon's use of football for political purposes.

110. Michael Weinreb, *Season of Saturdays: A History of College Football in 14 Games* (New York: Scribner, 2014), 75–90.

111. On the white evangelical entrance into the "God and country" gap left by mainline leaders after the 1950s, see Zubovich, *Before the Religious Right*, 242–247, 306–310; Hollinger, *Christianity's American Fate*, 90–106. For Biggie Munn's support of Graham, see his letter to Louis Shinger, January 11, 1971, CBMP, Box 801, Folder 6. Of course, theological convictions could lead some middlebrow mainliners to join in with evangelicals. Recall Branch Rickey,

who turned to the FCA in part because of his frustrations with liberal theology in his Methodist denomination. So, too, some middlebrow mainliners opted for a more cosmopolitan New Age approach to spirituality instead of a turn to evangelicalism.

112. Dewey King, "'Man, I Dig You'!," *Christian Athlete*, December 1972, 3.
113. King, "'Man, I Dig You,'" 2–5; John Drakeford, *The Awesome Power of the Listening Ear* (Waco, TX: Word Books, 1967).
114. Smith, *The Sons of Westwood*, 131–132. See also Kareem Abdul-Jabbar, *Coach Wooden and Me: Our 50-Year Friendship on and off the Court* (New York: Hachette, 2017).
115. "The 36th Chair," *Christian Athlete*, September 1969, 18–20.
116. Edwards, *The Revolt of the Black Athlete*, 49, 61–62.
117. Harry Edwards, *Sociology of Sport* (Homewood, IL: Dorsey Press, 1973), 148–152.
118. White, *Blood, Sweat, & Tears*, 210.
119. "Jake Gaither Addresses FCA Meeting," *Atlanta Daily World*, June 28, 1970, 7.
120. "A New Face in the League," *Christian Athlete*, October 1968, 2–4.
121. Prentice Gautt, "The Coach and the Black Athlete," *Christian Athlete*, October 1969, 12–13.
122. Jack Olsen, "The Anguish of a Team Divided," *Sports Illustrated*, July 29, 1968, 35.
123. "Sports Helps to Open Doors," *Daily Ardmoreite*, August 22, 1969, 7.
124. T. Berry, "For Thou Art with Me" (2010). Berry's essay, based on interviews from their shared hometown of Elgin, Texas, tells Westbrook's life story.
125. Murray Olderman, "Curry Found Self in Funeral March," *Morning News* (Wilmington, DE), May 3, 1968, 35.
126. George Plimpton and Bill Curry, *One More July* (New York: Harper & Row, 1977), 69. Gary Warner, *Competition* (Elgin, IL: David C. Cook, 1979), 150. Curry would eventually move back into the FCA fold as a coach in the 1980s.
127. Jackie Robinson, "Mixed Emotions over Boycott of Olympics," *New York Amsterdam News*, December 16, 1967, 17; Jackie Robinson, "Some Resolutions for the New Year," *New York Amsterdam News*, January 6, 1968, 13; "Robinson in State," *Greenville News* (Greenville, SC), October 22, 1968, 2.
128. Jackie Robinson, untitled acceptance speech, 1969, available at "How a Baseball Great Made Franklin Pierce's '69 Commencement Legendary," *Sentinel Source*, May 4, 2019.
129. Robinson, *I Never Had It Made*, xxiv; Long and Lamb, *Jackie Robinson*, 127–178.
130. Martin Luther King Jr., *Where Do We Go from Here: Chaos or Community?* (Boston: Beacon Press, 2010; originally published in 1967), 3–4.
131. Guridy, *The Sports Revolution*, 95.
132. John Wyngaard, "Erickson Backs President Negotiating with Power," *Green Bay Press-Gazette*, October 19, 1970, A-11.
133. Simon Henderson, *Sidelined: How American Sports Challenged the Black Freedom Struggle* (Lexington: University Press of Kentucky, 2013), 121–148. See also Hartmann, *Race, Culture, and the Revolt of the Black Athlete*, 207–270; Bass, *Not the Triumph but the Struggle*, 291–325.

Chapter 6

1. Gary Warner, "A Year after 'The Series,'" *Christian Athlete*, April 1977, 19.
2. Frank Deford, "Religion in Sport," *Sports Illustrated*, April 19, 1976, 88–102; "The Word According to Tom," *Sports Illustrated*, April 26, 1976, 54–69; "Reaching for the Stars," *Sports Illustrated*, May 3, 1976, 42–60.
3. On evangelicalism's rise to prominence in the 1970s, see Steven P. Miller, *The Age of Evangelicalism: America's Born-Again Years* (New York: Oxford University Press, 2014).
4. Worthen, *Apostles of Reason*, 264.
5. Robert Lipsyte, *SportsWorld: An American Dreamland* (New York: Quadrangle, 1975); James A. Michener, *Sports in America* (New York: Random House, 1976); Michael MacCambridge, *The Big Time: How the 1970s Transformed Sports in America* (New York: Grand Central Publishing, 2023).
6. Benjamin G. Rader, *In Its Own Image: How Television Has Transformed Sports* (New York: Free Press, 1984), 147; David A. Klatell and Norman Marcus, *Sports for Sale: Television, Money, and the Fans* (New York: Oxford University Press, 1988), 121, 130–132; Roberts and Olson, *Winning Is the Only Thing*, 126–127, 139; Howard P. Chudacoff, *Changing the Playbook: How Power, Profit, and Politics Transformed College Sports* (Urbana: University of Illinois Press, 2015), 51–54.

7. Roberts and Olson, *Winning Is the Only Thing*, 153–157; Michael Schiavone, *Sports and Labor in the United States* (Albany: State University of New York Press, 2015), 31, 58; Michael Oriard, *Brand NFL: Making and Selling America's Favorite Sport* (Chapel Hill: The University of North Carolina Press, 2007), 59, 102.

8. "Competition Comebackers," *Christian Athlete*, April 1975, 22; Roberts and Olson, *Winning Is the Only Thing*, 153–154.

9. Bill Bright, "Who Is Your Head Coach?," *Athletes in Action*, Spring 1967, 30.

10. Deford, "The Word According to Tom."

11. Turner, *Bill Bright and Campus Crusade for Christ*, 99–101.

12. Bill Bright, *Come Help Change the World* (Old Tappan, NJ: Revell, 1970), 131–139; Joe Smalley, *More than a Game* (San Bernardino, CA: Campus Crusade for Christ, 1981), 47–59.

13. Dave Hannah, "The Last Game," *Athletes in Action*, Winter 1971, 22; Sutton, *American Apocalypse*, 345–353; Hummel, *The Rise and Fall of Dispensationalism*, 244.

14. *One Way to Play Basketball* (San Diego, CA: Beta Boks, 1977), 139.

15. Smalley, *More than a Game*, 38.

16. Sutton, *American Apocalypse*.

17. *One Way to Play Basketball*, 139–143.

18. Smalley, *More than a Game*, 33–46. On AAU basketball, see Adolph H. Grundman, *The Golden Age of Amateur Basketball: The AAU Tournament, 1921–1968* (Lincoln, NE: Bison Books, 2004).

19. Smalley, *More than a Game*, 93–102.

20. Bright, *Come Help Change the World*, 134.

21. "Join the Athletes in Action Team," *Athletes in Action*, February 1968, 19.

22. Bill Bright, *Revolution Now!* (San Bernardino, CA: Campus Crusade for Christ, 1969), 18–25.

23. On Bright's conservative political orientation, see Williams, *God's Own Party*, 120–122; Turner, *Bill Bright and Campus Crusade for Christ*, 163–168.

24. Turner, *Bill Bright and Campus Crusade for Christ*, 144–145.

25. "Profiles," *Athletes in Action*, Winter 1971, 28. See also "Off-Season Offense," *Athletes in Action*, Winter 1969, 7; "While the White Man's Sleeping, We're Outside Playing Basketball," *Athletes in Action*, 1974, 20–22; Bright, *Come Help Change the World*, 138–139.

26. Curtis, *The Myth of Colorblind Christians*, 213.

27. Roberts and Olson, *Winning Is the Only Thing*, 62–63; Robert H. Boyle, "It's Just One Man's Family," *Sports Illustrated*, September 25, 1972; Michael MacCambridge, *America's Game: The Epic Story of How Pro Football Captured a Nation* (New York: Random House, 2004), 354–355.

28. Jeane Hoffman, "11 From Heaven: Praying Prime Force with Bruin Grid Men," *Los Angeles Times*, November 9, 1954, IV-2.

29. Ed Nichols, "Shore Sports," *Salisbury Times* (Salisbury, MD), February 7, 1957, 10.

30. Bill Glass, *Get in the Game* (Waco, TX: Word Books, 1965), 117–118.

31. Glass, *Get in the Game*, 76–77.

32. Glass, *Get in the Game*, 38–40, 47–48; The "spiritual daddy" line was from Watson Spoelstra to Bill Glass, February 1978, CFLP, Collection 455, Box 1, Folder 13.

33. Milton Gross, "Steelers' Buddy Dial at Home on Field, on Stage, in Pulpit," *Pittsburgh Press*, December 13, 1963, 43; Buddy Dial, "Beyond the Goal Post," *Guideposts*, September 1964, 6–7; Bill Wade, "The Most Powerful Witness," *Guideposts*, November 1964, 12–14.

34. "Professional Athletes Retreat," *Christian Athlete*, March 1964, 6–7; "Professional Athletes Report" (1965), CBMP, Box 520, Folder 46; Tom McEwen, "The Linebacker Carries a Bible," *Tampa Tribune*, February 23, 1964, 1-C.

35. L. Fisher, *God's Voice to the Pro* (Boca Raton, FL: Sports World Chaplaincy, 1969); Zola Levitt, *Somebody Called "Doc"* (Carol Stream, IL: Creation House, 1972).

36. Bob Terrell, "FCA's Influence Great," *Asheville Citizen*, October 24, 1964, 10.

37. Fisher, *God's Voice to the Pro*, 45.

38. Fisher, *God's Voice to the Pro*, 47–48, 83; "Line Coach for the Lord," *All Florida Magazine*, December 15, 1968, 10.

39. Fisher, *God's Voice to the Pro*, 100–101.

40. Fisher, *God's Voice to the Pro*, 48–49; Dave Sjodin, "'He-Man Religion," *Fort Lauderdale News*, January 6, 1968, 5B.

41. See, for example, Dave Tatham, "Boca's Eshleman Made Believers out of the Colts," *Palm Beach Post-Times*, November 12, 1967, 6D.

42. Peter Gent, *North Dallas Forty* (New York: William Morrow & Company, 1973), 230–231.

43. Bruce Buurmsa, "Pray Ball!," *Courier-Journal*, April 2, 1976, G-1; Randy Frame, "Christianity Comes of Age in the NFL," *Christianity Today*, January 13, 1984, 36–37.

44. Tom Skinner, "The U.S. Racial Crisis and World Evangelism," https://urbana.org/message/us-racial-crisis-and-world-evangelism. For background on Skinner, see Edward Gilbreath, *Reconciliation Blues: A Black Evangelical's Inside View of White Christianity* (Downers Grove, IL: InterVarsity Press, 2006), 56–72.

45. Barrie Doyle, "Super Goals," *Christianity Today*, January 5, 1973, 50–51; "Super Bowl Rivals Emphasize Spiritual Values," *New York Times*, January 6, 1973, 35; Tom Skinner, "Teamwork," *Christian Athlete*, January 1976, 2–3.

46. Pat Toomay, *The Crunch* (New York: W.W. Norton, 1975), 65–66.

47. On Zeoli's NFL ministry, see also Billy Zeoli, ed., *Great Football Pros on the Game of Life* (New York: Fleming H. Revell, 1972); Deford, "Reaching for the Stars."

48. Fisher, *God's Voice to the Pro*, 102–103; Turner, *Bill Bright & Campus Crusade for Christ*, 140.

49. Dick Forbes, "Religion, Sports: Working Parlay," *Cincinnati Enquirer*, February 15, 1976, D-6.

50. Jim Stump with Frank Martin, *The Power of One-on-One: Discovering the Joy and Satisfaction of Mentoring Others* (Grand Rapids, MI: Baker Books, 2014), 74. In 1974, Stump launched his own ministry called Sports Challenge.

51. Terry Bradshaw with David Diles, *Terry Bradshaw: Man of Steel* (Grand Rapids, MI: Zondervan, 1979), 122–124; Arlis Priest with Al Janssen, *Love Unlocks Every Door* (San Bernardino, CA: 1982), 135.

52. Ladd and Mathisen, *Muscular Christianity*, 158–160.

53. Levitt, *Somebody Called "Doc,"* 127; "A New Dimension," *Athletes in Action*, Fall 1971, 13; Priest, *Love Unlocks Every Door*, 127–131.

54. "Kick-Off for Christ," *Green Bay Press-Gazette*, July 10, 1971, A-5.

55. "Tackling the Pros," *Christianity Today*, February 22, 1976, 17; Priest, *Love Unlocks Every Door*, 130–134; Bill Giduz, "Jocks for Jesus," *Presbyterian Survey*, December 1978, 19–20.

56. Deford, "Religion in Sport," 95.

57. Deford, "Religion in Sport," 95.

58. Robert Schuster, "Tape 6," August 18, 2003, in Interviews of William E. Pannell, Collection 498 at Billy Graham Center Archives at Wheaton College, MP3 audio, 1:32:46. On Pannell, see also Curtis, *The Myth of Colorblind Christians*, 70–74.

59. Levitt, *Somebody Called "Doc,"* 147; Priest, *Love Unlocks Every Door*, 136.

60. Oriard, *Brand NFL*, 210.

61. "Ken Houston Is Oiler Safety Who Punishes Ball Carriers," *Johnson City Press*, December 18, 1969, 22; Ken Houston, "God Has Given Me a New Motivation for Playing Football," *Athletes in Action*, 1974, 31.

62. Gary Rausch, "All 'Quiet' on the Washington Front," *Independent Press-Telegram* (Long Beach, CA), August 18, 1971; Carver Gayton, "Carver Gayton Reflects on the Jim Owens Statue at Husky Stadium, University of Washington," *HistoryLink.org*, September 19, 2004, http://www.historylink.org/File/5745.

63. David L. Diles, *Twelfth Man in the Huddle* (Waco, TX: Word Books, 1976), 109–115.

64. Bobby Richardson with David Thomas, *Impact Player: Leaving a Lasting Legacy on and off the Field* (Carol Stream, IL: Tyndale House, 2012), 275; "Baseball Chapel's a Hit with Athletes," *Minneapolis Star*, September 2, 1977, 7B.

65. Gary Warner, "Play Ball! But First, Let Us Pray," *Christian Athlete*, August 1973, 22–23; Edward Plowman, "Dugout Disciples," *Christianity Today*, November 8, 1974, 39–40.

66. This summary of Baseball Chapel is derived from the Baseball Chapel materials in CFLP, Collection 455, Box 1, Folder 13. See also William C. Kashatus, "The Origins of Baseball Chapel and the Era of the Christian Athlete, 1973–1990," *Nine: A Journal of Baseball History and Social Policy Perspectives* 7, no. 2 (Spring 1999): 75–90.

67. Deford, "Reaching for the Stars."

68. Ladd and Mathisen, *Muscular Christianity*, 135–155. On aspects of the growing evangelical consumer subculture, see Du Mez, *Jesus and John Wayne*; Vaca, *Evangelicals Incorporated*; Leah Payne, *God Gave Rock and Roll to You: A History of Contemporary Christian Music* (New York: Oxford University Press, 2024).

69. Deford, "Religion in Sport," 102.

70. Priest, *Love Unlocks Every Door*, 133.

71. Turner, *Bill Bright and Campus Crusade for Christ*, 84–89; Migliazzo, *Mother of Modern Evangelicalism*, 31; Bright, ed., *Teacher's Manual*.

72. Bright, *Teacher's Manual*, 171, 178.

73. Bright, *Teacher's Manual*, 177, 189.

74. David R. Hannah, ed., *A Strategy Designed to Present the Claims of Christ through Charger Classics* (San Bernardino, CA: Campus Crusade for Christ, 1968), 14.

75. Norm Evans, "Dedication," in *Supergoal: Great Football Pros on the Game of Life*, ed. Billy Zeoli (Grand Rapids, MI: Fleming H. Revell, 1972), 105.

76. These developments reflected a broader therapeutic turn for popular forms of evangelical faith. See David Harrington Watt, *A Transforming Faith: Explorations of Twentieth-Century American Evangelicalism* (New Brunswick, NJ: Rutgers University Press, 1991), 15–31, 137–154; Miller, *The Age of Evangelicalism*, 22; Turner, *Bill Bright & Campus Crusade for Christ*, 101–103.

77. Giduz, "Jocks for Jesus," 21.

78. Gwilym S. Brown, "Winning One for the Ripper," *Sports Illustrated*, November 26, 1973, 46–54; Gary Warner, "Inside the Competitor," *Christian Athlete*, January 1975, 8.

79. Bill Glass, *My Greatest Challenge* (Waco, TX: Word Books, 1968), 61; Bill Glass, *Expect to Win* (Waco, TX: Word Books, 1981), 16.

80. Wes Neal, *The Handbook on Athletic Perfection* (Milford, MI: Mott Media, 1981), ix.

81. Wesley D. Neal, *The Making of an Athlete of God* (San Bernardino, CA: Campus Crusade for Christ, 1972).

82. Neal, *The Making of an Athlete of God*, III-3.

83. Blazer, *Playing for God*, 64.

84. Timothy W. Gallwey, *The Inner Game of Tennis* (New York: Random House, 1974).

85. Al Janssen, ed., *One Way to Play Football* (Atlanta: Cross Roads Books, 1979), 61.

86. Janssen, *One Way to Play Football*, 103, 204.

87. Deford, "Reaching for the Stars." See also Oriard, *Brand NFL*, 52; Berrett, *Pigskin Nation*, 159–180.

88. Watson Spoelstra's *Baseball Chapel* newsletter, November 2, 1975; Levitt, *Somebody Called "Doc,"* 127, 144–145; Priest, *Love Unlocks Every Door*, 131–133.

89. Norm Evans with Edwin Pope, *On the Line* (Old Tappan, NJ: Fleming H. Revell, 1976), 147; Turner, *Bill Bright and Campus Crusade for Christ*, 154–158; Dowland, *Family Values and the Rise of the Christian Right*, 129–156.

90. Evans, *On the Line*, 84.

91. Levitt, *Somebody Called "Doc,"* 145.

92. Du Mez, *Jesus and John Wayne*, 64.

93. Marabel Morgan, *The Total Woman* (Old Tappan, NJ: Revell, 1973), 68; Emily Suzanne Johnson, *This Is Our Message: Women's Leadership in the New Christian Right* (New York: Oxford University Press, 2019), 11–37.

94. Johnson, *This Is Our Message*, 31.

95. Morgan, *The Total Woman*, 67–68, 188; Susan Hemmingway, "Bucs' Wives Will Try a New Game Plan of Their Own," *Tampa Times*, October 20, 1977, 10.

96. Joyce Heard, "Dolphin Wife Tells How Book, God Helped Her," *Palm Beach Post*, May 10, 1974, C4.

97. Dowland, *Family Values*, 207–227.

98. Norm Evans, Ray Didinger, and Sonny Schwartz, *On God's Squad: The Story of Norm Evans* (Carol Stream, IL: Creation House, 1971), 181–182.

99. Evans, *On God's Squad*, 181.

100. Giduz, "Jocks for Jesus," 19–20.

101. Dave Meggyesy, *Out of Their League* (Berkeley, CA: Ramparts Press, 1970), 6. See also Jack Scott, *The Athletic Revolution* (New York: Free Press, 1971); Berrett, *Pigskin Nation*, 159–180.

102. "On the Sociological Dodgers," *Christian Century*, April 5, 1972, 383.

103. Eugence Bianchi, "The Superbowl Culture of Male Violence," *Christian Century*, September 18, 1974, 844.

104. "Sports: Are We Overdoing It?," *Christianity Today*, August 11, 1972, 22–23.

105. David Kucharsky, "It's Time to Think Seriously about Sports," *Christianity Today*, November 7, 1975, 18.

106. Nancy Woodhull, "Athletes Spread the Religious Word," *Detroit Free Press*, March 29, 1975, 5-C.

107. Bill Glass and William Pinson Jr., *Don't Blame the Game: An Answer to Super Star Swingers and a Look at What's Right with Sports* (Waco, TX: Word, 1972), 12, 21.

108. Glass, *Don't Blame the Game*, 84.

109. Diles, *Twelfth Man in the Huddle*, 72. See also "The Real Hero Is Jesus," *Christian Athlete*, September/October 1978, 14.

110. Staubach, "Foreword," in Glass and Pinson, *Don't Blame the Game*, 7.

111. Gary Warner, "The CA Turns Ten," *Christian Athlete*, May 1969, 23; Warner, *Competition*, 39–47.

112. Gary Warner, "Healthy Controversy and Change," *Christian Athlete*, July 1971, 23.

113. Jerry Pyle, "Sports and War," *Christian Athlete*, January 1972, 3–9.

114. Gary Warner, "The Sportsmonger," *Christian Athlete*, January 1972, 31.

115. Warner, *Competition*, 184–185; "Sports and War," *Christian Athlete*, March 1972, 6–7; "Beanballs 'n Backslaps," *Christian Athlete*, May 1972, 30.

116. "Beanballs 'n Backslaps," *Christian Athlete*, May 1972, 30.

117. Dick Harp to Bill Glass, February 18, 1972, CFLP, Collection 455, Box 4, Folder 6; Leonard E. LeSourd to Bill Glass, February 24, 1972, CFLP, Collection 455, Box 11, Folder 14. See also Warner, *Competition*, 184–185.

118. Gary Warner, "Building a Perspective," *Christian Athlete*, March 1975, 18–20.

119. "Beanballs 'n Backslaps," *Christian Athlete*, May 1974, 7.

120. David R. Swartz, *Moral Minority: The Evangelical Left in an Age of Conservatism* (Philadelphia: University Pennsylvania Press, 2012); Brantley W. Gasaway, *Progressive Evangelicals and the Pursuit of Social Justice* (Chapel Hill: University of North Carolina Press, 2014).

121. Gary Warner to Bill Glass, July 3, 1973, CFLP, Collection 455, Box 4, Folder 6. See also Warner, *Competition*, 137–140.

122. LeSourd to Glass, February 24, 1972.

123. "Door Interview: Gary Warner and Skip Stogsdill," *Wittenburg Door*, May/June 1975, 19–20.

124. The November and December 1976 issues of the *Christian Athlete* were devoted to problems in the structure and system of youth sports.

125. Gary Warner, "A Time for Hard Decisions," *Christian Athlete*, March 1975, 31.

126. Swartz, *Moral Minority*, 149–150; Murchison, *Caution to the Wind*.

127. "'Competition' Comebackers," *Christian Athlete*, April 1975, 22.

128. Gary Warner, "Goodbye, My Friends," *Christian Athlete*, December 1977, 31.

129. "Beanballs 'n Backslaps," *Christian Athlete*, May/June 1978, 18–19.

130. Watson Spoelstra, "Sunday Brunch at Jerry's Place," *Christianity Today*, March 12, 1976, 48–49; Dick Schaap, "Training Table," *Sport*, May 1976, 13.

131. "2/5/76 - Remarks at a Prayer Breakfast for Athletes," Box 23, President's Speeches and Statements, Gerald R. Ford Presidential Library; Gerald Ford, "In Defense of the Competitive Urge," *Sports Illustrated*, July 8, 1974, 16–23.

132. Williams, *God's Own Party*, 123–132, 193; Randall Balmer, *Redeemer: The Life of Jimmy Carter* (New York: Basic Books, 2014), 51–158.

Chapter 7

1. Linda Kay, "When Christianity Goes into the Locker Room," *Chicago Tribune*, October 17, 1982, 6.

2. John Carvalho, "AIA... Clearing Up the Initial Confusion," *Athletes in Action*, Spring 1984, 4.

3. Lars Dzikus, Robin Hardin, and Steven N. Waller, "Case Studies of Collegiate Sport Chaplains," *Journal of Sport and Social Issues* 36, no. 3 (2012): 268–293.

4. Grant Teaff with Louis and Kay Moore, *Winning: It's How You Play the Game* (Dallas: Word Books, 1985); Grant Teaff, *A Coach's Influence: Beyond the Game* (Waco, TX: American Football Coaches Association, 2012).

5. Atcheson, *Impact for Christ*, 74–89; Tom Osborne with John E. Roberts, *More than Winning* (Nashville, TN: Thomas Nelson, 1985); Bobby Bowden with Mark Schlabach, *Called to Coach: Reflections on Life, Faith and Football* (New York: Howard Books, 2011).

6. "FCA Big on Breakfast," *Sharing the Victory*, January/February 1984, 14.

7. Watson Spoelstra, *Baseball Chapel* newsletter, July 24, 1977; Pat Williams with James D. Denney, *Ahead of the Game: The Pat Williams Story* (Grand Rapids, MI: Revell, 2014), 215.

8. Tom Friend, "Gibbs Reconvenes the Breakfast Club," *Washington Post*, January 22, 1989, C-16; Watson Spoelstra, "Waddy's World," *Sports Spectrum*, January 1994, 5.

9. Travis Vogan, *ESPN: The Making of a Sports Media Empire* (Urbana: University of Illinois Press, 2015), 11–42.

10. William Endicott, "Born Again Ballplayers on Increase," *Los Angeles Times*, August 31, 1979, 28.

11. Sam Lacy, "Athletics and Religion," *New Journal and Guide*, May 25, 1983, A32. The racial diversity within the Christian athlete movement will be discussed more in Chapter 8.

12. Alan M. Goldenbach, "Tuning into the Gospel: How the Growth of Sports Television Popularized Public Prayer among Athletes" (master's thesis, University of Maryland, College Park, 2012), 7–26.

13. "An All-Loose Series," *Los Angeles Times*, October 9, 1979, 4.

14. Leonard Shapiro and Tom Friend, "Players Take a Moment," *Washington Post*, December 12, 1989, E4.

15. Watson Spoelstra, "Waddy's World," *Sports Spectrum*, January 1994, 5.

16. Thomas Neumann, "How 49ers, Giants Started Postgame Prayer Tradition 25 Years Ago," ESPN.com, December 3, 2015, https://www.espn.com/nfl/story/_/id/14276301/first-postg ame-prayer-san-francisco-49ers-new-york-giants-25th-anniversary.

17. Jim Reeves, "That Bat Rack Religion," *Fort Worth Star-Telegram*, February 8, 1981, 4B; Kashatus, "The Origins of Baseball Chapel and the Era of the Christian Athlete."

18. Kay, "When Christianity Goes into the Locker Room," 6. For examples of the Bears Christian clique, see Marie Merriweather, "Bears 'Stay Clean' with Religion," *Chicago Defender*, August 11, 1982, 24. Thank you to Lou Moore for providing me with this source.

19. On evangelical consumer subcultures in the 1980s, see Randall Balmer, *Mine Eyes Have Seen the Glory: A Journey into the Evangelical Subculture in America* (New York: Oxford University Press, 1989); Vaca, *Evangelicals Incorporated*; Payne, *God Gave Rock and Roll to You*. There were evangelical sports leagues at the small-college level, but they received little attention from the broader public.

20. "Man with a Message," *Sharing the Victory*, September/October 1989, 4; John Dodderidge, "From the Editor," *Sharing the Victory*, March 1991, 7.

21. Glenn Dickey, "Time to Think about Next Year," *San Francisco Chronicle*, August 13, 1979, 48.

22. Rick Reilly, "Save Your Prayers," *Sports Illustrated*, February 4, 1991, 86–87.

23. MacCambridge, *The Franchise*.

24. "Drollinger Passes Up $400,000 Offer from New Jersey Nets," Athletes in Action press release, March 15, 1978, CFLP, Collection 455, Box 20, Folder 13; Steve Dolan, "Ralph Drollinger Sticks by Beliefs," *Life News*, March 29, 1978, B-1.

25. Dallas Mavericks press release, June 10, 1980, CFLP, Collection 455, Box 20, Folder 13; Jan Hubbard, "Drollinger to Get Last Look after He Mends," *Fort Worth Star-Telegram*, November 2, 1980, 13B.

26. For background on Sonju, see "Sonju: A Businessman with Ties to Sports," *Buffalo News*, March 26, 1977, A-7; David Bauer, "Backboard Jungle," *D Magazine*, June 1980, 158–159. See Grem, *The Blessings of Business*, for more on ServiceMaster and its connections to evangelical business culture.

27. On "wildcat Christianity" see Dochuk, *Anointed with Oil*. Carter was not in the oil business. He got his business break from his mother, Mary Crowley, who built Home Interior and Gifts into a direct-sales empire. Yet he approached his leadership of the Mavericks with a similar style as the "wildcat" Christians Dochuk describes. See, for example, Randy Harvey, "The Good Guys Finish Last," *Inside Sports*, June 30, 1981, 74.

28. John Papanek, "Well Now, Looka Here," *Sports Illustrated*, October 27, 1980.

29. Skip Bayless, "Kiki May Provide Mavs' Cornerstone," *Dallas Morning News*, June 11, 1980, B1; Harvey, "The Good Guys Finish Last," 79; Gregg Patton, "Drollinger to Focus on Good Sports," *San Bernardino County Sun*, January 31, 1985, E1.

30. Carvalho, "AIA . . . Clearing Up the Initial Confusion," 4.

31. Skip Bayless, *God's Coach: The Hymns, Hype, and Hypocrisy of Tom Landry's Cowboys* (New York: Simon and Schuster, 1990), 19.

32. "Stogsdill Resigns as Editor," *Sharing the Victory*, November/December 1989, 21.

33. "A New TV Program Features Well-Known Christian Athletes," *Christianity Today*, June 14, 1985, 48.

34. John Carvalho, "Sports Spectrum, SportsFocus and Me," *Sports Page* blog, March 24, 2018, https://johncarvalhosports.com/2018/03/24/sports-spectrum-sportsfocus-and-me/; Ladd and Mathisen, *Muscular Christianity*, 225–230; Steve Cooper, "Ex-Athlete Takes a 'Second Look' at Christian TV," *San Bernardino County Sun*, June 27, 1987, D5.

35. "Why Isn't This Dodger Blue?" and "Master at the Mid-Court," *Second Look* 1, no. 2, 1987, 6, 15–18.

36. John MacArthur Jr., "Under the Influence," *Second Look* 1, no. 3, 1987, 18–20. For context on MacArthur, see Hummel, *The Rise and Fall of Dispensationalism*, 309–312.

37. Hamilton, *For the Glory*; Eric Liddell, *The Disciplines of the Christian Life* (Nashville, TN: Abingdon Press, 1985).

38. John MacArthur Jr., "Striving for the Ultimate Reward," *Second Look* 1, no. 4, 1987, 18.

39. Ladd and Mathisen, *Muscular Christianity*, 169–171.

40. Darrell Turner, "Religion a Halftime Option on Super Bowl Sunday," *Tampa Bay Times*, January 16, 1993, 4E.

41. Neal, *Handbook on Athletic Perfection*, ix.

42. Blazer, *Playing for God*, 56–67.

43. Joyce Simms, "You Can Lose and Still Be Perfect," *Athletes in Action*, Winter 1982, 36; Athletes in Action, *The Principles of Athletic Competition* (Lebanon, OH: Athletes in Action, 1995); William David Pubols, "An Evaluation of the Five Principles as Taught at Athletes in Action's Ultimate Training Camp" (doctoral project, Biola University, 2018).

44. Anthony Munoz, "A Talent for the Game," *Guideposts*, November 1986, 42–44; Katie Pontius, "Christian Athletes Handle Unique Problems," *Cedars*, March 2, 1989, 7.

45. "Priority Reading," *Christian Athlete*, January/February 1982, 16; Arthur L. Lindsay, *Influence: A History of the Nebraska Fellowship of Christian Athletes* (Kearney, NE: Cross Training Publishing, 2009), 60, 103, 207–208, 231. Several different editions of Wes Neal's *Handbook on Athletic Perfection* and *Handbook on Coaching Perfection* have been published by Cross Training since the 1990s.

46. "Books," *Athletes in Action*, Winter 1982, 30.

47. Neal, *Handbook on Athletic Perfection*, 192.

48. Edward E. Plowman, "Bill Gothard's Institute," *Christianity Today*, May 25, 1973, 44; "Bill Gothard Steps down during Institute Shakeup," *Christianity Today*, August 8, 1980, 46; Du Mez, *Jesus and John Wayne*, 74–78.

49. Neal, *Handbook on Athletic Perfection*, 195.

50. Neal, *Handbook on Athletic Perfection*, 199.

51. William C. Rhoden, *Forty Million Dollar Slaves: The Rise, Fall, and Redemption of the Black Athlete* (New York: Crown Publishers, 2006).

52. Shirl Hoffman, "The Sanctification of Sport," *Christianity Today*, April 4, 1986, 17. Shirl Hoffman, "The Athletae Dei: Missing the Meaning of Sport," Presentation to the Philosophic Society for Study of Sport, November 14, 1975, Kent State University; Hoffman, *Good Game*.

53. Hoffman, "The Sanctification of Sport," 17; Hoffman, "The Athletae Dei," 12–17.

54. Hoffman, "The Sanctification of Sport," 17.

55. "Stretching," *Sharing the Victory*, May/June 1988, 17. See also Lowrie McCown and Valerie Gin, *Focus on Sport in Ministry* (Marietta, GA: 360 Sports, 2003), 73.

56. "Letters," *Christianity Today*, June 13, 1986, 6.

57. For an insider account of the rise of Maranatha, see Bob Weiner with David Wimbish, *Take Dominion* (Old Tappan, NJ: Chosen Books, 1988). For context on the growth of the charismatic/Pentecostal movement in the United States, see Edith L. Blumhofer, *Restoring the Faith: The Assemblies of God, Pentecostalism, and American Culture* (Chicago: University of Illinois Press, 1993); John Maiden, *Age of the Spirit: Charismatic Renewal, the Anglo-World, and Global Christianity, 1945–1980* (New York: Oxford University Press, 2023).

58. Maiden, *Age of the Spirit*, 22–30.

59. "Experts Fault Maranatha Campus Ministries for Authoritarian Practices and Questionable Theology," *Christianity Today*, August 10, 1984, 36.

60. A. C. Green with J. C. Webster, *Victory* (Orlando, FL: Creation House, 1994), 60–62.

61. Randy Frame, "Maranatha Disbands as Federation of Churches," *Christianity Today*, March 19, 1990, 40; Rice Broocks, *Every Nation in Our Generation* (Lake Mary, FL: Creation House, 2002).

62. Leigh Montville, "Trials of David," *Sports Illustrated*, April 29, 1996, 90–104; Chris Tomasson, "Ex-NBA Player a Champion off the Court," *Akron Beacon Journal*, December 25, 2000, E1; David Aldridge, "In a Season of Challenge, Green Keeps the Faith," *Washington Post*, December 4, 1993, B7.

63. John Feinstein, *Next Man Up: A Year behind the Lines in Today's NFL* (New York: Little, Brown and Company, 2005), 266–270.

64. Eric Tiansay, "God in the NFL," *Charisma and Christian Life*, November 2002, 37–46.

65. Carolyn McCulley, "Champions for Christ Pulled into NFL Convert Controversy," *Christianity Today*, October 5, 1998, 34–35; Robert Elder, "Greg Feste's Trail of Fumbles," *Austin American-Statesman*, October 28, 2007, H1.

66. On the rise of prosperity gospel figures like Frederick Price, founder of the Crenshaw Christian Center, see Bowler, *Blessed*, 89, 202–203. Price counted former NFL great Rosey Grier as one of his followers.

67. Weiner, *Take Dominion*, 158; C. Peter Wagner, "Dominion! Kingdom Action Can Change the World," *Journal of the American Society for Church Growth* 18, no. 1 (2007): 37–48.

68. Weiner, *Take Dominion*, 160.

69. Brad Christerson and Richard Flory, *The Rise of Network Christianity: How Independent Leaders Are Changing the Religious Landscape* (New York: Oxford University Press, 2017).

70. Tiansay, "God in the NFL."

71. Green, *Victory*, 70; Weiner, *Take Dominion*, 244–246.

72. Leilani Diane Corpus, "Straight Arrow Who'll Straight-Arm You," *Sharing the Victory*, March/April 1989, 2–4; Green, *Victory*, 157–158.

73. Barry Hankins, *Francis Schaeffer and the Shaping of Evangelical America* (Grand Rapids, MI: Eerdmans, 2008), 165–178; Silliman, *Reading Evangelicals*, 59–63.

74. Hartman, *A War for the Soul of America*, 5.

75. David Burnham, "Morality: The Rules They Are a-Changin," *Second Look* 2, no. 2, 1988, 2.

76. John Erickson, "President's Perspective," *Sharing the Victory*, November/December 1982, 2. See also Bill Bright, "The Root of the Problem," *Athletes in Action*, Fall 1982, 18.

77. On the rise of the Christian Right, see especially Williams, *God's Own Party*. On the centrality of "family values" to the rise of the Christian Right, see Dowland, *Family Values and the Rise of the Christian Right*.

78. Jerry Falwell, "Why the Moral Majority?," *Moral Majority Capitol Report*, August 1979, 1–3. For background on Falwell, see Williams, *God's Own Party*, 43–47, 171–179.

79. Ladd and Mathisen, *Muscular Christianity*, 161–163; Baker, *Playing with God*, 214–217. An earlier example of an upstart evangelical school using sports to get public attention was Oral Roberts University, which had a brief run of national prominence in college basketball in the early 1970s. See Baker, *Playing with God*, 210–211.

80. Leigh Montville, "Thou Shalt Not Lose," *Sports Illustrated*, November 13, 1989, 82–86.

81. Dochuk, *From Bible Belt to Sunbelt*, 259–292.

82. "Pastor Says He's Teachable," *Press Democrat*, January 9, 1981, 9D.

83. Kenneth M. Duberstein memo, "Meeting with John Erickson, National President, and Anthony Wauterlek, Chairman of the Board of Trustees, Fellowship of Christian Athletes," January 15, 1982, Presidential Briefing Papers, Folder titled 01/18/1982, Box 12, Ronald Reagan Library.

84. Jack Kemp, "The Competition of Ideas," *Christian Athlete*, February 1973, 19.

85. Morton Kondracke and Fred Barnes, *Jack Kemp: The Bleeding-Heart Conservative Who Changed America* (New York: Sentinel, 2015); Michael Weisskopf, "Kemp's Racial Awakening," *Washington Post*, October 9, 1996, A1.

86. On LaHaye's support for the JBS, see Williams, *God's Own Party*, 72–74. For background and context on the JBS, see Edward H. Miller, *A Conspiratorial Life: Robert Welch, the John Birch Society, and the Revolution of American Conservatism* (Chicago: University of Chicago Press, 2022).

87. Gary Kauffman, "How Does a Nice Guy Like This Wind Up in the Majors?," *Athletes in Action*, Spring 1984, 38–41; Mike Granberry, "Three Padres Pitch Their Politics," *Los Angeles Times*, July 8, 1984, J1.

88. Dave Dravecky with C. W. Neal, *The Worth of a Man* (Grand Rapids, MI: Zondervan, 1996), 141–143. It is unclear how long Dravecky continued his JBS involvement. A reporter in 1989 claimed that Dravecky remained a member in good standing with a San Francisco chapter. See Martin Snapp, "Eastbay Ear," *Oakland Tribune*, August 21, 1989, C-4.

89. Skip Stogsdill, "Cookie-Cutter Christians," *Sharing the Victory*, May/June 1987, 23; Skip Stogsdill, "From the Editor," *Sharing the Victory*, November/December 1989, 6.

90. Smith, *A Coach's Life*, 257.

91. Roe Johnston, "No Challenge, No Adventure," *Sharing the Victory*, May/June 1985), 16–17.

92. "Beanballs n Backslaps," *Sharing the Victory*, July/August 1985, 20.

93. James T. Baker, "Are You Blocking for Me, Jesus?," *Christian Century*, November 5, 1975, 997–1001. On these differences between evangelicals and mainline/ecumenical leaders, see Hollinger, *Christianity's American Fate*, 103–104.

94. Kruse, *One Nation under God*, 203–237.

95. T. R. Reid, "Coaches Run Joint Play to Push School Prayer," *Washington Post*, March 1, 1984, A3; Walter Goodman, "Strongest Effort Yet to Put Organized Prayer in Schools," *New York Times*, March 8, 1984, A1; Kruse, *One Nation under God*, 275–184.

96. Jeff Prugh, "Anti-Prayer Ruling Loses on High School Gridirons," *Los Angeles Times*, December 7, 1980, J1; Tom Wheatley, "'Born Again' Coaching Stirs Uproar in Memphis," *St Louis Post-Dispatch*, November 18, 1984, F1; Tony Kornheiser, "Prayer Fine, but Not in Locker Room," *Washington Post*, August 31, 1985, D1.

97. Bill McCartney with Dave Diles, *From Ashes to Glory* (Nashville, TN: Thomas Nelson, 1990), 204.

98. Frank Pastore with Ellen Vaughn, *Shattered: Struck Down, but Not Destroyed* (Carol Stream, IL: Tyndale House, 2010), 156; "A Former Professional Athlete Contending for the Faith," *Torch*, Spring 1991, 11.

99. Frank Pastore, "Christian Conservatives Must Not Compromise," *Los Angeles Times*, November 5, 2004, B13.

100. Ralph Drollinger, *Oaks in Office: Biblical Essays for Political Leaders* (Ventura, CA: Nordskog Publishing, 2019); Katherine Stewart, *The Power Worshippers: Inside the Dangerous Rise of Religious Nationalism* (New York: Bloomsbury, 2020), 34–54.

101. For extensive evidence and analysis of this, see Krattenmaker, *Onward Christian Athletes*.

102. Ladd and Mathisen, *Muscular Christianity*, 242–243; Jay, *More than Just a Game*, 158–171.

103. Cahn, *Coming on Strong*, 254, 260–261. On the growth of women's sports in the 1970s, see also Susan Ware, *Game, Set, Match: Billie Jean King and the Revolution in Women's Sports* (Chapel Hill: University of North Carolina Press, 2011).

104. FCA Newsletter, July 30, 1956, BRP, Box 58, Folder 2; Patsy Neal, "The Greatest Coach of All," *Christian Athlete*, February 1964, 12–13.

105. John Erickson, 1972 report on FCA activity, CFLP, Collection 455, Box 4, Folder 6; Atcheson, *Impact for Christ*, 110–119.

106. "Competition with a Feminine Touch," *Christian Athlete*, May 1973, 13–15; Atcheson, *Impact for Christ*, 118.

107. Cindy Smith telephone interview with author, October 10, 2017.

108. Cindy Smith to Laurie Mabry, June 14, 1976, NPBP, Box 12. Correspondence between Smith and AIAW leaders can also be found in Box 52, Folder 30, and Box 30, Folder 35 of the AIAW papers.

109. Margot Polivy to Carole Mushier, October 30, 1979, AIAW, Box 30, Folder 35.

110. Mary Fo Festle, *Playing Nice: Politics and Apologies in Women's Sports* (New York: Columbia University Press, 1996), 165–227.

111. Cindy Smith telephone interview with author, October 10, 2017.

112. Marcia K. Burton, "A Feasibility Study of an AIA-USA Women's Basketball Team," master's thesis, Bowling Green State University, 1988. See also the Winter 1985 issue of *Athletes in Action* magazine.

113. Karen Drollinger, *Grace and Glory: Profiles of Faith and Courage in the Lives of Top Women Athletes* (Dallas: Word Publishing, 1990); Karen Rudolph Drollinger, "Ladies of the Eighties," *Second Look*, July/August 1989, 8–10. Madeline Manning Mims was an especially important pioneer in women's sports ministry and in the development of Olympic sports chaplaincy.

114. Drollinger, "Ladies of the Eighties," 18.

115. Blazer, *Playing for God*, 103–128.

116. Dowland, *Family Values and the Rise of the Christian Right*, 136–138; Sharp, *The Other Evangelicals*, 163–196.

117. "The Danvers Statement," in *Recovering Biblical Manhood and Womanhood: A Response to Evangelical Feminism*, ed. John Piper and Wayne Grudem (Wheaton, IL: Crossway Books, 1991), 469–472; Dowland, *Family Values and the Rise of the Christian Right*, 131–141.

118. Turner, *Bill Bright and Campus Crusade for Christ*, 209.

119. Allen Palmeri, "Baptist Influence Ripples through Ministry of FCA," *Baptist Press*, April 20, 2004, https://www.baptistpress.com/resource-library/news/baptist-influence-ripples-through-ministry-of-fca/; Hankins, *Uneasy in Babylon*, 230–239; Du Mez, *Jesus and John Wayne*, 168–169.

120. "God Didn't Create Women to Umpire—Astros Pitcher," *Los Angeles Times*, March 15, 1988, I-1.
121. Jill Lieber, "Some Say No Leica," *Sports Illustrated*, June 20, 1988, 48–53.
122. Cahn, *Coming on Strong*, 246–314.
123. Debbie Wall Larson, "A Lot to Be Proud of, a Long Way to Go," *Sharing the Victory*, January/February 1987, 16; Blazer, *Playing for God*, 118.
124. John Dodderidge, "Setting High Standards," *Sharing the Victory*, March 1991, 8–9.
125. Larson, "A Lot to Be Proud of, a Long Way to Go," 16.
126. Drollinger, *Grace and Glory*, xi.
127. Karry Kelley, "The Sky's the Limit," *Athletes in Action*, Winter 1982, 23.
128. Festle, *Playing Nice*, 235–245; Cahn, *Coming on Strong*, 185–206.
129. Drollinger, *Grace and Glory*, 179–180; Blazer, *Playing for God*, 129–156.
130. For examples, see Randy Frame, "The Homosexual Lifestyle: Is There a Way Out?," *Christianity Today*, August 9, 1985, 32–36; Randy Frame, "The Evangelical Closet," *Christianity Today*, November 5, 1990, 56–57. For context on evangelical approaches to LGBTQ people, see Sharp, *The Other Evangelicals*, 207–242; David J. Neumann, "'A Definitive but Unsatisfying Answer': The Evangelical Response to Gay Christians," *Religion and American Culture* 32, no. 1 (2022): 1–40, doi:10.1017/rac.2021.21.
131. April Nelson, "Lesbian Lust," *Christian Athlete*, May/June 1982, 24–26.
132. "Homosexuality and the Female Athlete," *Sharing the Victory*, May/June 1985, 8–9.
133. Pat Griffin, *Strong Women, Deep Closets: Lesbians and Homophobia in Sport* (Champaign, IL: Human Kinetics, 1998), 109–132.
134. Stewart, *The Power Worshippers*, 37; Neumann, "'A Definitive but Unsatisfying Answer'"; Sharp, *The Other Evangelicals*, 242–247.
135. Michael J. Smith, "The Double Life of a Gay Dodger," *Inside Sports*, October 1982, 57–63; David Kopay and Perry Deane Young, *The David Kopay Story: An Extraordinary Self-Revelation* (New York: Arbor House, 1977).
136. See, for example, Jane Leavy, "Scott McGregor and the Pulpit Pitch," *Washington Post*, July 19, 1988, B1; Dowland, *Family Values and the Rise of the Christian Right*, 159–172.
137. "McCartney Fights Gay Rights," *St. Louis Post-Dispatch*, February 12, 1992, 2D; Adam Teicher, "McCartney's Passion for Bible Dividing Boulder," *Kansas City Star*, October 4, 1992, C-2.
138. Liz Clarke, "Packer's White Stands by Remarks," *Washington Post*, March 27, 1998, D1.
139. Reggie White with Andrew Peyton Thomas, *Fighting the Good Fight* (Nashville, TN: Thomas Nelson Publishers, 1999); Gwen Knapp, "Acolytes of White Make War, Not Peace," *San Francisco Examiner*, February 14, 1999, B-3.
140. Krattenmaker, *Onward Christian Athletes*, 136–137.
141. Du Mez, *Jesus and John Wayne*, 153. PK has received substantial scholarly attention. One of the best sources is Dowland, *Family Values and the Rise of the Christian Right*, 207–227.
142. Aldridge, "In a Season of Challenge, Green Keeps the Faith," B7; Green, *Victory*, 131.
143. Scott D. Strednak Singer, "The Word Was Made Flesh: The Male Body in Sports Evangelism" (PhD diss., Temple University, 2016), 134–177.
144. Barry Sanders with Mark E. McCormick, *Barry Sanders: Now You See Him* (Covington, KY: Clerisy, 2005), 130.
145. "In Depth Topics: LGBT Rights," Gallup, https://news.gallup.com/poll/1651/gay-lesbian-rights.aspx.
146. Chris Defresne, "Does God Care Who Wins?," *Los Angeles Times*, February 21, 1999, D10.

Chapter 8

1. "White Speaks His Mind," *Knoxville News-Sentinel*, March 15, A4.
2. "People's Forum," *Green Bay Press-Gazette*, from March 19, 22, and 28, 1997.
3. "Opinions Aired on Reggie White's Speech to Students," *Knoxville News-Sentinel*, March 30, 1997, F4.
4. Marshall Frady, *Jesse: The Life and Pilgrimage of Jesse Jackson* (New York: Random House, 1996), 116–120; Gary Dorrien, *A Darkly Radiant Vision: The Black Social Gospel in the Shadow of MLK* (New Haven, CT: Yale University Press, 2023), 104–187.
5. Frady, *Jesse*, 264; See also Dorrien, *A Darkly Radiant Vision*, 104–187.
6. Robinson, *I Never Had It Made*, 270; Howard Bryant, *The Last Hero: A Life of Henry Aaron* (New York: Pantheon Books, 2010), 424.

7. Adam L. Bond, *The Imposing Preacher: Samuel DeWitt Proctor and Black Public Faith* (Minneapolis: Fortress Press, 2013), 23–27; Gilbreath, *Reconciliation Blues*, 112–129.

8. Nudelman, "He Blinks and Breathes and Beats 'em All," 8–10.

9. "Justice for Blacks in Sports Subject of Black Athletes Meet," *Atlanta Daily World*, March 27, 1973, 2.

10. "You Can Pray if You Want to," *Christianity Today*, August 12, 1977, 12.

11. Jesse L. Jackson Sr., "The Rainbow Nation," in *Keeping Hope Alive: Sermons and Speeches of Reverend Jesse L. Jackson Sr.*, ed. Grace Ji-Sun Kim (New York: Orbis Books, 2020).

12. "Aaron Hits Lack of Black Execs," *Chicago Defender*, June 13, 1987, 52; Merlisa Lawrence, "The Silent Minorities," *Sports Illustrated*, April 5, 1993, 108.

13. Frady, *Jesse*, 294, 492; Gilbreath, *Reconciliation Blues*, 112–129; "Jesse Jackson Spoke, but Not Many Listened," *Christianity Today*, March 7, 1986, 47; Dorrien, *A Darkly Radiant Vision*, 418–484.

14. Leah Wright Rigueur, *The Loneliness of the Black Republican* (Princeton, NJ: Princeton University Press, 2015), 305–306.

15. Maurice A. St. Pierre, "Reaganomics and Its Implications for African-American Family Life," *Journal of Black Studies* 21, no. 3 (March 1991): 325–340; Elizabeth Hinton, *From the War on Poverty to the War on Crime: The Making of Mass Incarceration in America* (Cambridge, MA: Harvard University Press, 2016), 307–332; Kenneth A. Briggs, "Black Churches Forging Coalition to Battle Economic and Social Ills," *New York Times*, December 12, 1982.

16. Frady, *Jesse*, 330–464; 484–487.

17. Jesse Jackson, "How We Respect Life Is the Over-riding Moral Issue," *Right to Life News*, January 1977, 207; Colman McCarthy, "Jackson's Reversal on Abortion," *Washington Post*, May 21, 1988; Frady, *Jesse*, 77–78.

18. Rigueur, *The Loneliness of the Black Republican*, 302–310; Joshua Farrington, *Black Republicans and the Transformation of the GOP* (Philadelphia: University of Pennsylvania Press, 2016), 230; Robert Joseph Taylor et al., "Black and White Differences in Religious Participation: A Multisample Comparison," *Journal for the Scientific Study of Religion* 35, no. 4 (December 1996): 403–410.

19. Adam J. Criblez, "White Men Playing a Black Man's Game: Basketball's 'Great White Hopes' of the 1970s," *Journal of Sport History* 42, no. 3 (Fall 2015): 371–381; Mark Armour and Daniel R. Levitt, "Baseball Demographics, 1947–2016," Society of American Baseball Research, https://sabr.org/bioproj/topic/baseball-demographics-1947-2012, accessed March 15, 2024; Oriard, *Brand NFL*, 210–249.

20. Howard Bryant, *The Heritage: Black Athletes, a Divided America, and the Politics of Patriotism* (Boston: Beacon Press, 2018), 52–99. See also Johnny Smith, *Jumpman: The Making and Meaning of Michael Jordan* (New York: Basic Books, 2023).

21. Andre Thornton with Al Janssen, *Triumph Born of Tragedy* (Eugene, OR: Harvest House Publishers, 1983).

22. "Indians' Andre Thornton Blasts Exec," *Afro-American*, September 13, 1980, 10; Ronnie Clark, "Andy Thornton Irked over Indians Failure to Promote Black Players," *Call and Post*, July 18, 10A; John Humenik, "Edwards Has Mixed Emotions," *The Times* (Munster, IN), July 17, 1987, B1.

23. Trudy S. Moore, "Athletes Come Together to Pray before They Play," *Jet*, May 3, 1982, 28–29; Reverend Henry Soles interviewed by Adele Hodge, August 23, 2002, The History Makers Digital Archive, http://www.thehistorymarkers.org/.

24. Henry Soles, "Confronting Change," *United Evangelical Action*, January/February 1985, 4–6.

25. Prentice Gautt, "Rumblings," *Sharing the Victory*, July/August 1985, 16–17.

26. Khalil Gibran Muhammad, *The Condemnation of Blackness: Race, Crime, and the Making of Modern Urban America* (Cambridge, MA: Harvard University Press, 2010).

27. William P. O'Hare, "Black Demographic Trends in the 1980s," *The Milbank Quarterly* 65, no. 1 (1987): 35–55; St. Pierre, "Reaganomics and Its Implications for African-American Family Life," 329–330.

28. Hinton, *From the War on Poverty to the War on Crime*, 19; Richard Rothstein, *The Color of Law: A Forgotten History of How Our Government Segregated America* (New York: Liveright, 2017).

29. Michelle Alexander, *The New Jim Crow: Mass Incarceration in the Age of Colorblindness* (New York: The New Press, 2010); Carl Suddler, *Presumed Criminal: Black Youth and the Justice System in Postwar New York* (New York: NYU Press, 2019).

30. John Erickson, "National Emphases for 1983," *Sharing the Victory*, January/February 1983, 14; John Dodderidge, "Inner City Survival," *Sharing the Victory*, January 1991, 22; Dave Burnham, "If I Should Die before I Win," *Second Look*, July/August 1990, 2.

31. Lena Williams, "U.S. Drive on Drugs Urged," *New York Times*, June 26, 1986, B9; Theresa Runstedtler, "Racial Bias: The Black Athlete, Reagan's War on Drugs, and Big-Time Sports Reform," *American Studies* 25, no. 3 (2016): 85–115.

32. Aaron Griffith, *God's Law and Order: The Politics of Punishment in Evangelical America* (Cambridge, MA: Harvard University Press, 2020), 145–152; 254–257.

33. Jones, *Gospel Trailblazer*, 211–212.

34. Ray Didinger, "For Heaven's Sake, He Quit the Eagles," *Philadelphia Daily News*, December 24, 1987, 63.

35. For background on Evans, see Shawn Varghese, "From Every Tribe, Tongue, and Nation: The Role of Dallas Theological Seminary in Shaping African American Evangelicalism" (PhD diss, University of Texas at Dallas, 2020), 173–219.

36. Deborah Kovach Caldwell, "Where There Is Vision," *Dallas Morning News*, October 26, 1996, 8A; Michael Fluent, "Tony Evans: A Formidable Salesman for God," *Fundamentalist Journal*, 5, no. 6 (June 1986), 39–40.

37. Anthony T. Evans, *America's Only Hope* (Chicago: Moody Press, 1990); Varghese, "From Every Tribe, Tongue, and Nation," 173–219.

38. Anthony T. Evans, "Developing Cross-Cultural Fellowship," *Sharing the Victory*, January/February 1991, 19; Evans, *America's Only Hope*, 153–159.

39. Fluent, "Tony Evans," 39–40.

40. Quoted in Hilde Løvdal Stephens, *Family Matters: James Dobson and Focus on the Family's Crusade for the Christian Home* (Tuscaloosa: The University of Alabama Press, 2019), 130; Kevin Blackistone, "Bishop Group Named," *Dallas Morning News*, December 9, 1986, 1A; Curtis, *The Myth of Colorblind Christians*, 177.

41. Rachael G. Warnock, *The Divided Mind of the Black Church: Theology, Piety and Public Witness* (New York: NYU Press, 2014), 140.

42. Warnock, *The Divided Mind of the Black Church*, 136; Mathews, *Doctrine and Race*; Bare, *Black Fundamentalists*.

43. On Cone's theological influence, see Dorrien, *A Darkly Radiant Vision*; Warnock, *The Divided Mind of the Black Church*.

44. Anthony Tyrone Evans, "A Biblical Critique of Selected Issues in Black Theology," (ThD diss, Dallas Theological Seminary, 1982), 326, 332.

45. Warnock, *The Divided Mind of the Black Church*, 136, 141. See also Dorrien, *A Darkly Radiant Vision*, 418–484.

46. Gib Twyman, "Urban Areas New Focus for FCA," *Kansas City Star*, May 25, 1989, B1.

47. "Carey Casey Named National Urban Director," *Sharing the Victory*, May/June 1988, 20; Norma Adams Wade, "Larger Ministry Beckons," *Dallas Morning News*, June 12, 1988, A34.

48. John Dodderidge, "Bridging the Gap," *Sharing the Victory*, January 1991, 4–5.

49. Twyman, "Urban Areas New Focus for FCA."

50. John Dodderidge, "From the Editor," *Sharing the Victory*, January 1991, 7; Dick Abel, "Head Coach's Corner," *Sharing the Victory*, January 1991, 3.

51. Michael O. Emerson and Christian Smith, *Divided by Faith: Evangelical Religion and the Problem of Race in America* (New York: Oxford University Press, 2000), 53–59; Curtis, *The Myth of Colorblind Christians*, 171–208; Andrea Smith, *Unreconciled: From Racial Reconciliation to Racial Justice in Christian Evangelicalism* (Durham, NC: Duke University Press, 2019).

52. Carey Casey, "I Was the Church's New Leader," *Leadership Journal*, Winter 1997, accessed via https://www.christianitytoday.com/pastors/1997/winter/7l1057.html.

53. Andrés Tapia, "The Myth of Racial Progress," *Christianity Today*, October 4, 1993, 16–27; John Perkins with Jo Kadlecek, *Resurrecting Hope: Powerful Stories of How God Is Moving to Reach Our Cities* (Ventura, CA: Regal Books, 1996), 67–79.

54. Ken Murray, "Door to a Better World," *Evening Sun*, December 21, 1990, C1; "The Door Sponsors Series on Issues Affecting Children," *Baltimore Sun*, September 30, 1994, 2B. On Ehrmann, see Jeffrey Marx, *Season of Life: A Football Star, a Boy, a Journey to Manhood* (New York: Simon & Schuster, 2004); Joe Ehrmann with Paula Ehrmann and Gregory Jordan, *InSideOut Coaching: How Sports Can Transform Lives* (New York: Simon & Schuster, 2011).

55. Marx, *Season of Life*, 33.

56. Dorothy Boulware, "Project Justice Is for All Seasons," *Afro-American*, December 19, 1998, A9.

57. McCartney, *From Ashes to Glory*, 210–212.
58. Bill McCartney, *Sold Out: Becoming Man Enough to Make a Difference* (Nashville, TN: Word Publishers, 1997), 177; Al Janssen and Larry K. Weeden, eds., *Seven Promises of a Promise Keeper* (Colorado Springs, CO: Focus on the Family Publishing, 1994), 164.
59. Soles interviewed by Adele Hodge, August 23, 2002.
60. Steve Hubbard, *Faith in Sports: Athletes and Their Religion on and off the Field* (New York: Doubleday, 1996), 108–118, 124–129.
61. Warnock, *The Divided Mind of the Black Church*, 151.
62. Curtis, *The Myth of Colorblind Christians*, 195–207; Dowland, *Family Values*, 215–223.
63. Jack Kemp and J. C. Watts Jr., "Better than Affirmative Action," *Washington Post*, July 8, 1997, A15.
64. J. C. Watts Jr., with Chriss Winston, *What Color Is a Conservative? My Life and My Politics* (New York: Perennial, 2002); Kondracke and Barnes, *Jack Kemp*.
65. McCartney, *Sold Out*, 180–181.
66. Bill McCartney, *Blind Spots: What You Don't See May Be Keeping Your Church from Greatness* (Wheaton, IL: Tyndale House, 2003), 129.
67. McCartney, *Blind Spots*, 53.
68. Curtis, *The Myth of Colorblind Christians*, 207.
69. Carolyn Click, "Promise Keepers Rally Billed as Life-Changing," *Charlotte Observer*, September 28, 1998, 2Y.
70. Ladd and Mathisen, *Muscular Christianity*, 228; Steve Henson, "Match Made in Heaven," *Los Angeles Times*, November 10, 1993; Stewart, *The Power Worshippers*, 37–38.
71. Perkins, *With Justice for All*, 78.
72. John MacArthur, "The Los Angeles Riots: A Biblical Perspective," May 3, 1992, accessed via https://www.gty.org/library/resources.
73. Griffith, *God's Law and Order*, 152–167, 218–569. Griffith shows that some white evangelicals were interested in criminal justice reform, but they tended to focus more on sentencing than policing.
74. Scott A. Bradley, *The Black Man: Cursed or Blessed?* (Chicago: Rivers of Life Ministry, 1993), iv.
75. Bradley, *The Black Man*, v, 97–99.
76. Bradley, *The Black Man*, 93.
77. Scott Bradley, "My Life with Da Bulls," *Sports Spectrum*, November 1993, 22–25.
78. "Racism Still Divides Black and White America," *Public Justice Report*, May/June 1991, accessed via https://www.cpjustice.org/public/page/content/racism_still_divides.
79. Rhoden, *Forty Million Dollar Slaves*, 138–144, 171–196; Adam Rittenberg, "Black Hires in College Football Leadership," ESPN, August 25, 2021, https://www.espn.com/espn/feature/story/_/id/31905530/the-history-black-hires-college-football-leadership.
80. Theresa Runstedtler, *Black Ball: Kareem Abdul-Jabbar, Spencer Haywood, and the Generation That Saved the Soul of the NBA* (New York: Bold Type Books, 2023).
81. Jane Gross, "N.B.A.'s Rebuilding Program Is Showing Results," *New York Times*, December 23, 1984, 5–3.
82. Al Janssen, "Businessman's Goal: Teach Athletes God's Love," *The Arizona Republic*, October 29, 1977, C1; Kay, "When Christianity Goes into the Locker Room."
83. Dan Sernoffsky, "Sixers' GM Has Priorities," *Daily News*, October 22, 1982, 15; Dave Brannon, *Slam Dunk* (Chicago: Moody Press, 1994), 9–11.
84. Julius Erving, "I Was Blessed before I Was Born," *Sharing the Victory*, January/February 1983, 3–4; Brannon, *Slam Dunk*, 67–79.
85. Fluent, "Tony Evans," 40; Neil Steinberg, "Chaplain Has His Own Game Plan," *Chicago Sun Times*, April 3, 1985, 39.
86. Marty James, "Basketball Still No. 1 for Terry," *Napa Valley Register*, August 4, 1993, 1B.
87. Tim Burke, "NBA's Big Money Doesn't Stack Up to Ministry," *Springfield Leader & Press*, September 14, 1982, C1.
88. Richie Whitt, "New Mavs Taking on Look of Enlightenment," *Fort Worth Star-Telegram*, June 30, 1996, C4; "Mavs Minutiae," *Fort Worth Star-Telegram*, March 8, 1998, C5.
89. Brad Townsend, "The Untold Story of Why the Original Mavs Played 'God Bless America,'" *Dallas Morning News*, February 13, 2021, 7C.
90. Kashatus, "The Origins of Baseball Chapel and the Era of the Christian Athlete, 1973–1990"; Krattenmaker, *Onward Christian Athletes*, 87–106.

91. Armour and Levitt, "Baseball Demographics, 1947–2016."
92. Dave Brannon and Joe Pellegrino, *Safe at Home* (Chicago: Moody Press, 1992).
93. Simonson, ed., *The Goal and the Glory*, 29–32.
94. Mike Yorkey with Jesse Florea and Joshua Cooley, *Playing with Purpose: Inside the Lives and Faith of the Major Leagues' Top Players* (Uhrichsville, OH: Barbour Pub., 2012).
95. Krattenmaker, *Onward Christian Athletes*, 196. See also Scholes, *Christianity, Race, and Sport*, 57–71.
96. For background on the limitations placed on Black quarterbacks, see Louis Moore, *The Great Black Hope: Doug Williams, Vince Evans, and the Making of the Black Quarterback* (New York: Public Affairs, 2024)
97. Tony Dungy with Nathan Whitaker, *Quiet Strength: The Principles, Practices, and Priorities of a Winning Life* (Carol Stream, IL: Tyndale House, 2007), 41–42, 58.
98. Dungy, *Quiet Strength*, 85, 208.
99. S. L. Price, "About Time," *Sports Illustrated*, June 10, 1996, 68–74.
100. Dungy, *Quiet Strength*, 98, 256, 292.
101. Aeneas Williams, *It Takes Respect* (Sisters, OR: Multnomah, 1998), 53–58.
102. Bowler, *Blessed*, 123–124.
103. Williams, *It Takes Respect*, 59, 76–77.
104. Williams, *It Takes Respect*, 102–03, 116–119; Pat Williams, *Souls of Steel: How to Build Character in Ourselves and Our Kids* (New York: FaithWords, 2008), 44.
105. Curtiss Paul DeYoung et al., *United by Faith: The Multiracial Congregation as an Answer to the Problem of Race* (New York: Oxford University Press, 2003), 91–95.
106. Don Banks, "A Christian Coalition," *Star Tribune*, October 12, 1997, C1, C14.
107. "'Million Man' Plan Divides Churches," *Los Angeles Times*, October 7, 1995, B10; Michael Janofsky, "Wary of Divisions, Leaders of Million Man March Play Down Farrakhan Role," *New York Times*, October 14, 1995, 8.
108. "Letters from Readers," *Star Tribune*, October 26, 1995, A24.
109. DeYoung, *United by Faith*, 94; Bob von Sternberg, "New Faces Are in Graham's Crowd Nowadays," *Star Tribune*, June 20, 1996, A20.
110. Clark Morphew, "Chaplain Rejoices at Olympics Assignment," *Charlotte Observer*, May 11, 1996, 3G; Don Banks, "Carter Is Honored for Community Service," *Star Tribune*, November 11, 1997, C4.
111. Cris Carter, *Born to Believe* (Upper Tantallon, Nova Scotia: Full Wits, 2000), 94–99.
112. Kent Youngblood and Kevin Selfert, "Chaplain Helps Team Cope with Some Tough Times," *Star Tribune*, September 22, 2001, C10.
113. White, *Fighting the Good Fight*, 191; Kevin Seifert, "NFL's Man of the Year Plans to Keep on Giving," *Star Tribune*, April 27, 2000, C1.
114. Reggie White with Jim Denney, *In the Trenches* (Nashville, TN: Thomas Nelson, 1996), 195.
115. White, *In the Trenches*, 198, 219.
116. Reggie White, *Broken Promises, Blinded Dreams: Taking Charge of Your Destiny* (Shippensburg, PA: Treasure House, 2003).
117. Krattenmaker, *Onward Christian Athletes*, 194–199.
118. Aaron Reiss, "Chaplain Strives to Be a Go-to Player," *Star Tribune*, August 13, 2017, C1.
119. Rick Morrissey, "Panthers, Bengals Try to Bridge Racial Gap," *Daily Oklahoman*, September 8, 1996, 7; Krattenmaker, *Onward Christian Athletes*, 195–196; Mark Packer, "Mitchell Filling Spiritual Need with Vols," *Knoxville News-Sentinel*, September 9, 2007, D2.
120. Samantha Holland interview with Michael Sylvester, "The Lenses Institute: See, Understand, Act," *Listener*, October 2018, podcast episode accessed via Spotify; Brooke Hempell and Susan Robinson interview with Alethea Lamberson, "Progress and Adversity in Ministry with Alethea Lamberson," *Race and Redemption*, May 2023, podcast episode accessed via Spotify.
121. Ron Brown, *Teamwork: Principles for Race Relations* (Grand Island, NE: Cross Training, 1999), 36.

Epilogue

1. For context on Tebow, see Scholes, *Christianity, Race, and Sports*, 59–71; Matthew G. Hawzen and Joshua I. Newman, "The Gospel According to Tim Tebow: Sporting Celebrity, Whiteness, and the Cultural Politics of Christian Fundamentalism in America," *Sociology of Sport Journal*, 34, no. 1 (2017): 12–24.

2. Marissa Payne, "Colin Kaepernick Refuses to Stand for National Anthem to Protest Police Killings," *Washington Post*, August 27, 2016, https://www.washingtonpost.com/news/early-lead/wp/2016/08/27/colin-kaepernick-refuses-to-stand-for-national-anthem-to-protest-police-killings/. For details and context on Kaepernick, see Bryant, *The Heritage*, 100–221; Scholes, *Christianity, Race, and Sports*, 75–91, 111–126.

3. Lari Latrice Martin, "Race, Mahmoud Abdul-Rauf, and Religious Realism," in Scholes and Balmer, eds., *Religion and Sport in North America*, 235–245.

4. Robinson, *I Never Had It Made*, xxiv.

5. Eric Reid, "Why Colin Kaepernick and I Decided to Take a Knee," *New York Times*, September 25, 2017, https://www.nytimes.com/2017/09/25/opinion/colin-kaepernick-football-protests.html.

6. Paul Emory Putz, "Black Christians Play a Crucial Role in Athlete Activism," *Christianity Today*, August 31, 2020, https://www.christianitytoday.com/ct/2020/august-web-only/nba-protests-christian-athletes-jacob-blake-fca-sports-mini.html; Paul Emory Putz, "The Role of Sports Ministries in the NFL Protests," *Religion & Politics*, October 17, 2017, https://religionandpolitics.org/2017/10/17/the-role-of-sports-ministries-in-the-nfl-protests/.

7. Alex Altman and Sean Gregory, "Inside Donald Trump's Latest Battle against the NFL," *TIME*, October 6, 2017, https://time.com/4960638/donald-trump-latest-battle-against-nfl/. On white evangelical support for Trump, see John Fea, *Believe Me: The Evangelical Road to Donald Trump* (Grand Rapids, MI: Eerdmans, 2018).

8. "John MacArthur's 'Statement on Social Justice' Is Aggravating Evangelicals," *Christianity Today*, September 12, 2018, https://www.christianitytoday.com/ct/podcasts/quick-to-listen/john-macarthur-statement-social-justice-gospel-thabiti.html; Chris Moody, "How Critical Race Theory Overran the Southern Baptist Convention," *NY Mag*, June 16, 2021, https://nymag.com/intelligencer/2021/06/critical-race-theory-divides-the-southern-baptist-convention.html.

9. Curtis Yee, "Cru Divided over Emphasis on Race," *Christianity Today*, June 3, 2021, https://www.christianitytoday.com/news/2021/june/cru-divided-over-emphasis-on-race.html; Nicole Alcindor, "Cru-Affiliated Race Ministry Is Shutting Down," *Christian Post*, August 4, 2021, https://www.christianpost.com/news/cru-affiliated-ministry-is-shutting-down-toxic-climate.html; "Progress and Adversity in Ministry with Alethea Lamberson," *Race and Redemption* podcast.

10. Stidger, "Introducing Branch Rickey," 45; Rickey, "Religious Education as Viewed from the Field of Sport," 1156.

11. Griswold, "You Don't Have to Be Born with It," 135.

12. Jeff Scholes uses Cornel West's phrase "Black prophetic fire" to describe Kaepernick in *Christianity, Race, and Sport*, 111–126.

Index

For the benefit of digital users, indexed terms that span two pages (e.g., 52–53) may, on occasion, appear on only one of those pages.